The Record of Helaman

A Teaching Commentary on The Book of Helaman

Volume 4

by

Monte S. Nyman

Distributed by:

Granite Publishing and Distribution, LLC
868 North 1430 West
Orem, Utah 84057
(801) 229-9023 • Toll Free (800) 574-5779
Fax (801) 229-1924

Page Layout & Design by Myrna Varga, The Office Connection, Inc.
Cover Design by Steve Gray

Cover Art
"All Present and Accounted for" by Clark Kelley Price
© Clark Kelley Price

ISBN: 1-932280-54-5
Library of Congress Control Number: 2004108037

Printed in the United States of America

10 9 8 7 6 5 4 3 2 1

Contents

List of Figures & Tables

Figure

Table

Preface

The Record of Helaman

The record of Helaman is really two records. The first record is the record of Helaman, son of Alma, "Comprising chapters 45 to 62 inclusive" (*superscription*, above Alma 45). Mormon also abridged the short record of Shiblon, brother of Helaman and another son of Alma (Alma 63). The second record is of the record of Helaman son of Helaman, and also his sons (*superscription* to the book of Helaman). Alma chapters 43 and 44 from the record of Alma has also been included in this volume because of its contents, a war in the eighteenth year of the reign of the judges.

Alma chapters 43 through 62 have been called the war years or section of the Book of Mormon. They constitute 53 pages, or ten percent, of the 531 pages of the entire Book of Mormon. The book of Helaman also contains much about war.

Why does the Book of Mormon say so much about war? On November 1, 1831, the Lord revealed that "the hour is not yet, but is nigh at hand, when peace shall be taken from the earth" (D&C 1:35). On December 25, 1832, the Lord revealed that beginning with the Civil War, war would be "poured out upon all nations." Thereafter, wars would continue until there comes "a full end of all nations" (D&C 87:1–6). In January 1847, following the martyrdom of Joseph and Hyrum Smith, the Lord said:

34 Thy brethren have rejected you and your testimony, even the nation that has driven you out;

35 And now cometh the day of their calamity, even the days of sorrow, like a woman that is taken in travail; and their sorrow shall be great unless they speedily repent, yea, very speedily.

36 For they killed the prophets, and them that were sent unto them; and they have shed innocent blood, which crieth from the ground against them. [D&C 136:34–36]

The innocent blood of these two great men seem to be connected to the civil war as the Spirit temporarily withdrew from the Americas. Nephi described similar things occurring because "the blood of the saints shall cry from the ground against [the Gentiles]" (2 Nephi 28:10).

The Book of Helaman warns of the secret combinations that were so prevalent in the fifty-one years prior to Christ's birth. The parallel to the Second Coming seems obvious as we approach the millennium.

Appreciation is expressed to my good friend Ron Grow for carefully reading the manuscript and offering many helpful suggestions. I take full responsibility for the principles and doctrines stated in the text except that which is quoted from others.

Introduction

T he title of this volume of the Book of Mormon commentary series would more appropriately be called "The Records of Helaman," since there are the two Helaman's whose records were abridged by Mormon. The first record abridged consisted of Alma chapters 45 through 63. The author was Helaman, the oldest son of Alma the younger. He kept the record for twenty-one years, from 73 B.C. through 51 B.C. These twenty-one years are known as the war years in the Book of Mormon, along with the previous year recorded in the book of Alma (Alma 43–44; 74 B.C.). These two chapters of Alma were included in this volume since the primary subject was war. The law of war, the cause of war, the principles of war, and the results of war are all included in this section of the Book of Mormon, and are very applicable to our day which is the prophesied time "of wars and rumors of wars" in the latter days (JS–Matthew). These chapters of Alma also include the abridged record of the two thousand stripling warriors, known as "the sons of Helaman." The young warriors set a wonderful example to follow for the Latter-day Saints who presently serve in the military service.

The sixty-third chapter of Alma informs us of the people moving into the land northward, and one Hagoth, a Nephite man who built ships and sailed away never to be heard of again. He is connected with the Polynesians of our day.

The second record of Helaman, abridged by Mormon, was kept

by Helaman, son of Helaman, and his sons. Their abridged record is the Book of Helaman in our present-day Book of Mormon. The first six chapters of Helaman were kept by Helaman and warn us of the secret combinations that do and will exist in the latter days. They also tell us how to avoid those secret combinations. Helaman chapters 7 through 12 are called the Prophecy of Helaman, the son of Helaman, and inform us of the relationship between God and man. Helaman chapters 13 through 16 are called the Prophecy of Samuel the Lamanite. These prophecies constitute his prophecies made from the walls of Zarahemla, and the results of his prophecies. The prophecies were basically about the destruction of the Nephites, and the coming of the Lord Jesus Christ in the Meridian of Time. The entire book of Helaman covers all but the last year of the fifty-two years preceding the birth of Christ.

There are twenty-one chapters of Alma, and sixteen chapters of Helaman discussed in this volume of this work (vol. 4). The thirty-seven chapters are again a light touch of history, as Nephi, son of Lehi, had instructed his brother Jacob to keep the records (see Jacob 1:2–3). Although basically an historical account, the record includes much "preaching which was sacred, or revelation which was great, or prophesying" as Nephi also instructed (Jacob 1:4). These three categories are summarized at the end of each chapter. It is often difficult to determine whether it is Helaman, Nephi, Samuel the Lamanite, or Mormon, as he is abridging, who inserts many precepts for the readers to apply to their lives. The Prophet Joseph Smith said, "The Book of Mormon was the most correct of any book on earth, and the keystone of our religion, and a man would get nearer to God by abiding by its precepts, than any other book" (*Teachings of the Prophet Joseph Smith*, 194; see also the Introduction to the Book of Mormon). Although there are many such precepts, the ones inserted by Helaman, Nephi, Samuel the Lamanite or Mormon are usually introduced with phrases such as "I will show unto you," or "thus we see."

There are also many points of doctrine taught throughout the Book of Mormon. Isaiah foretold that when the Book of Mormon came forth, "They also that erred in spirit shall come to understanding, and they that murmured shall learn doctrine" (Isaiah 29:24; 2 Nephi 27:35). In a revelation given on the day the Church was established, the Lord enumerated many doctrines that are found in the Book of Mormon (see D&C 20:17–36). President Boyd K. Packer has often stressed the importance of teaching doctrine to the Saints (see CR, Oct. 1986, 20; April 1997, 8; and April 2004). Therefore, the doctrines taught in each reading are summarized, along with helpful commentary by General Authorities in the end of each chapter. Hopefully the analysis of the Book of Mormon that follows will enlarge the reader's understanding of the record of these ancient peoples.

Chapter One

The Law of War

Alma 43–45

*H*istorical Setting: Before Alma instructed his sons (Alma 36–42), the record states: "and thus commenced a war betwixt the Lamanites and the Nephites, in the eighteenth year of the reign of the judges; and an account shall be given of their wars hereafter" (Alma 35:13). Mormon now gives us the account of that war. The three Book of Mormon chapters discussed in this reading include the events of that year, and Alma's turning over the record to his son Helaman in the beginning of the nineteenth year (see Alma 43:3; 44:24, and 45:2, 20). Mormon takes his information from the record of Alma and the beginning of the record of Helaman that "was written upon the [large] plates of Nephi" (Alma 44:24). The Lamanite armies came into the land of Zarahemla, and the battles took place on both sides of the river Sidon. Mormon focuses mainly on the principles that guided the Nephites in the beginning of "an exceedingly great" long (14 year) war (Alma 62:41).

Precepts of this Reading:

> And now the design of the Nephites was to support their lands, and their houses, and their wives, and their children, that they might preserve them from the hands of their enemies; and also that they might preserve their rights and their privileges, yea, and also their

liberty, that they might worship God according to their desires. [Alma 43:9]

45 Nevertheless, the Nephites were inspired by a better cause, for they were not fighting for monarchy nor power but they were fighting for their homes and their liberties, their wives and their children, and their all, yea, for their rites of worship and their church.

46 And they were doing that which they felt was the duty which they owed to their God; for the Lord had said unto them, and also unto their fathers, that: Inasmuch as ye are not guilty of the first offense, neither the second, ye shall not suffer yourselves to be slain by the hands of your enemies.

47 And again, the Lord has said that: Ye shall defend your families even unto bloodshed. Therefore for this cause were the Nephites contending with the Lamanites, to defend themselves, and their families, and their lands, their country, and their rights, and their religion. [Alma 43:45–47]

The law of war, revealed to the Prophet Joseph Smith in August 1833, was also given to the ancients (see D&C 98:33–38, quoted later). That the Nephites were some of the ancients to whom the law was previously revealed is confirmed in these chapters of Alma. An outline of the chapters of Alma discussed here is given as a preparation for a deeper study.

Outline • Alma 43–45

> 43:1–2   Alma and the sons of Alma go among the people to declare the word.

       a.   They preached truth according to the spirit of prophecy and revelation (v. 2).

       b.   They preached according to their calling after the holy order of God (v. 2).

> 43:3–14   An account of the wars between the Nephites and Lamanites.

       a.   The Zoramites became Lamanites, and the Nephites saw that the Lamanites were coming upon them (v. 4).

1.   The Nephites made preparations for war.

       2.   They gathered their armies to the land of Jershon.

   b. Thousands of Lamanites came into the Zoramite land of Antionum (vv. 5–8).

       1.   A man named Zerahemnah was their leader.

       2.   He appointed chief captains who were Zoramites and Amalikites because the Amalikites were of a more wicked and murderous disposition.

       3.   He wanted to preserve their hatred towards the Nephites and bring them unto subjection.

       4.   His design was to stir up the Lamanites to anger and usurp power over them, and gain power over the Nephites and bring them into bondage.

   c. The design of the Nephites was to support their lands, houses, wives and children, and preserve them from their enemies (vv. 9–10).

       1.   They desired to preserve their rights, privileges, liberty, and freedom to worship God.

       2.   The Lamanites would destroy those who worshipped the true and living God in spirit and in truth.

   d. The Nephites knew of the extreme hatred of the Lamanites towards the people of Ammon who had covenanted to not take up arms (vv. 11–14).

       1.   The Nephites would not allow the Lamanites to destroy the people of Ammon, and gave them lands for their inheritance.

       2.   The people of Ammon gave the Nephites a large portion of their substance to support their armies.

       3.   The Nephites withstood the Lamanites, who were of Laman, Lemuel, the sons of Ishmael, and the dissenters of the Nephites; who were Amalekites, Zoramites, and descendants of the priests of Noah.

       4.   Those descendants were almost as numerous as the Nephites.

➤ 43:15–24 The Nephites were prepared to meet the Lamanites in the land of Jershon.

    a.   The chief captain appointed to command all the armies of the Nephites was Moroni (vv. 16–17).

        1. He was twenty-five years old when he was appointed.

        2. Moroni's people met the Lamanites in the borders of Jershon armed with all manner of weapons of war.

    b.   The Lamanites saw that Moroni had prepared his people with breastplates, arm shields, head shields, and thick clothing (vv. 16–21).

        1. The army of Zerahemnah had only their weapons, and were naked except for a skin girded about their loin, except the Zoramites and Amalekites.

        2. They were extremely afraid of the Nephites although their numbers were much greater.

    c.   The Lamanites left the land of Antionum and journeyed into the wilderness by the head of the river Sidon to take possession of the land of Manti (vv. 22–24).

        1. The Lamanites supposed Moroni would not know where they had gone.

        2. Moroni sent spies to watch their camp.

        3. He also enquired of Alma to know where they would go.

        4. The word of the Lord told Alma where the Lamanites were, and where they might attack.

➤ 43:25–33 Moroni left part of his army in Jershon, and took the rest to Manti.

    a.   Moroni caused the people in the area of Manti to gather to defend their rights (vv. 26–28).

        1. He secreted his army in the valley near the river Sidon.

2.   He placed spies to know when the Lamanites would come.

  b. Moroni knew the desires of the Lamanites and the Nephites so he thought it no sin to defend them by stratagem (vv. 29–33).

    1.   He divided his army, placing part by the hill Riplah and the remainder he concealed in the valley west of the river Sidon by the borders of Manti.

    2.   He was prepared to meet the Lamanites.

➤ 43:34–47   The Lamanites came on the north past the hill Riplah where part of the army of Moroni was concealed.

  a. After the Lamanites passed the hill and began to cross the river Sidon, the Nephites, led by Lehi, encircled the Lamanites on the east and rear (vv. 35–38).

    1.   The Lamanites turned and began to contend with the army of Lehi.

    2.   The work of death commenced on both sides, but more so on the Lamanites because of the protective clothing of the Nephites.

  b. The Lamanites began to flee, and Lehi and his men drove them into the river (vv. 39–42).

    1.   The Lamanites crossed the river and Moroni and his men met them in the valley on the other side, and began to slay them.

    2.   The Lamanites began to flee towards Manti, and were met again by Moroni's men.

  c. The Lamanites fought with exceeding strength and courage heretofore unknown (vv. 43–44).

    1.   They were inspired by their Amalekite and Zoramite captains, and by Zarehemnah.

    2.   They fought like dragons, and many Nephites were slain.

  d. The Nephites were inspired by a better cause; their homes, liberties, wives and children, and their rights of worship and the church (vv. 45–47).

1. They were doing their duty that they owed to their God.

2. The Lord had said to them and their fathers that if they were not guilty of the first or second offence they should not let themselves be slain.

3. The Lord had said to defend their families even to bloodshed.

➤ 43:48–54 The Nephites were about to shrink from the Lamanite fierceness, but Moroni inspired their hearts with the thoughts of their lands, their liberty, and freedom from bondage.

    a. The Nephites turned upon the Lamanites and cried with one voice unto God for their liberty (vv. 49–53).

        1. In the same hour, the Lamanites began to flee into the waters of Sidon.

        2. The Lamanites were double in number, but were still driven into the river.

        3. The Lamanites were surrounded on the east by Lehi and on the west by Moroni, and were struck with terror.

    b. Moroni commanded his men to stop the shedding of blood (v. 54).

➤ 44:1–7 Moroni withdrew a pace from the Lamanites and spoke to Zarahemnah.

    a. You are in our hands, but we do not desire to slay you (vv. 1–2).

        1. We do not desire to bring you into bondage as you desire to do to us.

        2. You are angry with us because of our religion.

    b. The Lord is with us and has delivered you into our hands (vv. 3–4).

        1. This was done because of our religion and our faith in Christ.

        2. You see that you cannot destroy our faith, which is the true faith of God.

3.   God will support and preserve us as long as we are faithful.

      4.   He will not allow our destruction except we transgress and deny our faith.

  c. Moroni commands Zarahemnah in the name of God, who strengthens us and to whom we owe our happiness, to deliver up their weapons and not come to war again against us, and we will spare their lives (vv. 5–7).

      1.   If you will not do this, my men will make you extinct.

      2.   You will see who will have power and who will be brought into bondage.

➤ 44:8–9   Zarahemnah delivered up his weapons but said he would not take an oath (to not come again to war) that he knew he and his children would break.

  a. Zarahemnah agreed to depart into the wilderness or they would retain their swords and perish or conquer (v. 8).

  b. He said they are not of your faith and do not believe that God delivered them unto you, but it is your breastplates and shields that has preserved you (v. 9).

➤ 44:10–11   Moroni returned Zarahemnah's weapons and said we will end the conflict.

  a. Moroni would not recall his words and said, as the Lord liveth, you shall not depart unless you take the oath (v. 11).

  b. Moroni said they would spill their blood on the ground unless they submitted to the conditions he proposed (v. 11).

➤ 44:12–15   Zarahemnah rushed forward to slay Moroni with his sword, but one of Moroni's soldiers smote the sword and broke it.

  a. The soldier smote off the scalp of Zarahemnah and it fell to the ground, and Zarahemnah withdrew into the midst of his soldiers (v. 12).

  b. The soldier took the scalp, put it on the point of his

sword, and said: as the scalp of your chief has fallen, so shall you fall if you do not deliver up your weapons and depart with a covenant of peace (vv. 13–15).

1. Many threw their weapons at Moroni's feet and entered the covenant of peace.

2. As many as entered the covenant of peace were allowed to depart.

➤ 44:16–23　Zarahemnah was wroth and stirred up his remaining soldiers to contention with the Nephites.

a. Moroni was angry because of their stubbornness and commanded his people to slay them (vv. 17–19).

1. The Lamanite soldiers fell exceedingly fast because of the exposure of their bodies.

2. Zarahemnah cried mightily to Moroni, promising to covenant with them.

b. Moroni commanded the work of death to cease (vv. 20–21).

1. He took their weapons of war, after making a covenant of peace, and they were allowed to depart.

2. The dead could not be numbered because of the great amount of Lamanites and Nephites who were slain.

c. The dead were cast into the waters of Sidon and were carried into and buried in the depths of the sea (v. 22).

d. The armies of Moroni returned to their houses and lands (vv. 23–24).

1. The 18th year of the reign of the judges ended.

2. The record of Alma ended.

➤ Superscription: The people of Nephi, their wars and contentions, according to the record of Helaman (chapters 45–62).

➤ 45:1　The people rejoiced because the Lord had again delivered them out of the hands of their enemies.

a. The people of Nephi gave thanks to the Lord their God.

b.   They fasted and prayed much and worshipped God.

➤ 45:2–14   In the 19th year of the reign of the judges, Alma came to his son Helaman and asked if he believed Alma's words about the records that had been kept. Helaman said, yes.

     a.   Alma asked if he believed in Jesus Christ who should come. Helaman said he believed all the words which had been spoken (vv. 4–5).

     b.   Alma asked if he would keep the commandments. Helaman said he would do so with all his heart (vv. 6–7).

     c.   Alma said Helaman was blessed and the Lord would prosper him in the land (v. 8).

     d.   Alma prophesied but told Helaman not to make his prophecies known until they were fulfilled (vv. 9–14).

         1.   The Nephites shall dwindle in unbelief 400 years after Christ shall manifest himself unto them.

         2.   Wars, pestilences, famines and bloodshed, will bring extinction to the Nephites because of unbelief, works of darkness, lasciviousness, and iniquities.

         3.   Because they sin against light and knowledge, the fourth generation will not pass away before this happens.

         4.   The seed of those who are now numbered among the Nephites shall no longer be numbered among them.

         5.   Those not destroyed in that day shall be numbered with the Lamanites and become like them, except for a few who shall be called the disciples of the Lord.

         6.   The Lamanites shall pursue the disciples until they become extinct.

➤ 45:15–17   Alma blessed Helaman and his other sons, and also the earth for the righteous' sake.

     a.   Thus saith the Lord—Cursed unto destruction is the land to all who do wickedly, when they are fully ripe (v. 16).

         1.   This is the cursing or the blessing of God upon the land.

         2.   The Lord cannot look upon sin with the least degree of allowance.

    b.   Alma blessed the church and all those who shall stand fast in the faith (v. 17).

➤ **45:18–19** Alma departed from Zarahemla and was never heard from again, and no one knows of his death and burial.

    a.   He was a righteous man and the saying went abroad in the church that he was taken up by the Spirit, or buried by the hand of the Lord, even as Moses (v. 19).

    b.   The scriptures say the Lord took Moses unto himself, and we suppose the Lord took Alma unto himself (v. 19).

➤ **45:20–24** In the commencement of the nineteenth year of the reign of the judges, Helaman went among the people to declare the word unto them.

    a.   Because of wars and little dissensions and disturbances, it was expedient for a regulation to be made throughout the church (vv. 21–22).

         1.   He and his brethren went to all the cities to establish the church again.

         2.   They appointed priests and teachers over all the churches.

    b.   Their arose a contention and the people would not listen to the words of Helaman and his brethren (vv. 23–24).

         1.   They grew proud, being lifted up in pride because of their riches.

         2.   They grew rich in their own eyes and would not walk uprightly before God.

NOTES AND COMMENTARY

Introduction: When are members of the Church justified or

expected to go to war? President David O. McKay answered this question at the beginning of World War II.

"... there are conditions when entrance into war is justifiable, and when a Christian nation may, without violation of principles, take up arms against an opposing force.

Such a condition, however, is not a real or fancied insult given by one nation to another. When this occurs proper reparation may be made by mutual understanding, apology, or by arbitration.

Neither is there justifiable cause found in a desire or even a need for territorial expansion. The taking of territory implies the subjugation of the weak by the strong—the application of the jungle law.

Nor is war justified in an attempt to enforce a new order of government, or even to impel others to a particular form of worship, however better the government or eternally true the principles of the enforced religion may be.

There are, however, two conditions which may justify a truly Christian man to enter—mind you, I say enter, not begin—a war: (1) An attempt to dominate and to deprive another of his free agency, and, (2) Loyalty to his country. Possibly there is a third, viz., Defense of a weak nation that is being unjustly crushed by a strong, ruthless one.[1]

The chapters of Alma that we will examine verify the words of President McKay.

Alma 43:1–2 • Alma And His Sons Preach The Word

1 And now it came to pass that the sons of Alma did go forth among the people, to declare the word unto them. And Alma, also, himself, could not rest, and he also went forth.

2 Now we shall say no more concerning their preaching, except that they preached the word, and the truth, according to the spirit of

---

[1] General Conference, April 1942, the conference was a solemn assembly held in the temple for leaders only because of the restrictions of the war. The entire address is too long for inclusion here, but is obviously based on teachings of the Book of Mormon and other scriptures, pp. 70–74.

prophecy and revelation; and they preached after the holy order of
God by which they were called.

Apparently Alma does not deem it necessary to expand upon the
preaching at this time. Perhaps there was nothing taught that had not
been mentioned in previous accounts of their preaching. He does want
it known that they were guided by revelation and were under the
authority of the priesthood (v. 2).

Alma 43:3–8 • The Designs Of The Lamanites

3 And now I return to an account of the wars between the Nephites
and the Lamanites, in the eighteenth year of the reign of the judges.

4 For behold, it came to pass that the Zoramites became Lamanites;
therefore, in the commencement of the eighteenth year the people of
the Nephites saw that the Lamanites were coming upon them;
therefore they made preparations for war; yea, they gathered together
their armies in the land of Jershon.

5 And it came to pass that the Lamanites came with their thousands; and they came into the land of Antionum, which is the land
of the Zoramites; and a man by the name of Zerahemnah was their
leader.

6 And now, as the Amalekites were of a more wicked and murderous disposition than the Lamanites were, in and of themselves,
therefore, Zerahemnah appointed chief captains over the Lamanites,
and they were all Amalekites and Zoramites.

7 Now this he did that he might preserve their hatred towards the
Nephites, that he might bring them into subjection to the accomplishment of his designs.

8 For behold, his designs were to stir up the Lamanites to anger
against the Nephites; this he did that he might usurp great power over
them, and also that he might gain power over the Nephites by bringing
them into bondage.

Although the war was between the Nephites and the Lamanites,
it was engineered by the apostate Nephites. The Zoramites had
separated themselves from the Nephites and had previously trodden

down Korihor the anti-Christ (see Alma 30:59). The Zoramites, who had become Lamanites (Alma 43:4), had rejected the missionary efforts of Alma and his companions (see Alma 31–35). Although his lineage is not given, Zarahemnah was apparently a Lamanite since the Lamanites had come into the Zoramite land of Antionum (Alma 43:5).

The Amalekites had apostatized many years earlier, about 90 B.C., and were a people "after the order of the Nehors" (Alma 21:2–4). Zemnarihah's appointment of apostate captains of his armies to preserve hatred towards the Nephites (Alma 43:2–7) was contrary to the Nephite's custom of appointing captains who "had the spirit of revelation and also prophecy" (3 Nephi 3:19). Thus the battle of Satan and Michael that was begun in heaven, or in the pre-mortal life, commenced once more on the earth at this time (see Revelation 12:7). The desire of the Lamanites to bring the Nephites into bondage (Alma 43:8) had been their traditional aspiration through the years, and was a tool of Satan (see Mosiah 7:22; 9:10).

Alma 43:9–14 • The Design Of The Nephites

9 And now the design of the Nephites was to support their lands, and their houses, and their wives, and their children, that they might preserve them from the hands of their enemies; and also that they might preserve their rights and their privileges, yea, and also their liberty, that they might worship God according to their desires.

10 For they knew that if they should fall into the hands of the Lamanites, that whosoever should worship God in spirit and in truth, the true and the living God, the Lamanites would destroy.

11 Yea, and they also knew the extreme hatred of the Lamanites towards their brethren, who were the people of Anti-Nephi-Lehi, who were called the people of Ammon—and they would not take up arms, yea, they had entered into a covenant and they would not break it—therefore, if they should fall into the hands of the Lamanites they would be destroyed.

12 And the Nephites would not suffer that they should be destroyed; therefore they gave them lands for their inheritance.

13 And the people of Ammon did give unto the Nephites a large

portion of their substance to support their armies; and thus the Nephites were compelled, alone, to withstand against the Lamanites, who were a compound of Laman and Lemuel, and the sons of Ishmael, and all those who had dissented from the Nephites, who were Amalekites and Zoramites, and the descendants of the priests of Noah.

14 Now those descendants were as numerous, nearly, as were the Nephites; and thus the Nephites were obliged to contend with their brethren, even unto bloodshed.

The opposite of bondage is freedom, the desire of the Nephites (v. 9). It is also the contrast of Christ and Satan. Christ is the advocate of agency and Satan seeks to destroy agency (see Moses 4:1–4; Abraham 3:24–28). The Lamanites were following Satan's plan in being determined to destroy the Nephite's agency (Alma 43:10). A basic belief of The Church of Jesus Christ of Latter-day Saints is: "We claim the privilege of worshipping Almighty God according to the dictates of our own conscience, and allow all men the same privilege, let them worship how, where, or what they may." (Article of Faith 11). The Nephites had the same belief (Alma 43:9).

The people of Anti-Nephi-Lehi, or the people of Ammon (v. 11), were the Lamanite converts during the mission of the sons of Mosiah (see Alma 23:16–18). The desire of the Nephites was to also maintain freedom for their beloved Lamanite converts. These brethren had covenanted not to take up arms (Alma 43:11; Alma 26:6–19). However, they did support the cause of freedom in other ways (Alma 43:13). Their covenant should remind us of the pledge of allegiance: "I pledge allegiance to the flag of the United States of America and to the republic for which it stands, one nation under God, indivisible, with liberty and justice for all."

Alma 43:15–24 • Moroni, The Nephite Chief Captain

15 And it came to pass as the armies of the Lamanites had gathered together in the land of Antionum, behold, the armies of the Nephites were prepared to meet them in the land of Jershon.

16 Now, the leader of the Nephites, or the man who had been appointed to be the chief captain over the Nephites—now the chief captain took the command of all the armies of the Nephites—and his name was Moroni;

17 And Moroni took all the command, and the government of their wars. And he was only twenty and five years old when he was appointed chief captain over the armies of the Nephites.

18 And it came to pass that he met the Lamanites in the borders of Jershon, and his people were armed with swords, and with cimeters, and all manner of weapons of war.

19 And when the armies of the Lamanites saw that the people of Nephi, or that Moroni, had prepared his people with breastplates and with arm-shields, yea, and also shields to defend their heads, and also they were dressed with thick clothing—

20 Now the army of Zerahemnah was not prepared with any such thing; they had only their swords and their cimeters, their bows and their arrows, their stones and their slings; and they were naked, save it were a skin which was girded about their loins; yea, all were naked, save it were the Zoramites and the Amalekites;

21 But they were not armed with breastplates, nor shields—therefore, they were exceedingly afraid of the armies of the Nephites because of their armor, notwithstanding their number being so much greater than the Nephites.

22 Behold, now it came to pass that they durst not come against the Nephites in the borders of Jershon; therefore they departed out of the land of Antionum into the wilderness, and took their journey round about in the wilderness, away by the head of the river Sidon, that they might come into the land of Manti and take possession of the land; for they did not suppose that the armies of Moroni would know whither they had gone.

23 But it came to pass, as soon as they had departed into the wilderness Moroni sent spies into the wilderness to watch their camp; and Moroni, also, knowing of the prophecies of Alma, sent certain men unto him, desiring him that he should inquire of the Lord whither the armies of the Nephites should go to defend themselves against the Lamanites.

24 And it came to pass that the word of the Lord came unto Alma,

and Alma informed the messengers of Moroni, that the armies of the Lamanites were marching round about in the wilderness, that they might come over into the land of Manti, that they might commence an attack upon the weaker part of the people. And those messengers went and delivered the message unto Moroni.

Moroni had taken command at a very young age (v. 17). He died eighteen years after the account we are reading, in the 36th year of the reign of the judges (see Alma 63:3). Therefore, he may have been appointed some years before, or he would have been only forty-three or forty-four years of age at the time of his death. He had retired one to four years[2] earlier from his military position "to spend the remainder of his days in peace" (Alma 62:43).

Preparation is the mark of a good leader. To be prepared requires anticipation of the future, and Captain Moroni was always prepared for war against the Lamanites (Alma 43:18–21). As the account continues, the Lamanites copy the Nephites innovative methods, but we will see that Captain Moroni was a step ahead and always prepared with some new methods of defense that the Lamanites had not anticipated. On the other hand, the Lamanites still used their basic age-old customs of warfare (see Enos 1:20; Mosiah 10:8; Alma 3:5). They relied on the arm of human strength while Captain Moroni relied on the Lord.

The Lamanites also relied on their reasoning to gain power over the Nephites (Alma 43:22). Captain Moroni relied on revelation through the Lord's prophet for his defense (Alma 44:23). His faith was rewarded, and Alma received Captain Moroni's requested message from the Lord (v. 24). Captain Moroni began his preparation for the next Lamanite invasion.

---

[2] The war ended in the 31st year of the judges (Alma 62:39), and he retired between the end of that year and the 35th year. These years are summarized in Alma 62:40–52 with no specific years given.

Alma 43:25–33 • The Stratagem
Of Captain Moroni

25 Now Moroni, leaving a part of his army in the land of Jershon, lest by any means a part of the Lamanites should come into that land and take possession of the city, took the remaining part of his army and marched over into the land of Manti.

26 And he caused that all the people in that quarter of the land should gather themselves together to battle against the Lamanites, to defend their lands and their country, their rights and their liberties; therefore they were prepared against the time of the coming of the Lamanites.

27 And it came to pass that Moroni caused that his army should be secreted in the valley which was near the bank of the river Sidon, which was on the west of the river Sidon in the wilderness.

28 And Moroni placed spies round about, that he might know when the camp of the Lamanites should come.

29 And now, as Moroni knew the intention of the Lamanites, that it was their intention to destroy their brethren, or to subject them and bring them into bondage that they might establish a kingdom unto themselves over all the land;

30 And he also knowing that it was the only desire of the Nephites to preserve their lands, and their liberty, and their church, therefore he thought it no sin that he should defend them by stratagem; therefore, he found by his spies which course the Lamanites were to take.

31 Therefore, he divided his army and brought a part over into the valley, and concealed them on the east, and on the south of the hill Riplah;

32 And the remainder he concealed in the west valley, on the west of the river Sidon, and so down into the borders of the land Manti.

33 And thus having placed his army according to his desire, he was prepared to meet them.

Once more Mormon contrasts the desires of the Lamanites and the Nephites (vv. 29–30). In doing so, he illustrates another principle of Captain Moroni's leadership; "he thought it no sin that he should defend [the Nephites] by strategem" (v. 30). He was not using a common justification of our day, "the end justifies the means," but was illustrating his concern for fair play, as will be illustrated when the war continues. An astute leader, he was governed by principle. Captain Moroni was relying on his mental powers as well as his physical ones.

Alma 43:34–47 • The Law of War Revealed To The Ancients

34 And it came to pass that the Lamanites came up on the north of the hill, where a part of the army of Moroni was concealed.

35 And as the Lamanites had passed the hill Riplah, and came into the valley, and began to cross the river Sidon, the army which was concealed on the south of the hill, which was led by a man whose name was Lehi, and he led his army forth and encircled the Lamanites about on the east in their rear.

36 And it came to pass that the Lamanites, when they saw the Nephites coming upon them in their rear, turned them about and began to contend with the army of Lehi.

37 And the work of death commenced on both sides, but it was more dreadful on the part of the Lamanites, for their nakedness was exposed to the heavy blows of the Nephites with their swords and their cimeters, which brought death almost at every stroke.

38 While on the other hand, there was now and then a man fell among the Nephites, by their swords and the loss of blood, they being shielded from the more vital parts of the body, or the more vital parts of the body being shielded from the strokes of the Lamanites, by their breastplates, and their armshields, and their head-plates; and thus the Nephites did carry on the work of death among the Lamanites.

39 And it came to pass that the Lamanites became frightened, because of the great destruction among them, even until they began to flee towards the river Sidon.

40 And they were pursued by Lehi and his men; and they were driven by Lehi into the waters of Sidon, and they crossed the waters of Sidon. And Lehi retained his armies upon the bank of the river Sidon that they should not cross.

41 And it came to pass that Moroni and his army met the Lamanites in the valley, on the other side of the river Sidon, and began to fall upon them and to slay them.

42 And the Lamanites did flee again before them, towards the land of Manti; and they were met again by the armies of Moroni.

43 Now in this case the Lamanites did fight exceedingly; yea, never had the Lamanites been known to fight with such exceedingly great strength and courage, no, not even from the beginning.

44 And they were inspired by the Zoramites and the Amalekites, who were their chief captains and leaders, and by Zerahemnah, who was their chief captain, or their chief leader and commander; yea, they did fight like dragons, and many of the Nephites were slain by their hands, yea, for they did smite in two many of their head-plates, and they did pierce many of their breastplates, and they did smite off many of their arms; and thus the Lamanites did smite in their fierce anger.

45 Nevertheless, the Nephites were inspired by a better cause, for they were not fighting for monarchy nor power but they were fighting for their homes and their liberties, their wives and their children, and their all, yea, for their rites of worship and their church.

46 And they were doing that which they felt was the duty which they owed to their God; for the Lord had said unto them, and also unto their fathers, that: Inasmuch as ye are not guilty of the first offense, neither the second, ye shall not suffer yourselves to be slain by the hands of your enemies.

47 And again, the Lord has said that: Ye shall defend your families even unto bloodshed. Therefore for this cause were the Nephites contending with the Lamanites, to defend themselves, and their families, and their lands, their country, and their rights, and their religion.

Again anticipating the moves of the Lamanites, Captain Moroni laid the groundwork for the next defeat of the Lamanites (v. 25). The accompanying figure illustrates his strategy and how it worked. The numbers of the chart are briefly explained there.

The Lamanite leaders, apostate Nephites, inspired their people to be angry which resulted in strength and courage beyond their normal capacities (vv. 43–44). The Nephites were inspired by love of family, freedom, and their God. Thus, they were led by the word of God (vv. 45–46).

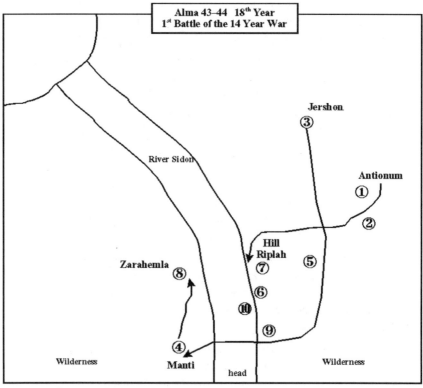

Alma 43–44 18ᵗʰ Year
1ˢᵗ Battle of the 14 Year War

Figure 1. Captain Moroni's Strategy

CAPTAIN MORONI'S STRATEGY
(numbers correspond with the chart)

1. The Lamanites gather to Antionum to battle the Nephites (Alma 43:15).
2. Moroni meets the Lamanites and in fear they depart for the land of Manti (Alma 43:18–22).
3. Moroni sends spies who see the Lamanites fleeing towards Manti. He

leaves part of his army to defend the land of Jershon (Alma 43:23–28).

4. Enroute to Manti Moroni's men split, under Lehi some camp east and south of the hill Riplah (Alma 43:31).

5. The remainder of Moroni's men continue to a valley on the west side of the river Sidon near the borders of Manti (Alma 43:32–33).

6. The Lamanites begin to cross the river Sidon (Alma 43:34–35).

7. Lehi's men attack the Lamanites from the rear on the east side of the river Sidon (Alma 43:35–40).

8. Moroni's men meet the Lamanites on the west bank of the river Sidon (Alma 43:41).

9. The Lamanites flee toward Manti but are cut off by Moroni (Alma 43:42–50).

10. The Lamanites are encircled on the west by Moroni, and on the east by Lehi (Alma 43:51–54).

The source of what the Lord had said (vv. 46–47) was undoubtedly the plates of brass. As stated under the precepts of this chapter, the ancients had been taught the law of war, and the Nephites were included among the ancients. There are two parts of the law quoted by Mormon, as he abridges the record. The first part, the defense of a nation against an enemy nation, was given more fully to the Prophet Joseph Smith:

> 33 And again, this is the law that I gave unto mine ancients, that they should not go out unto battle against any nation, kindred, tongue, or people, save I, the Lord, commanded them.

> 34 And if any nation, tongue, or people should proclaim war against them, they should first lift a standard of peace unto that people, nation, or tongue;

> 35 And if that people did not accept the offering of peace, neither the second nor the third time, they should bring these testimonies before the Lord;

> 36 Then I, the Lord, would give unto them a commandment, and justify them in going out to battle against that nation, tongue, or people.

> 37 And I, the Lord, would fight their battles, and their children's

battles, and their children's children's, until they had avenged themselves on all their enemies, to the third and fourth generation.

38 Behold, this is an ensample unto all people, saith the Lord your God, for justification before me. [D&C 98:33–38]

The lifting of the standard of peace is a condition presented to the aggressor. In Captain Moroni's situation, the lifting of the standard is recorded in the forty-fourth chapter of Alma, and will be discussed there.

The second part of the law of war, the defending of your families even unto bloodshed, had been practiced by Captain Moroni already. This part of the law appears to have been separated from the first part on the plates of brass as indicated by "again the Lord has said" (Alma 43:47). The significant point of this part of the law is that you do not have to wait for three offenses to defend yourself, your family, or your personal rights (v. 47). Captain Moroni's men had defended their people even unto bloodshed on both sides of the river Sidon (vv. 37–41).

Alma 43:48–54 • Captain Moroni Inspires His Men With Thoughts Of Freedom

48 And it came to pass that when the men of Moroni saw the fierceness and the anger of the Lamanites, they were about to shrink and flee from them. And Moroni, perceiving their intent, sent forth and inspired their hearts with these thoughts—yea, the thoughts of their lands, their liberty, yea, their freedom from bondage.

49 And it came to pass that they turned upon the Lamanites, and they cried with one voice unto the Lord their God, for their liberty and their freedom from bondage.

50 And they began to stand against the Lamanites with power; and in that selfsame hour that they cried unto the Lord for their freedom, the Lamanites began to flee before them; and they fled even to the waters of Sidon.

51 Now, the Lamanites were more numerous, yea, by more than double the number of the Nephites; nevertheless, they were driven

insomuch that they were gathered together in one body in the valley, upon the bank by the river Sidon.

52 Therefore the armies of Moroni encircled them about, yea, even on both sides of the river, for behold, on the east were the men of Lehi.

53 Therefore when Zerahemnah saw the men of Lehi on the east of the river Sidon, and the armies of Moroni on the west of the river Sidon, that they were encircled about by the Nephites, they were struck with terror.

54 Now Moroni, when he saw their terror, commanded his men that they should stop shedding their blood.

The leadership of Captain Moroni was again shown as he rallied his forces to drive the Lamanites into one body on the bank of the river Sidon (vv. 48–51). Certainly he had a captive audience to whom he raised the standard of liberty, the army of Lehi on the east bank and Captain Moroni's army on the west. Because the Lamanites were filled with terror, they were prepared to listen (vv. 51–54). Captain Moroni was evidently interested in more than victory, he desired peace with his Lamanite neighbors (v. 54).

Alma 44:1–7 • Captain Moroni Raises the Standard of Liberty

1 And it came to pass that they did stop and withdrew a pace from them. And Moroni said unto Zerahemnah: Behold, Zerahemnah, that we do not desire to be men of blood. Ye know that ye are in our hands, yet we do not desire to slay you.

2 Behold, we have not come out to battle against you that we might shed your blood for power; neither do we desire to bring any one to the yoke of bondage. But this is the very cause for which ye have come against us; yea, and ye are angry with us because of our religion.

3 But now, ye behold that the Lord is with us; and ye behold that he has delivered you into our hands. And now I would that ye should understand that this is done unto us because of our religion and our faith in Christ. And now ye see that ye cannot destroy this our faith.

4 Now ye see that this is the true faith of God; yea, ye see that God will support, and keep, and preserve us, so long as we are faithful unto

him, and unto our faith, and our religion; and never will the Lord
suffer that we shall be destroyed except we should fall into transgression and deny our faith.

5 And now, Zerahemnah, I command you, in the name of that all-
powerful God, who has strengthened our arms that we have gained
power over you, by our faith, by our religion, and by our rites of
worship, and by our church, and by the sacred support which we owe
to our wives and our children, by that liberty which binds us to our
lands and our country; yea, and also by the maintenance of the sacred
word of God, to which we owe all our happiness; and by all that is
most dear unto us—

6 Yea, and this is not all; I command you by all the desires which
ye have for life, that ye deliver up your weapons of war unto us, and
we will seek not your blood, but we will spare your lives, if ye will
go your way and come not again to war against us.

7 And now, if ye do not this, behold, ye are in our hands, and I
will command my men that they shall fall upon you, and inflict the
wounds of death in your bodies, that ye may become extinct; and then
we will see who shall have power over this people; yea, we will see
who shall be brought into bondage.

Captain Moroni was not guilty of the first offense according to
the law of war (Alma 43:46; D&C 98:34). His speech to his captive
audience included several important declarations relative to the law
of war. First, the Nephites did not desire to shed blood, the Lamanites
had initiated the war (D&C 98:34). Second, they did not want to bring
the Lamanites into bondage, which was the Lamanite design of the
war (Alma 44:2). The third point was about God and his people,
certainly the most important declaration of all (vv. 2–4). Captain
Moroni recognized that the Lord had fought the battle as the law of
war promised (D&C 98:37). He testified of the truth of the Nephite
religion, and because of their faith in that religion, with which the
Lamanites were angry, and their faith in Christ, the Nephites had been
supported (Alma 44:2–5). Certainly Alma or Captain Moroni had
brought their testimonies before the Lord (D&C 98:35). Captain
Moroni, who had the spirit of revelation and prophecy (see 3 Nephi
3:19), commanded Zarahemnah in the name of the all-powerful God

who had strengthened them to lay down their weapons (Alma 44:5–6). Does this not strongly imply that God had commanded Alma or Captain Moroni to go to war against the Lamanites as the law of war promised (D&C 98:36)? Last of all, Captain Moroni threatened Zarahemnah that he would resume the wounds of death if the standards of peace were rejected (Alma 44:7). He demanded an unconditional surrender. This was no political or economic war, but a war for the Lord and the freedom of his people. There must be no compromise with the devil and his servants.

Alma 44:8–15 • Zarahemnah Rejects The Conditions Of Peace

8 And now it came to pass that when Zerahemnah had heard these sayings he came forth and delivered up his sword and his cimeter, and his bow into the hands of Moroni, and said unto him: Behold, here are our weapons of war; we will deliver them up unto you, but we will not suffer ourselves to take an oath unto you, which we know that we shall break, and also our children; but take our weapons of war, and suffer that we may depart into the wilderness; otherwise we will retain our swords, and we will perish or conquer.

9 Behold, we are not of your faith; we do not believe that it is God that has delivered us into your hands; but we believe that it is your cunning that has preserved you from our swords. Behold, it is your breastplates and your shields that have preserved you.

10 And now when Zerahemnah had made an end of speaking these words, Moroni returned the sword and the weapons of war, which he had received, unto Zerahemnah, saying: Behold, we will end the conflict.

11 Now I cannot recall the words which I have spoken, therefore as the Lord liveth, ye shall not depart except ye depart with an oath that ye will not return again against us to war. Now as ye are in our hands we will spill your blood upon the ground, or ye shall submit to the conditions which I have proposed.

12 And now when Moroni had said these words, Zerahemnah retained his sword, and he was angry with Moroni, and he rushed forward that he might slay Moroni; but as he raised his sword, behold,

one of Moroni's soldiers smote it even to the earth, and it broke by the hilt; and he also smote Zerahemnah that he took off his scalp and it fell to the earth. And Zerahemnah withdrew from before them into the midst of his soldiers.

13 And it came to pass that the soldier who stood by, who smote off the scalp of Zerahemnah, took up the scalp from off the ground by the hair, and laid it upon the point of his sword, and stretched it forth unto them, saying unto them with a loud voice:

14 Even as this scalp has fallen to the earth, which is the scalp of your chief, so shall ye fall to the earth except ye will deliver up your weapons of war and depart with a covenant of peace.

15 Now there were many, when they heard these words and saw the scalp which was upon the sword, that were struck with fear; and many came forth and threw down their weapons of war at the feet of Moroni, and entered into a covenant of peace. And as many as entered into a covenant they suffered to depart into the wilderness.

Zarahemnah knew he was defeated, but he was not willing to meet all of the conditions of peace (v. 8). The sacredness of the oath among the people from whence the families of Lehi and Ishmael came in 600 B.C. is again shown. The oath was more sacred than death even among the Lamanites (v. 8). However, Zarahemnah lacked a commitment to and a knowledge of God. Once more he put the strength of man above the power of God (v. 9).

Captain Moroni's commitment to fair play, as suggested above (Alma 43:30), is now illustrated. In spite of the superior number of the Lamanites (see Alma 43:51), he returns the weapons to Zarahemnah (Alma 44:10) that there be no advantage to the Nephites. Perhaps he wanted to show that God was with them as he had testified.

Although it is not stated clearly that Moroni is raising the standard of liberty the second time, it is implied by the Lamanites not being allowed to depart unless they make the oath not to return in war. "As the Lord liveth" is a sacred part of an oath (see 1 Nephi 4:32). Moroni would not recall his words. The conditions of peace belong to the victor and were not to be altered. Surely he was not responsible for the second offense, the Lamanite attack about to begin (see Alma 43:46). The Lord would also fight this battle.

Again Zarahemnah rejects the standard of peace. If Captain Moroni did not raise the standard of peace a second time, it was raised through the soldier who had smitten off Zarahemnah's scalp (Alma 44:13–14). Even though Zarahemnah had rejected the peace offer, many others did not accept the second offer (v. 14). Nothing is said about the lineage of those who accepted the second offer, but from reasoning it seems they were Lamanites and not Zoramites or Amalekites. Some have speculated that this incident was the origin of scalping by latter-day Americans Indians. Dr Daniel H. Ludlow has commented:

> Recent evidence would seem to indicate the American Indian did not have a scalping tradition until after the coming of the white man—that is, until the seventeenth century A.D. Apparently it was the white man who started the scalping custom, when some of the early colonists offered money for the scalps or hair of dead Indians. In order to get even with the evil white men who killed Indians just for their scalps (in much the same way as they would kill a buffalo for its hide), the Indians started to kill and scalp the whites in return.[3]

Alma 44:16–24 • The War, The 18ᵗʰ Year, and The Record Of Alma Is Ended

> 16 Now it came to pass that Zerahemnah was exceedingly wroth, and he did stir up the remainder of his soldiers to anger, to contend more powerfully against the Nephites.
>
> 17 And now Moroni was angry, because of the stubbornness of the Lamanites; therefore he commanded his people that they should fall upon them and slay them. And it came to pass that they began to slay them; yea, and the Lamanites did contend with their swords and their might.
>
> 18 But behold, their naked skins and their bare heads were exposed to the sharp swords of the Nephites; yea, behold they were pierced and smitten, yea, and did fall exceedingly fast before the swords of

---

[3] *A Companion to Your Study of the Book of Mormon* [1976], 232.

the Nephites; and they began to be swept down, even as the soldier of Moroni had prophesied.

19 Now Zerahemnah, when he saw that they were all about to be destroyed, cried mightily unto Moroni, promising that he would covenant and also his people with them, if they would spare the remainder of their lives, that they never would come to war again against them.

20 And it came to pass that Moroni caused that the work of death should cease again among the people. And he took the weapons of war from the Lamanites; and after they had entered into a covenant with him of peace they were suffered to depart into the wilderness.

21 Now the number of their dead was not numbered because of the greatness of the number; yea, the number of their dead was exceedingly great, both on the Nephites and on the Lamanites.

22 And it came to pass that they did cast their dead into the waters of Sidon, and they have gone forth and are buried in the depths of the sea.

23 And the armies of the Nephites, or of Moroni, returned and came to their houses and their lands.

24 And thus ended the eighteenth year of the reign of the judges over the people of Nephi. And thus ended the record of Alma, which was written upon the plates of Nephi.

These verses are self-explanatory. In addition to the summary in the heading of the above verses, the prophecy of the soldier was fulfilled, Zarahemnah cried for an end and Moroni ended the mass killing. However, as the following chapter will show, it was short lived.

Superscription:

The account of the people of Nephi, and their wars and dissensions, in the days of Helaman, according to the record of Helaman, which he kept in his days. Comprising chapters 45 to 62 inclusive.

As previously explained, the two chapters from the record of Alma were included in this volume instead of volume 3 because of their subject of war that continues in the record of Helaman.

Alma 45:1–8 • The Records Are Turned Over To Helaman, Son Of Helaman

1 Behold, now it came to pass that the people of Nephi were exceedingly rejoiced, because the Lord had again delivered them out of the hands of their enemies; therefore they gave thanks unto the Lord their God; yea, and they did fast much and pray much, and they did worship God with exceedingly great joy.

2 And it came to pass in the nineteenth year of the reign of the judges over the people of Nephi, that Alma came unto his son Helaman and said unto him: Believest thou the words which I spake unto thee concerning those records which have been kept?

3 And Helaman said unto him: Yea, I believe.

4 And Alma said again: Believest thou in Jesus Christ, who shall come?

5 And he said: Yea, I believe all the words which thou hast spoken.

6 And Alma said unto him again: Will ye keep my commandments?

7 And he said: Yea, I will keep thy commandments with all my heart.

8 Then Alma said unto him: Blessed art thou; and the Lord shall prosper thee in this land.

The three questions asked of Helaman by Alma: Do you believe the words I told you about the past records (i.e., the records the Lord has commanded to be kept)? Do you believe in Jesus Christ who shall come? Will you follow my commandments to preserve and keep the records (vv. 2–6; see also Alma 37:1–10)? These should be guidelines for every keeper of historical records. The Lord and his Church command that records be kept that we may learn from the experiences of others rather than the school of hard knocks. Those who keep good records will be blessed, as Alma promised Helaman (v. 8)

Alma 45: 9–14 • The Prophecies Of Alma

9 But behold, I have somewhat to prophesy unto thee; but what I prophesy unto thee ye shall not make known; yea, what I prophesy unto thee shall not be made known, even until the prophecy is fulfilled; therefore write the words which I shall say.

10 And these are the words: Behold, I perceive that this very people, the Nephites, according to the spirit of revelation which is in me, in four hundred years from the time that Jesus Christ shall manifest himself unto them, shall dwindle in unbelief.

11 Yea, and then shall they see wars and pestilences, yea, famines and bloodshed, even until the people of Nephi shall become extinct—

12 Yea, and this because they shall dwindle in unbelief and fall into the works of darkness, and lasciviousness, and all manner of iniquities; yea, I say unto you, that because they shall sin against so great light and knowledge, yea, I say unto you, that from that day, even the fourth generation shall not all pass away before this great iniquity shall come.

13 And when that great day cometh, behold, the time very soon cometh that those who are now, or the seed of those who are now numbered among the people of Nephi, shall no more be numbered among the people of Nephi.

14 But whosoever remaineth, and is not destroyed in that great and dreadful day, shall be numbered among the Lamanites, and shall become like unto them, all, save it be a few who shall be called the disciples of the Lord; and them shall the Lamanites pursue even until they shall become extinct. And now, because of iniquity, this prophecy shall be fulfilled.

Alma's direction that Helaman not disclose his prophecies until they were fulfilled (v. 9), has implications for our day. Do the leaders in the Church today know more than they tell us? Why do they not tell us? The answer to the first question can only come from our leaders, but some day we will know the answer. The answer to the second question is probably because of the principle of agency. We are on the earth to be tested and learn for ourselves and from the records of others. Our leaders will give us guidance even though they do not tell us some of the things they know. We can also learn to be guided by the Spirit or receive personal revelation.

The things Alma prophesied were fulfilled and noted in the record at the time of their fulfillment, as we will now discuss. When the Savior visited the Nephites, he repeated the prophecy of the destruction of the Nephites in four hundred years from the time that Christ manifested himself to the Nephites (vv. 10–12; see 3 Nephi 27:32). "More than four hundred and twenty years [had] passed away since the sign was given of the coming of Christ" when Moroni, the son of Mormon the abridger of the record, recorded the last book of the Book of Mormon record (Moroni 10:1). The gradual destruction of the fourth generation is recorded in 4 Nephi and Mormon.

The surviving Nephites being numbered among the Lamanites (v. 14) was also a fulfillment. When Mormon, the abridger of the Book of Mormon, turned over the record to his son Moroni in A.D. 385 (Mormon 6:5), there were only "twenty and four [Nephites] who were with [Mormon], and a few who had escaped into the south countries" (Mormon 6:15). In A.D. 400, when Moroni begins to record upon the plates, "the Lamanites [had] hunted my people, the Nephites, . . .even until they are no more . . . And there are none that do know the true God save it be the disciples of Jesus" (Moroni 8:7, 10). We will leave further verification of these prophecies for the future volumes of this work, but sufficient is given to verify their fulfillment.

Alma 45:15–19 • Alma Departs out of the Land and Is Never Heard from Again

15 And now it came to pass that after Alma had said these things to Helaman, he blessed him, and also his other sons; and he also blessed the earth for the righteous' sake.

16 And he said: Thus saith the Lord God—Cursed shall be the land, yea, this land, unto every nation, kindred, tongue, and people, unto destruction, which do wickedly, when they are fully ripe; and as I have said so shall it be; for this is the cursing and the blessing of God upon the land, for the Lord cannot look upon sin with the least degree of allowance.

17 And now, when Alma had said these words he blessed the church, yea, all those who should stand fast in the faith from that time henceforth.

18 And when Alma had done this he departed out of the land of Zarahemla, as if to go into the land of Melek. And it came to pass that he was never heard of more; as to his death or burial we know not of.

19 Behold, this we know, that he was a righteous man; and the saying went abroad in the church that he was taken up by the Spirit, or buried by the hand of the Lord, even as Moses. But behold, the scriptures saith the Lord took Moses unto himself; and we suppose that he has also received Alma in the spirit, unto himself; therefore, for this cause we know nothing concerning his death and burial.

Alma apparently anticipated that he was at the end of his time on earth. In addition to turning over the records to his son Helaman, he gives a final blessing to his sons, the land, and the church. It was his final blessing whether he knew or not that it would be (vv. 15–17). The cursing of the earth for the wicked, as opposed to the blessing (v. 16) was not the same as when the Lord cursed "the ground for Adam's sake" (Genesis 3:17). Adam was to work the ground for his own benefit while the Nephite land would be destroyed if the commandments of God were not kept. The cursing or blessing to which Alma refers was given to the Nephites (2 Nephi 1:5–10) and the Jaredites (Ether 2:9–12), and is still applicable today in the Americas.

The mystery of Alma, son of Alma, departing and never being heard of again (Alma 45:18) led to the conclusion by some in the Nephite Church that he was taken up by the Spirit or translated (v. 19). His comparison to Moses leads us to examine what happened to Moses: "So Moses the servant of the LORD died there in the land of Moab, according to the word of the LORD. And he buried him in a valley in the land of Moab, over against Beth-peor: but no man knoweth of his sepulcher unto this day" (Deuteronomy 34:5–6). That there was also a controversy over Moses death or being translated is verified in the New Testament: "Yet Michael the archangel, when contending with the devil he disputed about the body of Moses, durst not bring against him a railing accusation, but said, The Lord rebuke thee" (Jude 1:9). Why would Michael[4] contend with the devil over Moses burial? If Moses was translated, it was for a purpose. The purpose was to have a physical body in order to lay on hands and transfer keys to a later generation before there was a resurrection. Moses did appear on the Mount of transfiguration for that purpose.

> 1 And after six days Jesus taketh Peter, James, and John his brother, and bringeth them up into an high mountain apart,
>
> 2 And was transfigured before them: and his face did shine as the sun, and his raiment was white as the light.
>
> 3 And, behold, there appeared unto them Moses and Elias talking with him. [Matthew 17:1–3]

The Prophet Joseph Smith informed us: "The Savior, Moses, and Elias gave the keys to Peter, James and John, on the mount, when they were transfigured before him" (*TPJS*, 158). The JST further verifies that Moses was translated: "So Moses the servant of the Lord died there in the land of Moab, according to the word of the Lord. *For the Lord took him unto his fathers,* in a valley in the land of Moab, over against Beth-peor; therefore no man knoweth of his sepulcher unto this day" (JST, Deuteronomy 34:5–6; italics designates changes).

The evidence supports that Moses was translated, but what about Alma. While we cannot say for sure that Alma was translated, there is a good possibility that he was. If he was it would have been for a similar purpose as Moses, to pass on keys of authority to a future generation. The unabridged plates of Nephi may answer that question (see 3 Nephi 26:9–11).

Alma 45:20–24 • Helaman and His Brethren Preach the Word

> 20 And now it came to pass in the commencement of the nineteenth year of the reign of the judges over the people of Nephi, that

---

[4] The Prophet Joseph Smith identified Adam as "Michael the Archangel, spoken of in the Scriptures" (*TPJS*, 157).

Helaman went forth among the people to declare the word unto them.

21 For behold, because of their wars with the Lamanites and the many little dissensions and disturbances which had been among the people, it became expedient that the word of God should be declared among them, yea, and that a regulation should be made throughout the church.

22 Therefore, Helaman and his brethren went forth to establish the church again in all the land, yea, in every city throughout all the land which was possessed by the people of Nephi. And it came to pass that they did appoint priests and teachers throughout all the land, over all the churches.

23 And now it came to pass that after Helaman and his brethren had appointed priests and teachers over the churches that there arose a dissension among them, and they would not give heed to the words of Helaman and his brethren;

24 But they grew proud, being lifted up in their hearts, because of their exceedingly great riches; therefore they grew rich in their own eyes, and would not give heed to their words, to walk uprightly before God.

Helaman took his commitment to Alma seriously. He was more than a record keeper, he obviously succeeded his father as the high priest of the church (see Alma 4:18) and went forth to establish the church, or strengthen it from the effects of the wars (vv. 21–22. The old problem of pride and riches again surfaces (v. 24; see Jacob 2:13; Alma 4:6). However, Helaman had left them without excuse. He had taught them the word of God.

SACRED WRITING

Preaching Which is Sacred:

Alma 44:1–7; 10–11   Captain Moroni to Zarahemnah on conditions of peace.

Prophesying:

Alma 45:9–16	Alma to Helaman on the downfall of the Nephites in A.D. 400.

Doctrines Learned:

Alma 43:46	The law of war requires the lifting of the standard of peace to the enemy three times.
Alma 43:47	You shall defend yourself, family, and personal rights even to bloodshed.
Alma 45:16	The land of the Americas is cursed to the wicked for the Lord cannot look upon sin with the least degree of allowance.
Alma 45:19	Moses was taken up by the Spirit, or translated.

General Authority Quotes:

President Gordon B. Hinckley • Alma 43:45–47

The nations of the earth have been divided over the present situation. Feelings have run strong. There have been demonstrations for and against. We are now a world Church with members in most of the nations which have argued this matter. Our people have had feelings. They have had concerns.

War, of course, is not new. The weapons change. The ability to kill and destroy is constantly refined. But there has been conflict throughout the ages over essentially the same issues.

The book of Revelation speaks briefly of what must have been a terrible conflict for the minds and loyalties of God's children. The account is worth repeating:

"And there was war in heaven: Michael and his angels fought against the dragon; and the dragon fought and his angels,

"And prevailed not; neither was their place found any more in heaven.

"And the great dragon was cast out, that old serpent, called the Devil, and Satan, which deceiveth the whole world: he was cast out into the earth, and his angels were cast out with him" (Revelation 12:7–9).

Isaiah speaks further concerning that great conflict (see Isaiah 14:12–20). Modern revelation gives additional light (see D&C 76:25–29), as does the book of Moses (see Moses 4:1–4), which tells of Satan's plan to destroy the agency of man.

We sometimes are prone to glorify the great empires of the past, such as the Ottoman Empire, the Roman and Byzantine Empires, and in more recent times, the vast British Empire. But there is a darker side to every one of them. There is a grim and tragic overlay of brutal conquest, of subjugation, of repression, and an astronomical cost in life and treasure.

The great English essayist Thomas Carlyle once ironically shared the observation, "God must needs laugh outright, could such a thing be, to see his wondrous manikins below" (quoted in Sartor Resartus [1836], 182). I think our Father in Heaven must have wept as He has looked down upon His children through the centuries as they have squandered their divine birthright in ruthlessly destroying one another.

In the course of history, tyrants have arisen from time to time who have oppressed their own people and threatened the world. Such is adjudged to be the case presently, and consequently great and terrifying forces with sophisticated and fearsome armaments have been engaged in battle.

Many of our own Church members have been involved in this conflict. We have seen on televisions and in the press tearful children clinging to their fathers in uniform, going to the battlefront. . . .

The question arises, "Where does the Church stand in all of this?"

First, let it be understood that we have no quarrel with the Muslim people or with those of any other faith. We recognize and teach that all the people of the earth are of the family of God. And as He is our Father, so are we brothers and sisters with family obligations one to another. . . .

But as citizens we are all under the direction of our respective national leaders. They have access to greater political and military intelligence than do the people generally. Those in the armed services are under obligation to their respective governments to execute the will of the sovereign. When they joined the military service, they entered into a contract by which they are presently bound and to which they have dutifully responded.

One of the Articles of Faith, which represents an expression of our doctrine, states, "We believe in being subject to kings, presidents, rulers, and magistrates, in obeying, honoring, and sustaining the law" (Articles of Faith 1:12).

But modern revelation states that we are to "renounce war and proclaim peace" (D&C 98:16). In a democracy we can renounce war and proclaim peace. There is opportunity for dissent. Many have been speaking out and doing so emphatically. That is their privilege. That is their right, so long as they do so legally. However, we all must also be mindful of another overriding responsibility, which I may add, governs my personal feelings and dictates my personal loyalties in the present situation.

When war raged between the Nephites and the Lamanites, the record states that "the Nephites were inspired by a better cause, for they were not fighting for . . . power but they were fighting for their homes and their liberties, their wives and their children, and their all, yea, for their rites of worship and their church.

"And they were doing that which they felt was the duty which they owed to their God" (Alma 43:45–46).

The Lord counseled them, "Defend your families even unto bloodshed" (Alma 43:47).

And Moroni "rent his coat; and he took a piece thereof, and wrote upon it—In memory of our God, our religion, and freedom, and our peace, our wives, and our children—and he fastened it upon the end of a pole.

"And he fastened on his head plate, and his breastplate, and his shields, and girded on his armor about his loins; and he took the pole, which had on the end thereof his rent coat, (and he called it the title of liberty) and he bowed himself to the earth, and he prayed mightily unto his God for the blessings of liberty to rest upon his brethren" (Alma 46:12–13).

It is clear from these and other writings that there are times and circumstances when nations are justified, in fact have an obligation, to fight for family, for liberty, and against tyranny, threat, and oppression.

When all is said and done, we of this Church are people of peace. We are followers of our Redeemer, the Lord Jesus Christ, who was the Prince of Peace. But even He said, "Think not that I am come to send peace on earth: I came not to send peace, but a sword" (Matthew 10:34).

This places us in the position of those who long for peace, who teach peace, who work for peace, but who also are citizens of nations and are subject to the laws of our governments. Furthermore, we are a freedom-loving people, committed to the defense of liberty wherever it is in jeopardy. I believe that God will not hold men and women in uniform responsible as agents of their government in carrying forward that which they are legally obligated to do. It may even be that He will hold us responsible if we try to impede or hedge up the way of those who are involved in a contest with forces of evil and repression.

Now, there is much that we can and must do in these perilous times. We can give our opinions on the merits of the situation as we see it, but never let us become a party to words or works of evil concerning our brothers and sisters in various nations on one side or the other. Political differences never justify hatred or ill will. I hope that the lord's people may be at peace one with another during times of trouble, regardless of what loyalties they may have to different governments or parties.

Let us pray for those who are called upon to bear arms by their respective governments and plead for the protection of heaven upon them that they may return to their loved ones in safety.

To our brothers and sisters in harm's way, we say that we pray for you. We pray that the Lord will watch over you and preserve you from injury and that you may return home and pick up your lives again. We know that you are not in that land of blowing sand and brutal heat because you enjoy the games of war. The strength of your commitment is measured by your willingness to give your very lives for that in which you believe.

We know that some have died, and others may yet die in this hot and deadly contest. We can do all in our power to comfort and bless those who lose loved ones. May those who mourn be comforted with that comfort which comes alone from Christ, the Redeemer. [CR April 2003, 82–84]

President Ezra Taft Benson • Alma 44:5

The right to property is based on scriptural precept (see D&C 134:2; Alma 44:5; Matthew 5:5; Isaiah 14:1). It recognizes that the earth belongs to the Lord, that He created it for man's blessing and benefit. Thus, man's desire to own property, his own home and goods, his own business, is desirable and good. Utopian and communitarian schemes that eliminate property rights are not only unworkable, they also deny to man his inherent desire to improve his station. They are therefore contrary to the pursuit of happiness. [*The Teachings of Ezra Taft Benson* (1988), 607]

President Joseph Fielding Smith • Alma 45:18–19

There are several important prophets who were granted the privilege of remaining on the earth. John the Revelator was one of those, and in the Doctrine and Covenants, section seven, is an account of this. Elijah evidently was another, for no living soul could have received the resurrection until after our Redeemer had opened the graves. The scriptural inference is that Moses also was translated as was Alma. In the case of Alma we read in the book of Alma the following:

(Quotes Alma 45:18–19)

It is a very reasonable thought to believe that both Moses and Alma, like Elijah and John, were translated to accomplish some work which the Lord had in store for them at some future day. [*Answers to Gospel Questions*, comp. Joseph Fielding Smith Jr., 5 vols. (1972) 5:38]

President Joseph Fielding Smith • Alma 45:19

. . . we understand why Elijah and Moses were preserved from death: because *they* had a *mission* to *perform*, and it had to be performed *before* the crucifixion of the Son of God, and *it could not be done in the spirit. They had to have tangible bodies.* Christ is the first fruits of the resurrection; therefore if any former prophets had a work to perform preparatory to the mission of the Son of God, or to the dispensation of the meridian of times, it was essential that they be preserved to fulfill that mission *in the flesh.* For that reason Moses *disappeared* from among the people and was taken up into the mountain, and the people *thought* he was buried by the Lord. The Lord preserved him, so that he could come at the proper time and *restore his keys*, on the heads of Peter, James, and John, who stood at the head of the dispensation of the meridian of time. He reserved Elijah from death that he might also come and bestow his keys upon the heads of Peter, James and John and prepare them for their ministry.

But, one says, the Lord could have waited until after his resurrection, and then they could have done it. It is quite evident, due to the fact that it did so occur, that it had to be done before; and there was a reason. There may have been other reasons, but there is one reason *why Moses and Elijah did*

not suffer death in the flesh, like other men do. [*Doctrines of Salvation*, comp.
Bruce R. McConkie, 3 vols. (1954–56), 2:110–11]

President Joseph Fielding Smith

Our question is, however, is there ever a time when war, or the taking
up of arms is justified?

Yes, there are such times. There have been many instances when the Lord
has justified the taking up of arms and has approved his people in their
obedience to such action. When it becomes necessary for a righteous people
to take arms against their enemies who are the aggressors, in protection of
their lives and in defense of their possessions, the Lord has approved. If you
will read the scriptures carefully, you will discover that the Lord commanded
his chosen people to prepare for war and even to be the aggressors in the
accomplishment of his purposes. Here are a few examples:

"And Israel vowed a vow unto the Lord, and said, If thou wilt indeed
deliver this people into my hand, then I will utterly destroy their cities.

"And the Lord hearkened to the voice of Israel, and delivered up the
Canaanites; and they utterly destroyed them and their cities: and he called
the name of place Hormah" (Numbers 21:2–3).

"And the Lord spake unto Moses, saying,

"Avenge the children of Israel of the Midianites: afterward shalt thou
be gathered unto thy people.

"And Moses spake unto the people, saying, Arm some of yourselves unto
the war, and let them go against the Midianites, and avenge the Lord of
Midian" (Numbers 31:1–3).

"When the Lord thy God shall bring thee into the land whither thou goest
to possess it, and hath cast out many nations before thee, and the Hittites,
and the Girgashites, and the Amorites, and the Canaanites, and the Perizzites,
and the Hivites, and the Jebusites, seven nations greater and mightier than
thou;

"And when the Lord thy God shall deliver them before thee; thou shalt
smite them, and utterly destroy them; thou shalt make no covenant with them,
nor shew mercy unto them.

"Neither shalt thou make marriages with them; thy daughter thou shalt not give unto his son, nor his daughter shalt though take unto they son" (Deuteronomy 7:1–3).

All through the Old Testament you will find commandments which were given to Israel to go to war. There were good reasons for this which may be discovered by reading these parts of the Bible.

The Lord has always upheld a people which righteously defends itself against wicked aggression. He has said that he cleansed this American continent by the shedding of blood and justified the American colonists in their war of the American Revolution. Through Samuel, the Lord commanded Israel to make war on Israel's enemies. [*Answers to Gospel Questions*, comp. Joseph Fielding Smith Jr., 5 vols. (1954–56), 3:50–55]

President Charles W. Penrose • Alma 43:45–47

True, Jesus Christ taught that non-resistance was right and praiseworthy and a duty under certain circumstances and conditions; but just look at him when he went into the temple, when he made that scourge of thongs, when he turned out the money-changers and kicked over their tables and told them to get out of the house of the Lord! "My house is a house of prayer," he said, "but ye have made it a den of thieves." Get out of here! Hear him crying, "Woe unto you Scribes, Pharisees, hypocrites, ye compass sea and land to make one proselyte, and then ye make him ten-fold more the child of hell than he was before." That was the other side of the spirit of Jesus. Jesus was no milksop. He was not to be trampled under foot. He was ready to submit when the time came for his martyrdom, and he was to be nailed on the cross as a sacrifice for the sins of the world, but he was ready at any time to stand up for his rights like a man. He is not only called "the Lamb slain from the foundation of the world," but also "the Lion of the Tribe of Judah," and He will be seen to be terrible by and by to his enemies.

Now while we are not particularly required to pattern after the "lion" side of his character unless it becomes necessary, the Lord does not expect us to . . . inculcate the spirit of war nor the spirit of bloodshed. In fact he has commanded us not to shed blood, but there are times and seasons, as we can find in the history of the world, in Bible and the Book of Mormon, when it is justifiable and right and proper and the duty of men to go forth in the defense of their homes and their families and maintain their privileges and rights by force of arms. On this subject I might read something to you if there were plenty of time, but you can read it yourselves when you get home. Read the 101st section of the Doctrine and Covenants, then read the 98th section.

In section 101 the Lord speaks about the constitution of this land. He says it was framed by wise men whom he raised up for that very purpose. What for? To maintain the rights and privileges "of all flesh." Not alone the people of this land. The principles of that great instrument are to go forth to the nations, and the time will come when they will prevail, just as sure as the sun shines even when it appears to be in darkness and the clouds are over it. [CR April, 1917, 19–22]

Challenges to Eternal Life:

1. Make a commitment to do your part in preserving your rights and privileges and those of your family that they may worship God according to their desires (Alma 43:9).

2. Seek the advice of the prophet by studying the latest conference addresses (Alma 43:23–24).

3. Study the law of war in Alma 43:46–47 and D&C 98:33–38 that you may know the Lord's will on the subject.

4. Study the prophecies that you may be prepared for the future (Alma 45:9–14).

5. Choose a challenge of your own from this reading and apply it to your life.

Chapter Two

If All Were Like Unto Moroni

Alma 46–49

*H*istorical Setting: In the nineteenth year of the reign of the judges,
after a brief period of peace, the second year of the fourteen-year
war commenced in the land of Zarahemla. Again it was centered
around apostate Nephite leaders. However, it was internal politicians
seeking for power that caused the war to commence.

Precepts of this Reading:

> 8 Thus we see how quick the children of men do forget the Lord
> their God, yea, how quick to do iniquity, and to be led away by the
> evil one.
>
> 9 Yea, and we also see the great wickedness one very wicked man
> can cause to take place among the children of men. [Alma 46:8–9]
>
> 17 Yea, verily, verily I say unto you, if all men had been, and were,
> and ever would be, like unto Moroni, behold, the very powers of hell
> would have been shaken forever; yea, the devil would never have
> power over the hearts of the children of men. [Alma 48:17]

Elder John A. Widtsoe made this insightful observation about the
Book of Mormon:

> The Book of Mormon does not deal with trivial things—the battles
> and contests, the conquests of the enemy and the treaties made, the
> many difficulties of history, form merely a background against which

the principles that really make the book are illustrated. The teachings of the Book of Mormon appear against a narrative of historical events, but the events are of little consequence in comparison with the lessons that are taught for man's guidance in any day. [CR, October 1927, 27]

Elder Widtsoe's observation is certainly demonstrated in the four chapters of Alma discussed here. An outline of those chapters follow in preparation for a deeper study.

OUTLINE • ALMA 46–49

> 46:1–10   As many as would not hearken to Helaman and his brethren were gathered together against them.

     a.   Those who were exceedingly wroth were determined to slay Helaman and his brethren (v. 2).

     b.   Amalickiah, a large and strong man, was their leader (vv. 3–6).

         1.   He was desirous to be a king, and those who were wroth were desirous that he be their king.

         2.   The greater part of them were the lower judges of the land who were seeking for power.

         3.   The lower judges were promised by Amalickiah that, if he became king, he would make them rulers over the people.

         4.   They were led to dissensions in spite of the high priests great care over the church.

         5.   Many believed in the flatteries of Amalickiah and dissented from the church.

         6.   The affairs of the people were precarious and dangerous in spite of their victory over the Lamanites.

     c.   Thus we see how quickly the Lord is forgotten and men are led away by the evil one into iniquity (v. 8).

     d.   We also see the great wickedness one wicked man can cause (v. 9).

>   e. Amalickiah was a man of cunning device and flattering words (v. 10).

          1. He sought to destroy the church.

          2. He sought to destroy the foundation of liberty God had granted the righteous in the land.

➤ **46:11–28** Moroni, the chief captain of the armies, was angry with Amalickiah.

      a. Moroni rent his coat and wrote upon a piece of it: In memory of our God, our religion, freedom, peace, and our wives and children; and fastened it to a pole (vv. 12–16).

          1. He put on his armor and took his "title of liberty" and bowed himself to the earth.

          2. He prayed mightily to God for the blessing of liberty to rest upon his brethren as long as Christians remained to possess the land.

          3. The true believers of Christ, who belonged to the church of God, were called Christians by those who did not belong to the church.

          4. Those of the true believers gladly took upon themselves the name of Christ.

      b. Moroni named all of the land south of the land Desolation, and all of the land in the north and the south, a chosen land and a land of liberty (v. 17).

      c. Moroni said God would not suffer those despised because they took the name of Christ to be trodden down and destroyed unless it was for transgression (v. 18).

      d. Moroni went forth waving the rent part of his garment for the people to see the writing, and cried with a loud voice to them: (vv. 19–20).

          1. Whosoever will maintain this title in the land let them come forth in the strength of the Lord.

          2. Let them enter into a covenant to maintain their rights and religion that God may bless them.

    e. The people ran together with their armor, rending their garments as a covenant to not forsake the Lord their God (vv. 21–22).

        1. If they transgressed the commandments of God and were ashamed to take upon them the name of Christ, let the Lord rend them as they had their garments.

        2. They cast their garments at the feet of Moroni as a covenant to be destroyed, even as their brethren in the land northward, if they fell into transgression.

    f. Moroni said they were a remnant of Jacob and of Joseph whose coat was rent by his brethren into many pieces, and let us remember to keep the commandments or we may be rent by our brethren and cast into prison, or sold or slain (vv. 23–27).

        1. Let us preserve our liberty as a remnant of Joseph.

        2. Let us remember the words of Jacob, before his death, that a remnant of Joseph would be preserved by the hand of God and taken unto himself, even as a remnant of Joseph's garment had been preserved and not decayed, while the remainder of the seed of Joseph shall perish as the remnant of his garment.

        3. Jacob's soul was grieved, but he had joy in the part of his son's seed that would be taken unto God.

        4. Who knows but that the remnant of Joseph that would perish are those who dissented from us, and it shall be us if we do not stand fast in the faith of Christ.

    g. Moroni went forth in all the land where there were dissenters to gather people to defend their liberty against Amalickiah and the Amalickiahites (v. 28).

➤ 46:29–37 Amalickiah saw the number of Moroni's people were more numerous than the Amalickiahites, and his people were doubtful of the justice of his cause, therefore he took his followers and departed into the land of Nephi.

a. Moroni sought to cut off the Amalickiahites, and bring them back and put Amalickiah to death (vv. 30–32).

        1. He knew that Amalickiah would stir up the Lamanites to come to battle against them that he might accomplish his purposes.

        2. He took his army into the wilderness and cut off the course of Amalickiah.

    b. Amalickiah fled with a small number of men and Moroni delivered the rest back into the land of Zarahemla (vv. 33–35).

        1. Moroni had power from the chief judge to establish and exercise authority over the Amalickiahites.

        2. Those who would not covenant to support the cause of government, and maintain a free government were put to death.

        3. But few denied the covenant of freedom.

➤ **46:38–41** Moroni caused the title of liberty to be hoisted upon every tower in the land possessed by the Nephites.

    a. Moroni planted the standard of liberty among the Nephites (v. 38).

        1. They maintained peace in the land until nearly the end of the nineteenth year of the reign of the judges.

        2. Helaman and the high priests maintained order and peace in the church for four years.

    b. Many died firmly believing their souls were redeemed by Jesus Christ (v. 39).

    c. Some died with fevers, which were very frequent at some seasons in the land (v. 40).

        1. The excellent qualities of many plants and roots had been prepared by God to remove the cause of diseases.

        2. Men were subjected to diseases because of the nature of the climate.

    d. Many died of old age, and those who died in the faith of Christ we suppose are happy (v. 41).

➤ 47:1–7 Amalickiah, and those who fled to the land of Nephi, stirred up the Lamanites to anger. Their king sent a proclamation throughout the land to go again to battle against the Nephites.

    a. The people feared to displease the king, but also feared the Nephites (vv. 2–3).

        1. The more part of them would not obey the king.

        2. The king was angry.

    b. He gave Amalickiah command of part of the army and commanded him to compel the Lamanites to arms (vv. 3–5).

        1. This was the desire of Amalickiah, for he had a plan to dethrone the king of the Lamanites.

        2. He had command of those who favored the king, and sought to gain favor of those who were disobedient.

        3. He went to a place called Onidah where the disobedient had fled when they saw the army.

    c. The disobedient Lamanites had appointed a leader, resolving to not go against the Nephites, and gathered to mount Antipas in preparation for battle (vv. 6–7).

➤ 47:8–16 Amalickiah did not intend to battle them but to gain their favor, place himself at the head, dethrone the king, and possess the kingdom.

    a. The Amalickiahites pitched their tents in the valley near mount Antipas (vv. 9–12).

        1. At night he sent a secret embassy to the mount desiring Lehonti, their leader, to come to the foot of the mount and speak with him.

        2. He sent the embassy three times, but Lehonti would not come.

        3. He then went near to Lehonti's camp and sent a fourth message for him to come and bring his guards with him.

b. Lehonti and his guards came down; Amalickiah desired him to come at night and surround Amalickiah's troops and he would give them into Lehonti's hands if he would make Amalickiah second in command over the whole army (vv. 13–16).

       1. Lehonti came and surrounded Amalickiah's troops who desired to fall in with Lehonti's troops as Amalickiah had desired.

       2. Amalickiah delivered his men as part of the plan to dethrone the king.

➤ 47:17–30 The custom of the Lamanites was to appoint the second leader to be the chief leader if the first was killed.

    a. Amalickiah had one of his servants administer poison by degrees to Lehonti, and he died (v. 18).

    b. Amalickiah was appointed their leader and chief commander (v. 19).

    c. Amalickiah marched his army to the chief city, Nephi, in the land of Nephi (vv. 20–24).

       1. The king came out to meet Amalickiah with his guards, supposing he had gathered a great army.

       2. Amalickiah sent his servants to meet the king, and they bowed in reverence to his greatness.

       3. The king put forth his hand to raise them, a custom of peace taken from the Nephites.

       4. The first one he raised stabbed the king in the heart, and he fell to the earth.

    d. The servants of the king fled, and Amalickiah's servants cried that the kings servants had stabbed him in the heart and fled (vv. 25–28).

       1. Amalickiah marched his army forth to see what had happened and found the king dead.

       2. Amalickiah pretended to be wroth and commanded those who loved the king to pursue the servants that they may be slain.

       3. All who loved the king pursued after the servants.

e. The servants saw the army coming and fled to the land
    of Zarahemla, and joined the people of Ammon.

    1. The army pursued the servants in vain.

    2. Amalickiah, by his fraud, gained the hearts of the
        people.

47:31–36 On the morrow, Amalickiah entered the city and took
possession of it.

a. The queen heard from an embassy sent by Amalickiah
    that the king had been slain by his servants who had
    escaped (vv. 32–33).

    1. The queen sent to Amalickiah desiring him to spare
        the people of the city.

    2. She desired him to come and bring witnesses to
        testify of the death of the king.

b. Amalickiah took the same servants with him who had
    slain the king (v. 34).

    1. They all testified that the king had been slain by his
        own servants.

    2. They said the servants had fled, which act testified
        against them.

    3. The queen was satisfied concerning the king's
        death.

c. Amalickiah sought the favor of the queen and took her
    to wife (vv. 35–36).

    1. Thus fraud and the assistance of the cunning ser-
        vants he obtained the kingdom.

    2. He was acknowledged king among all the Laman-
        ites.

    3. The Lamanites were composed of Lamanites,
        Lemuelites, Ishmaelites, and all the dissenters of
        the Nephites from Nephi to the present time.

d. The dissenters had the same knowledge of the Lord as
    the Nephites (v. 36).

    1. Not long after their dissension they became more

hardened, impenitent, wild, and ferocious than the Lamanites.

2. They drank in the traditions of the Lamanites.

3. They entirely forgot the Lord their God.

48:1–6   Amalickiah began to inspire the Lamanites against the people of Nephi.

    a.   Amalickiah appointed men to speak to the Lamanites from their towers against the Nephites (v. 1).

    b.   In the latter end of the nineteenth year, having become king of the Lamanites, he sought to become king over the Nephites as well as the Lamanites (vv. 11–13).

      1.   He had hardened the Lamanite hearts, and blinded their minds, and stirred them up to anger to go against the Nephites in battle.

      2.   He was determined by the greatness of the number of Lamanites to overpower the Nephites and bring them into bondage.

      3.   He appointed chief captains of the Zoramites because of their knowledge of the Nephites.

    c.   They moved toward the land of Zarahemla in the wilderness (v. 6).

48:7–18   While Amalickiah was obtaining power by fraud and deceit, Moroni had been preparing the people to be faithful to God.

    a.   Moroni had strengthened their armies, erected places of resort, banks of earth, and walls of stone all around the cities and borders (vv. 8–10).

      1.   He placed the greater number of men in the weaker fortifications.

      2.   He prepared them to support their liberty, lands, wives, children, and peace that they might live unto the Lord their God and maintain the cause of Christians.

    b.   Moroni was a strong and mighty man, of perfect understanding (vv. 11–13).

1. He did not delight in bloodshed.
2. His soul did delight in the liberty and freedom of his country, and his brethren from bondage.
3. His heart swelled in thanksgiving to God for the privileges and blessings he bestowed upon the people.
4. He labored for the welfare and safety of the people.
5. He was firm in the faith of Christ.
6. He had sworn with an oath to defend his people, rights, country, and religion even to the loss of his blood.

c. The Nephites were taught to defend themselves even to the shedding of blood if necessary, and were never to give an offence or raise a sword except to preserve their lives (vv. 14–16).

1. Their faith was that God would preserve them in the land if they kept his commandments.
2. God would warn them to flee or prepare for war according to their danger.
3. God would make it known where to go to defend themselves, and God would deliver them.
4. Moroni's heart swelled in doing good, in preserving his people, and resisting iniquity.

d. If all men had been, and were, and ever would be like Moroni, the very powers of hell would have been shaken forever (vv. 17–18).

1. The devil would never have power over the hearts of men.
2. He was like Ammon, the son of Mosiah, even the other sons of Mosiah, and also Alma and his sons, for they were all men of God.

➤ 48:19–25 Helaman and his brethren were no less serviceable, for they did preach the word of God, and baptize unto repentance all who hearkened to their words.

a. The Nephites humbled themselves and were highly

favored of the Lord, and thus they were free from war and contention for four years (v. 20).

- b. The Nephites were compelled in the latter end of the nineteenth year to contend with the Lamanites (vv. 21–23).
  1. Their wars with the Lamanites did not cease for many years in spite of their reluctance.
  2. They were sorry to take up arms and send so many people into the eternal world unprepared to meet God.
- c. The Nephites could not allow their wives and children to be massacred by those who were once their brethren (vv. 24–25).
  1. They had dissented from the church and joined the Lamanites.
  2. The Lord promised that if they kept the commandments they would prosper in the land.

➤ 49:1–11   In the nineteenth year, eleventh month, and the tenth day, the armies of the Lamanites were seen approaching the land of Ammonihah.

- a. The city had been rebuilt, Moroni had stationed an army by its borders, and had cast up dirt round about to shield them from arrows and stones with which the Lamanites fought (v. 2).
- b. The Lamanites had destroyed it once because of the iniquity of the people, and they supposed it would be an easy prey unto them (vv. 3–9).
  1. They were disappointed because of the high ridge of earth except by the entry.
  2. Their chief captains were astonished at the wisdom of the Nephite security.
  3. The Lamanites wore breastplates, thick skins to protect them, and had shields.
  4. The Nephites were prepared as never known among the children of Lehi.

c. The Lamanites were astonished at the preparation of the Nephites (vv. 9–11).

        1. If Amalickiah had come at the head, perhaps he would have attacked because he did not care for the blood of his people.

        2. The Lamanite chief captains durst not attack.

> 49:12–25 The Lamanites retreated and marched toward the city of Noah supposing it to be the next best place to attack.

    a. The Lamanites knew not that Moroni had fortified every city in the land, and they took an oath to destroy the city of Noah (v. 13).

    b. To their astonishment, Noah, hitherto a weak city, had been made a strong city by Moroni, even stronger than Ammonihah (vv. 14–15).

        1. Moroni had supposed they would be frightened by the city of Ammonihah.

        2. He supposed they would march to the former weak city of Noah.

    c. Moroni had appointed Lehi, who had battled the Lamanites on the east of the river Sidon, to be the chief captain of the city of Noah (vv. 16–17).

        1. The Lamanites were afraid of Lehi.

        2. They had taken an oath to attack the city and brought up their armies.

    d. The Lamanites could not get into the city except by the entrance because of the fortifications Moroni had prepared (vv. 18–21).

        1. The Nephites could destroy any who attempted to climb up.

        2. The strongest Nephite men had their swords and slings to defend themselves.

        3. The Lamanites were driven from the place of entry time after time and there was an immense slaughter.

    e. The Lamanites attempted to dig down the banks, but

instead their dead were filling up the ditches that had been dug (vv. 22–24).

    1.   They fought until all their chief captains were slain.

    2.   More than a thousand Lamanites were slain and not a single Nephite.

    3.   About fifty Nephites were wounded in their legs but were shielded otherwise.

  f. The Lamanites fled into the wilderness and returned to inform Amalickiah, who was a Nephite by birth, of their great loss (v. 25).

➤ 49:26–30   Amalickiah was exceedingly angry that his desire to conquer the Nephites had failed.

  a. Amalickiah cursed God and swore an oath to drink Moroni's blood (vv. 27–28).

    1.   Moroni kept the commandments of God by securing the safety of his people.

    2.   The people of Nephi thanked God for delivering them from the enemy.

  b. The nineteenth year of the judges ended (v. 29).

  c. There was continual peace and great prosperity in the church because of their heed and diligence to the word of God declared by those ordained by the holy order of God (v. 30).

NOTES AND COMMENTARY

Introduction: What is leadership? One definition is to get the job done better than you could do it yourself. There are many kinds of leadership, but we will focus on two extremes: First, the emotionally inspired leader that gets people to do what he wants them to do, whether it is the right thing or not. Second, the divinely inspired leader who accomplishes what the Lord desires. This kind of leadership may leave people without excuse for not doing what they should. We see both kinds of leadership in this reading. Captain Moroni is an example of inspired leadership. Moroni accomplished incredible things through the blessings of God. He also left the Nephite dissenters without excuse. Amalickiah is the other main example. He also accomplished much of what he desired, but his partner was the devil. As Korihor, he failed in the end (see Alma 30:60). There are other examples as well.

Alma 46:1–10 • Amalickiah Leads the Dissenters Against Helaman

1 And it came to pass that as many as would not hearken to the words of Helaman and his brethren were gathered together against their brethren.

2 And now behold, they were exceedingly wroth, insomuch that they were determined to slay them.

3 Now the leader of those who were wroth against their brethren was a large and a strong man; and his name was Amalickiah.

4 And Amalickiah was desirous to be a king; and those people who were wroth were also desirous that he should be their king; and they were the greater part of them the lower judges of the land, and they were seeking for power.

5 And they had been led by the flatteries of Amalickiah, that if they would support him and establish him to be their king that he would make them rulers over the people.

6 Thus they were led away by Amalickiah to dissensions, notwithstanding the preaching of Helaman and his brethren, yea, notwithstanding their exceedingly great care over the church, for they were high priests over the church.

7 And there were many in the church who believed in the flattering words of Amalickiah, therefore they dissented even from the church; and thus were the affairs of the people of Nephi exceedingly precarious and dangerous, notwithstanding their great victory which they had had over the Lamanites, and their great rejoicings which they had had because of their deliverance by the hand of the Lord.

8 Thus we see how quick the children of men do forget the Lord their God, yea, how quick to do iniquity, and to be led away by the evil one.

9 Yea, and we also see the great wickedness one very wicked man can cause to take place among the children of men.

10 Yea, we see that Amalickiah, because he was a man of cunning device and a man of many flattering words, that he led away the hearts of many people to do wickedly; yea, and to seek to destroy the church of God, and to destroy the foundation of liberty which God had granted unto them, or which blessing God had sent upon the face of the land for the righteous' sake.

Amalickiah's desire to be a king (v. 4) is a parallel to that of Amlici at the time of the commencement of Alma's [the father of Helaman] administration (see Alma 2:2). Amalickiah's natural man emphasis of physical prowess and strength (Alma 46:3) was supported by his mental capacity to use flattery (v. 5). Flattery is another characteristic of natural men such as Sherem (see Jacob 7:4), King Noah (see Mosiah 11:7), Alma the elder before his conversion (see Mosiah 27:8), and Korihor (see Alma 30:7). Amalickiah had his power hungry followers (Alma 46:4–5) just as Amlici and the others just mentioned (see the surrounding texts cited above). In spite of the warnings of Helaman and his brethren, the dissenters were believed by many church members (vv. 6–7). The pride of the natural men came into the church when the people began to prosper. At this time it was precarious and dangerous because of the ever threatening possibility of war with the Lamanites. The Lord has also warned the Church in this dispensation to beware of pride, the sin that eventually destroyed the Nephites. Their destruction had just been prophesied by Alma, the father of Helaman.[1]

The conditions described in these verses led Mormon to insert the two precepts of this chapter: the quickness of people to forget and be led away by the evil one (v. 8) and the great wickedness that can be caused by one very wicked man (v. 9). Amalickiah was certainly a servant of the devil. He sought wickedness for all, the destruction of the church, and the loss of liberty or agency of man (v. 10, see also

---

[1] See D&C 38:39; President Ezra Taft Benson Conference Address of April. 1989, and Alma 45:9–12.

Moses 4:3). On the other hand, we will also see the effect that one very righteous man can have in the personage of Captain Moroni, as the record continues. Of course, we should not overlook what Helaman was doing, although the record does not enlarge upon his work at this time.

Alma 46:11–18 • Captain Moroni and the Title of Liberty

11 And now it came to pass that when Moroni, who was the chief commander of the armies of the Nephites, had heard of these dissensions, he was angry with Amalickiah.

12 And it came to pass that he rent his coat; and he took a piece thereof, and wrote upon it—In memory of our God, our religion, and freedom, and our peace, our wives, and our children—and he fastened it upon the end of a pole.

13 And he fastened on his head-plate, and his breastplate, and his shields, and girded on his armor about his loins; and he took the pole, which had on the end thereof his rent coat, (and he called it the title of liberty) and he bowed himself to the earth, and he prayed mightily unto his God for the blessings of liberty to rest upon his brethren, so long as there should a band of Christians remain to possess the land—

14 For thus were all the true believers of Christ, who belonged to the church of God, called by those who did not belong to the church.

15 And those who did belong to the church were faithful; yea, all those who were true believers in Christ took upon them, gladly, the name of Christ, or Christians as they were called, because of their belief in Christ who should come.

16 And therefore, at this time, Moroni prayed that the cause of the Christians, and the freedom of the land might be favored.

17 And it came to pass that when he had poured out his soul to God, he named all the land which was south of the land Desolation, yea, and in fine, all the land, both on the north and on the south—A chosen land, and the land of liberty.

18 And he said: Surely God shall not suffer that we, who are despised because we take upon us the name of Christ, shall be trodden

down and destroyed, until we bring it upon us by our own transgressions.

The flag was probably first used in Persia (Iran) as a means of rallying people to a cause.[2] Theodore Herzl, the father of Zionism in modern-day Israel "attached great importance to the need for a flag. 'It is with a flag that people are led whithersoever one desires, even to the Promised Land. For a flag men live and die'."[3]

With all due respect to Betsy Ross, may we suggest that Captain Moroni produced the first American flag. Both flags represent freedom and peace for all. While Moroni's flag was in memory of the Nephite religion (v. 12), at the time the stars and stripes were adopted the restoration of the gospel of Jesus Christ had not yet happened. However, old glory does stand for freedom of religion and will fly into the millennium.[4]

Some have questioned Moroni's use of the word "Christians," citing the New Testament: "And the disciples were called Christians first in Antioch" (Acts 11:26). The law of Moses had been altered by the time of Christ's ministry, and had lost the symbolism of the law being a type and shadow of Christ (see John 5:39; 2 Nephi 25:25; Mosiah 13:27–32; 3 Nephi 15:4–5). Therefore, the use of the word "Christians" in Antioch was probably the first time it was used in the Meridian of Time. Certainly Christ was known in all dispensations, which fact will be firmly established when the truth is known. Adam knew of Christ (see Moses 6:57) and was taught by the Lord himself that "all things have their likeness, and all things are created and made to bear record of me, both things which are temporal, and things which are spiritual" (Moses 6:63). The Apostle Paul taught that God "preached before the gospel unto Abraham, saying, In thee shall all the nations be blessed" (Galatians 3:8). The covenant made to

[2] Hugh Nibley, "An Approach to the Book of Mormon," *Improvement Era,* April, 1954, see the entire argument.

[3] Abba Eban, "My People," *Behrman House*, Oct. 1996.

[4] See Brigham Young in General Authority Quotes.

Abraham, to which Paul refers, was made by Jehovah (see Abraham 2:8–11), who is one of the Old Testament names of Christ (see JST, Exodus 6:2–4). Christ was known to the Nephites in Old Testament times (see 1 Nephi 19:10; 2 Nephi 10:7) and to the Jaredites (Ether 3:14). What Mormon says about the believers being called Christians and gladly taking his name (Alma 46:14–15) is true of all dispensations of truth.

Captain Moroni's meaning of "all the land, both on the north and on the south—a chosen, and a land of liberty" (v. 17) reminds us of the Prophet Joseph's definition of Zion.

> You know there has been great discussions in relation to Zion—where it is, and where the gathering of the dispensation is, and which I am now going to tell you. The prophets have spoken and written upon it; but I will make a proclamation that will cover a broader ground. *The whole of America is Zion itself from north to south, and is described by the Prophets, who declare that it is the Zion where the mountain of the Lord should be, and that it should be the center of the land.* When Elders shall take up and examine the old prophecies in the Bible, they will see it. [*TPJS*, 362]

The Americas were the "choice above all other lands" occupied by the Jaredites (Ether 2:10–12), and the Nephites (see 2 Nephi 1:5). America is Zion, and the land of the New Jerusalem to be built there by the remnant of Joseph in the latter days (see Ether 13:6–8). God will not suffer (allow) the righteous on the land to be trodden down and destroyed (see Alma 26:18).

Alma 46:19–28 • Captain Moroni and the Remnant of Joseph

> 19 And when Moroni had said these words, he went forth among the people, waving the rent part of his garment in the air, that all might see the writing which he had written upon the rent part, and crying with a loud voice, saying:
>
> 20 Behold, whosoever will maintain this title upon the land, let them come forth in the strength of the Lord, and enter into a covenant

that they will maintain their rights, and their religion, that the Lord God may bless them.

21 And it came to pass that when Moroni had proclaimed these words, behold, the people came running together with their armor girded about their loins, rending their garments in token, or as a covenant, that they would not forsake the Lord their God; or, in other words, if they should transgress the commandments of God, or fall into transgression, and be ashamed to take upon them the name of Christ, the Lord should rend them even as they had rent their garments.

22 Now this was the covenant which they made, and they cast their garments at the feet of Moroni, saying: We covenant with our God, that we shall be destroyed, even as our brethren in the land northward, if we shall fall into transgression; yea, he may cast us at the feet of our enemies, even as we have cast our garments at thy feet to be trodden under foot, if we shall fall into transgression.

23 Moroni said unto them: Behold, we are a remnant of the seed of Jacob; yea, we are a remnant of the seed of Joseph, whose coat was rent by his brethren into many pieces; yea, and now behold, let us remember to keep the commandments of God, or our garments shall be rent by our brethren, and we be cast into prison, or be sold, or be slain.

24 Yea, let us preserve our liberty as a remnant of Joseph; yea, let us remember the words of Jacob, before his death, for behold, he saw that a part of the remnant of the coat of Joseph was preserved and had not decayed. And he said—Even as this remnant of garment of my son hath been preserved, so shall a remnant of the seed of my son be preserved by the hand of God, and be taken unto himself, while the remainder of the seed of Joseph shall perish, even as the remnant of his garment.

25 Now behold, this giveth my soul sorrow; nevertheless, my soul hath joy in my son, because of that part of his seed which shall be taken unto God.

26 Now behold, this was the language of Jacob.

27 And now who knoweth but what the remnant of the seed of Joseph, which shall perish as his garment, are those who have dissented from us? Yea, and even it shall be ourselves if we do not stand fast in the faith of Christ.

28 And now it came to pass that when Moroni had said these words he went forth, and also sent forth in all the parts of the land where there were dissensions, and gathered together all the people who were desirous to maintain their liberty, to stand against Amalickiah and those who had dissented, who were called Amalickiahites.

The effectiveness of Moroni's title of liberty gathering the people (v. 21) illustrates the love of freedom that is innate with man. The rending of the people's garments[5] as a covenant to not forsake the Lord (v. 21) also shows their love of the Lord and his religion. The people who were destroyed in "the land northward" (v. 22) refers to the remains of a great battle discovered by King Limhi's men while looking for the land of Zarahemla (see Mosiah 8:7–8). These people whose remains were found in the north are known later in the Book of Mormon as the Jaredites, whose records were abridged by Moroni, son of Mormon. The abridgment is called the book of Ether (see p. 487 in the Book of Mormon).

Captain Moroni now follows another principle of good leadership. He applies the scriptures unto his people. The Nephites were a remnant of Joseph through Lehi he being of Manasseh and Ishmael being of Ephraim[6](Alma 46:23–24). The Latter-day Saints are also a remnant of Joseph through Ephraim.[7] Therefore, the same passages of Genesis concerning Joseph, son of Jacob, should be applied to members of the Church today.

The account of Jacob, the father of the twelve tribes of Israel, and the torn coat of his son Joseph comes from Genesis 37. However, Moroni gives a fuller account, preserving some of the language and

[5] The rending (tearing) of one's garment was a tradition used in biblical times to show mourning, grief, or distress. See Geneses 37:29; 44:13; 2 Samuel 1:11.

[6] See vol.1 of this work *I Nephi Wrote this Record*, 1 Nephi 7:5 and commentary Lehi was of Manasseh (Alma 10:3) [2003], 91; and Ishmael was of Ephraim (*JD*, 23:184).

[7] See Wayne R. Shute, Monte S. Nyman, and Randy L. Bott, *Chosen of the Lord*, [1999]. The entire book supports Ephraim as the literal blood of the majority of the latter-day church members.

prophecies made by Jacob at that time (Alma 46:26). That these words, taken from the plates of brass, were once a part of the Bible are sustained by other ancient records. Dr. Hugh Nibley has written:

In the tenth century of our era the greatest antiquarian of the Moslem world, Muhammad ibn-Ibrahim ath-Tha'labi, collected in Persia a great many old tales and legends about the prophets of Israel. After the fall of Jerusalem and the scattering of the Jews, many of the sectaries, such as those that once lived around the Dead Sea, moved East to be under the protection of the Persians. Thus groups of Jews representing various sects and shades of belief were scattered all over central Asia in the Middle Ages, and it is from such, no doubt, that Tha'labi gets his amazing fund of information, which is worthy to be set up beside the most enlightening volumes of Apocrypha. Among other things, Tha'labi tells a number of stories, which we have not found anywhere else, about Jacob and the garment of Joseph. In one, Joseph's brethren bring his torn garment to their father as proof that he is dead, but Jacob after examining the garment, ("and there were in the garment of Joseph three marks or tokens when they brought it to his father") declares that the way the cloth is torn shows him that their story is not true; "Behold, if the bear had eaten him he surely would have rent his garment, and since he would (naturally) have fled towards the gate, verily the garment should have been torn behind. . . ." But since this is not the case it may be that Joseph still lives. Another account is the case of "the vizier" Potiphar, who by examining the tears in Joseph's garment knew that he was innocent and spared his life, "for he knew that if he (Joseph) had attacked his wife the tear would have been in front. . . ." So again his torn garment declared that Joseph should live.

Most significant is Tha'labi's discussion of the two remnants of Joseph's garment, from which we quote:

"And when Joseph had made himself known unto them (his brethren) he asked them about his father saying, 'What did my father after (I left)?' They answered, 'He lost his eyesight (from weeping).' Then he gave them his garment (*qamis*, long outer shirt). According to ad-Dahak that garment was of the weave (pattern, design) of Paradise, and the breath (spirit, odor) of Paradise was in it, *so that it never decayed* or in any way deteriorated (and that was) a sign (omen). And Joseph gave them that garment, and it was the very one that had belonged to Abraham, having already had a long history. And he said to them. 'Go, take this garment of mine and place it upon the face of my father so he may have sight again, and return (to me) with all your families. And when they had put Egypt behind them and come to Canaan their father Jacob said, 'Behold, I perceive the spirit (breath, odor) of Joseph, if you will not think me wandering in my mind and weakheaded from age. . . . (for) he knew that upon all the earth there was no spirit (breath, odor) of Paradise save in that garment alone. . . And as-Sadi says that Judah said to Joseph, 'It was I who took the garment bedaubed with blood to Jacob, and reported to him that the bear had eaten Joseph; so give me this day thy garment that I might tell him that thou art living, that I might cause him to rejoice now as greatly as I caused him to sorrow then. And Ibn-Abbas says that Judah took the garment and went forth in great haste, panting with exertion and anxiety . . . and when he brought the garment he laid it upon his face, so that his sight returned to him. And ad-Dahak says that his sight returned after blindness, and his strength after weakness, and youth after age, and joy after sorrow." ("then follows a dialogue between Jacob and the King of Death").

Note here that there were *two* remnants of Joseph's garment, one sent by *Joseph* to his father as a sign that he was still alive (since the garment *had not decayed*), and the other, torn and smeared with blood, brought by Judah to his father as a sign that Joseph was dead. Moroni actually quotes Jacob ("Now behold, this was the language of Jacob"). As saying: "Now behold, this giveth my soul sorrow; nevertheless, my soul hath joy in my son . . ." (Alma 46:25 f.) Compare this with Judah's statement in the Old World account, that the undecayed garment caused Jacob as much joy as the bloody garment caused him sorrow. In both accounts Jacob is described as being near to death—hence Judah's haste to reach him with the garment and make amends for the evil he had done.[8]

Thus the Book of Mormon makes known these plain and precious things, and the ancient records quoted above by Brother Nibley add a second witness to the Book of Mormon account.

---

[8] Hugh Nibley, *An Approach to the Book of Mormon,* Course of Study for the Melchizedek Priesthood Quorums of The Church of Jesus Christ of Latter-day Saints, Published by the Council of the Twelve Apostles, [1957], 186–188.

Captain Moroni's words again exemplify his leadership as he rallies his people to stand fast in the faith of Christ (v. 27). The people being gathered from all parts of the land again shows the basic love of freedom that is innate in humankind (v. 28).

Alma 46:29–37 • Amalickiah Departs to the Land of Nephi

29 And it came to pass that when Amalickiah saw that the people of Moroni were more numerous than the Amalickiahites—and he also saw that his people were doubtful concerning the justice of the cause in which they had undertaken—therefore, fearing that he should not gain the point, he took those of his people who would and departed into the land of Nephi.

30 Now Moroni thought it was not expedient that the Lamanites should have any more strength; therefore he thought to cut off the people of Amalickiah, or to take them and bring them back, and put Amalickiah to death; yea, for he knew that he would stir up the Lamanites to anger against them, and cause them to come to battle against them; and this he knew that Amalickiah would do that he might obtain his purposes.

31 Therefore Moroni thought it was expedient that he should take his armies, who had gathered themselves together, and armed themselves, and entered into a covenant to keep the peace—and it came to pass that he took his army and marched out with his tents into the wilderness, to cut off the course of Amalickiah in the wilderness.

32 And it came to pass that he did according to his desires, and marched forth into the wilderness, and headed the armies of Amalickiah.

33 And it came to pass that Amalickiah fled with a small number of his men, and the remainder were delivered up into the hands of Moroni and were taken back into the land of Zarahemla.

34 Now, Moroni being a man who was appointed by the chief judges and the voice of the people, therefore he had power according to his will with the armies of the Nephites, to establish and to exercise authority over them.

35 And it came to pass that whomsoever of the Amalickiahites

that would not enter into a covenant to support the cause of freedom, that they might maintain a free government, he caused to be put to death; and there were but few who denied the covenant of freedom.

36 And it came to pass also, that he caused the title of liberty to be hoisted upon every tower which was in all the land, which was possessed by the Nephites; and thus Moroni planted the standard of liberty among the Nephites.

37 And they began to have peace again in the land; and thus they did maintain peace in the land until nearly the end of the nineteenth year of the reign of the judges.

Amalickiah demonstrates an example of uninspired leadership. If the uninspired leader doesn't get his way, he dissents from the group and pulls away those who will follow with him (v. 29). Captain Moroni recognizes another trait of the uninspired leader, to stir up his followers to anger (v. 30). However, the efforts of Amalickiah were thwarted and the flag of liberty did wave (v. 36). Moroni's offer of "a covenant of freedom" or death (v. 35) is an example of the balance between justice and mercy explained by Alma (see Alma 42). Although there was peace in the land, it was short-lived.

Alma 46:38–41 • Helaman and the High Priests Maintain Order in the Church

38 And Helaman and the high priests did also maintain order in the church; yea, even for the space of four years did they have much peace and rejoicing in the church.

39 And it came to pass that there were many who died, firmly believing that their souls were redeemed by the Lord Jesus Christ; thus they went out of the world rejoicing.

40 And there were some who died with fevers, which at some seasons of the year were very frequent in the land—but not so much so with fevers, because of the excellent qualities of the many plants and roots which God had prepared to remove the cause of diseases, to which men were subject by the nature of the climate—

41 But there were many who died with old age; and those who died in the faith of Christ are happy in him, as we must needs suppose.

The four years of peace in the church (v. 38) were not maintained throughout the whole land. The fourteen-year war with the Lamanites continued in various places.

There are several lessons about death given by Mormon as he abridges the record. Those who firmly believed in Jesus Christ and went out of the world rejoicing (v. 39) reminds us of the Lord's declaration to the Prophet Joseph Smith: "those that die in me shall not taste of death, for it shall be sweet unto them" (D&C 42:46). The fevers causing death because of "the nature of the climate" gives us a second lesson. *God had prepared* many plants and roots to remove the cause of disease (v. 40; italics added). This writer has walked the medicinal paths of Guatemala and heard the guides' explanation of various cures for diseases from items grown therein. The practice of natural medicine seems to be one reason at least for retaining the traditional medicine man among the modern tribes of Native Americans today. Again, we turn to modern revelation. Those who "have not faith to be healed, but believe, shall be nourished with all tenderness, with herbs and mild food, and that not by the hand of an enemy" (D&C 42:43). There is a place for both faith and medicine in the Lord's eyes. The third lesson concerning death is to the aged. "Those who died in the faith of Christ are happy in him" (Alma 46:41). The Lord instructs us to "weep for the loss of them that die, but more especially for those that have not hope for a glorious resurrection" (D&C 42:45). Those we love are missed, but the knowledge of their happiness should make us happy as well.

Alma 47:1–7 • Amalickiah Stirs up the Lamanites to Battle

1 Now we will return in our record to Amalickiah and those who had fled with him into the wilderness; for, behold, he had taken those who went with him, and went up in the land of Nephi among the Lamanites, and did stir up the Lamanites to anger against the people of Nephi, insomuch that the king of the Lamanites sent a proclamation throughout all his land, among all his people, that they should gather themselves together again to go to battle against the Nephites.

2 And it came to pass that when the proclamation had gone forth among them they were exceedingly afraid; yea, they feared to displease the king, and they also feared to go to battle against the Nephites lest they should lose their lives. And it came to pass that they would not, or the more part of them would not, obey the commandments of the king.

3 And now it came to pass that the king was wroth because of their disobedience; therefore he gave Amalickiah the command of that part of his army which was obedient unto his commands, and commanded him that he should go forth and compel them to arms.

4 Now behold, this was the desire of Amalickiah; for he being a very subtle man to do evil therefore he laid the plan in his heart to dethrone the king of the Lamanites.

5 And now he had got the command of those parts of the Lamanites who were in favor of the king; and he sought to gain favor of those who were not obedient; therefore he went forward to the place which was called Onidah, for thither had all the Lamanites fled; for they discovered the army coming, and, supposing that they were coming to destroy them, therefore they fled to Onidah, to the place of arms.

6 And they had appointed a man to be a king and a leader over them, being fixed in their minds with a determined resolution that they would not be subjected to go against the Nephites.

7 And it came to pass that they had gathered themselves together upon the top of the mount which was called Antipas, in preparation to battle.

Captain Moroni's foreknowledge of Amalickiah stirring up the Lamanites (Alma 46:30) came to pass (Alma 47:1). Another uninspired principle of leadership is revealed by Amalickiah, his plan to dethrone the Lamanite king (v. 4). This power incentive is known today as "a hidden agenda," or one's "own agenda" that is secretly carried out. As far as this world goes, it originated with Satan. "For thou hast said in thy heart: I will ascend into heaven, I will exalt my throne above the stars of God; I will sit also upon the mount of the congregation, in the sides of the north; I will ascend above the heights of the clouds; I will be like the Most High" (2 Nephi 24:13–14; Isaiah 14:13–14).

Anyone who follows the power incentive principle "seeketh to become a law unto itself," a trait of those who become sons of perdition (D&C 88:35; see also vv. 32–34). The fearful Lamanites were the victims of the subtle and evil Amalickiah.

Alma 47:8–16 • Amalickiah Becomes Second in Command

8 Now it was not Amalickiah's intention to give them battle according to the commandments of the king; but behold, it was his intention to gain favor with the armies of the Lamanites, that he might place himself at their head and dethrone the king and take possession of the kingdom.

9 And behold, it came to pass that he caused his army to pitch their tents in the valley which was near the mount Antipas.

10 And it came to pass that when it was night he sent a secret embassy into the mount Antipas, desiring that the leader of those who were upon the mount, whose name was Lehonti, that he should come down to the foot of the mount, for he desired to speak with him.

11 And it came to pass that when Lehonti received the message he durst not go down to the foot of the mount. And it came to pass that Amalickiah sent again the second time, desiring him to come down. And it came to pass that Lehonti would not; and he sent again the third time.

12 And it came to pass that when Amalickiah found that he could not get Lehonti to come down off from the mount, he went up into the mount, nearly to Lehonti's camp; and he sent again the fourth time his message unto Lehonti, desiring that he would come down, and that he would bring his guards with him.

13 And it came to pass that when Lehonti had come down with his guards to Amalickiah, that Amalickiah desired him to come down with his army in the night-time, and surround those men in their camps over whom the king had given him command, and that he would deliver them up into Lehonti's hands, if he would make him (Amalickiah) a second leader over the whole army.

14 And it came to pass that Lehonti came down with his men and surrounded the men of Amalickiah, so that before they awoke at the

dawn of day they were surrounded by the armies of Lehonti.

15 And it came to pass that when they saw that they were surrounded, they plead with Amalickiah that he would suffer them to fall in with their brethren, that they might not be destroyed. Now this was the very thing which Amalickiah desired.

16 And it came to pass that he delivered his men, contrary to the commands of the king. Now this was the thing that Amalickiah desired, that he might accomplish his designs in dethroning the king.

The uninspired leader makes deals to improve his own position or power, but is, as Amalickiah was, disloyal to his associates. His own men were deceived by him and his own leader, the Lamanite king, was totally cheated.

Alma 47:17–30 • Amalickiah Gains the Hearts of the People by Fraud

17 Now it was the custom among the Lamanites, if their chief leader was killed, to appoint the second leader to be their chief leader.

18 And it came to pass that Amalickiah caused that one of his servants should administer poison by degrees to Lehonti, that he died.

19 Now, when Lehonti was dead, the Lamanites appointed Amalickiah to be their leader and their chief commander.

20 And it came to pass that Amalickiah marched with his armies (for he had gained his desires) to the land of Nephi, to the city of Nephi, which was the chief city.

21 And the king came out to meet him with his guards, for he supposed that Amalickiah had fulfilled his commands, and that Amalickiah had gathered together so great an army to go against the Nephites to battle.

22 But behold, as the king came out to meet him Amalickiah caused that his servants should go forth to meet the king. And they went and bowed themselves before the king, as if to reverence him because of his greatness.

23 And it came to pass that the king put forth his hand to raise

them, as was the custom with the Lamanites, as a token of peace, which custom they had taken from the Nephites.

24 And it came to pass that when he had raised the first from the ground, behold he stabbed the king to the heart; and he fell to the earth.

25 Now the servants of the king fled; and the servants of Amalickiah raised a cry, saying:

26 Behold, the servants of the king have stabbed him to the heart, and he has fallen and they have fled; behold, come and see.

27 And it came to pass that Amalickiah commanded that his armies should march forth and see what had happened to the king; and when they had come to the spot, and found the king lying in his gore, Amalickiah pretended to be wroth, and said: Whosoever loved the king, let him go forth, and pursue his servants that they may be slain.

28 And it came to pass that all they who loved the king, when they heard these words, came forth and pursued after the servants of the king.

29 Now when the servants of the king saw an army pursuing after them, they were frightened again, and fled into the wilderness, and came over into the land of Zarahemla and joined the people of Ammon.

30 And the army which pursued after them returned, having pursued after them in vain; and thus Amalickiah, by his fraud, gained the hearts of the people.

There are two principles of uninspired leadership disclosed here. The first principle is to "poison by degrees" (v. 18). Small amounts of poison are palatable whether administered physically, verbally, or intellectually. The victims are unaware of the poison until they are overcome. How many people are hooked on pornography or intellectual apostasy in one dose? Gradual exposure is addictive if no antidote is given.

The second principle of uninspired leadership in these verses is fraud. Fraud must be carefully planned and usually requires an accomplice to avoid disclosure. The servants of Amalickiah were a part of the dastardly murder of the Lamanite king (vv. 22–26). How many innocent people are victimized by the plots of wicked men (v. 29)? How many good unassuming people are led to support evil leaders (v. 30)?

Alma 47:31–36 • Amalickiah Marries the Lamanite Queen

31 And it came to pass on the morrow he entered the city Nephi with his armies, and took possession of the city.

32 And now it came to pass that the queen, when she had heard that the king was slain—for Amalickiah had sent an embassy to the queen informing her that the king had been slain by his servants, that he had pursued them with his army, but it was in vain, and they had made their escape—

33 Therefore, when the queen had received this message she sent unto Amalickiah, desiring him that he would spare the people of the city; and she also desired him that he should come in unto her; and she also desired him that he should bring witnesses with him to testify concerning the death of the king.

34 And it came to pass that Amalickiah took the same servant that slew the king, and all them who were with him, and went in unto the queen, unto the place where she sat; and they all testified unto her that the king was slain by his own servants; and they said also: They have fled; does not this testify against them? And thus they satisfied the queen concerning the death of the king.

35 And it came to pass that Amalickiah sought the favor of the queen, and took her unto him to wife; and thus by his fraud, and by the assistance of his cunning servants, he obtained the kingdom; yea, he was acknowledged king throughout all the land, among all the people of the Lamanites, who were composed of the Lamanites and the Lemuelites and the Ishmaelites, and all the dissenters of the Nephites, from the reign of Nephi down to the present time.

36 Now these dissenters, having the same instruction and the same information of the Nephites, yea, having been instructed in the same knowledge of the Lord, nevertheless, it is strange to relate, not long after their dissensions they became more hardened and impenitent, and more wild, wicked and ferocious than the Lamanites—drinking

in with the traditions of the Lamanites; giving way to indolence, and all manner of lasciviousness; yea, entirely forgetting the Lord their God.

The accomplices in Amalickiah's fraud now become his false witnesses (v. 34). The queen, believing Amalickiah has done her a big favor, is pulled into the ultimate conspiracy. She marries Amalickiah, allowing him to not only dethrone the Lamanite king (see Alma 47:4, 16), but also obtain the kingdom of the Lamanites "by his fraud, and the assistance of his cunning servants" (v. 35). It reminds us of the soap operas of today's television shows. Mormon's analysis of the Nephite dissenters entirely forgetting the Lord their God (v. 36) is a second witness to his previous precept. Those who "have been once enlightened by the Spirit of God" and fall away "become more hardened, and thus their state becomes worse" (Alma 24:30).

Alma 48:1–6 • Amalickiah Seeks to Reign Over Both Lamanites and Nephites

1 And now it came to pass that, as soon as Amalickiah had obtained the kingdom he began to inspire the hearts of the Lamanites against the people of Nephi; yea, he did appoint men to speak unto the Lamanites from their towers, against the Nephites.

2 And thus he did inspire their hearts against the Nephites, insomuch that in the latter end of the nineteenth year of the reign of the judges, he having accomplished his designs thus far, yea, having been made king over the Lamanites, he sought also to reign over all the land, yea, and all the people who were in the land, the Nephites as well as the Lamanites.

3 Therefore he had accomplished his design, for he had hardened the hearts of the Lamanites and blinded their minds, and stirred them up to anger, insomuch that he had gathered together a numerous host to go to battle against the Nephites.

4 For he was determined, because of the greatness of the number of his people, to overpower the Nephites and to bring them into bondage.

5 And thus he did appoint chief captains of the Zoramites, they

being the most acquainted with the strength of the Nephites, and their places of resort, and the weakest parts of their cities; therefore he appointed them to be chief captains over his armies.

6 And it came to pass that they took their camp, and moved forth toward the land of Zarahemla in the wilderness.

Amalickiah is still not satisfied. He desires complete power (v. 2). His methods to obtain that power illustrates another principle of uninspired leadership. He selects trained henchmen to go among the Lamanites and spread falsehoods and accusations against their Nephite brethren (v. 1). An extension of that same principle is followed in his appointment of the apostate Zoramites as his chief captains. Before contrasting Amalickiah with Captain Moroni, let us summarize the uninspired principles of Amalickiah in support of Mormon's precept of "the great wickedness one very wicked man can cause to take place among the children of men" (Alma 46:9).

PRINCIPLES OF UNINSPIRED LEADERSHIP

1. Flattery • Alma 45:23–46:8
2. Dissents from known truth • Alma 46:29–35
3. Stir up to anger-rebellion • Alma 46:30; 47:1
4. Power hungry-hidden agenda • Alma 47:4–16
5. Makes secret deals • Alma 47:13
6. Poisons by degrees • Alma 47:18
7. Fraud and deceit • Alma 47:22–30
8. False Witnesses • Alma 47:33–35
9. Trained spokesmen to accuse and control others • Alma 48:1–5

Alma 48:7–18 • Captain Moroni Prepares the People to Be Faithful

7 Now it came to pass that while Amalickiah had thus been obtaining power by fraud and deceit, Moroni, on the other hand, had been preparing the minds of the people to be faithful unto the Lord their God.

8 Yea, he had been strengthening the armies of the Nephites, and erecting small forts, or places of resort; throwing up banks of earth round about to enclose his armies, and also building walls of stone to encircle them about, round about their cities and the borders of their lands; yea, all round about the land.

9 And in their weakest fortifications he did place the greater number of men; and thus he did fortify and strengthen the land which was possessed by the Nephites.

10 And thus he was preparing to support their liberty, their lands, their wives, and their children, and their peace, and that they might live unto the Lord their God, and that they might maintain that which was called by their enemies the cause of Christians.

11 And Moroni was a strong and a mighty man; he was a man of a perfect understanding; yea, a man that did not delight in bloodshed; a man whose soul did joy in the liberty and the freedom of his country, and his brethren from bondage and slavery;

12 Yea, a man whose heart did swell with thanksgiving to his God, for the many privileges and blessings which he bestowed upon his people; a man who did labor exceedingly for the welfare and safety of his people.

13 Yea, and he was a man who was firm in the faith of Christ, and he had sworn with an oath to defend his people, his rights, and his country, and his religion, even to the loss of his blood.

14 Now the Nephites were taught to defend themselves against their enemies, even to the shedding of blood if it were necessary; yea, and they were also taught never to give an offense, yea, and never to raise the sword except it were against an enemy, except it were to preserve their lives.

15 And this was their faith, that by so doing God would prosper them in the land, or in other words, if they were faithful in keeping the commandments of God that he would prosper them in the land; yea, warn them to flee, or to prepare for war, according to their danger;

16 And also, that God would make it known unto them whither they should go to defend themselves against their enemies, and by so doing, the Lord would deliver them; and this was the faith of Moroni, and his heart did glory in it; not in the shedding of blood but

in doing good, in preserving his people, yea, in keeping the commandments of God, yea, and resisting iniquity.

17 Yea, verily, verily I say unto you, if all men had been, and were, and ever would be, like unto Moroni, behold, the very powers of hell would have been shaken forever; yea, the devil would never have power over the hearts of the children of men.

18 Behold, he was a man like unto Ammon, the son of Mosiah, yea, and even the other sons of Mosiah, yea, and also Alma and his sons, for they were all men of God.

Moroni's physical preparations of fortification (v. 8) were again one step ahead of the Lamanites. Moreover, it was for their spiritual well-being (v. 10), not a hidden agenda for personal power. "A man of perfect understanding" (v. 11) suggests Moroni lived by revelation and thus saw the whole picture. While he did not know all things, he recognized that God did, and so he sought to know that what he did was the will of the Lord. In contrast to Amalickiah, he did not delight in the shedding of blood (v. 11, cp. Alma 49:10), but was an advocate of freedom from bondage and slavery. Moroni recognized the "Lord's hand in all things" (D&C 59:21), and, like King Benjamin, he knew that those who are "in the service of [their] fellow beings . . . are only in the service of [their] God" (Alma 48:12, Mosiah 2:17). Mormon's faith in Christ is evident by his actions in defending his people (Alma 48:13).

The law of war had been taught to the Nephites (v. 14, see Alma 43:46–47), and they believed in the promise given to the land of the Americas that if they kept the commandments of God they would prosper (v. 15; see 2 Nephi 1:5–7; Ether 2:9–12). They also believed revelation was the guiding principle to face their threatened freedom (Alma 48:16).

Mormon's tribute of wishing all men were "like unto Captain Moroni," as he abridged the record (Alma 48:17), will be sustained as we continue to read the record. This tribute describes a soldier, a man of war who had become sanctified. It is not the position one holds, but what one does in that position. Sanctification comes to people "because of their yielding their hearts unto God" (Helaman 3:35). Moroni's life, as recognized many years later by Mormon as he abridges, is one to be emulated by all.

The Lord provides a few men like Captain Moroni in every dispensation. Mormon names a few of them who had previously labored among the Nephites (Alma 48:18). In our own dispensation, we could cite the latter-day prophets from Joseph Smith to Gordon B. Hinckley, and other Church leaders. However, we must not forget the founding fathers of the United States of America and other political, military, academic leaders, and various others. The Lord does and will provide inspired leaders. Our challenge is to follow and sustain them.

Alma 48:19–25 • The Work of Helaman and His Brethren

19 Now behold, Helaman and his brethren were no less serviceable unto the people than was Moroni; for they did preach the word of God, and they did baptize unto repentance all men whosoever would hearken unto their words.

20 And thus they went forth, and the people did humble themselves because of their words, insomuch that they were highly favored of the Lord, and thus they were free from wars and contentions among themselves, yea, even for the space of four years.

21 But, as I have said, in the latter end of the nineteenth year, yea, notwithstanding their peace amongst themselves, they were compelled reluctantly to contend with their brethren, the Lamanites.

22 Yea, and in fine, their wars never did cease for the space of many years with the Lamanites, notwithstanding their much reluctance.

23 Now, they were sorry to take up arms against the Lamanites, because they did not delight in the shedding of blood; yea, and this was not all—they were sorry to be the means of sending so many of their brethren out of this world into an eternal world, unprepared to meet their God.

24 Nevertheless, they could not suffer to lay down their lives, that

their wives and their children should be massacred by the barbarous cruelty of those who were once their brethren, yea, and had dissented from their church, and had left them and had gone to destroy them by joining the Lamanites.

25 Yea, they could not bear that their brethren should rejoice over the blood of the Nephites, so long as there were any who should keep the commandments of God, for the promise of the Lord was, if they should keep his commandments they should prosper in the land.

The work of Helaman and his brethren is again recognized by Mormon as he abridges (v. 19). Although war and threats of war continued, there was a four-year period within the land of Zarahemla where the church was prospering (vv. 20–22). The latter end of the nineteenth year of the reign of the judges is described in Alma 49. Thus the entire coverage of the Nephite record of this year is covered in Alma 45:20–49:30.

The sad summary of the end of the nineteenth year, the premature deaths of those unprepared to meet God and the barbarous cruelty of the apostate Nephites (Alma 48:23–24), is somewhat offset by the faith and commitment of the faithful among the Nephites.

The effects of one righteous man's leadership is likewise illustrated below.

PRINCIPLES OF INSPIRED LEADERSHIP

1. Raises the standards for freedom • Alma 46:11–22
2. Applies the scriptures to his people • Alma 46:23–28
3. Prepares the minds of the people • Alma 48:7
4. Fortifies them physically (and spiritually, emotionally, and mentally) • Alma 48:8–9
5. Perfect understanding through revelation • Alma 48:11, 15–16
6. Does not delight in the shedding of blood • Alma 48:11
7. Recognizes and gives thanks to God • Alma 48:12
8. Labors exceedingly for the welfare of his people • Alma 48:12
9. Firm in the faith of Christ • Alma 48:13–16

Alma 49:1–11 • Captain Moroni's Preparation Pays Off

1 And now it came to pass in the eleventh month of the nineteenth year, on the tenth day of the month, the armies of the Lamanites were seen approaching towards the land of Ammonihah.

2 And behold, the city had been rebuilt, and Moroni had stationed an army by the borders of the city, and they had cast up dirt round about to shield them from the arrows and the stones of the Lamanites; for behold, they fought with stones and with arrows.

3 Behold, I said that the city of Ammonihah had been rebuilt. I say unto you, yea, that it was in part rebuilt; and because the Lamanites had destroyed it once because of the iniquity of the people, they supposed that it would again become an easy prey for them.

4 But behold, how great was their disappointment; for behold, the Nephites had dug up a ridge of earth round about them, which was so high that the Lamanites could not cast their stones and their arrows at them that they might take effect, neither could they come upon them save it was by their place of entrance.

5 Now at this time the chief captains of the Lamanites were astonished exceedingly, because of the wisdom of the Nephites in preparing their places of security.

6 Now the leaders of the Lamanites had supposed, because of the greatness of their numbers, yea, they supposed that they should be privileged to come upon them as they had hitherto done; yea, and they had also prepared themselves with shields, and with breastplates; and they had also prepared themselves with garments of skins, yea, very thick garments to cover their nakedness.

7 And being thus prepared they supposed that they should easily overpower and subject their brethren to the yoke of bondage, or slay and massacre them according to their pleasure.

8 But behold, to their uttermost astonishment, they were prepared for them, in a manner which never had been known among the children of Lehi. Now they were prepared for the Lamanites, to battle after the manner of the instructions of Moroni.

9 And it came to pass that the Lamanites, or the Amalickiahites,

were exceedingly astonished at their manner of preparation for war.

10 Now, if king Amalickiah had come down out of the land of Nephi, at the head of his army, perhaps he would have caused the Lamanites to have attacked the Nephites at the city of Ammonihah; for behold, he did care not for the blood of his people.

11 But behold, Amalickiah did not come down himself to battle. And behold, his chief captains durst not attack the Nephites at the city of Ammonihah, for Moroni had altered the management of affairs among the Nephites, insomuch that the Lamanites were disappointed in their places of retreat and they could not come upon them.

The inspired Moroni was able to stop the Lamanite invasion without the shedding of blood. The Lamanite leaders were afraid to attack because of Moroni's new preparation and Amalickiah was not there to enrage them for battle (vv. 2, 5, 8–10). The Lamanites had copied from Moroni's previous preparations (v. 6), but they could not copy his new preparations because they were not inspired of God.

Alma 49:12–25 • The City of Noah is Successfully Defended

12 Therefore they retreated into the wilderness, and took their camp and marched towards the land of Noah, supposing that to be the next best place for them to come against the Nephites.

13 For they knew not that Moroni had fortified, or had built forts of security, for every city in all the land round about; therefore, they marched forward to the land of Noah with a firm determination; yea, their chief captains came forward and took an oath that they would destroy the people of that city.

14 But behold, to their astonishment, the city of Noah, which had hitherto been a weak place, had now, by the means of Moroni, become strong, yea, even to exceed the strength of the city Ammonihah.

15 And now, behold, this was wisdom in Moroni; for he had supposed that they would be frightened at the city Ammonihah; and as the city of Noah had hitherto been the weakest part of the land, therefore they would march thither to battle; and thus it was according to his desires.

16 And behold, Moroni had appointed Lehi to be chief captain over the men of that city; and it was that same Lehi who fought with the Lamanites in the valley on the east of the river Sidon.

17 And now behold it came to pass, that when the Lamanites had found that Lehi commanded the city they were again disappointed, for they feared Lehi exceedingly; nevertheless their chief captains had sworn with an oath to attack the city; therefore, they brought up their armies.

18 Now behold, the Lamanites could not get into their forts of security by any other way save by the entrance, because of the highness of the bank which had been thrown up, and the depth of the ditch which had been dug round about, save it were by the entrance.

19 And thus were the Nephites prepared to destroy all such as should attempt to climb up to enter the fort by any other way, by casting over stones and arrows at them.

20 Thus they were prepared, yea, a body of their strongest men, with their swords and their slings, to smite down all who should attempt to come into their place of security by the place of entrance; and thus were they prepared to defend themselves against the Lamanites.

21 And it came to pass that the captains of the Lamanites brought up their armies before the place of entrance, and began to contend with the Nephites, to get into their place of security; but behold, they were driven back from time to time, insomuch that they were slain with an immense slaughter.

22 Now when they found that they could not obtain power over the Nephites by the pass, they began to dig down their banks of earth that they might obtain a pass to their armies, that they might have an equal chance to fight; but behold, in these attempts they were swept off by the stones and arrows which were thrown at them; and instead of filling up their ditches by pulling down the banks of earth, they were filled up in a measure with their dead and wounded bodies.

23 Thus the Nephites had all power over their enemies; and thus the Lamanites did attempt to destroy the Nephites until their chief captains were all slain; yea, and more than a thousand of the Lamanites were slain; while, on the other hand, there was not a single soul of the Nephites which was slain.

24 There were about fifty who were wounded, who had been exposed to the arrows of the Lamanites through the pass, but they were shielded by their shields, and their breastplates, and their head-plates, insomuch that their wounds were upon their legs, many of which were very severe.

25 And it came to pass, that when the Lamanites saw that their chief captains were all slain they fled into the wilderness. And it came to pass that they returned to the land of Nephi, to inform their king, Amalickiah, who was a Nephite by birth, concerning their great loss.

The wisdom of Moroni again succeeds. Not only had he strengthened the weak (city of Noah), but he had appointed a chief captain who was feared by the Lamanites (vv. 16–17). The immense slaughter of the Lamanites (v. 21), including every chief captain, was unbelievable when contrasted with the Nephites not having one person slain (v. 23). Certainly the Lord was with Moroni and his army.

Alma 49:26–30 • Amalickiah Swears to Drink Moroni's Blood

26 And it came to pass that he was exceedingly angry with his people, because he had not obtained his desire over the Nephites; he had not subjected them to the yoke of bondage.

27 Yea, he was exceedingly wroth, and he did curse God, and also Moroni, swearing with an oath that he would drink his blood; and this because Moroni had kept the commandments of God in preparing for the safety of his people.

28 And it came to pass, that on the other hand, the people of Nephi did thank the Lord their God, because of his matchless power in delivering them from the hands of their enemies.

29 And thus ended the nineteenth year of the reign of the judges over the people of Nephi.

30 Yea, and there was continual peace among them, and exceedingly great prosperity in the church because of their heed and diligence which they gave unto the word of God, which was declared unto them by Helaman, and Shiblon, and Corianton, and Ammon and his brethren, yea, and by all those who had been ordained by the holy

order of God, being baptized unto repentance, and sent forth to preach among the people.

Amalickiah should have recognized he was fighting against his God, being an apostate Nephite. However, he had joined forces with Satan and was blind in his mind. He cursed God instead of turning to him (v. 27). His oath to drink Moroni's blood reminds us of Cain making an oath with Satan to kill Abel.

> 28 And it came to pass that Cain took one of his brothers' daughters to wife, and they loved Satan more than God.
>
> 29 And Satan said unto Cain: Swear unto me by thy throat, and if thou tell it thou shalt die; and swear thy brethren by their heads, and by the living God, that they tell it not; for if they tell it, they shall surely die; and this that thy father may not know it; and this day I will deliver thy brother Abel into thine hands.
>
> 30 And Satan sware unto Cain that he would do according to his commands. And all these things were done in secret. [Moses 5:28–30; see also Genesis 4:8]

On the other hand, the Nephite people recognized their God (v. 28), and Mormon, as he abridges, recognized the prosperity of the church because of the work of Helaman and his brethren (v. 30). We should also acknowledge the repentance of Corianton, as shown by his being listed with Helaman (v. 30). Thank God again for the principle of repentance.

SACRED WRITING

Prophesying:

Alma 46:23–27   Captain Moroni cites the prophecies of Jacob, father of Joseph sold into Egypt.

Doctrines Learned:

Alma 46:14   True believers were called Christians before the time of Christ.

Alma 46:17	All the land south and all the land north is a chosen land, the land of liberty.
Alma 46:24	Jacob prophesied that a remnant of Joseph would be preserved.
Alma 46:40	God prepares roots and plants to remove diseases.

General Authority Quotes:

Elder Ezra Taft Benson • Alma 46:10, 12–13, 36

In that sacred volume of scripture, the Book of Mormon, we note the great and prolonged struggle for liberty. We also note the complacency of the people and their frequent willingness to give up their liberty for the promises of a would-be provider. [CR, Oct. 1962, 14–5]

President Anthony W. Ivins • Alma 46:12

So long as there should be a band of Christians: . . . we have heard a great deal since the beginning of this devastating war, in regard to making the world safe for democracy. My appeal to you this morning is to make the world safe for Christianity, for if Christianity is safe, then is democracy safe also. Then is representative government by the people, and for the people, safe. Then are the principles of charity, and mercy, and justice safe, for these, and every other thing which the heart of man may desire in righteousness are made safe when the doctrines taught by the Redeemer are acknowledged to be the supreme law, and he the Law-giver.

So I appeal to you to reflect, and to resolve, in the words of Moroni which I have read, that so long as there is a band of Christians left in the world, they will gird on their armor, the armor of righteousness, that the word of the Lord may be advocated in every nation, and if necessary the arm of every Christian be steeled to fight for the perpetuity of these eternal truths upon which the salvation of the world depends today. God give victory to the armies which are fighting in defense of these principles. May he give strength to the Latter-day Saints to properly perform their part in this great struggle, and above all may he give power to spread these truths among all nations, until the world shall be converted, God's kingdom come, and his will be done upon earth, as it is in heaven. . . . [CR, Oct. 1918, 52–52]

President Brigham Young • Alma 46:12–13

When the day comes in which the Kingdom of God will bear rule, the flag of the United States will proudly flutter unsullied on the flag staff of liberty and equal rights, without a spot to sully its fair surface; the glorious flag our fathers have bequeathed to us will then be unfurled to the breeze by those who have power to hoist it aloft and defend its sanctity.

How long will it be before the words of the prophet Joseph will be fulfilled? He said if the Constitution of the United States were saved at all if must be done by this people. It will not be many years before these words come to pass. [*Discourses of Brigham Young*, sel. John A. Widtsoe (1941), 360]

Bishop Vaughn J. Featherstone • Alma 46:12–13

What a contrast to the attitude of some of our liberals! Someone asked me once how I felt about amnesty for the draft card burner and the deserter. I told him that I thought every one of them should be taken before General Moroni to be judged. We need to feel again what it means to be a citizen of the United States of America. We need to feel the thrill and sensation and have the swellings within our bosom about this country. The priesthood of God should be an example of patriotism and loyalty to our country. As I talk about the United States of America, each one should consider his homeland, his flag, and his country. The scriptures give us a description of a great, great soul when they describe Moroni. [CR, Oct. 1978, 9–10]

President Joseph Fielding Smith • Alma 46:17

We should put our faith in the Lord and keep his commandments, but the Lord has also told us to exercise works with our faith, and there is wisdom in getting counsel to help us to take care of our bodies, and when sick, to find the best methods of restoring them to health. A physician has a proper place in the Church as well as in the days of the apostles of old. They had physicians, one of them being Luke, author of one of the gospels. We should live so that we will have faith, but the Lord has advised that we call in nurses or others to assist when the occasion requires. [*Doctrines of Salvation,* comp. Bruce R. McConkie, 3 vols. (1954–56), 2:315]

Elder Mark E. Petersen • Alma 46:19–21

So, my dear young friends, I say to you, this is God's land. He raised it up specially as he has raised up no other nation. He has given us our flag. So far as I am concerned the flag of the United States is the flag of Almighty God. Old Glory to me stands for everything that the gospel of Christ stands for, because Old Glory was raised up because there was to be a restoration of the gospel. I cannot separate my flag and my religion. I would fight for my flag as I would fight for my religion.

The very best thing, I repeat, that we can do is to determine that we will be good Americans and good Latter-day Saints. Thereby we will fulfill the great destiny that God has given us, . . . ["Our Divine Destiny," Address given to BYU student body, Feb. 20, 1968]

Elder Ezra Taft Benson • Alma 48:17

Now, part of the reason we may not have sufficient priesthood bearers to save the Constitution, let alone to shake the powers of hell, is because unlike Moroni, I fear, our souls do not joy in keeping our country free, and we are not firm in the faith of Christ, nor have we sworn with an oath to defend our rights and the liberty of our country.

Moroni, raised a title of liberty and wrote upon it these words: "In memory of our God, our religion, and freedom, and our peace, our wives, and our children." Why didn't he write upon it: "Just live your religion; there's no need to concern yourselves about your freedom, your peace, your wives, or your children"? The reason he didn't do this was because all these things were a part of his religion, as they are of our religion today.

Should we counsel people, "Just live your religion. There's no need to get involved in the fight for freedom"? No, we should not, because our stand for freedom is a most basic part of our religion; this stand helped get us to this earth, and our reaction to freedom in this life will have eternal consequences. Man has many duties, but he has no excuse that can compensate for his loss of liberty.

As members of the church we have some close quarters to pass through if we are going to get home safely. We will be given a chance to choose between conflicting counsel given by some. That's why we must learn—and the sooner we learn, the better—to keep our eye on the Prophet, the President of the Church. [CR, Oct. 1966, 122]

Challenges to Eternal Life:

1. Be mindful of the moral character and teachings of community and national leaders before you choose to vote for or follow their counsel (Alma 46:8–9).

2. Analyze your spiritual food and see if the devil is administering a little poison by degrees such as pornography, alcohol, or drugs (Alma 47:18).

3. Review the description of Moroni and choose one characteristic of him that you would like to emulate and work towards (Alma 48:11–13).

4. Choose a challenge of your own from this reading and endeavor to work towards it.

Chapter Three

Principles of War
for a Nation

Alma 50:1–53:9

*H*istorical Setting: The four Book of Mormon chapters discussed
in this chapter (50–53) cover nine years, from the twentieth
through the twenty-eighth year of the reign of the judges. The ending
of chapter fifty-three (vv. 10–22) describes the sons of Ammon, the
sons of the Lamanite converts who entered into the war. These verses
fit the context of the following chapter and are included there. The
events of the four chapters included herein all take place in the various
lands of the greater land of Zarahemla and the land of Bountiful. These
lands were originally established by the Nephites, but are now being
invaded by the Lamanites.

Precepts of this Reading:

19 And thus we see how merciful and just are all the dealings of
the Lord, to the fulfilling of all his words unto the children of men;
yea, we can behold that his words are verified, even at this time, which
he spake unto Lehi, saying:

20 Blessed art thou and thy children; and they shall be blessed,
inasmuch as they shall keep my commandments they shall prosper
in the land. But remember, inasmuch as they will not keep my
commandments they shall be cut off from the presence of the Lord.
[Alma 50:19–20]

21 And we see that these promises have been verified to the people of Nephi; for it has been their quarrellings and their contentions, yea, their murderings, and their plunderings, their idolatry, their whoredoms, and their abominations, which were among themselves, which brought upon them their wars and their destructions.

22 And those who were faithful in keeping the commandments of the Lord were delivered at all times, whilst thousands of their wicked brethren have been consigned to bondage, or to perish by the sword, or to dwindle in unbelief, and mingle with the Lamanites.

23 But behold there never was a happier time among the people of Nephi, since the days of Nephi, than in the days of Moroni, yea, even at this time, in the twenty and first year of the reign of the judges. [Alma 50:21–23]

And thus because of iniquity amongst themselves, yea, because of dissensions and intrigue among themselves they were placed in the most dangerous circumstances. [Alma 53:9]

There are other important issues that the Nephites face at this time. Most of these issues are similar to issues that we face today as a nation, and the Book of Mormon teaches us the Lords' will concerning them. An outline of the Book of Mormon chapters follow as a preparation for a deeper study.

OUTLINE • ALMA 50:1–53:9

➤ 50:1–6   Moroni made preparations continually to defend his people against the Lamanites. In the twentieth year of the reign of the judges:

a.   Moroni's armies commenced digging up heaps of earth around all the cities (vv. 1–3).

1.   On top of these ridges of earth he built works of timbers to the height of a man.

2.   A frame of pickets, strong and high, was built upon the timbers round about.

b.   Moroni erected towers that overlooked the pickets and built places of security upon the towers to defend against stones and arrows, and they were able to cast stones from the top of the tower upon any who should approach. (vv. 4–5)

c. Moroni prepared strongholds against the coming of the enemy, around every city in the land (v. 6).

➤ 50:7–12   Moroni caused his armies to go forth and drive out all the Lamanites who were in the east wilderness into their own lands, which were south of Zarahemla.

a. The land of Nephi ran in a straight course from the east sea to the west (v. 8).

b. Moroni caused the inhabitants of Zarahemla to go into the east wilderness and possess the land even to the borders by the seashore (v. 9).

c. Moroni placed armies on the borders in the south, and erected fortifications to secure their armies and people (v. 10).

d. Moroni cut off all the strongholds of the Lamanites in the east wilderness and the west, fortifying the line between the Nephites and the Lamanites, between the lands of Zarahemla and the land of Nephi, running by the head of the river Sidon—the Nephites possessed all the land northward of the land Bountiful (v. 11).

e. Moroni and his armies increased daily because of the assurance of protection from the Lamanites (v. 12).

➤ 50:13–16   The Nephites began to build many cities during the twentieth year.

a. The Nephites built the city of Moroni by the east sea, and the city Nephihah between the cities of Moroni and Aaron, joining the borders of Moroni and Aaron (vv.13–14).

b. The Nephites built the city of Lehi, and many others on the north which was by the borders of the seashore (v. 15).

➤ 50:17–24   The Nephites prospered exceedingly, multiplied and waxed strong in the twenty-first year.

a. Thus we see how merciful and just are the dealings of the Lord to the fulfilling of his words (vv. 19–22).

        1. Lehi said those who kept the commandments would prosper and those who didn't would be cut off.

        2. Their quarrellings, contentions, murderings, plunderings, idolatry, whoredoms, and abominations among themselves had brought wars and destructions upon them.

        3. Those who were faithful and kept the commandments were delivered, while thousands of their wicked brethren perished by the sword, were in bondage, or dwindled in unbelief among the Lamanites.

    b. There never was a happier time among the people of Nephi than in the days of Moroni, in the twenty and first year of the reign of the judges (v. 23).

    c. The twenty-second and twenty-third year ended in peace (v. 24).

➤ 50:25–26 The twenty-fourth year was peaceful except for contention concerning the lands of Lehi and Morianton on the seashore.

    a. The people of Morianton claimed a part of the land of Lehi and took up arms against them (vv. 26–31).

        1. The people of Lehi fled to the camp of Moroni and appealed for protection for they were not in the wrong.

        2. The people of Morianton feared that the army of Moroni would come and destroy them.

        3. Their leader Morianton, urged them to flee northward to a land covered with large bodies of water.

        4. The plan would have taken effect, but Morianton was angry with one of his maidservants and beat her.

        5. She fled to the camp of Moroni and told him of their intentions to flee to the land northward.

    b. Moroni feared that the people of Bountiful would unite

with Morianton and obtain possession of those lands, which consequences would lead to the overthrow of their liberty (vv. 32–35).

1. Moroni sent an army to stop their flight north.
2. They met them at the borders of the land of Desolation by the narrow pass that led by the sea.
3. Moroni's army, led by Teancum, battled with Morianton's people, who were inspired by his wickedness.
4. Teancum slew Morianton and defeated his army, and took them prisoners back to Moroni, as the twenty-fourth year ended.

c. Morianton's people were restored to their land upon their covenant to keep the peace, and a union took place with the people of Lehi (v. 36).

➤ 50:37–40 Nephihah, the second chief judge, died having filled his seat with perfect uprightness before God.

a. Nephihah had refused to take possession of the records and sacred things, and Alma had conferred them on Helaman, his son (v. 38).
b. The son of Nephihah, Pahoran, was appointed chief judge and governor over the people with an oath and sacred ordinance (v. 39–40).

1. He was to keep the peace and the freedom of the people, and the sacred privilege to worship God.
2. He was to support and maintain the cause of God, and to bring the wicked to justice according to their crime.
3. He commenced his reign in the end of the twenty-fourth year.

➤ 51:1–10 The twenty-fifth year commenced in peace, but there began to be contention among the people concerning the chief judge Pahoran for a part of the people desired that a few particular points of the law should be altered; but Pahoran would not alter them.

a. Those who desired the law altered were angry and wanted Pahoran removed (vv. 4–5).

       1. They were called king-men.

       2. They wanted to alter the law, overthrow the free government, and establish a king.

    b. Those who supported Pahoran took upon them the name "freemen" and covenanted to maintain their rights, and privileges of their religion by a free government (v. 6).

    c. The contention was settled by the voice of the people who chose to retain Pahoran of the judgment seat (vv. 7–8).

       1. The people of liberty rejoiced.

       2. The king-men were put to silence and obliged to maintain the cause of freedom.

       3. Those in favor of kings were those of high birth, and sought to be kings.

       4. They were supported by those who sought power and authority over the people.

    d. The contention came at a critical time, for Amalickiah again stirred up the Lamanites to come against the Nephites, and he was preparing for war (vv. 9–10).

       1. He had sworn to drink the blood of Moroni.

       2. We shall see that his promise was rash.

➢ 51:11–21 Amalickiah's armies had many thousands slain, but he had gathered a wonderfully great army and did not fear to come down to Zarahemla.

    a. Amalickiah did himself head the army at the same time the Pahoran contentions were settled (v. 12).

    b. The king-men were glad in their hearts and refused to take up arms to defend the country (v. 13).

    c. Moroni was angry and sent a petition to the governor asking for power to compel those dissenters to defend their country or be put to death (vv. 14–16).

       1. His first care was to put an end to such contentions

and dissensions, which had previously been the cause of all their destruction.

   2. He was granted this power by the voice of the people.

d. Moroni commanded his army, and they went against the king-men and compelled them to defend their country or be put to death (vv. 17–21).

   1. They lifted their weapons of war against the men of Moroni and four thousand were put to death.

   2. The leaders who were not slain were cast into prison, for there was not time for their trials.

   3. The remainder yielded to the standard of liberty, and were compelled to hoist the title of liberty upon their towers and take up arms to defend the country.

e. Moroni put an end of those known as king-men (v. 21).

➤ 51:22–27 While Moroni was putting down the king-men, the Lamanites came into the land of Moroni (v. 22).

a. The Nephites in that city were not sufficiently strong; therefore Amalickiah took possession of the city, slaying many (v. 23).

b. Those who fled from the city of Moroni came to the city of Nephihah, and the people of the city of Lehi made preparation to defend the city of Nephihah (v. 24).

c. Amalickiah would not come first against Nephihah, but went on down the seashore taking possession of many cities, leaving men to maintain and defend them (vv. 25–27).

   1. The cities of Nephihah, Lehi, Morianton, Omner, Gid and Mulek, all on the east by the seashore, were all captured.

   2. Amalickiah had captured many cities that had been fortified by Moroni.

d. The Lamanites marched to the land Bountiful, driving and slaying many Nephites (vv. 28–32).

1.   They were met by Teancum, who had slain Morianton.

        2.   Teancum and his men were great warriors, and exceeded the Lamanites in strength and skill.

        3.   Teancum did harass and slay them until it was dark.

        4.   Teancum pitched his tents in the borders of Bountiful.

        5.   Amalickiah pitched his tents on the beach by the seashore.

    e.   Teancum and his servant went into the camp of Amalickiah by night (vv. 33–37).

        1.   Sleep had overpowered them because of their much fatigue.

        2.   Teancum stole privily into Amalickiah's tent and put a javelin into his heart.

        3.   Teancum returned and awoke his men and had them stand in readiness lest the Lamanites had awakened, ending the twenty-fifth year.

➤ 52:1–14   On the first day of the twenty-sixth year, the Lamanites awoke and found Amalickiah dead and Teancum ready for battle.

    a.   The Lamanites retreated into the city of Mulek and sought protection in their fortifications (v. 2).

    b.   Ammoron, the brother of Amalickiah, was appointed to reign in his stead, and he commanded his people to maintain those cities they had taken (vv. 3–4).

    c.   Teancum thought it not expedient to attack them in their forts (vv. 5–7).

        1.   He kept his men round about, casting up walls and preparing places of resort.

        2.   He thus prepared for war until Moroni sent many men to strengthen his army.

    d.   Moroni sent orders to retain all the prisoners as a ransom for those taken by the Lamanites (vv. 8–14).

1.   He also sent orders to fortify the land Bountiful and secure the narrow pass to the north.

    2.   He also sent desiring Teancum to be faithful in maintaining that quarter of land, and to scourge the Lamanites and possibly retake those cities.

    3.   He could not come to them for he was fighting the Lamanites by the west sea. King Ammoron had gone to the queen and told her of the death of his brother and had taken a large number to the borders of the west sea.

    4.   He was endeavoring to harass the Nephites in that part of the land.

    5.   The Nephites were in dangerous circumstances as the twenty and sixth year ended.

➤ 52:15–18   In the twenty-seventh year, Moroni was marching to Bountiful to assist Teancum, and he ordered Teancum to attack Mulek.

    a.   Teancum saw it was impossible to retake Mulek, so he returned to Bountiful to wait for Moroni that he might receive strength for his army (v. 17).

    b.   Moroni arrived in the latter end of the year.

➤ 52:19–40   In the beginning of the twenty-eighth year, Moroni, Teancum and many of the chief captains held a council of war on how to retake the city of Mulek.

    a.   The council sent embassies to Jacob, the Lamanite leader who was a Zoramite, to come out with his armies and meet them on the plains, but Jacob would not come (v. 20).

    b.   Moroni resolved a plan to decoy the Lamanites out of their strongholds (vv. 21–26).

        1.   Teancum took a small number of men and marched down near the seashore and Moroni by night marched in the wilderness and west of the city Mulek.

2. On the morrow, the Lamanite guards discovered Teancum and ran and told Jacob.
3. The Lamanite army pursued Teancum who retreated northward by the seashore.
4. They pursued Teancum with vigor and a part of Moroni's army retook Mulek.
5. Moroni marched with the remainder of his army to meet the Lamanites who pursued Teancum.

c. The Lamanites pursued Teancum to near the city of Bountiful where they met Lehi and a small army (vv. 27–32).
   1. The Lamanites fled in confusion when they saw Lehi's army.
   2. They were surrounded by Moroni on one hand, and Lehi on the other, both fresh and full of strength, while the Lamanites were wearied by their march.

d. Jacob, a Zoramite with an unconquerable spirit, led the Lamanites to battle with exceeding fury (vv. 33–37).
   1. Moroni and his men were more powerful and did not give way.
   2. Jacob was killed and Moroni was wounded.
   3. Lehi pressed upon their rear with such fury that the Lamanites in the rear gave up their weapons.
   4. Moroni told the other Lamanites to give up their weapons and their blood would not be shed.

e. Many including their chief captains, threw down their weapons, but some would not (vv. 38–40).
   1. Those who would not give up their swords were taken prisoners and bound and compelled to march to Bountiful.
   2. The number of prisoners exceeded more than the number slain on both sides.

➤ 53:1–9 Moroni set guards over the Lamanite prisoners and did compel them to go and bury their dead and the Nephite dead.

a. Moroni went to the city of Mulek with Lehi, and gave Lehi command of the city (v. 2).

      1. Lehi had been with Moroni in the more part of his battles, and they rejoiced in each other's safety.

      2. They were a lot alike and loved each other, and were loved by the people.

   b. The prisoners were marched back to Bountiful, and Teancum, by order of Moroni, had them dig a ditch around the city of Bountiful (vv. 3–5).

      1. They built a breastwork of timber on the inner bank, and encircled the city with a strong wall of timbers and earth.

      2. It became an exceeding stronghold, and the prisoners were guarded there.

      3. Moroni compelled the prisoners to labor because it was easy to guard them.

   c. Moroni had gained a victory over one of the greatest armies of the Lamanites, obtained the city of Mulek, which was one of the strongest holds of the Lamanites, and built a stronghold to retain prisoners (vv. 6–7).

      1. He did no more attempts to battle the Lamanites that year.

      2. He employed his men in preparing for war, making fortifications, and delivering their woman and children from famine and affliction.

   d. The Lamanites on the west sea south had gained some ground over the Nephite in the absence of Moroni (vv. 8–9).

      1. The Nephites had some intrigue that caused dissensions amongst themselves.

      2. The Nephites placed themselves in the most dangerous circumstances.

NOTES AND COMMENTARY

Introduction: When the Savior ministered on the earth in Jerusalem, he gave us one of the signs of his Second Coming: "And they shall hear of wars, and rumors of wars" (JS–Matthew 1:28). Since the coming forth of the Book of Mormon his prophecy has been and is still being fulfilled. Wars rage on in our day. The Book of Mormon chapters discussed herein teach us principles to guide us as a nation in maintaining our freedom in these days and years of war as the Second Coming draws nigh (see JS–History 1:40–41). Again we note that the historical incidents are the framework to teach principles that are more important than the minute details that may be difficult to follow or to remember. The following chapter of this work teaches individual principles that we must abide to maintain our freedom in this chosen land of America. The same principles will bring freedom to any other land if they are followed by the people.

Alma 50:1–6 • Captain Moroni Prepares Strongholds Around Every City—20th Year

1 And now it came to pass that Moroni did not stop making preparations for war, or to defend his people against the Lamanites; for he caused that his armies should commence in the commencement of the twentieth year of the reign of the judges, that they should commence in digging up heaps of earth round about all the cities, throughout all the land which was possessed by the Nephites.

2 And upon the top of these ridges of earth he caused that there should be timbers, yea, works of timbers built up to the height of a man, round about the cities.

3 And he caused that upon those works of timbers there should be a frame of pickets built upon the timbers round about; and they were strong and high.

4 And he caused towers to be erected that overlooked those works of pickets, and he caused places of security to be built upon those towers, that the stones and the arrows of the Lamanites could not hurt them.

5 And they were prepared that they could cast stones from the top thereof, according to their pleasure and their strength, and slay him who should attempt to approach near the walls of the city.

6 Thus Moroni did prepare strongholds against the coming of their enemies, round about every city in all the land.

A major first concern for every nation is civil defense. Should they build up their defenses against possible future attacks during times of peace? Captain Moroni followed the Boy Scout motto of "be prepared." In the nineteenth year of the reign of the judges, the war against the Lamanites ended. Moroni began "the commencement of the twentieth year" (v. 1) by physically building defensive structures for every city. The defensive measures were not simple, but involved multiple lines of protection. They were well thought out and beyond the expectations of the time.

Were Moroni's actions a pattern for Christian nations to follow? Some may cite the "First Presidency statement on Basing of MX Missile" in Utah and Nevada given on 5 May 1981 as refutation of Moroni's action. However, the First Presidency's concern was against the arms race of nations "building of vast arsenals of nuclear weaponry," with the capacity "to destroy in large measure our civilization."[1] There is a difference, in this writer's opinion, in preparing to defend and in preparing to destroy.

Alma 50:7–12 • Captain Moroni Cuts off the Strength and Power of the Lamanites

7 And it came to pass that Moroni caused that his armies should go forth into the east wilderness; yea, and they went forth and drove all the Lamanites who were in the east wilderness into their own lands, which were south of the land of Zarahemla.

8 And the land of Nephi did run in a straight course from the east sea to the west.

9 And it came to pass that when Moroni had driven all the Lamanites out of the east wilderness, which was north of the lands of their own possessions, he caused that the inhabitants who were in the land of Zarahemla and in the land round about should go forth

---

[1] See *Ensign*, June 1981 for the full statement.

into the east wilderness, even to the borders by the seashore, and possess the land.

10 And he also placed armies on the south, in the borders of their possessions, and caused them to erect fortifications that they might secure their armies and their people from the hands of their enemies.

11 And thus he cut off all the strongholds of the Lamanites in the east wilderness, yea, and also on the west, fortifying the line between the Nephites and the Lamanites, between the land of Zarahemla and the land of Nephi, from the west sea, running by the head of the river Sidon—the Nephites possessing all the land northward, yea, even all the land which was northward of the land Bountiful, according to their pleasure.

12 Thus Moroni, with his armies, which did increase daily because of the assurance of protection which his works did bring forth unto them, did seek to cut off the strength and the power of the Lamanites from off the lands of their possessions, that they should have no power upon the lands of their possession.

In addition to the physical buildup of defenses, Moroni analyzed the lay of the lands and the seas to fortify his people against the enemy. He drove out the Lamanites from inside his line of defense and placed his armies in position to protect the people against the power of the Lamanites armies (vv. 11–12).

The land of Nephi running from the east sea to the west (v. 8) should again be qualified geographically. The land did not necessarily run to the west sea, but to the west. The wilderness on the west may have ended the straight course. Similarly, the west sea did not necessarily run "by the head of the river Sidon," but the fortified line was "between the Nephites and the Lamanites, between the land of Zarahemla and the land of Nephi, from the west sea" (v. 11 compare Alma 22:32; Helaman 4:7). If the sea ran by the head of the river, it should have been to the south not the west. So much for geography until we get a fuller record.

Alma 50:13–16 • The Nephites Build Cities

13 And it came to pass that the Nephites began the foundation of a city, and they called the name of the city Moroni; and it was by the east sea; and it was on the south by the line of the possessions of the Lamanites.

14 And they also began a foundation for a city between the city of Moroni and the city of Aaron, joining the borders of Aaron and Moroni; and they called the name of the city, or the land, Nephihah.

15 And they also began in that same year to build many cities on the north, one in a particular manner which they called Lehi, which was in the north by the borders of the seashore.

16 And thus ended the twentieth year.

There were many cities being built as the twentieth year ended. Three of them were named and specific locations given. The three named cities are spoken of later, which is probably the reason that Mormon mentioned them as he abridged the record.

Alma 50:17–24 • The Promise Given to Lehi Is Verified 21st–24th Year

17 And in these prosperous circumstances were the people of Nephi in the commencement of the twenty and first year of the reign of the judges over the people of Nephi.

18 And they did prosper exceedingly, and they became exceedingly rich; yea, and they did multiply and wax strong in the land.

19 And thus we see how merciful and just are all the dealings of the Lord, to the fulfilling of all his words unto the children of men; yea, we can behold that his words are verified, even at this time, which he spake unto Lehi, saying:

20 Blessed art thou and thy children; and they shall be blessed, inasmuch as they shall keep my commandments they shall prosper in the land. But remember, inasmuch as they will not keep my commandments they shall be cut off from the presence of the Lord.

21 And we see that these promises have been verified to the people

of Nephi; for it has been their quarrellings and their contentions, yea, their murderings, and their plunderings, their idolatry, their whoredoms, and their abominations, which were among themselves, which brought upon them their wars and their destructions.

22 And those who were faithful in keeping the commandments of the Lord were delivered at all times, whilst thousands of their wicked brethren have been consigned to bondage, or to perish by the sword, or to dwindle in unbelief, and mingle with the Lamanites.

23 But behold there never was a happier time among the people of Nephi, since the days of Nephi, than in the days of Moroni, yea, even at this time, in the twenty and first year of the reign of the judges.

24 And it came to pass that the twenty and second year of the reign of the judges also ended in peace; yea, and also the twenty and third year.

The above eight verses describe three years, all of them prosperous. They were the last three of the four years of peace mentioned before (see Alma 48:20). Two of the three years are covered in one short verse (Alma 50:24). Mormon mentions the years to verify the promise of the Lord to Lehi regarding prosperity if God's commandments are kept, a precept to the reader (vv. 19–20). This conditional promise of prosperity has been a constant theme throughout the Book of Mormon (see 1 Nephi 4:14; 2 Nephi 1:9, 20; Jarom 1:9; Mosiah 1:7; Alma 9:13). However, Mormon's second precept, a contrast to the first (Alma 50:21–22), gives us the cause of wars. We will see that quarrellings and contentions were a major factor in the succeeding years of war. Notice that these were internal difficulties, not the Lamanite invasions. Contentions and quarreling in the political arena is magnified in our own day. Another contrast was given by Mormon between those who followed wickedness and those who kept the commandments (vv. 22–23). That contrast is also evident today. Never was there a happier time for the faithful since the days of Nephi (v. 23) in over 500 years. The unabridged record should give us specific reasons for the Nephites happiness instead of the generalization in these verses.

Alma 50:25–36 • An Illustration of the Cause of War

25 And it came to pass that in the commencement of the twenty and fourth year of the reign of the judges, there would also have been peace among the people of Nephi had it not been for a contention which took place among them concerning the land of Lehi, and the land of Morianton, which joined upon the borders of Lehi; both of which were on the borders by the seashore.

26 For behold, the people who possessed the land of Morianton did claim a part of the land of Lehi; therefore there began to be a warm contention between them, insomuch that the people of Morianton took up arms against their brethren, and they were determined by the sword to slay them.

27 But behold, the people who possessed the land of Lehi fled to the camp of Moroni, and appealed unto him for assistance; for behold they were not in the wrong.

28 And it came to pass that when the people of Morianton, who were led by a man whose name was Morianton, found that the people of Lehi had fled to the camp of Moroni, they were exceedingly fearful lest the army of Moroni should come upon them and destroy them.

29 Therefore, Morianton put it into their hearts that they should flee to the land which was northward, which was covered with large bodies of water, and take possession of the land which was northward.

30 And behold, they would have carried this plan into effect, (which would have been a cause to have been lamented) but behold, Morianton being a man of much passion, therefore he was angry with one of his maid servants, and he fell upon her and beat her much.

31 And it came to pass that she fled, and came over to the camp of Moroni, and told Moroni all things concerning the matter, and also concerning their intentions to flee into the land northward.

32 Now behold, the people who were in the land Bountiful, or rather Moroni, feared that they would hearken to the words of Morianton and unite with his people, and thus he would obtain possession of those parts of the land, which would lay a foundation for serious consequences among the people of Nephi, yea, which consequences would lead to the overthrow of their liberty.

33 Therefore Moroni sent an army, with their camp, to head the people of Morianton, to stop their flight into the land northward.

34 And it came to pass that they did not head them until they had come to the borders of the land Desolation; and there they did head them, by the narrow pass which led by the sea into the land northward, yea, by the sea, on the west and on the east.

35 And it came to pass that the army which was sent by Moroni, which was led by a man whose name was Teancum, did meet the people of Morianton; and so stubborn were the people of Morianton, (being inspired by his wickedness and his flattering words) that a battle commenced between them, in the which Teancum did slay Morianton and defeat his army, and took them prisoners, and returned to the camp of Moroni. And thus ended the twenty and fourth year of the reign of the judges over the people of Nephi.

36 And thus were the people of Morianton brought back. And upon their covenanting to keep the peace they were restored to the land of Morianton, and a union took place between them and the people of Lehi; and they were also restored to their lands.

The contention over land (v. 26) and the anger of Morianton (v. 30) led to the war between Morianton's people and Teancum (v. 35). Morianton's anger led to an example of the precept given above (v. 21)—quarreling and contentions among themselves caused war. Morianton "being a man of much passion" (v. 30) suggests his anger may have been a result of desiring to commit whoredoms, another cause of war, but we don't know for sure.

Alma 50:37–40 • The Appointment of the Third Chief Judge

37 And it came to pass that in the same year that the people of Nephi had peace restored unto them, that Nephihah, the second chief judge, died, having filled the judgment-seat with perfect uprightness before God.

38 Nevertheless, he had refused Alma to take possession of those records and those things which were esteemed by Alma and his fathers to be most sacred; therefore Alma had conferred them upon his son, Helaman.

39 Behold, it came to pass that the son of Nephihah was appointed to fill the judgment-seat, in the stead of his father; yea, he was appointed chief judge and governor over the people, with an oath and sacred ordinance to judge righteously, and to keep the peace and the freedom of the people, and to grant unto them their sacred privileges to worship the Lord their God, yea, to support and maintain the cause of God all his days, and to bring the wicked to justice according to their crime.

40 Now behold, his name was Pahoran. And Pahoran did fill the seat of his father, and did commence his reign in the end of the twenty and fourth year, over the people of Nephi.

Alma was the first chief judge and was replaced by Nephihah after serving for eight years (see Alma 4:11, 18). Nephihah served until the end of the twenty-fourth year, a period of almost sixteen years (see Alma 50:40) from the commencement of the ninth year to the end of the twenty-fourth year. The oath of office that Pahoran took as the third chief judge gives us guidelines for effective political leaders. Notice the positive emphasis on righteous judgment, peace and freedom, privilege of worship, and maintaining the cause of God (v. 39). Concentration on these matters would certainly reduce the number of wicked who needed to be brought to justice.

Alma 51:1–10 • The King-Men Versus the Freemen—25th Year

1 And now it came to pass in the commencement of the twenty and fifth year of the reign of the judges over the people of Nephi, they having established peace between the people of Lehi and the people of Morianton concerning their lands, and having commenced the twenty and fifth year in peace;

2 Nevertheless, they did not long maintain an entire peace in the land, for there began to be a contention among the people concerning the chief judge Pahoran; for behold, there were a part of the people who desired that a few particular points of the law should be altered.

3 But behold, Pahoran would not alter nor suffer the law to be altered; therefore, he did not hearken to those who had sent in their voices with their petitions concerning the altering of the law.

4 Therefore, those who were desirous that the law should be altered were angry with him, and desired that he should no longer be chief judge over the land; therefore there arose a warm dispute concerning the matter, but not unto bloodshed.

5 And it came to pass that those who were desirous that Pahoran should be dethroned from the judgment-seat were called king-men, for they were desirous that the law should be altered in a manner to overthrow the free government and to establish a king over the land.

6 And those who were desirous that Pahoran should remain chief judge over the land took upon them the name of freemen; and thus was the division among them, for the freemen had sworn or covenanted to maintain their rights and the privileges of their religion by a free government.

7 And it came to pass that this matter of their contention was settled by the voice of the people. And it came to pass that the voice of the people came in favor of the freemen, and Pahoran retained the judgment-seat, which caused much rejoicing among the brethren of Pahoran and also many of the people of liberty, who also put the king-men to silence, that they durst not oppose but were obliged to maintain the cause of freedom.

8 Now those who were in favor of kings were those of high birth, and they sought to be kings; and they were supported by those who sought power and authority over the people.

9 But behold, this was a critical time for such contentions to be among the people of Nephi; for behold, Amalickiah had again stirred up the hearts of the people of the Lamanites against the people of the Nephites, and he was gathering together soldiers from all parts of his land, and arming them, and preparing for war with all diligence; for he had sworn to drink the blood of Moroni.

10 But behold, we shall see that his promise which he made was rash; nevertheless, he did prepare himself and his armies to come to battle against the Nephites.

The king-men opposed the purpose of government, as outlined in Pahoran's oath (Alma 50:39). The few particular points of the law that the king-men wished to have altered are not stated (v. 2). However, they must have been a threat to the oath of the chief judge because

Pahoran would not change them. Furthermore, the king-men wanted to overthrow the free government that sought to maintain the rights and privileges of religion (v. 6). The king-men were of high birth and sought to exercise power and authority over the people (v. 8). Therefore it was freedom versus bondage, or restriction of agency (see v. 21). Being "of high birth" suggests institution of a class system or inequality of men. It further promotes a respect of persons according to worldly possessions (compare Alma 1:30). Amalickiah illustrates another warning against freedom, the making of rash promises (v. 10). These promises were obviously made to attract followers. Politics does not change, just the names of the people and the principles they promote.

Alma 51:11–21 • Amalickiah Assembles a Great Army

11 Now his armies were not so great as they had hitherto been, because of the many thousands who had been slain by the hand of the Nephites; but notwithstanding their great loss, Amalickiah had gathered together a wonderfully great army, insomuch that he feared not to come down to the land of Zarahemla.

12 Yea, even Amalickiah did himself come down, at the head of the Lamanites. And it was in the twenty and fifth year of the reign of the judges; and it was at the same time that they had begun to settle the affairs of their contentions concerning the chief judge, Pahoran.

13 And it came to pass that when the men who were called king-men had heard that the Lamanites were coming down to battle against them, they were glad in their hearts; and they refused to take up arms, for they were so wroth with the chief judge, and also with the people of liberty, that they would not take up arms to defend their country.

14 And it came to pass that when Moroni saw this, and also saw that the Lamanites were coming into the borders of the land, he was exceedingly wroth because of the stubbornness of those people whom he had labored with so much diligence to preserve; yea, he was exceedingly wroth; his soul was filled with anger against them.

15 And it came to pass that he sent a petition, with the voice of the people, unto the governor of the land, desiring that he should read

it, and give him (Moroni) power to compel those dissenters to defend their country or to put them to death.

16 For it was his first care to put an end to such contentions and dissensions among the people; for behold, this had been hitherto a cause of all their destruction. And it came to pass that it was granted according to the voice of the people.

17 And it came to pass that Moroni commanded that his army should go against those king-men, to pull down their pride and their nobility and level them with the earth, or they should take up arms and support the cause of liberty.

18 And it came to pass that the armies did march forth against them; and they did pull down their pride and their nobility, insomuch that as they did lift their weapons of war to fight against the men of Moroni they were hewn down and leveled to the earth.

19 And it came to pass that there were four thousand of those dissenters who were hewn down by the sword; and those of their leaders who were not slain in battle were taken and cast into prison, for there was no time for their trials at this period.

20 And the remainder of those dissenters, rather than be smitten down to the earth by the sword, yielded to the standard of liberty, and were compelled to hoist the title of liberty upon their towers, and in their cities, and to take up arms in defense of their country.

21 And thus Moroni put an end to those king-men, that there were not any known by the appellation of king-men; and thus he put an end to the stubbornness and the pride of those people who professed the blood of nobility; but they were brought down to humble themselves like unto their brethren, and to fight valiantly for their freedom from bondage.

Another national problem arises its ugly head—conscientious objectors and draft dodgers. These men were not like the Lamanite converts who buried their weapons of war as a covenant to God rather than harm another person. That covenant was based on past experiences of which they had repented and didn't want to risk returning to their sins (see Alma 24). The king-men wanted to overthrow the government of freedom (Alma 51:5). They refused to defend their country, and rejoiced over the Lamanites coming to battle (v. 13). The cause of their destruction hitherto (v. 16) is not specified but contention is always caused by Satan, "the father of contention" (3 Nephi 11:29). A study of previous encounters will show his presence always.

Moroni's petition was not to kill whoever chose not to fight. Notice that there was not time for a trial (Alma 51:19). Five years later, the men of Pachus, also king-men, "received their trial, according to the law" and those who would "fight against [their country], were put to death." This action was taken "for the safety of their country" (Alma 62:9–10). In a similar situation today, the same action may be justified. Notice also that the dissenters were given the choice to defend their country or be put to death (Alma 51:15). Moroni's actions put an end to the king-men and to the stubbornness and pride of those "who professed the blood of nobility" (v. 21).

Alma 51:22–27 • Amalickiah Captures the City of Moroni and Others

22 Behold, it came to pass that while Moroni was thus breaking down the wars and contentions among his own people, and subjecting them to peace and civilization, and making regulations to prepare for war against the Lamanites, behold, the Lamanites had come into the land of Moroni, which was in the borders by the seashore.

23 And it came to pass that the Nephites were not sufficiently strong in the city of Moroni; therefore Amalickiah did drive them, slaying many. And it came to pass that Amalickiah took possession of the city, yea, possession of all their fortifications.

24 And those who fled out of the city of Moroni came to the city of Nephihah; and also the people of the city of Lehi gathered themselves together, and made preparations and were ready to receive the Lamanites to battle.

25 But it came to pass that Amalickiah would not suffer the Lamanites to go against the city of Nephihah to battle, but kept them down by the seashore, leaving men in every city to maintain and defend it.

26 And thus he went on, taking possession of many cities, the city of Nephihah, and the city of Lehi, and the city of Morianton, and the

city of Omner, and the city of Gid, and the city of Mulek, all of which were on the east borders by the seashore.

27 And thus had the Lamanites obtained, by the cunning of Amalickiah, so many cities, by their numberless hosts, all of which were strongly fortified after the manner of the fortifications of Moroni; all of which afforded strongholds for the Lamanites.

The cities mentioned by name that were built earlier (Alma 50:13–15) and others as well are now captured by the Lamanites.[2] The strong defensive cities built by Captain Moroni have become the "strongholds for the Lamanites" (v. 27).

Alma 51:28–37 • Teancum Slays Amalickiah

28 And it came to pass that they marched to the borders of the land Bountiful, driving the Nephites before them and slaying many.

29 But it came to pass that they were met by Teancum, who had slain Morianton and had headed his people in his flight.

30 And it came to pass that he headed Amalickiah also, as he was marching forth with his numerous army that he might take possession of the land Bountiful, and also the land northward.

31 But behold he met with a disappointment by being repulsed by Teancum and his men, for they were great warriors; for every man of Teancum did exceed the Lamanites in their strength and in their skill of war, insomuch that they did gain advantage over the Lamanites.

32 And it came to pass that they did harass them, insomuch that they did slay them even until it was dark. And it came to pass that Teancum and his men did pitch their tents in the borders of the land Bountiful; and Amalickiah did pitch his tents in the borders on the beach by the seashore, and after this manner were they driven.

33 And it came to pass that when the night had come, Teancum and his servant stole forth and went out by night, and went into the camp of Amalickiah; and behold, sleep had overpowered them because

---

[2] The city of Mulek is not the same city as the city of Melek where Alma previously preached.

of their much fatigue, which was caused by the labors and heat of the day.

34 And it came to pass that Teancum stole privily into the tent of the king, and put a javelin to his heart; and he did cause the death of the king immediately that he did not awake his servants.

35 And he returned again privily to his own camp, and behold, his men were asleep, and he awoke them and told them all the things that he had done.

36 And he caused that his armies should stand in readiness, lest the Lamanites had awakened and should come upon them.

37 And thus endeth the twenty and fifth year of the reign of the judges over the people of Nephi; and thus endeth the days of Amalickiah.

Teancum found a way to celebrate New Year's Eve. He took out the old (Amalickiah) and then he awaked his sleeping men to bring in the new, whatever the New Year had to offer (vv. 33–36. See Alma 52:1 for the designation of New Year's Eve). Teancum was certainly entitled to be called one of the great Nephite warriors (Alma 51:31).

Alma 52:1–14 • Ammoron Succeeds Amalickiah—26th Year

1 And now, it came to pass in the twenty and sixth year of the reign of the judges over the people of Nephi, behold, when the Lamanites awoke on the first morning of the first month, behold, they found Amalickiah was dead in his own tent; and they also saw that Teancum was ready to give them battle on that day.

2 And now, when the Lamanites saw this they were affrighted; and they abandoned their design in marching into the land northward, and retreated with all their army into the city of Mulek, and sought protection in their fortifications.

3 And it came to pass that the brother of Amalickiah was appointed king over the people; and his name was Ammoron; thus king Ammoron, the brother of king Amalickiah, was appointed to reign in his stead.

4 And it came to pass that he did command that his people should

maintain those cities, which they had taken by the shedding of blood; for they had not taken any cities save they had lost much blood.

5 And now, Teancum saw that the Lamanites were determined to maintain those cities which they had taken, and those parts of the land which they had obtained possession of; and also seeing the enormity of their number, Teancum thought it was not expedient that he should attempt to attack them in their forts.

6 But he kept his men round about, as if making preparations for war; yea, and truly he was preparing to defend himself against them, by casting up walls round about and preparing places of resort.

7 And it came to pass that he kept thus preparing for war until Moroni had sent a large number of men to strengthen his army.

8 And Moroni also sent orders unto him that he should retain all the prisoners who fell into his hands; for as the Lamanites had taken many prisoners, that he should retain all the prisoners of the Lamanites as a ransom for those whom the Lamanites had taken.

9 And he also sent orders unto him that he should fortify the land Bountiful, and secure the narrow pass which led into the land northward, lest the Lamanites should obtain that point and should have power to harass them on every side.

10 And Moroni also sent unto him, desiring him that he would be faithful in maintaining that quarter of the land, and that he would seek every opportunity to scourge the Lamanites in that quarter, as much as was in his power, that perhaps he might take again by stratagem or some other way those cities which had been taken out of their hands; and that he also would fortify and strengthen the cities round about, which had not fallen into the hands of the Lamanites.

11 And he also said unto him, I would come unto you, but behold, the Lamanites are upon us in the borders of the land by the west sea; and behold, I go against them, therefore I cannot come unto you.

12 Now, the king (Ammoron) had departed out of the land of Zarahemla, and had made known unto the queen concerning the death of his brother, and had gathered together a large number of men, and had marched forth against the Nephites on the borders by the west sea.

13 And thus he was endeavoring to harass the Nephites, and to

draw away a part of their forces to that part of the land, while he had commanded those whom he had left to possess the cities which he had taken, that they should also harass the Nephites on the borders by the east sea, and should take possession of their lands as much as it was in their power, according to the power of their armies.

14 And thus were the Nephites in those dangerous circumstances in the ending of the twenty and sixth year of the reign of the judges over the people of Nephi.

The Nephites, under Teancum and Moroni, spent the entire twenty-sixth year building up their defenses and planning their strategy for future Lamanite invasions. The only principle of war stated in the above verses is concerning prisoners of war. Captain Moroni instructs Teancum to retain all Lamanite prisoners as a ransom for the Nephite prisoners taken by the Lamanites (v. 8). We will see the benefits of this later, but it was a measure to save the lives of their own soldiers. It also sustains the fact that Moroni did not delight in the shedding of blood (see Alma 48:11).

Alma 52:15–18 • Teancum Is Ordered to Attack the City of Mulek—27th Year

15 But behold, it came to pass in the twenty and seventh year of the reign of the judges, that Teancum, by the command of Moroni— who had established armies to protect the south and the west borders of the land, and had begun his march towards the land Bountiful, that he might assist Teancum with his men in retaking the cities which they had lost—

16 And it came to pass that Teancum had received orders to make an attack upon the city of Mulek, and retake it if it were possible.

17 And it came to pass that Teancum made preparations to make an attack upon the city of Mulek, and march forth with his army against the Lamanites; but he saw that it was impossible that he could overpower them while they were in their fortifications; therefore he abandoned his designs and returned again to the city Bountiful, to wait for the coming of Moroni, that he might receive strength to his army.

18 And it came to pass that Moroni did arrive with his army at the

land of Bountiful, in the latter end of the twenty and seventh year of the reign of the judges over the people of Nephi.

The initiative of Teancum in choosing not to attack the city of Mulek shows the reason why the Nephites chose chief captains who "had the spirit of revelation and also prophecy" (3 Nephi 3:19). The Lord, as well as Moroni, expected his leaders to make decisions as directed by the Spirit, according to the situation.

Alma 52:19–40 • The Chief Captains Hold a Council of War—28th Year

19 And in the commencement of the twenty and eighth year, Moroni and Teancum and many of the chief captains held a council of war—what they should do to cause the Lamanites to come out against them to battle; or that they might by some means flatter them out of their strongholds, that they might gain advantage over them and take again the city of Mulek.

20 And it came to pass they sent embassies to the army of the Lamanites, which protected the city of Mulek, to their leader, whose name was Jacob, desiring him that he would come out with his armies to meet them upon the plains between the two cities. But behold, Jacob, who was a Zoramite, would not come out with his army to meet them upon the plains.

21 And it came to pass that Moroni, having no hopes of meeting them upon fair grounds, therefore, he resolved upon a plan that he might decoy the Lamanites out of their strongholds.

22 Therefore he caused that Teancum should take a small number of men and march down near the seashore; and Moroni and his army, by night, marched in the wilderness, on the west of the city Mulek; and thus, on the morrow, when the guards of the Lamanites had discovered Teancum, they ran and told it unto Jacob, their leader.

23 And it came to pass that the armies of the Lamanites did march forth against Teancum, supposing by their numbers to overpower Teancum because of the smallness of his numbers. And as Teancum saw the armies of the Lamanites coming out against him he began to retreat down by the seashore, northward.

24 And it came to pass that when the Lamanites saw that he began

to flee, they took courage and pursued them with vigor. And while Teancum was thus leading away the Lamanites who were pursuing them in vain, behold, Moroni commanded that a part of his army who were with him should march forth into the city, and take possession of it.

25 And thus they did, and slew all those who had been left to protect the city, yea, all those who would not yield up their weapons of war.

26 And thus Moroni had obtained possession of the city Mulek with a part of his army, while he marched with the remainder to meet the Lamanites when they should return from the pursuit of Teancum.

27 And it came to pass that the Lamanites did pursue Teancum until they came near the city Bountiful, and then they were met by Lehi and a small army, which had been left to protect the city Bountiful.

28 And now behold, when the chief captains of the Lamanites had beheld Lehi with his army coming against them, they fled in much confusion, lest perhaps they should not obtain the city Mulek before Lehi should overtake them; for they were wearied because of their march, and the men of Lehi were fresh.

29 Now the Lamanites did not know that Moroni had been in their rear with his army; and all they feared was Lehi and his men.

30 Now Lehi was not desirous to overtake them till they should meet Moroni and his army.

31 And it came to pass that before the Lamanites had retreated far they were surrounded by the Nephites, by the men of Moroni on one hand, and the men of Lehi on the other, all of whom were fresh and full of strength; but the Lamanites were wearied because of their long march.

32 And Moroni commanded his men that they should fall upon them until they had given up their weapons of war.

33 And it came to pass that Jacob, being their leader, being also a Zoramite, and having an unconquerable spirit, he led the Lamanites forth to battle with exceeding fury against Moroni.

34 Moroni being in their course of march, therefore Jacob was determined to slay them and cut his way through to the city of Mulek.

But behold, Moroni and his men were more powerful; therefore they did not give way before the Lamanites.

35 And it came to pass that they fought on both hands with exceeding fury; and there were many slain on both sides; yea, and Moroni was wounded and Jacob was killed.

36 And Lehi pressed upon their rear with such fury with his strong men, that the Lamanites in the rear delivered up their weapons of war; and the remainder of them, being much confused, knew not whither to go or to strike.

37 Now Moroni seeing their confusion, he said unto them: If ye will bring forth your weapons of war and deliver them up, behold we will forbear shedding your blood.

38 And it came to pass that when the Lamanites had heard these words, their chief captains, all those who were not slain, came forth and threw down their weapons of war at the feet of Moroni, and also commanded their men that they should do the same.

39 But behold, there were many that would not; and those who would not deliver up their swords were taken and bound, and their weapons of war were taken from them, and they were compelled to march with their brethren forth into the land Bountiful.

40 And now the number of prisoners who were taken exceeded more than the number of those who had been slain, yea, more than those who had been slain on both sides.

The strategy used by Moroni to capture the city of Mulek is outlined in the following diagram.

1. Teancum marches near the seashore, retreats northward (v. 22).
2. Moroni marches in the wilderness on the west of the city of Mulek (v. 22)
3. The Lamanites pursue Teancum (vv. 23–24).
4. Moroni takes possession of the city of Mulek (vv. 25–26).
5. Moroni Marches with part of his army to meet the returning Lamanites (v. 26).
6. Lehi, with fresh men, marches from Bountiful to meet the Lamanites. The Lamanites fled (vv. 27–31).

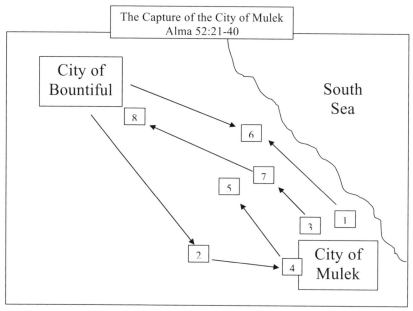

Figure 2. The Capture of the City of Mulek

7. The Lamanites battle, but throw down their weapons (vv. 32–38).
8. Many prisoners taken back to Bountiful (vv. 39–40).

Many lives were saved. Moroni did not delight in the shedding of blood. Freedom was maintained for the Nephites, and many Lamanites, although prisoners, were exposed to the real and righteous Nephite culture.

Alma 53:1–9 • The City of Mulek Given to Lehi

1 And it came to pass that they did set guards over the prisoners of the Lamanites, and did compel them to go forth and bury their dead, yea, and also the dead of the Nephites who were slain; and Moroni placed men over them to guard them while they should perform their labors.

2 And Moroni went to the city of Mulek with Lehi, and took

command of the city and gave it unto Lehi. Now behold, this Lehi was a man who had been with Moroni in the more part of all his battles; and he was a man like unto Moroni, and they rejoiced in each other's safety; yea, they were beloved by each other, and also beloved by all the people of Nephi.

3 And it came to pass that after the Lamanites had finished burying their dead and also the dead of the Nephites, they were marched back into the land Bountiful; and Teancum, by the orders of Moroni, caused that they should commence laboring in digging a ditch round about the land, or the city, Bountiful.

4 And he caused that they should build a breastwork of timbers upon the inner bank of the ditch; and they cast up dirt out of the ditch against the breastwork of timbers; and thus they did cause the Lamanites to labor until they had encircled the city of Bountiful round about with a strong wall of timbers and earth, to an exceeding height.

5 And this city became an exceeding stronghold ever after; and in this city they did guard the prisoners of the Lamanites; yea, even within a wall which they had caused them to build with their own hands. Now Moroni was compelled to cause the Lamanites to labor, because it was easy to guard them while at their labor; and he desired all his forces when he should make an attack upon the Lamanites.

6 And it came to pass that Moroni had thus gained a victory over one of the greatest of the armies of the Lamanites, and had obtained possession of the city of Mulek, which was one of the strongest holds of the Lamanites in the land of Nephi; and thus he had also built a stronghold to retain his prisoners.

7 And it came to pass that he did no more attempt a battle with the Lamanites in that year, but he did employ his men in preparing for war, yea, and in making fortifications to guard against the Lamanites, yea, and also delivering their women and their children from famine and affliction, and providing food for their armies.

8 And now it came to pass that the armies of the Lamanites, on the west sea, south, while in the absence of Moroni on account of some intrigue amongst the Nephites, which caused dissensions amongst them, had gained some ground over the Nephites, yea, insomuch that they had obtained possession of a number of their cities in that part of the land.

9 And thus because of iniquity amongst themselves, yea, because of dissensions and intrigue among themselves they were placed in the most dangerous circumstances.

Another lesson is given regarding prisoners of war. Moroni kept them busy. It was easy to guard them while they were working (v. 5), but it was a benefit for all. The prisoners were able to get physical exercise. The burying of the dead helped with sanitation and personal comforts. Lack of proper burial at the city of Ammonihah after it was destroyed by the Lamanites caused the city to be unlivable. "So great was the scent thereof that the people did not go in to possess the land of Ammonihah for many years. And it was called Desolation of Nehors" (Alma 16:11). Time would pass more quickly when they were kept busy, and the needed improvements were made in the defenses of the Nephites. The prisoner's work did not endanger their lives, but it may also have had an unintended benefit for the Lamanites as a whole when these prisoners learned the methods of defense used by the Nephites. Other benefits will be shown in the future chapters.

Another example of the cause of war is shown as intrigues and dissensions of the Nephites on the west sea placed the people in dangerous circumstances (Alma 53:9). The iniquity among them is an example of the second precept given to us by Mormon, as he abridges the record. He said quarrellings and contentions "brought upon them their wars and their destructions" (Alma 50:21). Mormon leaves the sequential account at this point to tell us of the young Lamanite soldiers, which is the subject of the following chapter.

Sacred Writing

Doctrines Learned:

Alma 51:19   Conscientious objectors are ordinarily given a trial to determine why they will not defend their country.

General Authority Quotations

The First Presidency • Alma 50:21

War is basically selfish. Its roots feed in the soil of envy, hatred, desire for domination. Its fruit, therefore, is always bitter. They who cultivate and propagate it spread death and destruction, and are enemies of the human race.

War originates in the hearts of men who seek to despoil, to conquer, or to destroy other individuals or groups of individuals. Self exaltation is a motivating factor; force, the means of attainment. War is rebellious action against moral order. . . .

Even though we sense the hellish origin of war, even though we feel confident that war will never end war, yet under existing conditions we find ourselves as a body committed to combat this evil thing. With other loyal citizens we serve our country as bearers of arms, rather than to stand aloof to enjoy a freedom for which others have fought and died. [CR, April 1942, 1, 5]

Elder Boyd K. Packer • Alma 51:5–7, 13–21

To Maintain the Cause of Freedom: It is to you, our brethren in the armed forces, that I speak. Nor is the man who serves the only one concerned. There are wives and there are parents who never, never cease to love their children or fear for them.

A man answering the call now is not left in total comfort that all will sustain him. There have emerged in our society groups composed mostly of rest-less, unchallenged young people. In the name of peace and love and brotherhood, they criticize those who, obedient to the laws of the land, have answered the call to military duty. It is puzzling to see them renouncing their obligation, repudiating their citizenship responsibilities. They declare on moral grounds, as an act of virtue, that they will not serve. One can be sensitive, even sympathetic, to their feelings, for war is an ugly thing—a heinous, hideous, ugly thing! Strangely, it is a pursuit to which mankind has turned again and again and again. The wicked have generated it, and the innocent have ultimately been provoked by it.

The Lord said: "Therefore, renounce war and proclaim peace. . . ." (D&C 98:16.) I would that all men would remain at peace. [CR, April 1968, 33]

Bishop Robert L. Simpson • Alma 51:5–7, 13–21

Do you have this problem, young men? This is a problem stated by a young man who contemplates military call-up. This is what he says: "Didn't the Savior teach peace? To me, peace means no fighting. I am not sure about our present military involvements." I say to this young man, the following facts helped me and they may be helpful to you:

Where the Book of Mormon talks about a land choice above all others, I believe it.

When we are taught that our founding forefathers prayed for and received inspiration as they framed our Constitution, I believe it.

When a prophet suggests that the gospel could best be restored in a land of freedom and democracy, I believe it.

When the standard works of the Church instruct me about obeying, honoring, and sustaining the law, I want to do it. I even believe that our elected national leaders are basically honest men and base their decision upon what they believe to be for the good of the people as they see it.

Last but not least, I also believe that a prophet of God will let me know about any change of policy in the foregoing line of reasoning. Young men, to whatever country your citizenship commitment might be, you honor it, you obey it, you sustain it. To do otherwise would be contrary to the law and order; and law and order is the basis of the priesthood, wherever it is established. ["Sustaining the Laws," in Conference Report, Oct. 1970, 101]

Challenges to Eternal Life:

1. Eliminate quarrellings, contentions, and iniquity from your associations so that God will deliver you at all times and you will find happiness (Alma 50:21–23; 53:9).

2. As you review political platforms and candidates compare them with the oath taken by Pahoran to serve as chief judge and vote accordingly (Alma 50:39).

3. Make a personal covenant with God to maintain the rights and privileges by a free government and involve yourself in grass roots politics (Alma 51:6).

4. Choose a challenge of your own from this reading and apply it to your life.

Chapter Four

The 2000 Stripling Warriors

Alma 53:10–58:41

*H*istorical Setting: Alma's record discussed in these chapters is covering two different parts of the land. Alma chapter 53–55 is an account of the war on the eastern side of the land of Zarahemla in the twenty-eighth and twenty-ninth year of the reign of the judges. Chapter 56 begins the thirteenth year, but shifts to the western side of the land of Zarahemla. The time period also shifts back to the twenty-sixth year and continues through the twenty-ninth year of the judges. The information of the western part of the war comes from an epistle that was written by Helaman to Moroni. If the two areas are kept in mind, it should not be confusing when the years are mentioned.

Precepts of this Reading:

20 And they were all young men, and they were exceedingly valiant for courage, and also for strength and activity; but behold, this was not all—they were men who were true at all times in whatsoever thing they were entrusted.

21 Yea, they were men of truth and soberness, for they had been taught to keep the commandments of God and to walk uprightly before him. [Alma 53:20–21]

Nevertheless, we may console ourselves in this point, that they have died in the cause of their country and of their God, yea, and they are happy. [Alma 56:11]

47 Now they never had fought, yet they did not fear death; and they did think more upon the liberty of their fathers than they did upon their lives; yea, they had been taught by their mothers, that if they did not doubt, God would deliver them.

48 And they rehearsed unto me the words of their mothers, saying: We do not doubt our mothers knew it. [Alma 56:47–48]

Yea, and they did obey and observe to perform every word of command with exactness; yea, and even according to their faith it was done unto them; and I did remember the words which they said unto me that their mothers had taught them. [Alma 57:21]

Now this was the faith of these of whom I have spoken; they are young, and their minds are firm, and they do put their trust in God continually. [Alma 57:27]

10 Therefore we did pour out our souls in prayer to God, that he would strengthen us and deliver us out of the hands of our enemies, yea, and also give us strength that we might retain our cities, and our lands, and our possessions, for the support of our people.

11 Yea, and it came to pass that the Lord our God did visit us with assurances that he would deliver us; yea, insomuch that he did speak peace to our souls, and did grant unto us great faith, and did cause us that we should hope for our deliverance in him. [Alma 58:10–11]

40 But behold, they have received many wounds; nevertheless they stand fast in that liberty wherewith God has made them free; and they are strict to remember the Lord their God from day to day; yea, they do observe to keep his statutes, and his judgments, and his commandments continually; and their faith is strong in the prophecies concerning that which is to come.

41 And now, my beloved brother, Moroni, may the Lord our God, who has redeemed us and made us free, keep you continually in his presence; yea, and may he favor this people, even that ye may have success in obtaining the possession of all that which the Lamanites have taken from us, which was for our support. And now, behold, I

close mine epistle. I am Helaman, the son of Alma. [Alma 58:40–41]

The example set by the sons of Helaman, as the sons of the Lamanite converts became known, is the pattern that should be followed by the young Latter-day Saint men of today, whether in the armed forces or battling against the evils of our day. An outline of the contents of the six chapters of Alma to be discussed below follows, as a preparation for a deeper study.

OUTLINE • ALMA 53:10–58:41

➤ 53:10–23   Concerning the people of Ammon, Lamanites who were converted unto the Lord, and who were brought to Zarahemla and ever since protected by the Nephites.

    a. The people of Ammon had taken an oath to never take up arms and shed blood (vv. 11–15).

        1. When they saw the dangers and afflictions the Nephites bore for them, they desired to take up arms and defend their country.

        2. They were persuaded by Helaman and his brethren to not break their oath.

        3. Helaman was afraid they would lose their souls.

    b. The people of Ammon had many sons who had not entered into their father's covenant but who willingly entered into a covenant to fight for the liberty of the Nephites (vv. 17–18).

        1. To protect the land to the laying down of their lives.

        2. To fight in all cases to protect the Nephites and themselves from bondage.

    c. There were two thousand of the sons of Ammon who entered into this covenant (vv. 19–21).

        1. They had never been a disadvantage to the Nephites, but now became a great support.

        2. They took their weapons and desired that Helaman be their leader.

        3.   They were all young men, valiant for courage, strength, and activity.

        4.   They were true at all times in whatever thing they were entrusted.

        5.   They were men of truth and soberness, having been taught to keep the commandments of God and walk uprightly before him.

   d.   Helaman marched at the head of these stripling warriors to support the Nephites on the south by the west sea as the twenty-eighth year ended (vv. 22–23).

➤ 54:1–14   In the twenty-ninth year Ammoron sent to Moroni desiring to exchange prisoners.

   a.   Moroni rejoiced because he desired that the provisions for the prisoners be used to support his own people, and he desired for his own people to strengthen his army (vv. 2–3).

        1.   The Lamanites had taken many woman and children, and there were no children or women among the prisoners of Moroni.

        2.   Moroni resolved upon a stratagem to obtain as many prisoners as possible.

   b.   Moroni wrote this epistle and sent it back through the same servant who had delivered Moroni's epistle from Ammoron. He said: (vv. 5–14)

        1.   Your brother waged a war against my people and you are still determined to carry on.

        2.   The justice of God and the sword of his almighty wrath hangs over you except you repent and withdraw your armies.

        3.   I would tell you of the awful hell that awaits to receive murderers such as you and your brother if you were capable of hearkening to them.

        4.   You once rejected those things and fought against

the people of the Lord, and I expect you will do it again.

5. Except you repent and withdraw your armies, God will visit you with death, for we will retain our lands and maintain our religion and the cause of God.

6. I suppose I talk in vain or that you are a child of hell, and I will not exchange prisoners except you deliver up a man, his wife, and children for one of our prisoners.

c. If you will not thus exchange prisoners, I will come with my armies and even arm my woman and children and follow you into your own lands and destroy you from off the face of the earth (vv. 12–14).

1. I am angry. You have sought to murder us and we have only defended ourselves.

2. I am Moroni, a leader of the people of the Nephites.

➤ 54:15–24   Ammoron was angry and wrote another epistle unto Moroni saying:

a. I am Ammoron, king of the Lamanites, the brother of Amalickiah whom you murdered (vv. 16–17).

1. I will avenge his blood and come with my armies for I fear not your threatening.

2. Your fathers wronged their brethren and robbed them of their right of government.

b. If the Nephites will lay down their arms and be governed by those whose right it is to govern, we will lay down our weapons and be at war no more (vv. 18–24).

1. I will exchange prisoners according to your request that I may preserve food for my men of war.

2. We will wage an eternal war to subject the Nephites to our authority or to their eternal extinction.

3. We know not God nor do you, but if there is such a being, he made us as well as you.

4. If there is a hell or a devil, will he not send you

there to dwell with my brother whom you murdered, whom you hinted had gone to this place?

5. I am a descendant of Zoram, whom your fathers pressed and brought out of Jerusalem.

6. I am a bold Lamanite who hath waged this war to avenge their wrongs and obtain their right to the government.

➤ 55:1–3   Moroni was angry over the epistle from Ammoron. Ammoron had a perfect knowledge of his fraud, and knew he did not have a just cause to wage war.

    a. Moroni refused to exchange prisoners unless Ammoron withdrew his purpose (v. 2).

    b. Moroni knew where the Nephite prisoners were guarded, and he would seek death among the Lamanites until they would sue for peace (v. 3).

➤ 55:4–27   Moroni searched for a descendant of Laman among them and found one named Laman, one of the servants of the king who was murdered by Amalickiah.

    a. Laman and a small number of men went to the guards over the Nephite prisoners in the city of Gid (vv. 6–14).

        1. In the evening, they saw him coming and they hailed him.

        2. He said he was a Lamanite and they had escaped from the Nephites and had brought some of their wine with them.

        3. The Lamanites asked for some of the wine, but Laman suggested they keep it until they went to battle which made them more desirous for the wine.

        4. The guards were weary and wanted to drink it now because they would receive more wine in their rations to strengthen them for battle.

        5. Laman let them have the wine; they drank freely and became drunken.

    a. Laman and his men returned and reported what had happened (vv. 15–20).

1. Moroni took weapons of war to the city of Gid and cast them into the Nephite prisoners.
2. As many as were able to use a weapon of war were armed in perfect silence, and even if the Lamanites had awakened they were drunken and could have been slain.
3. Moroni did not delight in bloodshed but in saving his people from destruction, and would not destroy the drunken Lamanites.
4. The armed prisoners had power to gain possession within the city.

c. Moroni and his men withdraw a pace, and in the nighttime surrounded the armies of the Lamanites (vv. 21–24).

1. When the Lamanites awoke they were surrounded by Nephites, and the prisoners were armed within.
2. The chief captains collected the weapons, cast them at the feet of the Nephites, and pleaded for mercy.
3. Moroni took them prisoners of war, possessed the city, and liberated the Nephite prisoners, who joined his army, increasing their strength.

d. The Lamanite prisoners commenced strengthening the fortifications about the city of Gid (vv. 25–26).

1. Upon completion of the fortification, the prisoners were taken to Bountiful.
2. That city was guarded with an exceeding strong force.

e. In spite of the intrigues of the Lamanites, the Nephites kept protecting the prisoners they had taken, and maintained the ground they had retaken (v. 27).

➤ 55:28–35 The Nephites began again to be victorious, and to reclaim their rights and privileges.

a. The Lamanites attempted to encircle them by night, but in so doing lost many prisoners (v. 29).

b. The Lamanites attempted to administer wine to the

Nephites and destroy them with poison or drunkenness (vv. 30–32).

1. The Nephites were not slow to remember the Lord in their afflictions.
2. They would not partake of the wine save they first gave some to the Lamanite prisoners.
3. If the wine would poison a Lamanite it would poison a Nephite.

c. Moroni made preparations to attack the city Morianton (vv. 33–34).

1. The Lamanites had made it a stronghold.
2. They continually brought new forces and new provisions into the city.

d. Thus ended the twenty-ninth year (v. 35).

➤ 56:1–20 Moroni received an epistle from Helaman concerning the people in the west quarter of the land, on the second day of the first month of the thirtieth year.

a. Two thousand sons of Ammon came down in the twenty-sixth year and Helaman marched at their head to the city of Judea to assist Antipus, the leader in that part of the land (he reviews the past—see 53:10–22) (vv. 2–12).

1. Helaman joined "his sons" to the army of Antipus.
2. His army had been reduced by a vast number being slain.
3. They died in the cause of their country and their God and are happy.
4. The Lamanites had killed all but the chief captains who they kept as their prisoners.

b. The Lamanites had obtained the cities of Manti, Zeezrom, Cumeni, and Antiparah (vv. 13–17).

1. Antipus' men were toiling to fortify the city of Judea, being depressed in body and spirit because they fought by day and toiled by night.
2. They were determined to conquer or die, and those

sons of Helaman gave them great hope and much joy.

c. When the Lamanites saw the increase in Antipus' army, Ammoron compelled them not to come against the city of Judea in battle (vv. 18–20).

   1. The Nephites were favored of the Lord, for had the Lamanites come they may have been destroyed.

   2. Ammoron commanded the Lamanites to maintain the cities they had taken.

➤ 56:23–48 In the twenty-seventh year, The Nephites had prepared the city and themselves for defense.

a. The Nephites wanted the Lamanites to come against them, instead of having to attack their strongholds (vv. 21–26).

   1. Their spies watched day and night that the Lamanites not pass them and attack other cities northward.

   2. The Nephite cities to the north were not strong and the army of Judea hoped to attack the Lamanites in the rear after they passed.

   3. The Lamanites dared not pass them nor march against other cities.

b. In the second month our fathers brought us many provisions from the fathers of the sons of Helaman. Two thousand men came from Zarahemla, and thus we had ten thousand men and provisions (vv. 27–33).

   1. The Lamanites were fearful and tried to put an end to our receiving provisions and strength.

   2. Antipus ordered Helaman and his sons to march to a neighboring city as if carrying provisions.

   3. They marched past the city of Antiparah, as if going by the seashore.

   4. Antipus marched forth with part of his army after our army had left.

c. The strongest Lamanite army was stationed in Antiparah, and they followed our army (vv. 34–42).

1. Helaman fled northward and led the strongest Lamanite army away.

2. After considerable distance, the Lamanites saw the army of Antipus pursuing, and they pursued Helaman in a straight course, probably to destroy them before Antipus' army caught them.

3. Helaman marched for two days, camping at night, and on the third morning of the seventh month the Lamanites halted.

d. Helaman knew not if Antipus had overtaken the Lamanites, or if they had halted so that he would come against them (vv. 43–46).

1. Helaman asked if his sons would go to battle against the Lamanites, and he had never seen such great courage.

2. He called them his sons for they are all very young.

3. They said to him: Father, our God is with us and he will not allow us to fall.

4. We would not slay our brethren if they would leaves us alone, let us go lest they overpower the army of Antipus.

e. The sons had never fought but they did not fear death, thinking more of liberty than their lives (vv. 47–48).

1. Their mothers had taught them that if they did not doubt, God would deliver them.

2. They said: We do not doubt our mothers knew it.

➤ 56:49–54 Helaman returned with his warriors and Antipus had overtaken the Lamanites, and a terrible battle had commenced.

a. Anitpus' army was weary from their long march in so short a time, and would have fallen had we not returned (vv. 50–54).

1. Antipus and many leaders had fallen by the sword and the men were confused.

2. The Lamanite army was pursuing them, and my army came on their rear and began slaying them.

3.   The Lamanites turned on us and the army of Antipus took courage and attacked them again.

    4.   The armies of both Helaman and Antipus surrounded the Lamanites and did slay them.

    5.   The Lamanites threw down their weapons and surrendered.

  b. Helaman numbered his young men, fearing many had been slain (vv. 55–56).

    1.   Not one soul of them had fallen.

    2.   They had fought with the strength of God.

    3.   Never were men known to have fought with such miraculous strength.

  c. The prisoners were sent to Zarahemla with a part of Antipus' army. The remainder of his army joined Helaman and marched back to Judea (v. 57).

➤ 57:1–5   Ammoron sent an epistle saying he would deliver up the city of Antiparah in exchange for the prisoners we had taken in the recent battle.

  a. Helaman responded that his forces could take the city so he would only exchange prisoners (v. 2).

  b. Ammoron refused to exchange prisoners so preparations for war were made (v. 3).

  c. The people of Antiparah fled the city, thus it fell into the Nephite hands (v. 4).

  d. The twenty-eighth year ended (v. 5).

➤ 57:6–36   In the twenty-ninth year, a supply of provisions and an addition of six thousand men to our army were received from Zarahemla. Sixty sons of Ammon also came to join Helaman's band of two thousand.

  a. The Nephites were strong and had plenty of provisions so they desired to battle the Lamanite army placed at Cumeni (vv. 6–12).

    1.   We surrounded the city a little before they were to receive provisions.

2. We camped around the city many nights and the Lamanites attempted to slay us many times, but each time their blood was spilt.

3. Their provisions finally arrived, but we took them and made the men poisoners.

4. The Lamanites were determined to defend the city, so it was expedient to take the supplies to Judea, and the new provisions to Zarahemla.

5. In not many days the Lamanites lost hope and gave up the city of Cumeni.

b. The prisoners were so numerous that the Nephites had to employ all their forces to contain them or put them to death (vv. 13–16).

1. They would break out in great numbers and fight with clubs and stones, and two thousand of them were killed.

2. We determined to send them to Zarahemla to be guarded by a part of our men.

c. On the morrow, the guards returned just in time to save us from falling to the Lamanites (vv. 17–18).

1. Ammoron had sent new supplies and also a numerous army.

2. We did not inquire concerning the prisoners because of the expedient battle.

➤ 57:19–27 Helaman's little band of two thousand sixty fought desperately while others of the army were about to give way.

a. Helaman's band did obey and observe every command with exactness according to their faith.

1. Helaman remembered what they said their mothers had taught them.

2. Helaman's band and the returning guards of the prisoners were responsible for the victory.

3. The Lamanites were driven back to Manti, the Nephites retained Cumeni, but suffered great losses.

b. Helaman ordered the wounded to be taken from among the dead to dress their wounds (vv. 24–27).

1. Two hundred of Helaman's sons had fainted from loss of blood.

2. To the astonishment and joy of the army not one had perished.

3. Neither was there one soul who had not been wounded.

4. A thousand Nephites were slain, but all of Helaman's sons survived because of the miraculous power of God and their faith.

5. They were young and their minds were firm, and they trusted in God continually.

➤ 57:28–35　Helaman inquired of Gid, the chief captain, concerning the prisoners being taken to Zarahemla.

a. Gid met the spies of the Nephite armies who warned us of the coming Lamanite army to Cumeni (vv. 30–34).

1. The prisoners took courage and ran in a body toward our swords, killing a greater number, but the remainder escaped.

2. The guards could not overtake them so they sped towards Cumeni.

b. The Nephites were again delivered from their enemies, thanks to God (v. 35).

➤ 57:37　Helaman was filled with joy because of the goodness of God, and trusted that the souls of those slain had entered into the rest of God.

➤ 58:1–12　Helaman's next object was to obtain the city of Manti, but they could not decoy the Lamanites as before, for they remembered the former decoy, and the Lamanites were too numerous to attack.

a. It was expedient to maintain the land the Nephites had regained, thus they waited for strength and supplies from Zarahemla (vv. 3–7).

    1. Helaman sent an embassy to the governor to acquaint him with our circumstances.

    2. The Lamanites were receiving strength and provisions from day to day.

    3. The Lamanites were trying to destroy us by stratagem, but we could not do battle because of their strongholds.

    4. These difficulties continued for many months until we were about to perish for want of food.

  b. The Nephites did receive food guarded by an army of two thousand, who joined them, but this was all the assistance they received (vv. 8–12).

    1. They knew not the cause for not sending more. They feared the judgments of God would come upon them to their overthrow and destruction.

    2. They poured out their souls to God to strengthen and deliver them.

    3. The Lord did visit them with assurance of deliverance through peace to their souls.

    4. Their small force took courage and determined to maintain the cause of freedom.

➤ 58:13–31 The Nephites went forth with all their might against the city of Manti.

  a. The Lamanites saw the Nephites on their borders and sent out spies to determine their numbers (vv. 14–15).

    1. They saw the Nephites were not numerous.

    2. They came out to battle supposing they could destroy the Nephites.

  b. Helaman had Gid and Teomner and a small number of men secrete themselves on the right, and he put left the remainder of his army in the wilderness on the left (vv. 16–19).

    1. Helaman's men retreated and the Lamanites followed them with speed.

2. The Lamanites passed by Gid and Teomner and did not discover them.

    c. Gid and Teomner cut off the Lamanite spies that they could not return to the city (vv. 20–25).

        1. Gid and Teancum rushed the city, destroyed the guards, and possessed the city.

        2. The Lamanites saw Helaman was leading them to Zarahemla, and retreated back the way they came and camped for the night.

    d. Helaman's people did not sleep but marched to Manti by another way, and on the morrow arrived to the city of Manti before the Lamanites (vv. 26–31).

        1. The city of Manti was taken without the shedding of blood.

        2. The Lamanites saw the Nephites and fled into the wilderness, but took many woman and children out of the land.

        3. The cities which the Lamanites had taken were all now in Nephite possession.

        4. The Nephite women and children returned to their homes, except those taken prisoners by the Lamanites.

➤ 58:32–41   Helaman's armies were too small to maintain so great a number of cities and possessions.

    a. The armies trusted in God who had given them victory (vv. 33–35).

        1. They did not know why the government did not grant them more strength.

        2. They did not know if the Nephites were unsuccessful and had drawn away the forces from their sector.

    b. The armies feared there was some faction in the government that caused no more assistance to come to them (vv. 36–38).

    1.   They trusted God would deliver them in spite of the weakness of their armies.

    2.   In the latter end of the twenty-ninth year, the Lamanites had fled and the Nephites were in possession of their lands.

c,   The sons of the people of Ammon were with Helaman in the city of Manti, and the Lord had supported them insomuch that not one soul had been slain (vv. 39–40).

    1.   They had received many wounds but stood fast in the liberty of God.

    2.   They were strict to remember God from day to day, and to keep his statutes, judgments, and commandments continually.

    3.   Their faith was strong in the prophecies of what was to come.

d,   Helaman asked God, who had redeemed them and made them free, to keep Moroni continually in his presence, and favor this people to obtain all the lands the Lamanites had taken from them (v. 41).

e.   Helaman, son of Alma, closed his epistle (v. 41).

NOTES AND COMMENTARY

Introduction: Chapter three of this work emphasized principles to guide a nation during war and threats of war. This chapter will show the principles to guide individuals as they face the problems brought about by war.

Alma 53:10–17 • Concerning the Lamanite People of Ammon—28th Year

10 And now behold, I have somewhat to say concerning the people of Ammon, who, in the beginning, were Lamanites; but by Ammon and his brethren, or rather by the power and word of God, they had been converted unto the Lord; and they had been brought down into the land of Zarahemla, and had ever since been protected by the Nephites.

11 And because of their oath they had been kept from taking up arms against their brethren; for they had taken an oath that they never would shed blood more; and according to their oath they would have perished; yea, they would have suffered themselves to have fallen into the hands of their brethren, had it not been for the pity and the exceeding love which Ammon and his brethren had had for them.

12 And for this cause they were brought down into the land of Zarahemla; and they ever had been protected by the Nephites.

13 But it came to pass that when they saw the danger, and the many afflictions and tribulations which the Nephites bore for them, they were moved with compassion and were desirous to take up arms in the defence of their country.

14 But behold, as they were about to take their weapons of war, they were overpowered by the persuasions of Helaman and his brethren, for they were about to break the oath which they had made.

15 And Helaman feared lest by so doing they should lose their souls; therefore all those who had entered into this covenant were compelled to behold their brethren wade through their afflictions, in their dangerous circumstances at this time.

16 But behold, it came to pass they had many sons, who had not entered into a covenant that they would not take their weapons of war to defend themselves against their enemies; therefore they did assemble themselves together at this time, as many as were able to take up arms, and they called themselves Nephites.

The Nephites' love for their converted brethren of the Lamanites was demonstrated by the protection they furnished for them (vv. 11–12). The sacredness of an oath among these Israelite people is again shown by Helaman and his brethren persuading the converts to not break their oath (vv. 14–15). The young sons calling themselves Nephites (v. 16) takes us back to the name of Anti-Nephi-Lehi. As suggested in volume 3 of this work, the name probably refers to following the mirror or image of Nephi and Lehi (see vol. 3 Alma 23:17–18 and commentary). These young sons were just as devout in their willingness to fight for their liberty as their fathers had been in refraining to fight (v. 17). Both of their dedications were ruled by the situation. The parents were not merely opposed to war, but were concerned for their eternal lives (v. 11 see also Alma 24:12–16). The young soldiers were governed by their love for liberty (Alma 53:17).

Alma 53:18–23 • Mormon's Assessment of the Lamanite Sons

17 And they entered into a covenant to fight for the liberty of the Nephites, yea, to protect the land unto the laying down of their lives; yea, even they covenanted that they never would give up their liberty, but they would fight in all cases to protect the Nephites and themselves from bondage.

18 Now behold, there were two thousand of those young men, who entered into this covenant and took their weapons of war to defend their country.

19 And now behold, as they never had hitherto been a disadvantage to the Nephites, they became now at this period of time also a great support; for they took their weapons of war, and they would that Helaman should be their leader.

20 And they were all young men, and they were exceedingly valiant for courage, and also for strength and activity; but behold, this was not all—they were men who were true at all times in whatsoever thing they were entrusted.

21 Yea, they were men of truth and soberness, for they had been taught to keep the commandments of God and to walk uprightly before him.

22 And now it came to pass that Helaman did march at the head of his two thousand stripling soldiers, to the support of the people in the borders of the land on the south by the west sea.

23 And thus ended the twenty and eighth year of the reign of the judges over the people of Nephi.

Mormon's assessment of the young men never having been at a disadvantage, probably reflects their willingness to work with their parents behind the scene. Their support (v. 19) will be shown by Mormon, as he abridges the record (see v. 22 for a beginning). Their dedication to the truth (vv. 20–21) is attributed to what they had been taught (v. 21). The precept given by Mormon tells the reader that our children should be taught the same commitment to the keeping of the commandments as these stripling soldiers, to help them become children of truth and soberness.

Alma 54:1–14 • Moroni's Conditions for Exchanging Prisoners—29th Year

1 And now it came to pass in the commencement of the twenty and ninth year of the judges, that Ammoron sent unto Moroni desiring that he would exchange prisoners.

2 And it came to pass that Moroni felt to rejoice exceedingly at this request, for he desired the provisions which were imparted for the support of the Lamanite prisoners for the support of his own people; and he also desired his own people for the strengthening of his army.

3 Now the Lamanites had taken many women and children, and there was not a woman nor a child among all the prisoners of Moroni, or the prisoners whom Moroni had taken; therefore Moroni resolved upon a stratagem to obtain as many prisoners of the Nephites from the Lamanites as it were possible.

4 Therefore he wrote an epistle, and sent it by the servant of Ammoron, the same who had brought an epistle to Moroni. Now these are the words which he wrote unto Ammoron, saying:

5 Behold, Ammoron, I have written unto you somewhat concerning this war which ye have waged against my people, or rather which thy brother hath waged against them, and which ye are still determined to carry on after his death.

6 Behold, I would tell you somewhat concerning the justice of God, and the sword of his almighty wrath, which doth hang over you except ye repent and withdraw your armies into your own lands, or the land of your possessions, which is the land of Nephi.

7 Yea, I would tell you these things if ye were capable of hearkening unto them; yea, I would tell you concerning that awful hell that awaits to receive such murderers as thou and thy brother have been, except ye repent and withdraw your murderous purposes, and return with your armies to your own lands.

8 But as ye have once rejected these things, and have fought against the people of the Lord, even so I may expect you will do it again.

9 And now behold, we are prepared to receive you; yea, and except you withdraw your purposes, behold, ye will pull down the wrath of that God whom you have rejected upon you, even to your utter destruction.

10 But, as the Lord liveth, our armies shall come upon you except ye withdraw, and ye shall soon be visited with death, for we will retain our cities and our lands; yea, and we will maintain our religion and the cause of our God.

11 But behold, it supposeth me that I talk to you concerning these things in vain; or it supposeth me that thou art a child of hell; therefore I will close my epistle by telling you that I will not exchange prisoners, save it be on conditions that ye will deliver up a man and his wife and his children, for one prisoner; if this be the case that ye will do it, I will exchange.

12 And behold, if ye do not this, I will come against you with my armies; yea, even I will arm my women and my children, and I will come against you, and I will follow you even into your own land, which is the land of our first inheritance; yea, and it shall be blood for blood, yea, life for life; and I will give you battle even until you are destroyed from off the face of the earth.

13 Behold, I am in my anger, and also my people; ye have sought to murder us, and we have only sought to defend ourselves. But behold, if ye seek to destroy us more we will seek to destroy you; yea, and we will seek our land, the land of our first inheritance.

14 Now I close my epistle. I am Moroni; I am a leader of the people of the Nephites.

Although Moroni rejoiced over the possibility to exchange prisoners (v. 2), he used strategy to get as many of his own people freed as possible (v. 3). The Nephites had not taken women and children prisoners probably because the Lamanite army was in the Nephite lands and their women and children were not part of the army. On the other hand, the Lamanites taking of women and children may have been an attempt to get the Nephites to surrender more quickly because of the desire to regain their people. Whatever the reasons were for either side, Moroni once more lifts the standard of liberty for the Lamanites to meet his conditions, otherwise the war would continue. The law of war required the standard of peace to be raised three times. The testimonies of the standard having been raised was to be brought before the Lord. The Lord would then fight their battle (see D&C 98:34–37). Moroni's telling Ammoron of the justice of God (Alma 54:5) seems to refer to the Lord fighting their battles (vv. 6–9). Moroni's threats (vv. 9–10; 12), conditions and purposes of the war (vv. 11–13) fit the law of war as given to the Nephites and revealed anew in these latter days. (see D&C 98:34–37; Alma 43:45–47 and commentary in chapter one) Ammoron should have known this law since he was once a Nephite (Alma 54:8).

Alma 54:15–24 • Ammoron's Angry Reply

15 Now it came to pass that Ammoron, when he had received this epistle, was angry; and he wrote another epistle unto Moroni, and these are the words which he wrote, saying:

16 I am Ammoron, the king of the Lamanites; I am the brother of Amalickiah whom ye have murdered. Behold, I will avenge his blood upon you, yea, and I will come upon you with my armies for I fear not your threatenings.

17 For behold, your fathers did wrong their brethren, insomuch that they did rob them of their right to the government when it rightly belonged unto them.

18 And now behold, if ye will lay down your arms, and subject yourselves to be governed by those to whom the government doth rightly belong, then will I cause that my people shall lay down their weapons and shall be at war no more.

19 Behold, ye have breathed out many threatenings against me and my people; but behold, we fear not your threatenings.

20 Nevertheless, I will grant to exchange prisoners according to your request, gladly, that I may preserve my food for my men of war; and we will wage a war which shall be eternal, either to the subjecting

the Nephites to our authority or to their eternal extinction.

21 And as concerning that God whom ye say we have rejected, behold, we know not such a being; neither do ye; but if it so be that there is such a being, we know not but that he hath made us as well as you.

22 And if it so be that there is a devil and a hell, behold will he not send you there to dwell with my brother whom ye have murdered, whom ye have hinted that he hath gone to such a place? But behold these things matter not.

23 I am Ammoron, and a descendant of Zoram, whom your fathers pressed and brought out of Jerusalem.

24 And behold now, I am a bold Lamanite; behold, this war hath been waged to avenge their wrongs, and to maintain and to obtain their rights to the government; and I close my epistle to Moroni.

Ammoron by resorting to the traditions of the Lamanites in his reply (vv. 17–18; 21–22), shows his total rejection of his religion, his culture, and his God. His acceptance of Moroni's offer to exchange prisoners (v. 20) reflects a condition of desperation that was probably brought on by the Lamanites previous defeats. His claim to be a descendant of Zoram may have been true since Zoram was numbered with the Nephites and given all the blessings of Nephi (see 2 Nephi 1:31–32). It may also have been made up as an excuse for his joining the Lamanites. His denial of God and the devil (vv. 21–22) is another cause of war, a precept given by Mormon earlier (see Alma 50:21).

Alma 55:1–14 • Captain Moroni Rejects Ammoron's Offer

1 Now it came to pass that when Moroni had received this epistle he was more angry, because he knew that Ammoron had a perfect knowledge of his fraud; yea, he knew that Ammoron knew that it was not a just cause that had caused him to wage a war against the people of Nephi.

2 And he said: Behold, I will not exchange prisoners with Ammoron save he will withdraw his purpose, as I have stated in my

epistle; for I will not grant unto him that he shall have any more power than what he hath got.

3 Behold, I know the place where the Lamanites do guard my people whom they have taken prisoners; and as Ammoron would not grant unto me mine epistle, behold, I will give unto him according to my words; yea, I will seek death among them until they shall sue for peace.

4 And now it came to pass that when Moroni had said these words, he caused that a search should be made among his men, that perhaps he might find a man who was a descendant of Laman among them.

5 And it came to pass that they found one, whose name was Laman; and he was one of the servants of the king who was murdered by Amalickiah.

6 Now Moroni caused that Laman and a small number of his men should go forth unto the guards who were over the Nephites.

7 Now the Nephites were guarded in the city of Gid; therefore Moroni appointed Laman and caused that a small number of men should go with him.

8 And when it was evening Laman went to the guards who were over the Nephites, and behold, they saw him coming and they hailed him; but he saith unto them: Fear not; behold, I am a Lamanite. Behold, we have escaped from the Nephites, and they sleep; and behold we have taken of their wine and brought with us.

9 Now when the Lamanites heard these words they received him with joy; and they said unto him: Give us of your wine, that we may drink; we are glad that ye have thus taken wine with you for we are weary.

10 But Laman said unto them: Let us keep of our wine till we go against the Nephites to battle. But this saying only made them more desirous to drink of the wine;

11 For, said they: We are weary, therefore let us take of the wine, and by and by we shall receive wine for our rations, which will strengthen us to go against the Nephites.

12 And Laman said unto them: You may do according to your desires.

13 And it came to pass that they did take of the wine freely; and

it was pleasant to their taste, therefore they took of it more freely; and
it was strong, having been prepared in its strength.

14 And it came to pass they did drink and were merry, and by and
by they were all drunken.

How Moroni knew that Ammoron had "a perfect knowledge" of
his fraud (v. 1) is not stated. Perhaps that knowledge was based on
their acquaintance before Ammoron had apostatized, or he may have
known by the Spirit, the Holy Ghost. The man named Laman, who
was chosen by Moroni to free the prisons, had been a victim of Amalickiah's fraud. Ten years earlier, the nineteenth year of the judges, he
had fled to the Nephites after the king of the Lamanites had been killed
by one of Amalickiah's servants, and then placed the blame on the
king's servants (see Alma 46:37; 47:22–29). Undoubtedly he had
earned the trust of Moroni in those ten years. Laman's cleverness in
getting the Lamanite guards drunk is admirable, and a lesson the
Nephites learned from and used later (see Alma 55:30–31).

Alma 55:15–24 • The City of Gid Taken Without Shedding of Blood

15 And now when Laman and his men saw that they were all
drunken, and were in a deep sleep, they returned to Moroni and told
him all the things that had happened.

16 And now this was according to the design of Moroni. And
Moroni had prepared his men with weapons of war; and he went to
the city Gid, while the Lamanites were in a deep sleep and drunken,
and cast in weapons of war unto the prisoners, insomuch that they
were all armed;

17 Yea, even to their women, and all those of their children, as
many as were able to use a weapon of war, when Moroni had armed
all those prisoners; and all those things were done in a profound
silence.

18 But had they awakened the Lamanites, behold they were
drunken and the Nephites could have slain them.

19 But behold, this was not the desire of Moroni; he did not delight
in murder or bloodshed, but he delighted in the saving of his people

from destruction; and for this cause he might not bring upon him injustice, he would not fall upon the Lamanites and destroy them in their drunkenness.

20 But he had obtained his desires; for he had armed those prisoners of the Nephites who were within the wall of the city, and had given them power to gain possession of those parts which were within the walls.

21 And then he caused the men who were with him to withdraw a pace from them, and surround the armies of the Lamanites.

22 Now behold this was done in the night-time, so that when the Lamanites awoke in the morning they beheld that they were surrounded by the Nephites without, and that their prisoners were armed within.

23 And thus they saw that the Nephites had power over them; and in these circumstances they found that it was not expedient that they should fight with the Nephites; therefore their chief captains demanded their weapons of war, and they brought them forth and cast them at the feet of the Nephites, pleading for mercy.

24 Now behold, this was the desire of Moroni. He took them prisoners of war, and took possession of the city, and caused that all the prisoners should be liberated, who were Nephites; and they did join the army of Moroni, and were a great strength to his army.

The leadership of Moroni again is evident. Certainly the "profound silence" (v. 17) was a learned characteristic. Perhaps this incident or the previous training was passed down to future generations, since the characteristic was evident in the Native American tribes after the discovery of the Americas in modern times.

Once more the character of Moroni is shown as he is careful not to shed blood (v. 19; see 48:11). We see in the same verse his faith in Christ by his concern for justice (see Alma 48:13).

Moroni had accomplished his desire to free his own prisoners, and had done so without further loss of life (v. 24; see also 54:2–3).

Alma 55:25–35 • Captain Moroni
Further Strengthen His Cities

25 And it came to pass that he did cause the Lamanites, whom he had taken prisoners, that they should commence a labor in strengthening the fortifications round about the city Gid.

26 And it came to pass that when he had fortified the city Gid, according to his desires, he caused that his prisoners should be taken to the city Bountiful; and he also guarded that city with an exceedingly strong force.

27 And it came to pass that they did, notwithstanding all the intrigues of the Lamanites, keep and protect all the prisoners whom they had taken, and also maintain all the ground and the advantage which they had retaken.

28 And it came to pass that the Nephites began again to be victorious, and to reclaim their rights and their privileges.

29 Many times did the Lamanites attempt to encircle them about by night, but in these attempts they did lose many prisoners.

30 And many times did they attempt to administer of their wine to the Nephites, that they might destroy them with poison or with drunkenness.

31 But behold, the Nephites were not slow to remember the Lord their God in this their time of affliction. They could not be taken in their snares; yea, they would not partake of their wine, save they had first given to some of the Lamanite prisoners.

32 And they were thus cautious that no poison should be administered among them; for if their wine would poison a Lamanite it would also poison a Nephite; and thus they did try all their liquors.

33 And now it came to pass that it was expedient for Moroni to make preparations to attack the city Morianton; for behold, the Lamanites had, by their labors, fortified the city Morianton until it had become an exceeding stronghold.

34 And they were continually bringing new forces into that city, and also new supplies of provisions.

35 And thus ended the twenty and ninth year of the reign of the judges over the people of Nephi.

We are given an example of Moroni using the prisoners of war to his advantage. As stated before, the prisons were easier to guard while they were doing labor (see 53:6).

The Lamanites again try to copy the Nephite successes but are not successful. The difference is summarized by Mormon's observation that the Nephites were not slow to remember the Lord their God (v. 31). They went to battle under the influence of the Spirit of God. As stated above, they learned also from the mistakes of the Lamanites and their partaking of the wine (vv. 31–32; see vv. 9–14). Moroni apparently was aware of the Lamanite movements in the city of Morianton through his spy system (vv. 33–34; see Alma 43:23).

Alma 56:1–12 • Two Thousand Sons of Ammon—26th Year

1 And now it came to pass in the commencement of the thirtieth year of the reign of the judges, on the second day in the first month, Moroni received an epistle from Helaman, stating the affairs of the people in that quarter of the land.

2 And these are the words which he wrote, saying: My dearly beloved brother, Moroni, as well in the Lord as in the tribulations of our warfare; behold, my beloved brother, I have somewhat to tell you concerning our warfare in this part of the land.

3 Behold, two thousand of the sons of those men whom Ammon brought down out of the land of Nephi—now ye have known that these were descendants of Laman, who was the eldest son of our father Lehi;

4 Now I need not rehearse unto you concerning their traditions or their unbelief, for thou knowest concerning all these things—

5 Therefore it sufficeth me that I tell you that two thousand of these young men have taken their weapons of war, and would that I should be their leader; and we have come forth to defend our country.

6 And now ye also know concerning the covenant which their fathers made, that they would not take up their weapons of war against their brethren to shed blood.

7 But in the twenty and sixth year, when they saw our afflictions

and our tribulations for them, they were about to break the covenant which they had made and take up their weapons of war in our defence.

8 But I would not suffer them that they should break this covenant which they had made, supposing that God would strengthen us, insomuch that we should not suffer more because of the fulfilling the oath which they had taken.

9 But behold, here is one thing in which we may have great joy. For behold, in the twenty and sixth year, I, Helaman, did march at the head of these two thousand young men to the city of Judea, to assist Antipus, whom ye had appointed a leader over the people of that part of the land.

10 And I did join my two thousand sons, (for they are worthy to be called sons) to the army of Antipus, in which strength Antipus did rejoice exceedingly; for behold, his army had been reduced by the Lamanites because their forces had slain a vast number of our men, for which cause we have to mourn.

11 Nevertheless, we may console ourselves in this point, that they have died in the cause of their country and of their God, yea, and they are happy.

12 And the Lamanites had also retained many prisoners, all of whom are chief captains, for none other have they spared alive. And we suppose that they are now at this time in the land of Nephi; it is so if they are not slain.

Although the epistle to Captain Moroni from Helaman was written in the thirteenth year of the judges, it is describing the twenty-sixth year. The fathers of these young men had made a covenant to bury their weapons of war (see Alma 24), but the new generation did not feel bound by their fathers' covenant (see Alma 53:16–17). The first assignment of these sons was to defend the city of Judea (Alma 56:9). The consolation proposed by Helaman that the slain Nephites were happy (v. 11) was stated again by him regarding a later battle. After the second battle, he gave the reason for their supposed happiness as their probability of having entered into the rest of their God (see Alma 57:36). The rest of the Lord "is the fullness of his glory" (D&C 84:24). Even later, Captain Moroni declares without equivocation that the righteous who were slain did enter into the rest of the Lord (Alma 60:13). The same condition of righteousness would apply to Helaman's suppositions. The Lamanites slaying of all but the chief captains (Alma 56:12) may have been because with the trading of prisoners they felt chief captains would be more valuable to trade with the Nephites.

Alma 56:13–20 • Four Cities Captured on the West Quarter

13 And now these are the cities of which the Lamanites have obtained possession by the shedding of the blood of so many of our valiant men;

14 The land of Manti, or the city of Manti, and the city of Zeezrom, and the city of Cumeni, and the city of Antiparah.

15 And these are the cities which they possessed when I arrived at the city of Judea; and I found Antipus and his men toiling with their might to fortify the city.

16 Yea, and they were depressed in body as well as in spirit, for they had fought valiantly by day and toiled by night to maintain their cities; and thus they had suffered great afflictions of every kind.

17 And now they were determined to conquer in this place or die; therefore you may well suppose that this little force which I brought with me, yea, those sons of mine, gave them great hopes and much joy.

18 And now it came to pass that when the Lamanites saw that Antipus had received a greater strength to his army, they were compelled by the orders of Ammoron to not come against the city of Judea, or against us, to battle.

19 And thus were we favored of the Lord; for had they come upon us in this our weakness they might have perhaps destroyed our little army; but thus were we preserved.

20 They were commanded by Ammoron to maintain those cities which they had taken. And thus ended the twenty and sixth year. And in the commencement of the twenty and seventh year we had prepared our city and ourselves for defence.

In the Nephites' weakened condition, both physically and mentally, their determination (v. 17) must be admired. Helaman's recognition of the Lord's favor of the Nephites through the arrival of the two thousand young troops shows their dependence upon the Lord as well (v. 19).

Alma 56:21–42 • The Strategy of the Nephites—27th Year

21 Now we were desirous that the Lamanites should come upon us; for we were not desirous to make an attack upon them in their strongholds.

22 And it came to pass that we kept spies out round about, to watch the movements of the Lamanites, that they might not pass us by night nor by day to make an attack upon our other cities which were on the northward.

23 For we knew in those cities they were not sufficiently strong to meet them; therefore we were desirous, if they should pass by us, to fall upon them in their rear, and thus bring them up in the rear at the same time they were met in the front. We supposed that we could overpower them; but behold, we were disappointed in this our desire.

24 They durst not pass by us with their whole army, neither durst they with a part, lest they should not be sufficiently strong and they should fall.

25 Neither durst they march down against the city of Zarahemla; neither durst they cross the head of Sidon, over to the city of Nephihah.

26 And thus, with their forces, they were determined to maintain those cities which they had taken.

27 And now it came to pass in the second month of this year, there was brought unto us many provisions from the fathers of those my two thousand sons.

28 And also there were sent two thousand men unto us from the land of Zarahemla. And thus we were prepared with ten thousand men, and provisions for them, and also for their wives and their children.

29 And the Lamanites, thus seeing our forces increase daily, and provisions arrive for our support, they began to be fearful, and began

to sally forth, if it were possible to put an end to our receiving provisions and strength.

30 Now when we saw that the Lamanites began to grow uneasy on this wise, we were desirous to bring a stratagem into effect upon them; therefore Antipus ordered that I should march forth with my little sons to a neighboring city, as if we were carrying provisions to a neighboring city.

31 And we were to march near the city of Antiparah, as if we were going to the city beyond, in the borders by the seashore.

32 And it came to pass that we did march forth, as if with our provisions, to go to that city.

33 And it came to pass that Antipus did march forth with a part of his army, leaving the remainder to maintain the city. But he did not march forth until I had gone forth with my little army, and came near the city Antiparah.

34 And now, in the city Antiparah were stationed the strongest army of the Lamanites; yea, the most numerous.

35 And it came to pass that when they had been informed by their spies, they came forth with their army and marched against us.

36 And it came to pass that we did flee before them, northward. And thus we did lead away the most powerful army of the Lamanites;

37 Yea, even to a considerable distance, insomuch that when they saw the army of Antipus pursuing them, with their might, they did not turn to the right nor to the left, but pursued their march in a straight course after us; and, as we suppose, it was their intent to slay us before Antipus should overtake them, and this that they might not be surrounded by our people.

38 And now Antipus, beholding our danger, did speed the march of his army. But behold, it was night; therefore they did not overtake us, neither did Antipus overtake them; therefore we did camp for the night.

39 And it came to pass that before the dawn of the morning, behold, the Lamanites were pursuing us. Now we were not sufficiently strong to contend with them; yea, I would not suffer that my little sons should fall into their hands; therefore we did continue our march, and we took our march into the wilderness.

40 Now they durst not turn to the right nor to the left lest they should be surrounded; neither would I turn to the right nor to the left lest they should overtake me, and we could not stand against them, but be slain, and they would make their escape; and thus we did flee all that day into the wilderness, even until it was dark.

41 And it came to pass that again, when the light of the morning came we saw the Lamanites upon us, and we did flee before them.

42 But it came to pass that they did not pursue us far before they halted; and it was in the morning of the third day of the seventh month.

Where Helaman had learned his strategy maneuvers is not given to us, but it reminds us of the taking of the city of Mulek on the east quarter of the land (see Alma 52:19–40). However, Mormon's purpose was not to teach us the strategy of war, but to exemplify the faith of the young sons of the people of Ammon. The above verses seem self-explanatory.

Alma 56:43–48 • The Faith Instilled by Mothers

43 And now, whether they were overtaken by Antipus we knew not, but I said unto my men: Behold, we know not but they have halted for the purpose that we should come against them, that they might catch us in their snare;

44 Therefore what say ye, my sons, will ye go against them to battle?

45 And now I say unto you, my beloved brother Moroni, that never had I seen so great courage, nay, not amongst all the Nephites.

46 For as I had ever called them my sons (for they were all of them very young) even so they said unto me: Father, behold our God is with us, and he will not suffer that we should fall; then let us go forth; we would not slay our brethren if they would let us alone; therefore let us go, lest they should overpower the army of Antipus.

47 Now they never had fought, yet they did not fear death; and they did think more upon the liberty of their fathers than they did upon their lives; yea, they had been taught by their mothers, that if they did not doubt, God would deliver them.

48 And they rehearsed unto me the words of their mothers, saying: We do not doubt our mothers knew it.

Helaman giving his young soldiers a choice in their going to battle (v. 44) is unusual in most armies. The officer in command usually gives the orders and soldiers must follow or face court-martial. The relationship between Helaman and his young sons is well-defined. The father son relationship is also exemplary for all bloodline fathers and sons. Helaman credits his sons with courage. Their answer to him exemplifies their faith in God (vv. 45–46). Of course courage and faith go hand in hand. While their source of faith is rightfully recognized as coming from their mothers, they were certainly aware of the importance of liberty to their fathers (vv. 47–48). They were obviously raised in good homes. The hand that rocked their cradles as well as the teaching of their fathers had produced valiant sons. They, too, had been born of goodly parents (see 1 Nephi 1:1).

Alma 56:49–57 • The Sons Courage and Faith Pays Off

49 And it came to pass that I did return with my two thousand against these Lamanites who had pursued us. And now behold, the armies of Antipus had overtaken them, and a terrible battle had commenced.

50 The army of Antipus being weary, because of their long march in so short a space of time, were about to fall into the hands of the Lamanites; and had I not returned with my two thousand they would have obtained their purpose.

51 For Antipus had fallen by the sword, and many of his leaders, because of their weariness, which was occasioned by the speed of their march—therefore the men of Antipus, being confused because of the fall of their leaders, began to give way before the Lamanites.

52 And it came to pass that the Lamanites took courage, and began to pursue them; and thus were the Lamanites pursuing them with great vigor when Helaman came upon their rear with his two thousand, and began to slay them exceedingly, insomuch that the whole army of the Lamanites halted and turned upon Helaman.

53 Now when the people of Antipus saw that the Lamanites had turned them about, they gathered together their men and came again upon the rear of the Lamanites.

54 And now it came to pass that we, the people of Nephi, the people of Antipus, and I with my two thousand, did surround the Lamanites, and did slay them; yea, insomuch that they were compelled to deliver up their weapons of war and also themselves as prisoners of war.

55 And now it came to pass that when they had surrendered themselves up unto us, behold, I numbered those young men who had fought with me, fearing lest there were many of them slain.

56 But behold, to my great joy, there had not one soul of them fallen to the earth; yea, and they had fought as if with the strength of God; yea, never were men known to have fought with such miraculous strength; and with such mighty power did they fall upon the Lamanites, that they did frighten them; and for this cause did the Lamanites deliver themselves up as prisoners of war.

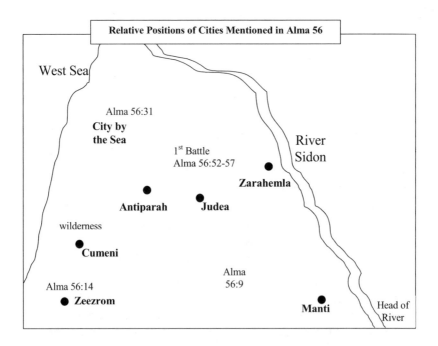

Figure 3. Relative Positions of Cities Mentioned in Alma 56

57 And as we had no place for our prisoners, that we could guard them to keep them from the armies of the Lamanites, therefore we sent them to the land of Zarahemla, and a part of those men who were not slain of Antipus, with them; and the remainder I took and joined them to my stripling Ammonites, and took our march back to the city of Judea.

Zero casualties amazed even Helaman. No doubt the power of God was their strength. It brought sufficient fear upon the Lamanites to cause their surrender (v. 56). No wonder Helaman adopted them as his sons.

Alma 57:1–5 • Ammoron Offers the City of Antiparah for Prisoners—28th Year

1 And now it came to pass that I received an epistle from Ammoron, the king, stating that if I would deliver up those prisoners of war whom we had taken that he would deliver up the city of Antiparah unto us.

2 But I sent an epistle unto the king, that we were sure our forces were sufficient to take the city of Antiparah by our force; and by delivering up the prisoners for that city we should suppose ourselves unwise, and that we would only deliver up our prisoners on exchange.

3 And Ammoron refused mine epistle, for he would not exchange prisoners; therefore we began to make preparations to go against the city of Antiparah.

4 But the people of Antiparah did leave the city, and fled to their other cities, which they had possession of, to fortify them; and thus the city of Antiparah fell into our hands.

5 And thus ended the twenty and eighth year of the reign of the judges.

Apparently Ammoron considered his Nephite prisoners, who were all chief captains (see Alma 56:12), valuable bargaining power. However, knowing the strength of his position, he was only interested in freeing his own people who had been taken prisoner. His reasoning was sound, and he retook Antiparah without shedding of blood. We assume the twenty-eighth year (v. 5) was spent in regrouping and bargaining.

Alma 57:6–12 • The Capture of Cumeni, Second City—29ᵗʰ Year

6 And it came to pass that in the commencement of the twenty and ninth year, we received a supply of provisions, and also an addition to our army, from the land of Zarahemla, and from the land round about, to the number of six thousand men, besides sixty of the sons of the Ammonites who had come to join their brethren, my little band of two thousand. And now behold, we were strong, yea, and we had also plenty of provisions brought unto us.

7 And it came to pass that it was our desire to wage a battle with the army which was placed to protect the city Cumeni.

8 And now behold, I will show unto you that we soon accomplished our desire; yea, with our strong force, or with a part of our strong force, we did surround, by night, the city Cumeni, a little before they were to receive a supply of provisions.

9 And it came to pass that we did camp round about the city for many nights; but we did sleep upon our swords, and keep guards, that the Lamanites could not come upon us by night and slay us, which they attempted many times; but as many times as they attempted this their blood was spilt.

10 At length their provisions did arrive, and they were about to enter the city by night. And we, instead of being Lamanites, were Nephites; therefore, we did take them and their provisions.

11 And notwithstanding the Lamanites being cut off from their support after this manner, they were still determined to maintain the city; therefore it became expedient that we should take those provisions and send them to Judea, and our prisoners to the land of Zarahemla.

12 And it came to pass that not many days had passed away before the Lamanites began to lose all hopes of succor; therefore they yielded up the city unto our hands; and thus we had accomplished our designs in obtaining the city Cumeni.

The addition of supplies and men brought a desire for another battle. Helaman now shows how they accomplished their desire (vv. 7–8). His desire to show Captain Moroni is not a precept to the reader as "I will show unto you" usually is used. It was not an insert by Mormon, but Helaman explaining in the epistle what they accomplished. However, we can certainly learn from it. One of the principles that brought victory in the second battle, retaking the city of Cumeni, was to cut off the Lamanites supplies (v. 10). The same is true in any battle. In the war against addiction, pornography, terrorism, or many other evil influences it is essential to cut off the supply of the sources. Again, the city is taken without the shedding of blood.

Alma 57:13–18 • The Numerous Prisoners of War

13 But it came to pass that our prisoners were so numerous that, notwithstanding the enormity of our numbers, we were obliged to employ all our force to keep them, or to put them to death.

14 For behold, they would break out in great numbers, and would fight with stones, and with clubs, or whatsoever thing they could get into their hands, insomuch that we did slay upwards of two thousand of them after they had surrendered themselves prisoners of war.

15 Therefore it became expedient for us, that we should put an end to their lives, or guard them, sword in hand, down to the land of Zarahemla; and also our provisions were not any more than sufficient for our own people, notwithstanding that which we had taken from the Lamanites.

16 And now, in those critical circumstances, it became a very serious matter to determine concerning these prisoners of war; nevertheless, we did resolve to send them down to the land of Zarahemla; therefore we selected a part of our men, and gave them charge over our prisoners to go down to the land of Zarahemla.

17 But it came to pass that on the morrow they did return. And now behold, we did not inquire of them concerning the prisoners; for behold, the Lamanites were upon us, and they returned in season to save us from falling into their hands. For behold, Ammoron had sent

to their support a new supply of provisions and also a numerous army of men.

18 And it came to pass that those men whom we sent with the prisoners did arrive in season to check them, as they were about to overpower us.

The principle of causing the Lamanites to labor "because it was easy to guard them" (Alma 53:5) was not effective with the large number of prisoners that had been taken. What happened on the way to taking the prisoners down to the land of Zarahemla (Alma 57:16–17) is disclosed below (vv. 30–34).

Alma 57:19–23 • The Second Battle of the Sons of Helaman

19 But behold, my little band of two thousand and sixty fought most desperately; yea, they were firm before the Lamanites, and did administer death unto all those who opposed them.

20 And as the remainder of our army were about to give way before the Lamanites, behold, those two thousand and sixty were firm and undaunted.

21 Yea, and they did obey and observe to perform every word of command with exactness; yea, and even according to their faith it was done unto them; and I did remember the words which they said unto me that their mothers had taught them.

22 And now behold, it was these my sons, and those men who had been selected to convey the prisoners, to whom we owe this great victory; for it was they who did beat the Lamanites; therefore they were driven back to the city of Manti.

23 And we retained our city Cumeni, and were not all destroyed by the sword; nevertheless, we had suffered great loss.

The faith of the sons of Helaman is again exemplified. The results of their faith illustrates a principle we are promised in the New Testament and by the Prophet Joseph Smith. The principle was: The sons obeyed and observed "to perform every word with exactness" (v. 21). James, the New Testament apostle taught: "for whosoever shall, save in one point, keep the whole law, he is guilty of all" (JST, James 2:10). The Prophet Joseph adds a second witness. In answer to the question: "Can we not be saved without going through all those ordinances?" Joseph answered: "Any person who is exalted to the highest mansion [kingdom] has to abide a celestial law, and the whole law too" (*TPJS*, 331). On the other side of the question, the Prophet Joseph taught: "The devil has no power over us only as we permit him. The moment we revolt at anything which comes from God, the devil takes power" (*TPJS*, 181).

The faith of these sons of Helaman, which was based upon the teachings of their mothers (Alma 57:21), brought about the Nephite victory (v. 22). The Lord has given us a similar promise in this dispensation. "I, the Lord, am bound when ye do what I say; but when ye do not what I say, ye have no promise" (D&C 82:10). That such promises extend to all walks of life is shown in another revelation: "There is a law, irrevocably decreed in heaven before the foundations of this world, upon which all blessings are predicated—And when we obtain any blessing from God, it is by obedience to that law upon which it is predicated" (D&C 130:20–21).

We must not assume that those who were killed (Alma 57:23) did not keep the commandments. Although they apparently did not have as much faith as their young brothers, they did receive eternal rewards for defending their country (see Alma 56:11 and 57:36 below).

Alma 57:24–27 • All the Sons of Helaman Are Wounded

24 And it came to pass that after the Lamanites had fled, I immediately gave orders that my men who had been wounded should be taken from among the dead, and caused that their wounds should be dressed.

25 And it came to pass that there were two hundred, out of my two thousand and sixty, who had fainted because of the loss of blood; nevertheless, according to the goodness of God, and to our great astonishment, and also the joy of our whole army, there was not one

soul of them who did perish; yea, and neither was there one soul among them who had not received many wounds.

26 And now, their preservation was astonishing to our whole army, yea, that they should be spared while there was a thousand of our brethren who were slain. And we do justly ascribe it to the miraculous power of God, because of their exceeding faith in that which they had been taught to believe—that there was a just God, and whosoever did not doubt, that they should be preserved by his marvelous power.

27 Now this was the faith of these of whom I have spoken; they are young, and their minds are firm, and they do put their trust in God continually.

That all of the sons received many wounds (v. 25) illustrates that they were all involved in the battle and did not resist combat. So must we be involved in the battle of evil. As Edmund Burke said: "The only thing necessary for the triumph of evil is for good men to do nothing."[1]

"The joy[2] of our whole army" over none of the sons being killed shows the great love they had for these young soldiers. The army also recognized the power of God as the son's protector, which surely increased their faith.

The firm minds of these young sons of Helaman and the putting of their trust in God continually is another great lesson for the young Latter-day Saint military people. Whether it be in a literal battle for their country, or in the battle of evil, they must follow this example if they want to survive the conflict. A firm mind, (v. 27) is one that knows and is determined to follow the laws of God, or at least the ones he does know. As the Prophet Joseph said: ". . . We cannot keep all the commandments without first knowing them, and we cannot expect

---

[1] Letter to William Smith, January 9, 1795; as quoted in "Second Century Address" by President Spencer W. Kimball, Oct. 10, 1975 Brigham Young University at the dedication of Carillon Tower and bells.

[2] The Book of Mormon editions up to the 1981 edition read "and also the foes of our whole army." This was probably due to a typing error in the original manuscript. Oliver Cowdery wrote in long hand as the Prophet Joseph dictated. This writer, having seen copies of Oliver's handwriting, could imagine how joy could have been misread as foes.

to know all, or more than we now know unless we comply with or keep those we have already received" (*TPJS*, 256).

To put our trust in God continually (v. 27) is to know the source and recognize a revelation. The Prophet Joseph Smith further said:

> That which is wrong under one circumstance, may be, and often is, right under another. . . . God said, 'thou shalt not kill;' at another time He said "Thou shalt utterly destroy." This is the principle on which the government of heaven is conducted—by revelation adapted to the circumstances in which the children of the kingdom are placed. Whatever God requires is right, no matter what it is, although we may not see the reason thereof till long after the events transpire. If we seek first the kingdom of God, all good things will be added. [*TPJS*, 256]

Alma 57:28–36 • The Prisoners Escape Is Explained

28 And now it came to pass that after we had thus taken care of our wounded men, and had buried our dead and also the dead of the Lamanites, who were many, behold, we did inquire of Gid concerning the prisoners whom they had started to go down to the land of Zarahemla with.

29 Now Gid was the chief captain over the band who was appointed to guard them down to the land.

30 And now, these are the words which Gid said unto me: Behold, we did start to go down to the land of Zarahemla with our prisoners. And it came to pass that we did meet the spies of our armies, who had been sent out to watch the camp of the Lamanites.

31 And they cried unto us, saying—Behold, the armies of the Lamanites are marching towards the city of Cumeni; and behold, they will fall upon them, yea, and will destroy our people.

32 And it came to pass that our prisoners did hear their cries, which caused them to take courage; and they did rise up in rebellion against us.

33 And it came to pass because of their rebellion we did cause that our swords should come upon them. And it came to pass that they did in a body run upon our swords, in the which, the greater number of

them were slain; and the remainder of them broke through and fled
from us.

34 And behold, when they had fled and we could not overtake
them, we took our march with speed towards the city Cumeni; and
behold, we did arrive in time that we might assist our brethren in
preserving the city.

35 And behold, we are again delivered out of the hands of our
enemies. And blessed is the name of our God; for behold, it is he that
has delivered us; yea, that has done this great thing for us.

36 Now it came to pass that when I, Helaman, had heard these
words of Gid, I was filled with exceeding joy because of the goodness
of God in preserving us, that we might not all perish; yea, and I trust
that the souls of them who have been slain have entered into the rest
of their God.

The guards not having time before to explain their early return from
taking the prisoners to the land of Zarahemla (v. 17), it is now told
(vv. 28–34). The explanation is sufficient and reasonable and needs
no further explanation. The lesson for us is two-fold: First, Gid
recognized the hand of God in their lives (v. 35); and Helaman trusted
in God that the souls of those slain had entered into the rest of God"
(v. 36). A similar promise regarding this two-fold lesson is also given
in modern revelation.

21 And in nothing doth man offend God, or against none is his
wrath kindled, save those who confess not his hand in all things, and
obey not his commandments.

23 But learn that he who doeth the works of righteousness shall
receive his reward, even peace in this world and eternal life in the
world to come. [D&C 59:21, 23]

Alma 58:1–7 • Helaman's Object Was
to Retake the City of Manti

1 And behold, now it came to pass that our next object was to
obtain the city of Manti; but behold, there was no way that we could
lead them out of the city by our small bands. For behold, they

remembered that which we had hitherto done; therefore we could not decoy them away from their strongholds.

2 And they were so much more numerous than was our army that we durst not go forth and attack them in their strongholds.

3 Yea, and it became expedient that we should employ our men to the maintaining those parts of the land which we had regained of our possessions; therefore it became expedient that we should wait, that we might receive more strength from the land of Zarahemla and also a new supply of provisions.

4 And it came to pass that I thus did send an embassy to the governor of our land, to acquaint him concerning the affairs of our people. And it came to pass that we did wait to receive provisions and strength from the land of Zarahemla.

5 But behold, this did profit us but little; for the Lamanites were also receiving great strength from day to day, and also many provisions; and thus were our circumstances at this period of time.

6 And the Lamanites were sallying forth against us from time to time, resolving by stratagem to destroy us; nevertheless we could not come to battle with them, because of their retreats and their strongholds.

7 And it came to pass that we did wait in these difficult circumstances for the space of many months, even until we were about to perish for the want of food.

How many months Helaman and his men waited for assistance is not given (v. 7). The morale of an army is certainly affected by their physical needs and their feelings of being supported by the government. In a letter to John Hancock on September 24, 1776, George Washington had many soldiers of the same rank with different pay. Congress was paying men unfairly. In his letter he wrote ". . . unless some speedy and effectual measures are adopted by Congress, our cause will be lost."[3] "Difficult circumstances" (v. 7) aptly describes the conditions of Helaman and his sons.

---

[3] *The Spirit of Seventy-six*, edited by Henry Steel Commage, Castle Books, [1958], 480.

Alma 58:8–12 • The Nephites Pour Out Their Souls to God

8 But it came to pass that we did receive food, which was guarded to us by an army of two thousand men to our assistance; and this is all the assistance which we did receive, to defend ourselves and our country from falling into the hands of our enemies, yea, to contend with an enemy which was innumerable.

9 And now the cause of these our embarrassments, or the cause why they did not send more strength unto us, we knew not; therefore we were grieved and also filled with fear, lest by any means the judgments of God should come upon our land, to our overthrow and utter destruction.

10 Therefore we did pour out our souls in prayer to God, that he would strengthen us and deliver us out of the hands of our enemies, yea, and also give us strength that we might retain our cities, and our lands, and our possessions, for the support of our people.

11 Yea, and it came to pass that the Lord our God did visit us with assurances that he would deliver us; yea, insomuch that he did speak peace to our souls, and did grant unto us great faith, and did cause us that we should hope for our deliverance in him.

12 And we did take courage with our small force which we had received, and were fixed with a determination to conquer our enemies, and to maintain our lands, and our possessions, and our wives, and our children, and the cause of our liberty.

Because of lack of assistance and embarrassments, the Nephites turned to their God (vv. 8–10). This was not a case of seeking help only in time of need, but of turning to him after all attempts to help themselves were exhausted. That they had been continually praying is illustrated by the assurances given them from God after they turned to him (v. 11). Their example illustrates the New Testament teaching: "The effectual fervent prayer of a righteous man availeth much" (James 5:16). The peace that came to the souls of the Nephites (v. 11) reminds us of Oliver Cowdery crying unto the Lord concerning the truth of the Book of Mormon and the Lord answered: "Did I not speak peace to your mind concerning the matter? What greater witness can you have than from God?" (D&C 6:23). Faith, as a principle of action, is exemplified in the courage and determination to conquer their enemies and preserve their liberty (Alma 58:12). The *Lectures on Faith* teach that "Faith is the moving cause of all action" (1:12).

Alma 58:13–31 • The Nephites Retake Manti

13 And thus we did go forth with all our might against the Lamanites, who were in the city of Manti; and we did pitch our tents by the wilderness side, which was near to the city.

14 And it came to pass that on the morrow, that when the Lamanites saw that we were in the borders by the wilderness which was near the city, that they sent out their spies round about us that they might discover the number and the strength of our army.

15 And it came to pass that when they saw that we were not strong, according to our numbers, and fearing that we should cut them off from their support except they should come out to battle against us and kill us, and also supposing that they could easily destroy us with their numerous hosts, therefore they began to make preparations to come out against us to battle.

16 And when we saw that they were making preparations to come out against us, behold, I caused that Gid, with a small number of men, should secrete himself in the wilderness, and also that Teomner and a small number of men should secrete themselves also in the wilderness.

17 Now Gid and his men were on the right and the others on the left; and when they had thus secreted themselves, behold, I remained, with the remainder of my army, in that same place where we had first pitched our tents against the time that the Lamanites should come out to battle.

18 And it came to pass that the Lamanites did come out with their numerous army against us. And when they had come and were about to fall upon us with the sword, I caused that my men, those who were with me, should retreat into the wilderness.

19 And it came to pass that the Lamanites did follow after us with great speed, for they were exceedingly desirous to overtake us that

they might slay us; therefore they did follow us into the wilderness; and we did pass by in the midst of Gid and Teomner, insomuch that they were not discovered by the Lamanites.

20 And it came to pass that when the Lamanites had passed by, or when the army had passed by, Gid and Teomner did rise up from their secret places, and did cut off the spies of the Lamanites that they should not return to the city.

21 And it came to pass that when they had cut them off, they ran to the city and fell upon the guards who were left to guard the city, insomuch that they did destroy them and did take possession of the city.

22 Now this was done because the Lamanites did suffer their whole army, save a few guards only, to be led away into the wilderness.

23 And it came to pass that Gid and Teomner by this means had obtained possession of their strongholds. And it came to pass that we took our course, after having traveled much in the wilderness towards the land of Zarahemla.

24 And when the Lamanites saw that they were marching towards the land of Zarahemla, they were exceedingly afraid, lest there was a plan laid to lead them on to destruction; therefore they began to retreat into the wilderness again, yea, even back by the same way which they had come.

25 And behold, it was night and they did pitch their tents, for the chief captains of the Lamanites had supposed that the Nephites were weary because of their march; and supposing that they had driven their whole army therefore they took no thought concerning the city of Manti.

26 Now it came to pass that when it was night, I caused that my men should not sleep, but that they should march forward by another way towards the land of Manti.

27 And because of this our march in the night-time, behold, on the morrow we were beyond the Lamanites, insomuch that we did arrive before them at the city of Manti.

28 And thus it came to pass, that by this stratagem we did take possession of the city of Manti without the shedding of blood.

29 And it came to pass that when the armies of the Lamanites did

arrive near the city, and saw that we were prepared to meet them, they were astonished exceedingly and struck with great fear, insomuch that they did flee into the wilderness.

30 Yea, and it came to pass that the armies of the Lamanites did flee out of all this quarter of the land. But behold, they have carried with them many women and children out of the land.

31 And those cities which had been taken by the Lamanites, all of them are at this period of time in our possession; and our fathers and our women and our children are returning to their homes, all save it be those who have been taken prisoners and carried off by the Lamanites.

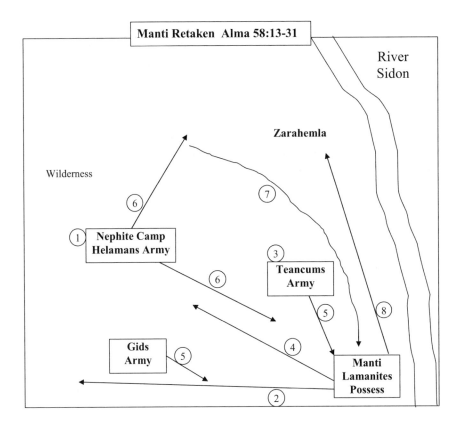

Figure 4. Manti Retaken

The step-by-step process of retaking the city is illustrated in Figure 4. The numbers correspond with the figure above.

1. Nephites camp in the wilderness (Alma 58:13).

2. Lamanites send out spies (Alma 58:14–15).

3. Gid and Teancum secrete themselves in the wilderness (Alma 58:16–17).

4. The Nephites retreat; the Lamanites follow them towards Zarahemla (Alma 58:18–19).

5. Gid and Teancum cut off the Lamanite spies, go to Manti, overcome the guards, and retake the city (Alma 58:20–23).

6. Helaman's army continues towards Zarahemla, Lamanites retreat towards Manti and camp in the wilderness (Alma 58:23–25).

7. Helaman's army travels all night to Manti (Alma 58:26).

8. Manti is retaken without shedding of blood, the Lamanites flee carrying away many women and children (Alma 58:27–31).

Thus the third city is retaken without blood being shed: Antiparah (Alma 57:4), Cumeni (Alma 57:12), and Manti (Alma 58:28). However, there were many Lamanites killed and some Nephites in battles outside of the cities and as prisoners of war (see Alma 56:52; 57:14; 57:26).

Alma 58:32–38 • Why Doesn't the Government Grant Us More?—29th Year

32 But behold, our armies are small to maintain so great a number of cities and so great possessions.

33 But behold, we trust in our God who has given us victory over those lands, insomuch that we have obtained those cities and those lands, which were our own.

34 Now we do not know the cause that the government does not grant us more strength; neither do those men who came up unto us know why we have not received greater strength.

35 Behold, we do not know but what ye are unsuccessful, and ye

have drawn away the forces into that quarter of the land; if so, we do not desire to murmur.

36 And if it is not so, behold, we fear that there is some faction in the government, that they do not send more men to our assistance; for we know that they are more numerous than that which they have sent.

37 But, behold, it mattereth not—we trust God will deliver us, notwithstanding the weakness of our armies, yea, and deliver us out of the hands of our enemies.

38 Behold, this is the twenty and ninth year, in the latter end, and we are in the possession of our lands; and the Lamanites have fled to the land of Nephi.

Helaman is the underdog in spite of their three victories (v. 32). He is also confused over his lack of support from the government (v. 34). Nevertheless, they maintain their faith and trust in God (v. 38). Helaman and his sons had been at war for four years (see Alma 56:9; 58:38).

Alma 58:39–41 • Stand Fast in the Liberty of God

39 And those sons of the people of Ammon, of whom I have so highly spoken, are with me in the city of Manti; and the Lord had supported them, yea, and kept them from falling by the sword, insomuch that even one soul has not been slain.

40 But behold, they have received many wounds; nevertheless they stand fast in that liberty wherewith God has made them free; and they are strict to remember the Lord their God from day to day; yea, they do observe to keep his statutes, and his judgments, and his commandments continually; and their faith is strong in the prophecies concerning that which is to come.

41 And now, my beloved brother, Moroni, may the Lord our God, who has redeemed us and made us free, keep you continually in his presence; yea, and may he favor this people, even that ye may have success in obtaining the possession of all that which the Lamanites have taken from us, which was for our support. And now, behold, I close mine epistle. I am Helaman, the son of Alma.

Again Helaman praises his stripling warriors. Their faith in the teachings of their mothers was honored by God, not even one of the two thousand and sixty young men lost his life (v. 39). Although many wounds were received, they stood fast in the liberty that God had granted unto them (v. 39). They stand as witnesses to our young people of today who face military service and war. First, they were strict to remember God from day to day (v. 40). They sought his protection, and recognized his hand in all things (v. 35). Theirs was not just a Sunday religion. They observed the statutes (laws), avoided the judgments (warnings), and followed his commandments continually (v. 40). Finally, they had faith in the prophecies of the future (v. 40). We have similar prophecies concerning the Americas today. If we serve the God of this land, we will not be swept off from the land. We will be free from bondage and captivity by all other nations (see Ether 2:8–12). These promises are applicable to everyone whether members of His Church or not, and whether in the military or not.

The ending of Helaman's epistle to Moroni shows his concern for all of the Nephite people, as well as Moroni (Alma 58:41). His leadership must have also inspired the young warriors.

Table 1 • Alma 56–58
Battles of the 2060 Sons of Helaman

CITIES RETAKEN	CONDITIONS	RESULTS	PRINCIPLES
1. City of Judea 56:9–19	• Replenish the army of Antipus	• No fighting	56:11, 19
2. City of Antiparah 56:30–56	• Led the Lamanites out followed by Antipus return and battle Lamanites	• Not one soul fallen	56:44–48
3. City of Cumeni chap. 57	• Surrounded and captured the Lamanites supplies • City surrendered • Prisoners sent to Zarahemla	• 200 fainted • All wounded • 1000 Nephites slain	57:21, 26–27

CITIES RETAKEN	CONDITIONS	RESULTS	PRINCIPLES
	• Lamanites attack • Guards of prisoners return	• Not one son of Helaman slain	
4. City of Manti chap. 58	• Armies of Gid and Teomner hid • Helaman gets Lamanites army to pursue • Gid and Teomner capture city • Lamanites stop and sleep • Helaman and army return at night • Lamanites return and find city captured	• Posses the city without the shedding of blood	58:10–12 58:35–40

SACRED WRITING

Preaching Which Is Sacred:

Alma 53:10–23   Mormon describes the sons of Helaman.

Alma 58:33–41   Helaman describes the Nephite stand on liberty.

Revelation Which Is Great:

Alma 58:10–12   The Lord assures deliverance to the sons of Helaman.

Doctrines Learned:

Alma 56:11   Those who die in defending the cause of their country and their God are happy.

General Authority Quotes

President George Albert Smith • Alma 53:19–22

Their Mothers Had Taught Them: I am thinking of the experience of the Nephites, when they were having their perilous troubles, and how just two thousand and sixty boys, striplings as Helaman called them, were brought face to face with men of experience and training in warfare, and they went forward without any question, and when they were gathered from the battlefield, everyone of them having been wounded, after a series of battles, two hundred of them having fainted from the loss of blood, not one had lost his life. When the question was asked, "How could you do it? How could you have the faith?" those boys, like the ones that are going out now, no doubt, eighteen years and a little older, smilingly remarked, "We knew, our mothers knew" (see Alma 57:19–22).

I think that is one of the greatest tributes that has ever been paid to motherhood—that in circumstances such as they were experiencing, when they were surrounded by enemies, they could train their children to have that faith in God that would carry them through and would bring them home without losing their lives.

I have been asking myself the question, "Have the mothers of Israel been preparing their sons?" Have they been teaching these boys that must represent us on the battlefield, that they too, can be preserved; that God will take care of them if they are in the line of their duty, and I want to say that if our mothers have, the fathers have much to be grateful for, because some fathers do not take much time to teach these children things like that in these days. [CR, April 1943, 89–90]

The First Presidency • Alma 53:20

True at All Times in Whatsoever Thing They Were Entrusted: To our young men who go into service, no matter whom they serve or where, we say live clean, keep the commandments of the Lord, pray to Him constantly to preserve you in truth and righteousness, live as you pray, and then whatever betides you the Lord will be with you and nothing will happen to you that will not be to the honor and glory of God and to your salvation and exaltation. There will come into your hearts from the living of the pure life you pray for, a joy that will pass your powers of expression or understanding. The Lord will be always near you; He will comfort you; you will feel His presence in the hour of your greatest tribulation; He will guard and protect you to the full extent that accords with His all-wise purpose. Then, when the conflict is over and you return to your homes, having lived the righteous life, how great will be your happiness—whether you be of the victors or of the vanquished—that you have lived as the Lord commanded. You will return so disciplined in righteousness that there-after all Satan's wiles and stratagems will leave you untouched. Your faith and testimony will be strong beyond breaking. You will be looked up to and revered as having passed through the fiery furnace of trial and temptation and come forth unharmed. Your brethren will look to you for counsel, support, and guidance. You will be the anchors to which thereafter the youth of Zion will moor their faith in man. [CR, April 1942, 96]

President David O. McKay • Alma 53:20

That is a great story (Alma 53:20), and an inspiration to young men in all the world.

Now, the application—Do you realize that we made a promise, a covenant at the water's edge? You and I are pretty well along in years, some of you, but we remember our baptism on our eighth birthday. There was a sense that came to us that we would not swear after that baptism, that we would do whatever our parents asked us to do, that we would do our part, or render service in the Church when called upon to do it. We were only children at eight years of age, that is true, but I can remember those feelings and sentiments as clearly as though they were yesterday. Don't you?

Later we realized what that covenant is. We buried the "old man," with all of his weaknesses, his jealousies, his tendency to slander, that we might come forth and walk in the newness of life. We refer to it now as the covenant made at the water's edge.

You made it, you gave your word. Is your word your bond? I ask the Church, and especially the men who hold the Priesthood.

Again, every Sunday in Sacrament meeting we give our word of honor, that we are willing to take upon us the name of the Son, that we will always remember him, that we will keep his commandments which he has given us, that we may have his Spirit to be with us. What a covenant! And we make it in the presence of God whom we are worshipping that day.

Another promise: do you remember what you said when you took your sweet wife though the Temple, your confidence in her, her purity, her worthiness was supreme—as pure as a snowflake, as spotless as a sunbeam, as worthy of motherhood as the purest of virgins. And she had that same confidence in you, as a husband and father; and together you stood in the House of the Lord and covenanted with each other that you would be true.

Is your word your bond? If so, then there should be no divorces, and the man who, because of his tendency to drink, abuses his wife and severs that connection, the man who, through desire to gratify his passion, becomes untrue to his wife, violates his word. There is not other explanation for it. [CR, Oct. 1952, 89–90]

Elder M. Russell Ballard • Alma 56:56; 57:25–26

Imagine that! These inexperienced young men were so spiritually and physically prepared, and so powerful, that they frightened their foes into surrendering! Although all 2,000 of the young men were wounded in battle at one time or another, not one was killed (see Alma 57:25). . . .

Brethren, today we are fighting a battle that in many ways is more perilous, more frightened with danger than the battle between the Nephites and the Lamanites. Our enemy is cunning and resourceful. We fight against Lucifer, the father of all lies, the enemy of all that is good and right and holy. Truly we live in a time of which Paul prophesied, when "men shall be lovers of their own selves, covetous, boasters, proud, blasphemers, disobedient to parents, unthankful, unholy, without natural affection, trucebreakers, false accusers, incontinent, fierce, despisers of those that are good, . . .lovers of pleasures more than lovers of God; having a form of godliness, but denying the power thereof: from such turn away" (2 Timothy 3:2–5).

Does this sound familiar, brethren? To me it sounds like a night of prime-time television.

These are "perilous times." We battle literally for the souls of men. The enemy is unforgiving and relentless. He is taking eternal prisoners at an alarming rate. And he shows no sign of letting up.

While we are profoundly grateful for the many members of the Church who are doing great things in the battle for truth and right, I must honestly tell you it still is not enough. We need much more help. And so, as the people of Ammon looked to their sons for reinforcement in the war against the Lamanites, we look to you, my young brethren of the Aaronic Priesthood. We need you. Like Helaman's 2,000 stripling warriors, you also are the spirit sons of God, and you too can be endowed with power to build up and defend

His kingdom. We need you to make sacred covenants, just as they did. We need you to be meticulously obedient and faithful, just as they were.

What we need now is the greatest generation of missionaries in the history of the Church. We need worthy, qualified, spiritually energized missionaries who, like Helaman's 2,000 stripling warriors, are "exceedingly valiant for courage, and also for strength and activity" and who are "true at all times in whatsoever thing they [are] entrusted" (Alma 53:20).

Listen to those words, my young brethren: valiant, courage, strength, active, true. We don't need spiritually weak and semi committed young men. We don't need you to just fill a position; we need your whole heart and soul. We need vibrant, thinking, passionate missionaries who know how to listen to and respond to the whisperings of the Holy Spirit. This isn't a time for spiritual weaklings. We cannot send you on a mission to be reactivated, reformed, or to receive a testimony. We just don't have time for that. We need you to be filled with "faith, hope, charity and love, with an eye single to the glory of God" (D&C 4:5). [CR, Oct. 2002, 51–52]

President Ezra Taft Benson • Alma 53:10–23

My young brethren, I counsel each of you to draw close to your own mother. Respect her. Honor her. Receive your mother's counsel as she loves and instructs you in righteousness. And honor and obey your father as he stands as the head of the home emulating his manly qualities. [*The Teachings of Ezra Taft Benson* (1988), 520]

Challenges to Eternal Life:

1. Make a commitment to keep the commandments of God and be true at all times in whatsoever thing you are entreated (Alma 53:10–21).

2. As you face temptation or trial remember what the mothers of the sons of Helaman taught—if they did not doubt God would deliver them. Pass that teaching on to your children (Alma 56:47).

3. Resolve to observe and perform every word of command with exactness that you may enter into the rest of the Lord (Alma 57:21).

4. When you are wounded in your fight against evil remember to stand fast in the liberty God has given you (Alma 58:40).

5. Choose a challenge of your own from this reading and apply it to your life.

Chapter Five

Principles of War

Alma 59:1–62:41

*H*istorical Setting: The above chapters of Alma return to the thirtieth year of the reign of the judges, and to the east coast of the land of Zarahemla. Alma chapters 56 through 58 had discussed to the twenty-sixth year of the judges and an account of the battles on the western front. There are two years covered in this reading, the thirtieth year and the thirty-first year.

Precepts of this Reading:

Or do ye suppose that the Lord will still deliver us, while we sit upon our thrones and do not make use of the means which the Lord has provided for us? [Alma 60:21]

Therefore, my beloved brother, Moroni, let us resist evil, and whatsoever evil we cannot resist with our words, yea, such as rebellions and dissensions, let us resist them with our swords, that we may retain our freedom, that we may rejoice in the great privilege of our church, and in the cause of our Redeemer and our God. [Alma 61:14]

But behold, because of the exceedingly great length of the war between the Nephites and the Lamanites many had become hardened, because of the exceedingly great length of the war; and many were softened because of their afflictions, insomuch that they did humble themselves before God, even in the depth of humility. [Alma 62:41]

The reading of these chapters ends the large war section of the Book of Mormon that has been the subject of this volume so far. There were other wars both before and after this section of Alma, but not like this section of Alma. An outline of Alma 59:1–62:41 follows as a preparation for a deeper study.

OUTLINE • ALMA 59:1–62:41

➤ 59:1–4   In the thirtieth year, after reading Helaman's epistle, Captain Moroni rejoiced in Helaman's success in obtaining the lands that were lost, and made it known to the people round about.

      a.   Moroni immediately sent an epistle to Pahoran desiring men to be gathered to go strengthen Helaman in maintaining the repossessed lands (v. 3).

      b.   Moroni began to lay plans to obtain the remainder of the cities taken by the Lamanites (v. 4).

➤ 59:5–13   As Moroni was preparing, the people of Nephihah were attacked by the Lamanites, who began to slay them.

      a.   The Lamanite armies were so numerous that the people were obliged to flee, and they came and joined the army of Moroni (v. 8).

      b.   Moroni supposed men would be sent to assist Nephihah to maintain the city, knowing it was easier to keep the city from falling than to retake it (vv. 9–12).

           1.   He retained all his forces to maintain the places he had recovered.

           2.   He was sorrowful and began to doubt because of the people's wickedness, if they might not fall into the hands of their brethren.

           3.   His chief captains doubted and marveled over the wickedness of the people because of the success of the Lamanites over them.

      c.   Moroni was angry with the government because of their indifference concerning the freedom of the country (v. 13).

➤ 60:1–13   Moroni writes again to Pahoran, the chief judge and the governor, and also to those chosen by the people to govern and manage the war.

   a. Moroni condemned those who had been appointed to gather and arm men to go against the Lamanites (vv. 2–5).

      1. Both he and Helaman and their men had suffered exceedingly: hunger, thirst, and fatigue.

      2. Thousands had fallen by the sword, while it could have been otherwise had they rendered strength and succor to our armies.

   b. Moroni desired to know the cause of their great neglect and thoughtless state (vv. 6–11).

      1. Can you sit in a thoughtless stupor, while thousands of your brethren are being murdered?

      2. They have looked to you for protection and you might have saved them.

      3. You withheld provisions, while they bled out their lives for the welfare of this people.

      4. The blood of thousands shall come upon your heads for vengeance.

      5. Do you suppose you can do nothing and the exceeding goodness of God will deliver you?

   c. It is vain to suppose that your brethren have been killed because of their wickedness? (vv. 12–13).

      1. Many have fallen by the sword to your condemnation.

      2. The Lord suffers the righteous to be slain that his judgment and justice may come upon the wicked.

      3. The righteous who are slain enter into the rest of the Lord.

➤ 60:14–19   Moroni feared the judgments of God would come on this people because of the government's slothfulness.

    a. If not for the wickedness that commenced at our head, the Nephite's enemies could have had no power over us (vv. 15–16).

        1. The king-men and their desire for power and authority caused contention among ourselves.

        2. Had the king-men been true to the cause of freedom and united with us, our enemies would have been disbursed.

    b. The Lamanites are coming and possessing our lands, murdering our people and carrying our wives and children away captive because of the wickedness of the king-men (vv. 17–19).

        1. We know not but what you seek for authority and are traitors to your country.

        2. Have you neglected us because you are in the heart of the country and are secure?

➢ 60:20–27 Have the leaders forgotten the commandments of the Lord, and the many times he has delivered our fathers out of the hands of our enemies?

    a. Will the Lord deliver us when we do not make use of the means the Lord has provided? (v. 21).

    b. Will you sit in idleness while tens of thousands surround you in idleness and thousands in the borders are falling wounded and bleeding? (v. 22).

    c. Will God look upon us as guiltless while ye sit still and behold these things? (vv. 23–27).

        1. God has said that the inward vessel shall be cleansed first and then the outer vessel.

        2. Except ye repent and send food and men to us and Helaman, we will contend no more with the Lamanites until we have first cleansed the inward vessel, the great head of government.

        3. Show me the true spirit of freedom or I will leave part of my freemen with a blessing of God upon them, and come unto you and stir up insurrections

among you until those who usurp power and authority become extinct.

➤ 60:28–33 Moroni does not fear the governor's power and authority, but it is his God under whose commandment he defends this country that he fears.

    a. The sword of justice hangs over you even to your destruction (vv. 29–31).

        1. Moroni awaits your assistance and relief or he will come and smite you.

        2. The Lord will not suffer you to live and wax strong in iniquities and destroy his righteous people.

    b. Will the Lord come in judgment upon the Lamanites when it is the tradition of their fathers that caused their hatred? (vv. 32–33).

        1. Those who dissented from us have increased their hatred.

        2. You know you transgress the laws of God and trample them under your feet.

        3. The Lord has told us to go to battle against the governors if they do not repent.

➤ 60:34–36 Moroni, was constrained according to the covenant he had made to keep the commandments of God.

    a. Adhere to the word of God and send men and provisions.

        1. If not, Moroni will come speedily, for God will not suffer them to perish with hunger.

        2. God will give us food, even if by the sword.

    b. Moroni is your chief captain (v. 36).

        1. He seeks not power but to pull it down.

        2. He seeks not for honor of the world, but the glory of God and the freedom and welfare of his country.

        3. He closes his epistle.

➤ 61:1–8   Moroni soon received an epistle from Pahoran, the chief
            governor.

    a. Pahoran does not joy in their great affliction, it grieves
        his soul (vv. 2–5).

        1. There are numerous ones who do joy in your afflic-
            tions and have rebelled against me and the freemen.

        2. They have sought to take the judgment seat and are
            the cause of this great iniquity.

        3. They have used great flattery, and have led away
            the hearts of many people.

        4. They have withheld our provisions and daunted the
            freemen from coming to you.

        5. They have driven me out, and I have fled with many
            men to the land of Gideon.

    b. Pahoran sent a proclamation throughout that part of the
        land and many flocked to him daily in defense of their
        country and their freedom (vv. 6–8).

        1. Those in rebellion durst not come against us to
            battle.

        2. They have possession of Zarahemla and have
            appointed a king over them.

        3. The king has written the king of the Lamanites, and
            entered and alliance with him.

        4. The king will enable the Lamanites to conquer
            Zarahemla, and he will be the king under the
            Lamanites.

➤ 61:9–13   Moroni, you censured me in your epistle, but I am not angry,
            I rejoice in the greatness of your heart.

    a. Pahoran does not seek for power but to retain his
        judgment seat that he may preserve the rights and liberty
        of his people (vv. 9).

        1. His soul stands fast in that liberty in the which God
            has made us free.

        2. We will resist wickedness even to bloodshed.

3. We would not shed the blood of the Lamanites if they would stay in their own land.

      4. We would not shed the blood of our brethren if they did not rebel against us.

  b. Pahoran said they would subject themselves to bondage if God commanded them, but God does not command them to subject themselves to their enemies, but to trust in him and he will deliver (v. 13).

61:14–18 Moroni, let us resist evil such as rebellions and dissensions, first with our words, and then resist them with our swords, to retain freedom in the cause of the church and our Redeemer and our God.

  a. Moroni, come speedily to me with a few of your men (vv. 15–16).

      1. Leave the remainder in charge of Lehi and Teancum; with power to conduct the war there according to the Spirit of God, which is the spirit of freedom in them.

      2. I have sent a few provisions unto them, that they may not perish.

  b. Moroni, gather whatever force you can in your march here, and we will go speedily against those dissenters in the strength of God according to our faith (vv. 17–18).

      1. We will take possession Zarahemla and obtain more food to send to Lehi and Teancum.

      2. We will go forth against the enemy in the strength of the Lord, and end this great iniquity.

61:19–21 Moroni, I joy in your epistle for I was worried about what to do.

  a. Moroni, you said except they repent, the Lord hath commanded you to go against them (v. 20).

  b. Strengthen Lehi and Teancum and God will deliver them and all who stand fast in the liberty of God (v. 21).

➤ 62:1–2   Moroni's heart took courage and was filled with joy over the epistle from Pahoran because of his faithfulness.

    a. Pahoran was not a traitor to the freedom and cause of his country (v. 1).

    b. Moroni mourned over the iniquity of those who drove Pahoran from the judgment-seat in rebellion against God and their country (v. 2).

➤ 62:3–6   Moroni took a small number of men, gave Lehi and Teancum command, and took his march towards Gideon.

    a. Moroni raised the standard of liberty in every place he entered (v. 14).

    b. Thousands flocked to Moroni's standard and took up swords in defense of their freedom (v. 5).

    c. Moroni came to Gideon and united his forces with Pahoran (v. 6).

       1. They became stronger than the men of Pachus.

       2. Pachus was the king of the dissenters who had driven out the freemen.

➤ 62:7–11   Moroni and Pahoran went to Zarahemla and battled Pachus.

    a. Pachus was slain, his men taken prisoner, and Pahoran was restored to his judgment-seat (v. 8–10).

       1. The men of Pachus received their trial according to the law, as well as the king-men who were in prison.

       2. Those who would not take up arms in defense of their country were put to death.

       3. This was strictly observed for the safety of the country.

    b. The thirtieth year ended, Moroni and Pahoran having restored peace to Zarahemla (v. 11).

➤ 62:12–26   In the commencement of the thirty-first year, Moroni immediately sent provisions, and an army of six thousand men to Helaman.

a. Moroni also sent an army of six thousand men and provisions to Lehi and Teancum (v. 13).

    b. Moroni and Pahoran left a large army in Zarahemla and marched with another large army to overthrow the city of Nephihah (vv. 14–18).

       1. Enroute they encountered many Lamanites, slew many, and took their provisions and weapons.

       2. They caused the remaining four thousand to enter into a covenant to make no more war against the Nephites.

       3. They sent them to dwell with the people of Ammon.

       4. They continued their march and camped in the plains of Nephihah, which was near to that city.

    c, Moroni was anxious for the Lamanites to come out to battle, but they were afraid (vv. 19–26).

       1. At night Moroni went to the top of the wall to spy and found the Lamanites asleep by the east entrance.

       2. He returned and prepared strong cords and ladders to let them down into the city.

       3. Moroni's men returned to the city and let themselves down on the west where the Lamanites were not camped.

       4. When the Lamanites awoke and saw the army of Moroni, they fled out by the pass.

       5. Moroni pursued them, slew many, took others prisoners, and some escaped to the land of Moroni.

       6. Moroni and Pahoran obtained the city without the loss of one soul of the Nephites.

➤ 62:27–32   Many of the Lamanite prisoners were desirous to join the people of Ammon.

    a. The prisoners joined the Ammonites and began to labor exceedingly in raising crops and animals (v. 28).

    b. The Nephites were relived of the great burden of all the Lamanite prisoners (v. 29).

    c. Moroni having reduced the Lamanite army and increased his own, marched to the land of Lehi (vv. 30–32).

       1. The Lamanites saw them coming and fled.

       2. Moroni pursued them from city to city until they met Lehi and Teancum.

       3. The Lamanites fled from Lehi and Teancum to the borders by the seashore, the land of Moroni.

➤ 62:33–38 The armies of the Lamanites were all gathered into one body in the land of Moroni, and Ammoron, their king, was with them.

    a. Moroni, Lehi, and Teancum camped their armies encircling the Lamanites by the wilderness on the south and the wilderness on the east (vv. 34–36).

       1. The Nephites and the Lamanites were very weary from the march and slept.

       2. However, Teancum, being very angry with Ammoron and Amalickiah as the cause of this great and lasting war, went and let himself down inside the city.

       3. Teancum went from place to place until he found Ammoron, the king, and cast a javelin at him, piercing him near the heart.

       4. The king awakened his servants before he died, and they pursued and slew Teancum.

    b. Lehi and Moroni were very sorrowful over Teancum's death.

       1. He had fought valiantly for his country, a true friend of liberty.

       2. He had suffered many sore afflictions.

    c. On the morrow, Moroni slew many Lamanites and drove them out of the land, and they did not return at that time (v. 38).

➤ 62:39–41   The thirty-first year ended having had wars, bloodshed, famine and affliction for many years.

    a.   There had been murders, contentions, dissensions, and all manner of iniquities (v. 40).

    b.   Because of the prayers of the righteous, they were spared (v. 40).

    c.   Because of the length of the war many had become hardened (v. 41).

    d.   Many were softened because of their afflictions, and did humble themselves before God (v. 41).

NOTES AND COMMENTARY

Introduction: What is the longest war in history? The longest war is the battle over good and evil that began in the pre-mortal life (see Revelation 12:7). Since that time, there have, been periodically many long physical wars, but the war of good and evil has been fought continuously. One of the signs to precede the Second Coming of Christ is that "they shall hear of wars, and rumors of wars" (JS–History 1:28). We are living in that day. The principles of war taught in these chapters of Alma are just as applicable to our day as they were to Helaman and Captain Moroni and their people. As we discuss these chapters of Alma, we will emphasize those principles that should govern us in war and also in the war against evil.

Alma 59:1–4 • Moroni Plans to Retake Other Cities from the Lamanites—30ᵗʰ Year

1 Now it came to pass in the thirtieth year of the reign of the judges over the people of Nephi, after Moroni had received and had read Helaman's epistle, he was exceedingly rejoiced because of the welfare, yea, the exceeding success which Helaman had had, in obtaining those lands which were lost.

2 Yea, and he did make it known unto all his people, in all the land round about in that part where he was, that they might rejoice also.

3 And it came to pass that he immediately sent an epistle to Pahoran, desiring that he should cause men to be gathered together to strengthen Helaman, or the armies of Helaman, insomuch that he might with ease maintain that part of the land which he had been so miraculously prospered in regaining.

4 And it came to pass when Moroni had sent this epistle to the land of Zarahemla, he began again to lay a plan that he might obtain the remainder of those possessions and cities which the Lamanites had taken from them.

These verses are self-explanatory. Nothing succeeds like success. The two great leaders were a catalyst to each other.

Alma 59:5–8 • The Lamanites Capture the City of Nephihah

5 And it came to pass that while Moroni was thus making preparations to go against the Lamanites to battle, behold, the people of Nephihah, who were gathered together from the city of Moroni and the city of Lehi and the city of Morianton, were attacked by the Lamanites.

6 Yea, even those who had been compelled to flee from the land of Manti, and from the land round about, had come over and joined the Lamanites in this part of the land.

7 And thus being exceedingly numerous, yea, and receiving strength from day to day, by the command of Ammoron they came forth against the people of Nephihah, and they did begin to slay them with an exceedingly great slaughter.

8 And their armies were so numerous that the remainder of the people of Nephihah were obliged to flee before them; and they came even and joined the army of Moroni.

The city of Nephihah had only been in existence for ten years. It was established in the twentieth year of the judges (see Alma 50:14, 16). The city's inhabitants gathered together for protection because the war with the Lamanites was on both fronts (vv. 5–6). The inhabitants were no match for the numerous Lamanites (v. 8).

Alma 59:9–13 • Doubt Arises Because of the Wickedness of the People

9 And now as Moroni had supposed that there should be men sent to the city of Nephihah, to the assistance of the people to maintain that city, and knowing that it was easier to keep the city from falling into the hands of the Lamanites than to retake it from them, he supposed that they would easily maintain that city.

10 Therefore he retained all his force to maintain those places which he had recovered.

11 And now, when Moroni saw that the city of Nephihah was lost he was exceedingly sorrowful, and began to doubt, because of the wickedness of the people, whether they should not fall into the hands of their brethren.

12 Now this was the case with all his chief captains. They doubted and marveled also because of the wickedness of the people, and this because of the success of the Lamanites over them.

13 And it came to pass that Moroni was angry with the government, because of their indifference concerning the freedom of their country.

The first principle of war identified in this section is Moroni's knowing that it is easier to keep the city from falling than to retake it (v. 9). One of the reasons this is true is that there is only one battle in defending the city, but if the city is lost there are two battles—the first to lose it and second one to retake it. Therefore, the losses are heavier both in lives and destruction of property. In the battle against evil, the principle is the same. It is easier to prevent sin than it is to repent of sin. Also there is the destruction of character and virtue in yielding to sin. The cause of the fall of the city was wickedness, as recognized by Moroni and the chief captains (vv. 11–12). We prevent wickedness by abstaining "from all appearance of evil" (1 Thessalonians 5:22). Jesus taught us to pray that we not be led away into temptation but "deliver us from evil" (3 Nephi 13:12; Matthew 6:12). Moroni's anger is vented in the following epistle.

Alma 60:1–5 • Captain Moroni Chastises Pahoran, the Chief Judge

1 And it came to pass that he wrote again to the governor of the land, who was Pahoran, and these are the words which he wrote, saying: Behold, I direct mine epistle to Pahoran, in the city of Zarahemla, who is the chief judge and the governor over the land, and also to all those who have been chosen by this people to govern and manage the affairs of this war.

2 For behold, I have somewhat to say unto them by the way of condemnation; for behold, ye yourselves know that ye have been appointed to gather together men, and arm them with swords, and with cimeters, and all manner of weapons of war of every kind, and send forth against the Lamanites, in whatsoever parts they should come into our land.

3 And now behold, I say unto you that myself, and also my men, and also Helaman and his men, have suffered exceedingly great sufferings; yea, even hunger, thirst, and fatigue, and all manner of afflictions of every kind.

4 But behold, were this all we had suffered we would not murmur nor complain.

5 But behold, great has been the slaughter among our people; yea, thousands have fallen by the sword, while it might have otherwise been if ye had rendered unto our armies sufficient strength and succor for them. Yea, great has been your neglect towards us.

Moroni was the chief captain of all of the Nephite armies (see Alma 43:16). He was directly responsible to Pahoran. Not knowing the cause of their being neglected, he extended his complaint to all those chosen as leaders of the people (vv. 1–2), as a careful reading of the text will show.

Another great characteristic of Captain Moroni is shown in his willingness to suffer (vv. 3–4), but he would not tolerate undeserved suffering upon those whom he was responsible to protect (v. 5).

Alma 60:6–13 • Moroni Desires to Know the Cause

6 And now behold, we desire to know the cause of this exceedingly great neglect; yea, we desire to know the cause of your thoughtless state.

7 Can you think to sit upon your thrones in a state of thoughtless stupor, while your enemies are spreading the work of death around you? Yea, while they are murdering thousands of your brethren—

8 Yea, even they who have looked up to you for protection, yea, have placed you in a situation that ye might have succored them, yea, ye might have sent armies unto them, to have strengthened them, and have saved thousands of them from falling by the sword.

9 But behold, this is not all—ye have withheld your provisions from them, insomuch that many have fought and bled out their lives because of their great desires which they had for the welfare of this people; yea, and this they have done when they were about to perish with hunger, because of your exceedingly great neglect towards them.

10 And now, my beloved brethren—for ye ought to be beloved; yea, and ye ought to have stirred yourselves more diligently for the welfare and the freedom of this people; but behold, ye have neglected them insomuch that the blood of thousands shall come upon your heads for vengeance; yea, for known unto God were all their cries, and all their sufferings—

11 Behold, could ye suppose that ye could sit upon your thrones, and because of the exceeding goodness of God ye could do nothing and he would deliver you? Behold, if ye have supposed this ye have supposed in vain.

12 Do ye suppose that, because so many of your brethren have been killed it is because of their wickedness? I say unto you, if ye have supposed this ye have supposed in vain; for I say unto you, there are many who have fallen by the sword; and behold it is to your condemnation;

13 For the Lord suffereth the righteous to be slain that his justice and judgment may come upon the wicked; therefore ye need not suppose that the righteous are lost because they are slain; but behold, they do enter into the rest of the Lord their God.

Moroni reminds Pahoran and us of the responsibility of the government for the lives of people in any conflict. The Lord holds the leader accountable. The value of human life in the eyes of God is primary (v. 10). Again we are reminded of God's justice being in balance with his mercy (v. 11). Earlier in the Book of Mormon we read of the Lord holding us accountable for teaching the people (2 Nephi 9:44; Jacob 1:19), now we read of the physical accountability. Condemnation will come on leaders who do not act according to God's laws (Alma 60:12).

The eternal principle of justice is taught by Moroni. In modern times the question asked by many is answered. Why do bad things happen to good people? We are all on earth to be tested (see Abraham 3:25–26). The Lord allows the righteous to be killed in order for the principle of agency to exist. In the words of President Harold B. Lee: It was "not by his will; He permits it."[4] Those who are the victims of other's agency will not be punished or lose any eternal possibilities. Again we are taught; "they do enter into the rest of the Lord their God" (Alma 60:13). The rest of the Lord is "the fullness of his glory" (D&C 84:24). The Prophet Joseph Smith taught: "All your losses will be made up to you in the resurrection, provided you continue faithful. By the vision of the Almighty I have seen it" (*TPJS*, 296). The same will be true of missed opportunities. Through the spirit world and the millennium all missed opportunities will be given to those whose lives were cut short.[5]

Alma 60:14–19 • Fear of the Judgments of God

14 And now behold, I say unto you, I fear exceedingly that the judgments of God will come upon this people, because of their exceeding slothfulness, yea, even the slothfulness of our government, and their exceedingly great neglect towards their brethren, yea, towards those who have been slain.

---

[4] *The Teachings of Harold B. Lee*, ed. Clyde J. Williams [1996], 187.

[5] See Spencer W. Kimball, *Tragedy or Destiny*.

15 For were it not for the wickedness which first commenced at our head, we could have withstood our enemies that they could have gained no power over us.

16 Yea, had it not been for the war which broke out among ourselves; yea, were it not for these king-men, who caused so much bloodshed among ourselves; yea, at the time we were contending among ourselves, if we had united our strength as we hitherto have done; yea, had it not been for the desire of power and authority which those king-men had over us; had they been true to the cause of our freedom, and united with us, and gone forth against our enemies, instead of taking up their swords against us, which was the cause of so much bloodshed among ourselves; yea, if we had gone forth against them in the strength of the Lord, we should have dispersed our enemies, for it would have been done, according to the fulfilling of his word.

17 But behold, now the Lamanites are coming upon us, taking possession of our lands, and they are murdering our people with the sword, yea, our women and our children, and also carrying them away captive, causing them that they should suffer all manner of afflictions, and this because of the great wickedness of those who are seeking for power and authority, yea, even those king-men.

18 But why should I say much concerning this matter? For we know not but what ye yourselves are seeking for authority. We know not but what ye are also traitors to your country.

19 Or is it that ye have neglected us because ye are in the heart of our country and ye are surrounded by security, that ye do not cause food to be sent unto us, and also men to strengthen our armies?

The principles given to individuals are also applicable to nations. "The devil has no power over us only as we permit him. The moment we revolt at anything which comes from God, the devil takes power (*TPJS*, 181). Thus, Moroni declared that the success of the Lamanites in capturing the Nephites cities and bringing suffering to Nephite people was due to the desire of the king-men seeking power and authority internally (vv. 15–17). The rise of the king-men is recorded in Alma 51 and was discussed in chapter three of this work.

Moroni raised the question of loyalty to the present leaders. Were they guilty of the same desires that the king-men had? Were they traitors to their country? Were they more concerned with their own security than with their constituents? These are all good questions. The answers to these questions come in Alma 61, but the same questions might be posed to modern-day politicians.

Alma 60:20–27 • Have Ye Forgotten the Commandments of God

20 Have ye forgotten the commandments of the Lord your God? Yea, have ye forgotten the captivity of our fathers? Have ye forgotten the many times we have been delivered out of the hands of our enemies?

21 Or do ye suppose that the Lord will still deliver us, while we sit upon our thrones and do not make use of the means which the Lord has provided for us?

22 Yea, will ye sit in idleness while ye are surrounded with thousands of those, yea, and tens of thousands, who do also sit in idleness, while there are thousands round about in the borders of the land who are falling by the sword, yea, wounded and bleeding?

23 Do ye suppose that God will look upon you as guiltless while ye sit still and behold these things? Behold I say unto you, Nay. Now I would that ye should remember that God has said that the inward vessel shall be cleansed first, and then shall the outer vessel be cleansed also.

24 And now, except ye do repent of that which ye have done, and begin to be up and doing, and send forth food and men unto us, and also unto Helaman, that he may support those parts of our country which he has regained, and that we may also recover the remainder of our possessions in these parts, behold it will be expedient that we contend no more with the Lamanites until we have first cleansed our inward vessel, yea, even the great head of our government.

25 And except ye grant mine epistle, and come out and show unto me a true spirit of freedom, and strive to strengthen and fortify our armies, and grant unto them food for their support, behold I will leave a part of my freemen to maintain this part of our land, and I will leave

the strength and the blessings of God upon them, that none other power can operate against them—

26 And this because of their exceeding faith, and their patience in their tribulations—

27 And I will come unto you, and if there be any among you that has a desire for freedom, yea, if there be even a spark of freedom remaining, behold I will stir up insurrections among you, even until those who have desires to usurp power and authority shall become extinct.

As Americans and as Latter-day Saints we should be asked the same question that Moroni asked Pahoran. Have we forgotten the captivity of our fathers (v. 20). The Revolutionary War brought freedom to the American colonies. The fathers led the Latter-day Saints from New York to Kirtland; from Kirtland to Missouri; from Missouri to Nauvoo; and from Nauvoo to the Rocky Mountains.

In the war against terrorism—or the war against evil—we must "make use of the means the Lord has provided for us" (v. 21). We must take precautions against terrorism and not sit idly by. We must avoid the temptations of pornography, cheating, lying, greed, and the quest for power that persists among us by the thousands and ten thousands who surround us and do nothing (v. 22).

The source of Moroni's quote "the inward vessel shall be cleansed first, and then shall the outer vessel be cleansed also" (v. 23) is obviously from the plates of brass and was among the "many plain and precious things taken out of the [Bible]" (1 Nephi 13:28). It is, however, another principle of war as well as of life. President Ezra Taft Benson has commented on this verse: "The proud do not change or improve, but defend their position by rationalization. Repentance means change, and it takes a humble person to change."[6] In the final battle against evil, which will end with the destruction of the wicked by the coming of Christ, it will commence with the members of the Church. The Lord has revealed:

---

[6] Ezra Taft Benson, *The Teachings of Ezra Taft Benson* [1988], 72.

23 Verily, verily, I say unto you, darkness covereth the earth, and gross darkness the minds of the people, and all flesh has become corrupt before my face.

24 Behold, vengeance cometh speedily upon the inhabitants of the earth, a day of wrath, a day of burning, a day of desolation, of weeping, of mourning, and of lamentation; and as a whirlwind it shall come upon all the face of the earth, saith the Lord.

25 And upon my house shall it begin, and from my house shall it go forth, saith the Lord;

26 First among those among you, saith the Lord, who have professed to know my name and have not known me, and have blasphemed against me in the midst of my house, saith the Lord. [D&C 112:23–26]

Moroni's suggestion of the Nephites first cleansing their inner vessel of government is followed by a threat (Alma 60:24–27). He was going to "make use of the means which the Lord [had] provided for [him]" (v. 21). We may not have the forces or sources available to use that Moroni had, but we do have the gospel to hold up by our example and through the teaching of those who will listen. We also have freedoms within our country that we must support through election of honest, wise, and good men to local and national political offices. Furthermore, we must give them our support after they are elected (see D&C 98:9–10).

Alma 60:28–33 • It Is My God Whom I Fear

28 Yea, behold I do not fear your power nor your authority, but it is my God whom I fear; and it is according to his commandments that I do take my sword to defend the cause of my country, and it is because of your iniquity that we have suffered so much loss.

29 Behold it is time, yea, the time is now at hand, that except ye do bestir yourselves in the defence of your country and your little ones, the sword of justice doth hang over you; yea, and it shall fall upon you and visit you even to your utter destruction.

30 Behold, I wait for assistance from you; and, except ye do administer unto our relief, behold, I come unto you, even in the land of Zarahemla, and smite you with the sword, insomuch that ye can have no more power to impede the progress of this people in the cause of our freedom.

31 For behold, the Lord will not suffer that ye shall live and wax strong in your iniquities to destroy his righteous people.

32 Behold, can you suppose that the Lord will spare you and come out in judgment against the Lamanites, when it is the tradition of their fathers that has caused their hatred, yea, and it has been redoubled by those who have dissented from us, while your iniquity is for the cause of your love of glory and the vain things of the world?

33 Ye know that ye do transgress the laws of God, and ye do know that ye do trample them under your feet. Behold, the Lord saith unto me: If those whom ye have appointed your governors do not repent of their sins and iniquities, ye shall go up to battle against them.

Moroni justified his threat to cleanse the government through the commandment of God (v. 28). As a church, we have been given the same guidelines, to us and all people. After lifting the standards of peace to our enemies three times, the Lord directs:

36 Then I, the Lord, would give unto them a commandment, and justify them in going out to battle against that nation, tongue, or people.

37 And I, the Lord, would fight their battles, and their children's battles, and their children's children's, until they had avenged themselves on all their enemies, to the third and fourth generation.

38 Behold, this is an ensample unto all people, saith the Lord your God, for justification before me. [D&C 98:36–38]

As a church, we must look to our leaders to know when and how to go to battle, both for a country and in the battle of evil. We should find comfort in the Lord's promise to fight our battle when we are commanded to fight. Of course, we must do our part.

"The sword of justice" (v. 29) also hangs over the heads of the nations of the Americas. He has warned whatever nation that possesses these lands to "serve God, or they shall be swept off when the fullness of his wrath cometh upon them, and the fullness of his wrath cometh upon them when they are ripened in iniquity" (Ether 2:9). The Lord will determine when that ripeness comes, but the nations certainly seems to be going in that direction. Probably, most Americans know they are transgressing the commandments of God (Alma 60:23), and certainly those who are members of the Church who transgress know they are transgressing. "The Lord cannot look upon sin with the least degree of allowance" (D&C 1:31; see also Alma 13:12).

Alma 60:34–36 • Moroni Is Constrained by His Covenants

34 And now behold, I, Moroni, am constrained, according to the covenant which I have made to keep the commandments of my God; therefore I would that ye should adhere to the word of God, and send speedily unto me of your provisions and of your men, and also to Helaman.

35 And behold, if ye will not do this I come unto you speedily; for behold, God will not suffer that we should perish with hunger; therefore he will give unto us of your food, even if it must be by the sword. Now see that ye fulfil the word of God.

36 Behold, I am Moroni, your chief captain. I seek not for power, but to pull it down. I seek not for honor of the world, but for the glory of my God, and the freedom and welfare of my country. And thus I close mine epistle.

Moroni's actions sustained his words in these verses. He was a true American. As stated in the comments under Alma 48:10–17, although he was involved in the shedding of blood, he did not delight in doing so and was a sanctified man. He yielded his heart to God (see Helaman 3:35).

Alma 61:1–8 • Pahoran Answers Captain Moroni's Epistle

1 Behold, now it came to pass that soon after Moroni had sent his epistle unto the chief governor, he received an epistle from Pahoran, the chief governor. And these are the words which he received:

2 I, Pahoran, who am the chief governor of this land, do send these words unto Moroni, the chief captain over the army. Behold, I say unto you, Moroni, that I do not joy in your great afflictions, yea, it grieves my soul.

3 But behold, there are those who do joy in your afflictions, yea, insomuch that they have risen up in rebellion against me, and also those of my people who are freemen, yea, and those who have risen up are exceedingly numerous.

4 And it is those who have sought to take away the judgment-seat from me that have been the cause of this great iniquity; for they have used great flattery, and they have led away the hearts of many people, which will be the cause of sore affliction among us; they have withheld our provisions, and have daunted our freemen that they have not come unto you.

5 And behold, they have driven me out before them, and I have fled to the land of Gideon, with as many men as it were possible that I could get.

6 And behold, I have sent a proclamation throughout this part of the land; and behold, they are flocking to us daily, to their arms, in the defence of their country and their freedom, and to avenge our wrongs.

7 And they have come unto us, insomuch that those who have risen up in rebellion against us are set at defiance, yea, insomuch that they do fear us and durst not come out against us to battle.

8 They have got possession of the land, or the city, of Zarahemla; they have appointed a king over them, and he hath written unto the king of the Lamanites, in the which he hath joined an alliance with him; in the which alliance he hath agreed to maintain the city of Zarahemla, which maintenance he supposeth will enable the Lamanites to conquer the remainder of the land, and he shall be placed king over this people when they shall be conquered under the Lamanites.

The situation in the seat of government was grave. As Moroni had supposed, the inner vessel needed to be cleansed. However, it was not the chief governor, but the king-men, to whom Moroni referred in his epistle (Alma 60:16). They had risen in rebellion again (Alma 61:3–5). Notice their use of flattery (v. 4), another tactic of Satan.

Pahoran was not sitting idly on his throne, as Moroni had supposed, (Alma 6:11, 21), but was rallying the freemen to defend their freedom and retain Pahoran on the throne (Alma 61:5–6). The king-men had finally attained their original plan, which was to have a king rule over them (vv. 6–8; compare Alma 51:5).

Alma 61:9–13 • The Character of Pahoran

9 And now, in your epistle you have censured me, but it mattereth not; I am not angry, but do rejoice in the greatness of your heart. I, Pahoran, do not seek for power, save only to retain my judgment-seat that I may preserve the rights and the liberty of my people. My soul standeth fast in that liberty in the which God hath made us free.

10 And now, behold, we will resist wickedness even unto bloodshed. We would not shed the blood of the Lamanites if they would stay in their own land.

11 We would not shed the blood of our brethren if they would not rise up in rebellion and take the sword against us.

12 We would subject ourselves to the yoke of bondage if it were requisite with the justice of God, or if he should command us so to do.

13 But behold he doth not command us that we shall subject ourselves to our enemies, but that we should put our trust in him, and he will deliver us.

Although Moroni had been wrong about Pahoran, we must admire Pahoran, for his calmness and demeanor in his reply (v. 9). The natural man would have retaliated in anger and informed Moroni how wrong he was. Instead, Pahoran reaffirmed his commitment to preserve the freedom of his people and resist wickedness even unto bloodshed (vv. 9–10). He also reaffirmed his faith in doing God's will and placing his trust in him (vv. 11–13). Certainly, Pahoran had faith unto salvation: "An actual knowledge that the course of life which one is pursuing is according to His will" (*Lectures on Faith,* 3:5). His name could well be added to Ammon and the other sons of Messiah, and Alma and his sons as "men of God" (Alma 48:18).

Alma 61:14–18 • Pahoran Instructs Captain Moroni

14 Therefore, my beloved brother, Moroni, let us resist evil, and whatsoever evil we cannot resist with our words, yea, such as rebellions and dissensions, let us resist them with our swords, that we may retain our freedom, that we may rejoice in the great privilege of our church, and in the cause of our Redeemer and our God.

15 Therefore, come unto me speedily with a few of your men, and leave the remainder in the charge of Lehi and Teancum; give unto them power to conduct the war in that part of the land, according to the Spirit of God, which is also the spirit of freedom which is in them.

16 Behold I have sent a few provisions unto them, that they may not perish until ye can come unto me.

17 Gather together whatsoever force ye can upon your march hither, and we will go speedily against those dissenters, in the strength of our God according to the faith which is in us.

18 And we will take possession of the city of Zarahemla, that we may obtain more food to send forth unto Lehi and Teancum; yea, we will go forth against them in the strength of the Lord, and we will put an end to this great iniquity.

As the commander-in-chief the Nephite armies, Pahoran gives his chief captain his orders. In doing so, he gives us another principle of war, one that had been given many years before by Alma: "whatsoever evil we cannot resist with our words, . . . let us resist with our swords" (v. 14; compare 31:5). However, he recognized that even war should be conducted "according to the Spirit of God" (v. 15). His equating the Spirit of God with the spirit of freedom (v. 15) is consistent with revelation. "The Spirit of truth is of God" (D&C 93:26; compare D&C 88:6–13; John 15:26). Pahoran is also making "use of the means which the Lord has provided for [them]" (Alma 61:16–18; 60:21).

Alma 61:19–21 • Pahoran Finds Joy in Moroni's Epistle

19 And now, Moroni, I do joy in receiving your epistle, for I was somewhat worried concerning what we should do, whether it should be just in us to go against our brethren.

20 But ye have said, except they repent the Lord hath commanded you that ye should go against them.

21 See that ye strengthen Lehi and Teancum in the Lord; tell them to fear not, for God will deliver them, yea, and also all those who stand fast in that liberty wherewith God hath made them free. And now I close mine epistle to my beloved brother, Moroni.

Pahoran found in Moroni's epistle the answer to his worries, and undoubtedly to his prayers (v. 19). We also learn from each other as the Lord gives both of us inspiration. Pahoran wants Moroni to strengthen Lehi and Teancum in the same way (v. 21). Both Pahoran and Moroni believed that "with God all things are possible" (Matthew 19:26; see also Mark 9:23).

Alma 62:1–6 • Thousands Flock to the Standard of Liberty

1 And now it came to pass that when Moroni had received this epistle his heart did take courage, and was filled with exceedingly great joy because of the faithfulness of Pahoran, that he was not also a traitor to the freedom and cause of his country.

2 But he did also mourn exceedingly because of the iniquity of those who had driven Pahoran from the judgment-seat, yea, in fine because of those who had rebelled against their country and also their God.

3 And it came to pass that Moroni took a small number of men, according to the desire of Pahoran, and gave Lehi and Teancum

command over the remainder of his army, and took his march towards the land of Gideon.

4 And he did raise the standard of liberty in whatsoever place he did enter, and gained whatsoever force he could in all his march towards the land of Gideon.

5 And it came to pass that thousands did flock unto his standard, and did take up their swords in the defence of their freedom, that they might not come into bondage.

6 And thus, when Moroni had gathered together whatsoever men he could in all his march, he came to the land of Gideon; and uniting his forces with those of Pahoran they became exceedingly strong, even stronger than the men of Pachus, who was the king of those dissenters who had driven the freemen out of the land of Zarahemla and had taken possession of the land.

Moroni's actions affirm what King Mosiah, son of Benjamin had taught: "It is not common that the voice of the people desireth anything contrary to that which is right" (Mosiah 29:26). Thousands of people came to the defense of freedom as Moroni marched to the land of Gideon (Alma 62:3–5). Truth and righteousness did and will prevail.

Alma 62:7–11 • Moroni and Pahoran Restore Peace to the Land

7 And it came to pass that Moroni and Pahoran went down with their armies into the land of Zarahemla, and went forth against the city, and did meet the men of Pachus, insomuch that they did come to battle.

8 And behold, Pachus was slain and his men were taken prisoners, and Pahoran was restored to his judgment-seat.

9 And the men of Pachus received their trial, according to the law, and also those king-men who had been taken and cast into prison; and they were executed according to the law; yea, those men of Pachus and those king-men, whosoever would not take up arms in the defence of their country, but would fight against it, were put to death.

10 And thus it became expedient that this law should be strictly observed for the safety of their country; yea, and whosoever was found denying their freedom was speedily executed according to the law.

11 And thus ended the thirtieth year of the reign of the judges over the people of Nephi; Moroni and Pahoran having restored peace to the land of Zarahemla, among their own people, having inflicted death upon all those who were not true to the cause of freedom.

This was the fifth major battle in this section of the Book of Mormon. Unlike the first rebellion of the king-men, the men of Pachus, the now deceased king of the dissenters, were given a trial (vv. 8–9; compare 51:19). Although not stated, it is implied that those who repented or who would not fight against the country were not executed (see vv. 16–17 below). While execution may seem harsh, the thousands who had been killed, and the threat of many more that would yet be killed had the law not been carried out, justifies their execution. To paraphrase the message of the Spirit to Nephi, son of Lehi: "It is better that [these who deny freedom] should perish than that a nation should dwindle and perish [in war]" (1 Nephi 4:13).

Alma 62:12–18 • Assistance Sent to Helaman on the West Front—31st Year

12 And it came to pass in the commencement of the thirty and first year of the reign of the judges over the people of Nephi, Moroni immediately caused that provisions should be sent, and also an army of six thousand men should be sent unto Helaman, to assist him in preserving that part of the land.

13 And he also caused that an army of six thousand men, with a sufficient quantity of food, should be sent to the armies of Lehi and Teancum. And it came to pass that this was done to fortify the land against the Lamanites.

14 And it came to pass that Moroni and Pahoran, leaving a large body of men in the land of Zarahemla, took their march with a large body of men towards the land of Nephihah, being determined to overthrow the Lamanites in that city.

15 And it came to pass that as they were marching towards the land, they took a large body of men of the Lamanites, and slew many of them, and took their provisions and their weapons of war.

16 And it came to pass after they had taken them, they caused them to enter into a covenant that they would no more take up their weapons of war against the Nephites.

17 And when they had entered into this covenant they sent them to dwell with the people of Ammon, and they were in number about four thousand who had not been slain.

18 And it came to pass that when they had sent them away they pursued their march towards the land of Nephihah. And it came to pass that when they had come to the city of Nephihah, they did pitch their tents in the plains of Nephihah, which is near the city of Nephihah.

Whether the large body of Lamanites were slain in battle or captured and then slain is not stated in the text (v. 25). It is assumed they were killed in battle, but they were also offered a covenant of peace, to no more take up their weapons of war (v. 16). That there were four thousand not slain illustrates the desire for freedom that also existed among the Lamanites. The people of Ammon (v. 17) were those Lamanites who had previously entered into such a covenant (see Alma 24). Freedom is an innate desire until taken away through disobedience and the traditions of man (see D&C 93:39). A major battle was building to take place at Nephihah (v. 18).

Alma 62:19–26 • Nephihah Taken Without Shedding of Blood

19 Now Moroni was desirous that the Lamanites should come out to battle against them, upon the plains; but the Lamanites, knowing of their exceedingly great courage, and beholding the greatness of their numbers, therefore they durst not come out against them; therefore they did not come to battle in that day.

20 And when the night came, Moroni went forth in the darkness of the night, and came upon the top of the wall to spy out in what part of the city the Lamanites did camp with their army.

21 And it came to pass that they were on the east, by the entrance; and they were all asleep. And now Moroni returned to his army, and caused that they should prepare in haste strong cords and ladders, to be let down from the top of the wall into the inner part of the wall.

22 And it came to pass that Moroni caused that his men should march forth and come upon the top of the wall, and let themselves down into that part of the city, yea, even on the west, where the Lamanites did not camp with their armies.

23 And it came to pass that they were all let down into the city by night, by the means of their strong cords and their ladders; thus when the morning came they were all within the walls of the city.

24 And now, when the Lamanites awoke and saw that the armies of Moroni were within the walls, they were affrighted exceedingly, insomuch that they did flee out by the pass.

25 And now when Moroni saw that they were fleeing before him, he did cause that his men should march forth against them, and slew many, and surrounded many others, and took them prisoners; and the remainder of them fled into the land of Moroni, which was in the borders by the seashore.

26 Thus had Moroni and Pahoran obtained the possession of the city of Nephihah without the loss of one soul; and there were many of the Lamanites who were slain.

Once more Moroni outsmarts the Lamanites, and again he obtains the city without the loss of his soldiers. This was the sixth battle described in these chapters of Alma.

Alma 62:27–32 • The Prisoners Join the People of Ammon

27 Now it came to pass that many of the Lamanites that were prisoners were desirous to join the people of Ammon and become a free people.

28 And it came to pass that as many as were desirous, unto them it was granted according to their desires.

29 Therefore, all the prisoners of the Lamanites did join the people of Ammon, and did begin to labor exceedingly, tilling the ground,

raising all manner of grain, and flocks and herds of every kind; and thus were the Nephites relieved from a great burden; yea, insomuch that they were relieved from all the prisoners of the Lamanites.

30 Now it came to pass that Moroni, after he had obtained possession of the city of Nephihah, having taken many prisoners, which did reduce the armies of the Lamanites exceedingly, and having regained many of the Nephites who had been taken prisoners, which did strengthen the army of Moroni exceedingly; therefore Moroni went forth from the land of Nephihah to the land of Lehi.

31 And it came to pass that when the Lamanites saw that Moroni was coming against them, they were again frightened and fled before the army of Moroni.

32 And it came to pass that Moroni and his army did pursue them from city to city, until they were met by Lehi and Teancum; and the Lamanites fled from Lehi and Teancum, even down upon the borders by the seashore, until they came to the land of Moroni.

Again we see that many of the Lamanite prisoners desired freedom (vv. 27–28). They also became a great benefit to the Nephite economy (v. 29). Moroni continued his conquest of the cities that had been captured by the Lamanites (vv. 30–32).

Alma 62:33–38 • The Final Battle Between Moroni and the Lamanites

33 And the armies of the Lamanites were all gathered together, insomuch that they were all in one body in the land of Moroni. Now Ammoron, the king of the Lamanites, was also with them.

34 And it came to pass that Moroni and Lehi and Teancum did encamp with their armies round about in the borders of the land of Moroni, insomuch that the Lamanites were encircled about in the borders by the wilderness on the south, and in the borders by the wilderness on the east.

35 And thus they did encamp for the night. For behold, the Nephites and the Lamanites also were weary because of the greatness of the march; therefore they did not resolve upon any stratagem in the night-time, save it were Teancum; for he was exceedingly angry with Ammoron, insomuch that he considered that Ammoron, and

Amalickiah his brother, had been the cause of this great and lasting war between them and the Lamanites, which had been the cause of so much war and bloodshed, yea, and so much famine.

36 And it came to pass that Teancum in his anger did go forth into the camp of the Lamanites, and did let himself down over the walls of the city. And he went forth with a cord, from place to place, insomuch that he did find the king; and he did cast a javelin at him, which did pierce him near the heart. But behold, the king did awaken his servants before he died, insomuch that they did pursue Teancum, and slew him.

37 Now it came to pass that when Lehi and Moroni knew that Teancum was dead they were exceedingly sorrowful; for behold, he had been a man who had fought valiantly for his country, yea, a true friend to liberty; and he had suffered very many exceedingly sore afflictions. But behold, he was dead, and had gone the way of all the earth.

38 Now it came to pass that Moroni marched forth on the morrow, and came upon the Lamanites, insomuch that they did slay them with a great slaughter; and they did drive them out of the land; and they did flee, even that they did not return at that time against the Nephites.

It seems ironic that Captain Moroni's final battle was fought over the land of Moroni (v. 34). The city of Moroni was built about ten years earlier (see Alma 50:13). It was probably named after Moroni since the Nephites named their cities after the founders (see Alma 8:7). Amalickiah was an apostate Nephite and had caused the war, as Teancum considered (Alma 62:35, see Alma 46:10). Ammoron was his brother and had carried on the apostate wickedness after Amalickiah's death, as the previous chapters have described (see Alma 52:3). The courage and determination of Teancum to end the life of Ammoron is admirable (v. 36). The short but final tribute to Teancum for having fought valiantly for his country as a true friend to liberty, under the trying circumstances (v. 37), was well deserved. We have but a brief account of the final battle, but it was a decisive victory (v. 38).

Alma 62:39–41 • A Summary
of the War of Many Years

39 And thus ended the thirty and first year of the reign of the judges over the people of Nephi; and thus they had had wars, and bloodsheds, and famine, and affliction, for the space of many years.

40 And there had been murders, and contentions, and dissensions, and all manner of iniquity among the people of Nephi; nevertheless for the righteous' sake, yea, because of the prayers of the righteous, they were spared.

41 But behold, because of the exceedingly great length of the war between the Nephites and the Lamanites many had become hardened, because of the exceedingly great length of the war; and many were softened because of their afflictions, insomuch that they did humble themselves before God, even in the depth of humility.

The war with the Lamanites began in the eighteenth year of the reign of the judges (see Alma 43:3). It ended in the thirty-first year of the same era (Alma 62:39). That is a fourteen-year period. While there were some periods of peace in some areas, there was war to some extent during all of this time.

The war with the Lamanites was basically caused by the wickedness of the apostate Nephites. It was also a war between good and evil (v. 40). The righteous were spared in both the Lamanite war and the war between good and evil because of the prayers of the righteous (v. 40, compare 45:15–16). The Lord had inspired their leaders. The battle of good and evil still continues.

The aftereffects of the war was twofold. Many hearts were hardened and many hearts were softened (v. 41). Again, the same results come from the war of good and evil. We may turn against God and ask why he allows war to happen, and make accusations and rationalizations, as did Ammoron (see Alma 54:15–24), or we can be like the sons of Helaman and turn to God in humility and seek his help. The accounts of the wars are included in the Book of Mormon to teach us these lessons.

Sacred Writing

Preaching Which is Sacred:

Alma 60:1–36	Captain Moroni to Pahoran.
Alma 61:1–21	Pahoran's patriotic reply to Moroni.

Doctrines Learned:

Alma 60:13	The Lord allows the righteous to be slain that his justice and judgment may come upon the wicked.
Alma 60:23	The righteous who are slain (in defense of freedom) enter into the rest of God.
Alma 61:14	Whatever evil you cannot resist with your words ye shall resist with the sword.
Alma 62:40	The prayers of the righteous can save a people.

General Authority Quotes

Elder Boyd K. Packer • Alma 60:11

Recently a college student about to graduate, and under notice from the selective service, came to my office. Confused and worried, he told me of the pressure from fellow students and from faculty members to refuse induction, to leave the country, if necessary. When the issues are so confusing—and they are confusing—what can a man do? How can he know which way to turn?

First, the scriptures are not silent on the subject. These are not new issues; 75 years B.C., the Nephites faced such a challenge. There encircled them an ominous threat to liberty, the home, the family, and their rights of worship. While our present dilemma is not quite like theirs, all too soon the very circumstances they faced could come upon us. We would do well at least to ponder the words of their prophets: "Behold," said Moroni, "could ye suppose that ye could sit upon your thrones, and because of the exceeding goodness of God ye could do nothing and he would deliver you? Behold, if ye have supposed this you have supposed in vain" (Alma 60:11).

These Nephites faced not only the hostility of invading enemies, but also indifference, dissension, and corruption in their own land. But the record confirms that "they were doing that which they felt was the duty which they owed to their God; for the Lord had said unto them and also unto their fathers, that: Inasmuch as ye are not guilty of the first offense, neither the second, ye shall not suffer yourselves to be slain by the hand of your enemies.

"And again, the Lord had said that: ye shall defend your families even unto bloodshed. Therefore for this cause were the Nephites contending with the Lamanites, to defend themselves, and their families, and their lands, their country, and their rights, and their religion" (Alma 43:46–47). [CR, April 1968, 33–34]

The First Presidency • Alma 60:12–13

Do Enter Into the Rest of the Lord Their God: In this terrible war now waging, thousands of our righteous young men in all parts of the world and in many countries are subject to a call into the military service of their own countries. Some of these, so serving, have already been called back to their heavenly home; others will almost surely be called to follow. But 'behold,' as Moroni said, 'the righteous of them who serve and are slain do enter into the rest of the Lord their God,' and of them the Lord has said "those that die in me shall not taste of death, for it shall be sweet unto them." (D&C 42:46.) Their salvation and exaltation in the world to come will be secure. That in their work of destruction they will be striking at their brethren will not be held against them. That sin, as Moroni of old said, is to the condemnation of those who 'sit in their places of power in a state of thoughtless stupor,' those rulers in the world who in a frenzy of hate and lust for unrighteous power and dominion over their fellow men, have put into motion eternal forces they do not comprehend and cannot control. God, in His own due time, will pass sentence upon them. [CR, April 1942, 95–96]

President Harold B. Lee • Alma 60:12–13

The sin, as Moroni of old said, is upon those who sit in their places of power and "in a state of thoughtless stupor" (Alma 60:7), in a frenzy of hate, who lust for unrighteous power and dominion over their fellowmen, and who have put into motion eternal forces that they do not comprehend or cannot control. God in His own due time will pass sentence upon such leaders.

Therefore, let us endeavor to banish all bitterness from our hearts and to rest judgment with God, as did the Apostle Paul when he wrote, "Vengeance is mine; I will repay, saith the Lord" (Romans 12:19). [*The Teachings of Harold B. Lee,* 359]

President Ezra Taft Benson • Alma 60:23

As we cleanse the inner vessel, there will have to be changes made in our own personal lives, in our families, and in the Church (see Alma 60:23). The proud do not change to improve, but defend their position by rationalizing. Repentance means change, and it takes a humble person to change. But we can do it. [*The Teachings of Ezra Taft Benson,* 72]

Challenges To Eternal Life:

1. Evaluate your life situations and determine the means the Lord has provided for you to deliver yourself from evil and make a commitment to use those means (Alma 60:21).
2. Make sure that you resist evil with your words and the broad swords of the Spirit (Alma 61:14).
3. Call on the Lord in the depths of humility to help you recognize and resist evil (Alma 62:41).
4. Choose a challenge of your own from this reading and apply it to your life.

Chapter Six

The Polynesians

Alma 62:42–63:17

*H*istorical Setting: Alma 62:42–52 is a brief synopsis of the thirty-second through the thirty-fifth years of the reign of the judges, a period of four years. These eleven verses are less than one page of the Book of Mormon. Alma 63 is a brief synopsis of the next four years, the thirty-sixth through the thirty-ninth year of the reign of the judges. The first five years describes the people and conditions in the land of Zarahemla. Shiblon, the son of Helaman became the record keeper. The next two years speaks mainly of a group of people who migrated to the land northward where one of the men had built a ship and sailed northward. The ship returned and other ships were built. Many more people sailed northward and were never heard of again. The last year, the thirty-ninth, basically tells of the sacred records being turned over to Helaman, the son of Helaman.

Precepts of this Reading:

There are no stated precepts in these two chapters, but Alma 62:48–51 describe the prosperity of the land of Zarahemla as the Nephites kept the commandments. This condition is a major theme running throughout the Book of Mormon after Nephi was promised by the Lord: "And inasmuch as ye shall keep my commandments, ye shall prosper, and shall be led to a land of promise" (1 Nephi 2:20).

Another special interest of this reading is the account of Hagoth building ships and sailing away. The belief that his people were the origin of the Polynesians in the islands of the Pacific will be treated herein. An outline of the reading follows as a preparation for a deeper study.

OUTLINE • ALMA 62:42–63:17

➤ 62:42–52   Moroni returned to Zarahemla and Helaman returned to the place of his inheritance, and peace was established once more among the Nephites

        a.   Moroni yielded up the command of his armies to his son Moronihah (vv. 43–44).

            1.   He retired to his own house to spend the remainder of his days in peace.

            2.   Pahoran returned to his judgment seat.

        b.   Helaman again preached the word of God unto the people (vv. 44–46).

            1.   Because of wars and contentions, a regulation was needed again in the church.

            2.   He and his brethren preached with much power, which convinced many of their wickedness, and they repented and were baptized.

            3.   The church was established again throughout the land.

        c.   Regulations were made in the law, and judges and chief judges were chosen (v. 47).

        d.   The people of Nephi again prospered, multiplied, waxed strong, and grew rich (vv. 48–51).

            1.   They were not lifted up in pride.

            2.   They were not slow to remember God.

            3.   They humbled themselves before God.

            4.   They remembered the Lord had delivered them from death, bonds, prisons, afflictions, and out of the hands of their enemies.

5. They prayed continually and the Lord did bless them according to his word.

    e. Helaman died in the thirty-fifth year of the judges (v. 42).

➢ 63:1–3   In the thirty-sixth year Shiblon took possession of the sacred things delivered unto Helaman by Alma.

    a. Shiblon was a just man, walking uprightly before God, doing good continually and keeping the commandments of God, as also did his brother (v. 2).

    b. Moroni died also and the thirty-sixth year ended (v. 3).

➢ 63:4–9   In the thirty-seventh year, five thousand and four hundred men with their wives and children departed from Zarahemla into the land northward.

    a. Hagoth, a curious man, built a large ship on the borders of Bountiful, by the land Desolation, and launched into the west sea, by the narrow neck that led into the north (vv. 5–6).

        1. Many men, woman, and children, with much provisions, sailed northward.

        2. The thirty-seventh year ended.

    b. In the thirty-eighth year, Hagoth built other ships (vv. 7–9).

        1. The first ship returned.

        2. Many more people entered into the ship, and with much provisions sailed northward.

        3. They were never heard of more and it was supposed they drowned in the sea.

        4. One other ship did sail forth and no one knows where it went.

        5. In this year many people went into the land northward.

➢ 63:10–17   In the thirty-ninth year, Shiblon died and Corianton sailed north to carry provisions to those who had previously left.

  a. Before his death, Shiblon conferred the sacred things upon Helaman, son of Helaman (vv. 11–13).

    1. The engravings in the possession of Helaman were written and sent forth to all the land save those parts Alma had commanded they not go forth.

    2. These things were kept sacred and were to be handed down from generation to generation.

  b. There were some dissenters who went to the Lamanites and stirred them up to anger against the Nephites (vv. 14–16).

    1. They came down with a numerous army against the army of Moronihah and were beaten and driven back to their own lands, suffering much loss.

    2. The thirty-ninth year ended.

  c. The account of Alma, and Helaman his son, and also Shiblon his son ended (v. 17).

NOTES AND COMMENTARY

Introduction: When and where did the belief that the Polynesian people are the descendents of Hagoth originate? These questions will be answered in this chapter, but first we will discuss the end of the record of Helaman son of Alma.

Alma 62:42–47 • Peace Established Among the People of Nephi

42 And it came to pass that after Moroni had fortified those parts of the land which were most exposed to the Lamanites, until they were sufficiently strong, he returned to the city of Zarahemla; and also Helaman returned to the place of his inheritance; and there was once more peace established among the people of Nephi.

43 And Moroni yielded up the command of his armies into the hands of his son, whose name was Moronihah; and he retired to his own house that he might spend the remainder of his days in peace.

44 And Pahoran did return to his judgment-seat; and Helaman did take upon him again to preach unto the people the word of God; for

because of so many wars and contentions it had become expedient that a regulation should be made again in the church.

45 Therefore, Helaman and his brethren went forth, and did declare the word of God with much power unto the convincing of many people of their wickedness, which did cause them to repent of their sins and to be baptized unto the Lord their God.

46 And it came to pass that they did establish again the church of God, throughout all the land.

47 Yea, and regulations were made concerning the law. And their judges, and their chief judges were chosen.

All but Moroni returned to their former positions among the Nephites. Moroni's retirement (v. 43) indicates he was older, although he may have retired because he was suffering from war injuries. His being replaced by his son Moronihah also indicates he was older. The Lamanite war lasted fourteen years. If Alma was only twenty-four years old when the war began (see Alma 43:17 and commentary), it does not seem possible that his son would have been old enough to have succeeded his father as the commander of all the Nephite armies (Alma 62:43). Again we conclude that Moroni's appointment to head the army at age twenty-five had occurred some years before the fourteen-year war with the Lamanites began.

A regulation "made again in the church" (v. 44) seems to refer to bringing a uniformity of beliefs and practices. Perhaps the stress of the war had led to a modification of principles and ordinances or even a neglect of them. Helaman first preached to the people to align them with correct principles, and then baptized them to bring them to a covenant with God (v. 45). Helaman had done the same thing in the nineteenth year of the judges after the first year of the Lamanite war (see Alma 45:20–21). Thus the church was established again throughout the land in both cases (v. 46; 45:22). A similar action was taken in the political arena of the Nephites (Alma 62:47).

Alma 62:48–52 • The People
Begin to Prosper Again

48 And the people of Nephi began to prosper again in the land, and began to multiply and to wax exceedingly strong again in the land. And they began to grow exceedingly rich.

49 But notwithstanding their riches, or their strength, or their prosperity, they were not lifted up in the pride of their eyes; neither were they slow to remember the Lord their God; but they did humble themselves exceedingly before him.

50 Yea, they did remember how great things the Lord had done for them, that he had delivered them from death, and from bonds, and from prisons, and from all manner of afflictions and he had delivered them out of the hands of their enemies.

51 And they did pray unto the Lord their God continually, insomuch that the Lord did bless them, according to his word, so that they did wax strong and prosper in the land.

52 And it came to pass that all these things were done. And Helaman died, in the thirty and fifth year of the reign of the judges over the people of Nephi.

There were three areas for measurement of prosperity listed by Mormon, as he abridged the record. The first was the family, they "began to multiply" (v. 48). The second was "to wax exceedingly strong" (v. 48). The meaning of wax as used herein is to increase or grow, thus indicating the Nephites were building their cities and communication. To be strong implies unity. Therefore they were united politically and socially. The third measurement of prosperity was becoming "rich." To become rich (v. 48), is to prosper in material goods. They also resisted the Nephite tendency to let their material goods lead them to pride (v. 49; see also Jacob 2:13; Alma 4:6). Their spiritual lives also were in a growth mode. They recognized the hands of the Lord in their prosperity as the Lord desired them to do (vv. 49–50; cp. D&C 59:21). Their prayers to God were apparently prayers of thanks, as well as asking for his direction (Alma 62:51).

Helaman's (son of Alma) reign ended in peace and happiness after many years of suffering and affliction. Great was his contribution to the progress of the Nephites at this time and throughout his life.

Alma 63:1–3 • Shiblon Takes the Sacred Records

> 1 And it came to pass in the commencement of the thirty and sixth year of the reign of the judges over the people of Nephi, that Shiblon took possession of those sacred things which had been delivered unto Helaman by Alma.
>
> 2 And he was a just man, and he did walk uprightly before God; and he did observe to do good continually, to keep the commandments of the Lord his God; and also did his brother.
>
> 3 And it came to pass that Moroni died also. And thus ended the thirty and sixth year of the reign of the judges.

Again, little is said of Shiblon. Alma's blessing to him was short (Alma 38) when compared to the one given to Helaman (Alma 36–37), but his reward was apparently the same as was Helaman's. He was a good man (Alma 63:2). The brother indicated here (v. 2) seems to be Corianton. If it does refer to Corianton, it is evident he had repented. However, that brother may have been a reference to Helaman.

Moroni's death, five years after the war ended (v. 3), may have been from war afflictions or from age as discussed before. He would have been only forty-four years of age if appointed chief captain at age twenty-five (see comments under Alma 62:43). Again we opt for an older age.

Alma 63:4–6 • Hagoth an Exceedingly Curious Man – 37th Year

> 4 And it came to pass that in the thirty and seventh year of the reign of the judges, there was a large company of men, even to the amount of five thousand and four hundred men, with their wives and their children, departed out of the land of Zarahemla into the land which was northward.

5 And it came to pass that Hagoth, he being an exceedingly curious man, therefore he went forth and built him an exceedingly large ship, on the borders of the land Bountiful, by the land Desolation, and launched it forth into the west sea, by the narrow neck which led into the land northward.

6 And behold, there were many of the Nephites who did enter therein and did sail forth with much provisions, and also many women and children; and they took their course northward. And thus ended the thirty and seventh year.

The land northward is not given a name. How the first large group traveled (v. 4) is not given. We assume it was by land since the ship is mentioned in verse five and seems to be mentioned as a unique way of travel. Also, Hagoth seems to be labeled as "exceedingly curious" because he built "an exceedingly large ship." The "narrow neck of land which led into the land northward" (v. 5; see also Alma 22:32), implies there may have been a second narrow neck of land.

Alma 63:7–9 Other Ships Built and People Migrate Northward – 38th Year

7 And in the thirty and eighth year, this man built other ships. And the first ship did also return, and many more people did enter into it; and they also took much provisions, and set out again to the land northward.

8 And it came to pass that they were never heard of more. And we suppose that they were drowned in the depths of the sea. And it came to pass that one other ship also did sail forth; and whither she did go we know not.

9 And it came to pass that in this year there were many people who went forth into the land northward. And thus ended the thirty and eighth year.

The total number of people who sailed away (vv. 6–7) must have been large. The text indicates there were others who went northward by other means of travel (v. 9). We must wait for the fuller record to be revealed (see 3 Nephi 26:6–11) from which we may learn more of those people.

Those who were never heard of again (v. 8) are believed to be the people in the islands of the sea known today as Polynesians. There is no evidence of this belief in the Book of Mormon, but it comes from statements of General Authorities of the Church and patriarchal blessings given to members of the Church in those islands. The First Presidency has never made an official statement concerning the Polynesian ancestry. However, there have been many statements made at various times.

At the dedication of the Hawaiian temple by President Heber J. Grant, on November 27, 1919, he said:

> "We thank Thee, that thousands and tens of thousands of the descendants of Lehi, in this favored land, have come to a knowledge of the gospel, many of whom have endured faithfully to the end of their lives. We thank Thee, our Father and our God, that those who are living and who have embraced the gospel are now to have the privilege of entering into this holy house, and laboring for the salvation of the souls of their ancestors."[1]

Dedicatory prayers of temples are considered to be revelatory (see section heading D&C 109). The above prayer does not identify these descendents of Lehi as Hagoth's people, but other statements of General Authorities and patriarchal blessings do identify them as such (see General Authority Quotes in the end of this chapter).

Dr. Paul R. Cheesman, and his wife Millie, my colleague and good friends, spent many years of research regarding the Polynesian peoples. He gave his purpose in their research: Paul is now deceased.

> "The purpose of this chapter has been to bring together collected research, to analyze some of the theories concerning the origin of the Polynesian Islands, with special emphasis on the theory given in the Book of Mormon, namely, an American origin.

[1] *Improvement Era*, vol. 23, No. 4, February, 1920 as published in *Temples of the Most High*. N. B. Lundwal, 154, 158.

In the past, some scientists have rejected an American-Polynesian connection, while others have deliberately avoided exploring the possibility of such a connection. Today, however, there are many leading scientists and ethnologists who concur as to a Polynesian-American relationship. This change has very likely resulted because of more recent archeological findings and more exact scientific methods being available in ethnology, particularly that of blood grouping. We do not claim that all Polynesian people originated from the American Indian. Their culture is cosmopolitan, and we accept the diffusion theory not looking to one independent origin. However, more emphasis can now be placed upon the American origin theory which has been rejected in the past."[2]

Dr. Cheesman quoted several scholars of today, who are not members of The Church of Jesus Christ of Latter-day Saints, to show the American-Polynesian connection. We will quote just three of them.

"There are innumerable traits in aboriginal American cultures whose parallelism with Oceanic and Asiatic traits is very difficult to explain, except on the grounds of common origin and transference. At the same time there are in Polynesia many traits apparently related to American rather than to western Oceanic or Asiatic culture. In consideration of these facts, as a Pacific ethnologist with an admitted Polynesian bias, I have no hesitation in saying that for me the balance of evidence favours the likelihood of transference of cultural traits from Polynesia to America and vice versa."[3]

"Thor Heyerdahl's vivid adventure narrative, the best seller, *Kon Tiki*, proved that ancient Peruvians could have crossed the Pacific east to west in their pre-historic balsa rafts, a feat once thought to be well nigh impossible. Heyerdahl believes not only that they did this, but that Polynesian population and culture were thus derived from South America, carried about A.D. 500 by the legendary Peruvian culture-hero, the blond god Viracocha and his fellow migrants. Six hundred

---

[2] Paul R. Cheesman and Millie F. Cheesman, *Early America and the Polynesians* [Provo, Utah: Promised Land Publications, 1975], 21.

[3] E.S.C. Handy, *Marqueson Legends,* B. P. Bishop mus. Bull, 69, Honolulu Hawaii, 1930, p. 104, as quoted in Paul R. Cheesman and Millie F. Cheesman, *Early America and the Polynesians* [Provo, Utah: Promised Land Publications, 1975], 10.

years later, according to Heyerdahl, "Caucasian-like" but also slightly Mongoloid Kwakiutl Indians from the North American northwest coast invaded Hawaii, merged with the Peruvian migrants, and formed the present Oceanic or Maori-Polynesian race and culture in these islands. He bases this on the resemblance between the pre-Incaic name for Viracocha, said to be "Con-Tici" or "illa Tici," and the Polynesian god "Tiki"; on what he fancies to be similar art styles in Polynesia and ancient Peru; on early accounts of light-skinned natives on Easter Island, and of fair, bearded, culture heroes in Peru, with fair, bearded, or aquiline-nosed people depicted in South and Central American pre-historic art (whom the Lost Tribes of Israel theorists consider to be Israelites); on the distribution of the sweet potato and the gourd, domesticated on both sides of the Pacific before the European discovery; and on the similarity of art styles between Northwest Coast aboriginal America and Polynesia."[4]

"His [Heyerdahl's] theory is founded on evidence more substantial than legend, for here on certain Pacific islands and atolls where Kon-Tiki is still revered are other appurtenances of his culture: pyramids, for example; also panpipes and helmets; and proof that irrigation, trepanning, and head deformation were practiced. Also these same Pacific islanders knew that the earth was round. 'Whence,' asks Heyerdahl, 'had the Polynesians obtained their vast astronomical knowledge and their calendar, which was calculated with astonishing thoroughness? Certainly not from Melanesian or Malayan peoples to the westward.

But the same old vanished race, the "white and bearded men," who had taught Aztecs, Mayas, and Incas their amazing culture in America, had evolved a curiously similar calendar and a similar astronomical knowledge which Europe in those times could not match'."[5]

Certainly there is much evidence of a connection between some of the Polynesians and the Book of Mormon peoples. Hagoth is the

---

[4] Paul R. Cheesman and Millie F. Cheesman, *Early America and the Polynesians* [Provo, Utah: Promised Land Publications, 1975], 12–13.

[5] Constance Irwin, *Fair Gods and Stone Faces* [New York: St. Martin's Press, 1963], 310–11, as quoted in Paul R. Cheesman and Millie F. Cheesman, *Early America and the Polynesians* [Provo, Utah: Promised Land Publications, 1975], 13.

only Book of Mormon reference to which the evidence may be connected.

Alma 63:9–17 • The Records Transferred to Helaman Son of Helaman – 39th Year

9 And it came to pass that in this year there were many people who went forth into the land northward. And thus ended the thirty and eighth year.

10 And it came to pass in the thirty and ninth year of the reign of the judges, Shiblon died also, and Corianton had gone forth to the land northward in a ship, to carry forth provisions unto the people who had gone forth into that land.

11 Therefore it became expedient for Shiblon to confer those sacred things, before his death, upon the son of Helaman, who was called Helaman, being called after the name of his father.

12 Now behold, all those engravings which were in the possession of Helaman were written and sent forth among the children of men throughout all the land, save it were those parts which had been commanded by Alma should not go forth.

13 Nevertheless, these things were to be kept sacred, and handed down from one generation to another; therefore, in this year, they had been conferred upon Helaman, before the death of Shiblon.

14 And it came to pass also in this year that there were some dissenters who had gone forth unto the Lamanites; and they were stirred up again to anger against the Nephites.

15 And also in this same year they came down with a numerous army to war against the people of Moronihah, or against the army of Moronihah, in the which they were beaten and driven back again to their own lands, suffering great loss.

16 And thus ended the thirty and ninth year of the reign of the judges over the people of Nephi.

17 And thus ended the account of Alma, and Helaman his son, and also Shiblon, who was his son.

The record of Helaman, son of Alma, is ended and Helaman's son, Helaman continues the record. Thus Alma chapters forty-five through sixty-two, eighteen chapters, are an abridgement of the record of Helaman, son of Alma, but included in the book of Alma (see superscription of Alma 45). The sixty-third chapter was abridged from the record of Helaman, but was written by Shiblon, the brother of Helaman (v. 17, see also v.1). Alma sixty-three covers just four years of the Nephite account, the thirty-fifth through the thirty-ninth, the years lived by Shiblon after Helaman died.

That the Nephite people had the opportunity to read some of the records has not been mentioned before (Alma 63:12), although it has been assumed. There were some records that were not made accessible (vv. 12–13).

All of the historical facts mentioned in the above verses are general and need no further commentary.

Sacred Writing

General Authority Quotes

Elder Mark E. Petersen • Alma 63:5–8

As Latter-day Saints we have always believed that the Polynesians are descendants of Lehi and blood relatives of the American Indians, despite the contrary theories of other men. For that reason, from the beginning of our Church history we have had more than an ordinary interest in them as a people. But now that interest is even more keen. Recent research on the part of world-recognized scientists and scholars has focused a new light upon them, and writings of early explorers in both America and Polynesia have become available now for detailed study.

The new knowledge which has been developed shows that the Polynesians without any reasonable doubt did come from America, that they are closely related to the American Indian in many respects, and that even their traditions and genealogies bear that out.

. . . Pronounced as are these views establishing the relationship of Polynesian and American Indians, there are equally impressive data now available to disprove the theory that the Polynesians originated in the Orient and came eastward from Indonesia, Maxaya, and nearby lands. Let us just mention a few of the convincing points of evidence.

Most of you have seen the great stone pyramids, or photographs of them, discovered by archaeologists in Mexico, Central, and South America. Pyramids of almost identical structure, both in plan and material, if not in size, have been found in Polynesia. I saw some of them myself within the last month.

Stone roadways, so characteristic of the pre-Inca period of America, are found to be duplicated in some of the Pacific Islands. Giant stone statues such as are found in the lands of South America and among the Incas are now discovered in the Polynesian Islands, with characteristics and markings so similar that few can doubt their common origin. This includes many of the structures found on Easter Island.

The sweet potato of the Pacific Islands, known in Polynesia as the *kumara* or *kamalla*, as it is called in Tonga, is now found by botanists to be the identical plant which is native to South America with impressive evidence as to the manner in which it was transported from Peru to the Pacific Islands.

Cotton, coconuts, pineapples, and papaya are likewise being traced from Polynesia to America by botanists who now announce that the Polynesian varieties of these plants are but offshoots of the parent plants in America.

The ocean currents have been observed in our time to carry drifting objects to Polynesia from two places in America, one being the Pacific Northwest and the other the Central and South American region. Large Pacific Northwest pine logs have been traced in the drifting currents of the Pacific Ocean from the Vancouver area of North America to the Hawaiian, Marshall, and Caroline Islands. Hawaiians and other Polynesians have made canoes from these drifted pine logs and in them have traveled from island to island. There are no such trees growing in Polynesia. They came by ocean currents from the Pacific Northwest of America.

This is the more notable when it is observed that customs and household articles characteristic of the Indians of the Pacific Northwest of America have been found on a wide scale in Polynesia. [CR, April 1962]

Elder Spencer W. Kimball • Alma 63:5–8

And They Were Never Heard of More: I hope I may help to make the whole world weep for the children of Lehi. Can one refrain from tears as he contemplates the fall of these people who have been brought down from culture and achievement to illiteracy and degradation; from kings and emperors, to slavery and serfdom; from landowners of vast continents, to indigent wards of governments and peons—from sons of God with knowledge of God, to rude savages, victims of superstition, and from builders of temples to dwellers in dirt hogans.

The predictions concerning the scattering of the early American was fulfilled to the letter. Not long before the birth of Christ, a great man by the name of Hagoth left continental America with colonies of people. He . . . went forth and built him an exceedingly large ship . . .and launched it forth into the west sea, . . .

And behold, there were many of the Nephites who did . . . sail forth with much provisions, and also many women and children; and they took their course northward. . . .

And the next year:

. . . this man built other ships. And the first ship did also return, and many more people did enter into it; . . . and set out again to the land northward.

And it came to pass that they were never heard of more. . . . And . . . one other ship also did sail forth. . . . (Alma 63:5–8).

It has been thought by many people that they went to the Pacifica Islands. And the scripture would so indicate:

But great are the promises of the lord unto them who are upon the isles of the sea; wherefore as it says isles, there must needs be more than this, and they are inhabited also by our brethren (2 Nephi 10:21).

Elder Cowley and I visited some of these peoples on the "isles of the sea" and found them developing and progressing and doing well. [CR, April 1947, 145–146]

Elder Matthew Cowley • Alma 63:5–8

This Man Built Other Ships: . . . You know, in the 63rd chapter of Alma, there is a little story which tells of Hagoth who was such an exceedingly curious man that he built a boat, and he went out on the seas, and he came back. He built other boats, and then finally the boats went forth and never returned. We are told in The Book of Mormon the place where those ships were built was near a narrow neck of land.

When I was on my first mission as a young boy, I used to ask the old-timers out there, "Where did you come from?" They would say (in Maori), "We cam from the place where the sweet potato grows wild, where it is not planted, does not have to be cultivated."

There is only one place in all the world where the sweet potato grows wild, and that is within the environs of that narrow neck of land where Hagoth built his ships. They will tell you that they came from several degrees of distance (Maori). On degree of distance, a greater degree of distance, and then a far greater degree of distance.

The Maori scholars tell you that . . . (spoken in Maori) means the place where the spirits are joined. But I have a little different interpretation of that. *Wairua* in the Maori language means "spirit." *Wairua* also means "two waters," *wai* meaning water, *rua* meaning two.

In the Hawaiian language *Wailua* means "two waters"; in the Samoan language *Vailua* means "two waters." The word for spirit in those other languages isn't *Wairua*, the same as in the Maori language.

The Maori scholars say that they came from a far distant place, where the spirits are joined, or where the body returns to the spirit. But I say, knowing the story of Hagoth as I do, that they came from the joining of two waters, a narrow neck of land between two bodies of water which joins those two great continents. [*Matthew Cowley—Speaks*, 114–115]

President Howard W. Hunter

We know that the Lord inspired a valiant group of his children to leave America to travel to Tahiti and from there populate other areas, including this beautiful land [New Zealand]. . . . They followed true principles, had faith in themselves and trusted completely in the Lord. They were successful in what was an extraordinarily difficult mission. Many here today are the benefactors of their courage and conviction, their determination and obedience.

It has been the position of the Church that Polynesians are related to the American Indians as descendants of Father Lehi, having migrated to the Pacific from America. Elder Mark E. Petersen, speaking on this subject in General Conference, said:

"As Latter-day Saints we have always believed that the Polynesians are descendants of Lehi and blood relatives of the American Indians, despite the contrary theories of other men" (in Conference Report, April 1962, 112).

Our belief in this regard is scriptural (see Alma 63:4–10). [*The Teachings of Howard W. Hunter*, 57]

Challenges to Eternal Life:

1. As you prosper in your various phases of life, remember to recognize and thank the Lord for your blessings (Alma 62:49).

2. Endeavor to walk uprightly before God, observe to do good continually, and to keep his commandments (Alma 63:2).

3. Choose a challenge of your own from this reading and apply it to your life.

Chapter Seven

Lessons from History

Helaman 1–3

*H*istorical Setting: The Book of Helaman covers fifty-one years of history, beginning with the fortieth year through the ninetieth year of the reign of the judges (52 B.C. through 1 B.C.). Helaman chapters 1–3 covers the first fourteen years (52 B.C. through 39 B.C.). Alma's two sons: Helaman and Shiblon, both of whom kept the sacred records (see Alma 63:11), have died and the records are turned over to Helaman, son of Helaman, who was commissioned to add to the records that had been kept (see Alma 63:11). The records kept by Alma's two sons were called the record of Helaman (Alma 45–63). The record that Helaman, son of Helaman, kept was called the book of Helaman.

The setting is in the land of Zarahemla, but there are again wars between the Lamanites whose central location is the land of Nephi. The Nephites also continue some migrations to the land northward, which had begun in the thirty-seventh year and thirty-eighth year of the reign of the judges.

Precepts of this Reading:

> And behold, in the end of this book ye shall see that this Gadianton did prove the overthrow, yea, almost the entire destruction of the people of Nephi. [Helaman 2:13]

Thus we may see that the Lord is merciful unto all who will, in the sincerity of their hearts, call upon his holy name. [Helaman 3:27]

Yea, thus we see that the gate of heaven is open unto all, even to those who will believe on the name of Jesus Christ, who is the Son of God. [Helaman 3:28]

29 Yea, we see that whosoever will may lay hold upon the word of God, which is quick and powerful, which shall divide asunder all the cunning and the snares and the wiles of the devil, and lead the man of Christ in a strait and narrow course across that everlasting gulf of misery which is prepared to engulf the wicked—

30 And land their souls, yea, their immortal souls, at the right hand of God in the kingdom of heaven, to sit down with Abraham, and Isaac, and with Jacob, and with all our holy fathers, to go no more out. [Helaman 3:29–30]

Nevertheless they did fast and pray oft, and did wax stronger and stronger in their humility, and firmer and firmer in the faith of Christ, unto the filling their souls with joy and consolation, yea, even to the purifying and the sanctification of their hearts, which sanctification cometh because of their yielding their hearts unto God. [Helaman 3:35]

These fourteen years, beginning fifty-one years before the birth of Christ, had many of the same challenges that we have faced and will continue to face in a similar time period before the Second Coming of Christ. We must liken these words unto ourselves for our profit and learning even as Nephi admonished us to liken the words of Isaiah unto his people (see 1 Nephi 19:23). An outline of these three chapters of Helaman follows, as a preparation for a more thorough study.

OUTLINE • HELAMAN 1–3

Superscription: the wars, contentions and dissensions of the Nephites, and the prophecies of many holy prophets, before the coming of Christ, according to the record of Helaman, son of Helaman, and the records of his sons.

a. An account of the Lamanite conversions, their righteousness, and the wickedness and abominations of the Nephites.

      b. It is called the book of Helaman.

➤ 1:1–13   A serious difficulty began among the Nephites in the fortieth year of the judges.

      a. Pahoran had died and there was a serious contention concerning who among his sons should have the judgment-seat (vv. 2–4).

          1. Those who contended for the judgment-seat were Pahoran, Paanchi, and Pacumeni.

          2. These were not all of his sons, but these three caused the divisions among the people.

      b. Pahoran was appointed by the voice of the people to be the chief judge and governor (vv. 5–8).

          1. Pacumeni united with the voice of the people.

          2. Paanchi and his followers were wroth, and he was about to flatter his people to rebellion.

          3. He was taken and tried by the people and condemned to death for seeking to destroy the liberty of the people.

      c. Kishkumen went to the judgment-seat and murdered Pahoran (vv. 9–12).

          1. He was pursued by Pahoran's servants but they did not overtake him.

          2. He and his group entered into a covenant, swearing by their everlasting maker to tell no man.

          3. Kishkumen was disguised at the time he murdered Pahoran.

          4. His group mingled among the people but could not be disclosed.

          5. As many as were found were put to death.

      d. Pacumeni was appointed chief judge and governor to succeed his brother by the voice of the people (v. 13).

➤ 1:14–21   In the forty-first year, the Lamanites armed themselves and
            came down to battle the Nephites.

            a.   The Lamanites were led by Coriantumr, a descendant
                 of Zarahemla, a large and mighty Nephite dissenter (vv.
                 15–17).

                 1.   Tubaloth, son of Ammoron, King of the Lamanites
                      sent him because of his strength and wisdom.

                 2.   He stirred up his people to anger, and caused them
                      to march to Zarahemla to battle.

            b.   Because of contention and difficulty in the government,
                 the Nephites had not kept sufficient guards in the land
                 (vv. 18–19).

                 1.   They did not suppose the Lamanites dared attack
                      Zarahemla, the heart of their lands.

                 2.   Coriantumr came with such speed that the Nephites
                      had no time to gather their armies.

            c.   Coriantumr marched his whole army into the city,
                 slaying everyone who opposed them, and took posses-
                 sion of the city (vv. 20–21).

                 1.   Pacumeni, the chief judge fled to the walls of the
                      city.

                 2.   Coriantumr smote him against the wall and he died.

➤ 1:22–34   Coriantumr took courage from his success, and went forth
            against all the land.

            a,   Coriantumr marched a large army toward Bountiful
                 seeking to obtain the north parts of the land (vv. 23–27).

                 1.   They went to the center of the land supposing it was
                      their greatest strength.

                 2.   The Nephites could not assemble except in small
                      groups.

                 3.   The Nephite strong armies were guarding the
                      borders of the land, and thus Moronihah had an
                      advantage.

4.   The Lamanites were slaying men, women, and children, as they went conquering cities along the way.

      b.   Moroni sent Lehi with an army to meet them before they reached Bountiful (vv. 28–32).

            1.   Lehi headed them off and they began to retreat to Zarahemla.

            2.   Moronihah met them in retreat and many were slain, including Coriantumr.

            3.   The Lamanites were completely surrounded by the Nephites.

            4.   Coriantumr had plunged the Lamanites into the midst of the Nephites, and they yielded themselves as prisoners.

      c.   Moronihah took possession of Zarahemla again and the Lamanite prisoners were sent out of the land in peace as the forty-first year ended (vv. 33–34).

➤ 2:1–11   In the forty-second year, there was no one to fill the judgment-seat, and there was contention again over who should be elected.

      a.   Helaman, son of Helaman was appointed by the voice of the people to fill the judgment-seat (vv. 2–3).

            1.   Kishkumen, who had murdered Pahoran, lay in wait to destroy Hela man and was supported by his band.

            2.   The secret band had entered into a covenant that no one should know Kishkumen's wickedness.

      b.   Gadianton was exceedingly expert in many words, and also in his craft, to carry on the secret work of murder and robbery (vv. 4–5).

            1.   He became the leader of the band of Kishkumen.

            2.   He flattered them and Kishkumen, to place him in the judgment-seat, and he would place them in power and authority among the people.

            3.   Therefore, Kishkumen sought to destroy Helaman.

    c. Kishkumen went to the judgment-seat to kill Helaman (vv. 6–9).

        1. A servant of Helaman, having learned of Kishkumen's plans through disguise, met him and gave him a sign.

        2. Kishkumen made his object known and asked the servant to conduct him to the judgment-seat.

        3. The servant, knowing Kishkumen's evil plans, agreed to take him.

        4. The servant stabbed Kishkumen that he fell dead, and the servant ran and told Helaman all he had seen, heard, and done.

    d. Helaman sent to take the band of robbers and secret murderers that they might be executed according to the law (vv. 10–11).

        1. Gadianton feared Kishkumen had been destroyed, and the band followed him out of the land by a secret way.

        2. Helaman could not find them.

➤ 2:12–14 As the forty-second year ended, Mormon added that more shall be spoken of Gadianton hereafter.

    a. In the end of this book, Gadianton proved the overthrow, almost the entire destruction of the people of Nephi (v. 13).

    b. Not the end of the book of Helaman, but the end of the book of Nephi from which he had abridged the record (v. 14).

➤ 3:1–12 In the forty-third year through the forty-fifth year, there was no contention among the people of Nephi.

    a. In the forty-sixth year there was much contention and many dissensions among the people (vv. 3–6).

        1. A great many departed Zarahemla and went to inherit the land northward.

2. They traveled an exceedingly great distance to large bodies of water and many rivers.

    3. They spread forth into all parts that had not been rendered desolate by the many previous inhabitants.

    4. The land was called desolate only because of there being little or no timber.

  b. The people became expert in the working of cement, and built and dwelt in houses of cement (vv. 7–12).

    1. They multiplied and spread from the land southward to the land northward.

    2. They began to cover the face of the whole earth, from the sea south to the sea north, from the sea west to the sea east.

    3. In the northland they dwelt in tents and cement houses, and preserved whatever trees that grew for building later.

    4. There was much timber sent to them by shipping, and they build many cities of wood and cement.

    5. Many people of Ammon (Lamanites by birth) went to this land (v. 12).

3:13–16 There were many records kept by many people, which were particular and very large.

  a. A hundredth part of their proceedings—their wars, preaching and prophecies; and their building of ships, temples, synagogues, sanctuaries and their righteousness and wickedness—could not be contained in this work (v. 14).

  b. There were many books and records kept chiefly by the Nephites (v. 15).

  c. The records were handed down from generation to generation by the Nephites until they fell into transgression and mixed with the Lamanites and were no more Nephites (v. 16).

3:17–22 The forty-sixth year passed and there was great contention in the forty-seventh and forty-eighth years.

     a.   Helaman did fill the judgment-seat with justice and equity (v. 20).

         1.   He observed the statues, judgments, and commandments of God.

         2.   He did right in the sight of God continually, walked in the ways of his father, and did prosper in the land.

     b.   He had two sons, the eldest named Nephi and the youngest named Lehi who grew up unto the Lord (v. 21).

     c.   Wars and contentions began to cease in the latter end of the forty-eighth year (v. 22).

➤ 3:23–26   In the forty-ninth year, there was continual peace except for secret combinations that Gadianton had established in the more settled parts of the land, which were not known to the government, and so they were not destroyed out of the land.

     a.   There was great prosperity in the church; thousands joined being baptized unto repentance (v. 24).

     b.   Many blessings were poured out that astonished even the high priests and the teachers (v. 25).

     c.   The work prospered unto baptizing and uniting to the church tens of thousands (v. 26).

➤ 3:27–32   Mormon drew three conclusions, identified by "thus we see."

     a.   The Lord is merciful unto all who call on his holy name in sincerity (v. 27).

     b.   The gate of heaven (baptism) is open to all who believe on Jesus Christ (v. 28).

     c.   Whosoever will lay hold of the word of God, which is quick and powerful, which will cut through the cunning snares and wiles of the devil and lead the man of God in a strait and narrow course across the gulf of misery that engulfs the wicked (vv. 29–10).

         1.   Their immortal souls will arrive at the right had of God in the kingdom of heaven.

2.   They will sit down with Abraham, Isaac, Jacob, and all our holy fathers, to go out no more.

    d.   There was continual rejoicing in all the land possessed by the Nephites in the remainder of the forty-ninth year, and continual peace and great joy in the fiftieth year (vv. 31–32).

➤ 3:33–36   In the fifty-first year there was peace also, except pride began to enter into the hearts of those who professed to belong to the church of God (v. 36).

    a.   The Nephites persecuted many of their brethren, causing the more humble part of the people to suffer persecutions and affliction (v. 34).

    b.   The humble fasted and prayed oft, waxed stronger and stronger in humility, firmer and firmer in the faith of Christ, filling their souls with joy and consolation (v. 35).

       1.   Purifying and sanctifying their hearts.

       2.   Which comes by yielding their hearts to God.

    c.   The fifty-second year ended in peace, except that great pride had got into the hearts of the people because of their riches and prosperity (v. 36).

➤ 3:37   In the fifty-third year, Helaman died and his eldest son Nephi began to reign in his stead.

    a.   He filled the judgment-seat with justice and equity.

    b.   He kept the commandments of God and walked in the way of his father.

NOTES AND COMMENTARY

Introduction: It has been said that those who do not learn from history will have to repeat that history. The problems of these chapters in Helaman have certainly been the problems of the past sixty plus years and will undoubtedly continue until the Second Coming of Christ. The Book of Mormon gives us the solution to these problems. The book of Helaman begins with the problems of contention over government, secret combinations, war, dissensions in the church and pride. As we study these chapters, we are shown how the Nephites met these challenges, and thus shows us how we can meet them, both individually and collectively.

Superscription

An account of the Nephites. Their wars and contentions, and their dissensions. And also the prophecies of many holy prophets, before the coming of Christ, according to the records of Helaman, who was the son of Helaman, and also according to the records of his sons, even down to the coming of Christ. And also many of the Lamanites are converted. An account of their conversion. An account of the righteousness of the Lamanites, and the wickedness and abominations of the Nephites, according to the record of Helaman and his sons, even down to the coming of Christ, which is called the book of Helaman.

The record of Helaman, son of Helaman, covers 29 years (40–68 of the reign of the judges). His record is in the first six chapters of the present editions of the Book of Mormon (1981). The record does not say which of the two sons of Helaman, Nephi or Lehi, kept the record, but they kept it for twenty-two years. Thus the book of Helaman covers fifty-one years. Chapter seven through twelve are labeled "The Prophecy of Nephi, son of Helaman" in another superscription above chapter seven. Chapter thirteen through fifteen are labeled "The prophecy of Samuel, the Lamanite to the Nephites" in the third superscription in the book of Helaman. The conversion of the Lamanites is recorded in Helaman chapter five. The coming of Christ, mentioned twice in the above superscription, is his birth in the eastern hemisphere, not his visit to the Nephites.

Helaman 1:1–8 • Contention
Over Government

1 And now behold, it came to pass in the commencement of the fortieth year of the reign of the judges over the people of Nephi, there began to be a serious difficulty among the people of the Nephites.

2 For behold, Pahoran had died, and gone the way of all the earth; therefore there began to be a serious contention concerning who should have the judgment-seat among the brethren, who were the sons of Pahoran.

3 Now these are their names who did contend for the judgment-seat, who did also cause the people to contend: Pahoran, Paanchi, and Pacumeni.

4 Now these are not all the sons of Pahoran (for he had many), but these are they who did contend for the judgment-seat; therefore, they did cause three divisions among the people.

5 Nevertheless, it came to pass that Pahoran was appointed by the voice of the people to be chief judge and a governor over the people of Nephi.

6 And it came to pass that Pacumeni, when he saw that he could not obtain the judgment-seat, he did unite with the voice of the people.

7 But behold, Paanchi, and that part of the people that were desirous that he should be their governor, was exceedingly wroth; therefore, he was about to flatter away those people to rise up in rebellion against their brethren.

8 And it came to pass as he was about to do this, behold, he was taken, and was tried according to the voice of the people, and condemned unto death; for he had raised up in rebellion and sought to destroy the liberty of the people.

The contentions over the judgment-seat reminds us of the party politics of our own day. Pacumeni is a good example for a government by the voice of the people. Once the people had spoken, he united with the voice of the people giving the newly formed government an opportunity to fulfill their role, as we assume, they had advocated in their campaign. The condemnation of Paanchi unto death is not enlarged upon in the text, but we again make an assumption, it was more than just a disagreement over who was the best qualified to govern. The destruction of liberty is the plan of Lucifer for which he was cast out (see Moses 4:3). "A third part of the hosts of heaven" followed Satan (D&C 29:36–37).

Helaman 1:9–13 • Kishkumen Murdered
Pahoran on the Judgment-Seat

9 Now when those people who were desirous that he should be their governor saw that he was condemned unto death, therefore they were angry, and behold, they sent forth one Kishkumen, even to the judgment-seat of Pahoran, and murdered Pahoran as he sat upon the judgment-seat.

10 And he was pursued by the servants of Pahoran; but behold, so speedy was the flight of Kishkumen that no man could overtake him.

11 And he went unto those that sent him, and they all entered into a covenant, yea, swearing by their everlasting Maker, that they would tell no man that Kishkumen had murdered Pahoran.

12 Therefore, Kishkumen was not known among the people of Nephi, for he was in disguise at the time that he murdered Pahoran. And Kishkumen and his band, who had covenanted with him, did mingle themselves among the people, in a manner that they all could not be found; but as many as were found were condemned unto death.

13 And now behold, Pacumeni was appointed, according to the voice of the people, to be a chief judge and a governor over the people, to reign in the stead of his brother Pahoran; and it was according to his right. And all this was done in the fortieth year of the reign of the judges; and it had an end.

The second problem to emerge at this period of time was the organization of a secret combination. Kishkumen and his band followed Satan as well. Secret combinations originated in the world with Satan's covenant with Cain to slay his brother Abel (see Helaman 6:26–27; Moses 5:29–33; Genesis 4:8–15). For the Nephite conspirators to swear "by their everlasting Maker" (Helaman 1:11) was not only ironic but blasphemous. Such are the tactics of Satan. Dr. Daniel C. Peterson, Professor of Arabic at Brigham Young University, has noted:

"Intriguingly, the Nephites record tells us it was a religious oath 'swearing by their everlasting Maker' (Helaman 1:11). This seems odd to those of us unaccustomed to thinking of murder as a religious act. But the very word assassin was given to us by a religious sect of the medieval Near East who bore it as a name. The 'Assassin' carried out daring murders for many years from mixed religious and political motives."[1]

That those who were found were put to death again emphasizes the seriousness of their sins towards the freedom of the people.

The appointment of Pacumeni was another evidence of his character. His previous actions had apparently earned their trust. "According to his right" (v. 13) suggests further a patriarchal order of government in the reign of the judges. There were exceptions at times, but those exceptions came by revelation. Alma was the first judge, and the selection of Nephihah as the second judge was implied to be by revelation (see Alma 46:15–17) The third judge was Pahoran, who was the son of Nephihah, and his two sons, Pahoran and Pacumeni, were his successors. Helaman, son of Helaman, was the next judge. There is no record of why he was appointed other than by the voice of the people (Helaman 2:2). Since he was the record keeper and apparently the high priest of the church, we assume he was appointed through revelation. Helaman was succeeded by his son, Nephi, another patriarchal succession (Helaman 3:36–37). Nephi appointed Cezoram, who was not in the family line but must have been a righteous man. It was probably revealed to Nephi that Cezoram should be his successor (Helaman 5:1–4).

Helaman 1:14–21 • The Results of Contention in the Government

14 And it came to pass in the forty and first year of the reign of the judges, that the Lamanites had gathered together an innumerable army of men, and armed them with swords, and with cimeters and with bows, and with arrows, and with head-plates, and with breast-plates, and with all manner of shields of every kind.

---

[1] Daniel C. Peterson, *Studies in Scripture Vol. 8 Alma to Moroni*, ed. Kent P. Jackson [1988], 94.

15 And they came down again that they might pitch battle against the Nephites. And they were led by a man whose name was Coriantumr; and he was a descendant of Zarahemla; and he was a dissenter from among the Nephites; and he was a large and a mighty man.

16 Therefore, the king of the Lamanites, whose name was Tubaloth, who was the son of Ammoron, supposing that Coriantumr, being a mighty man, could stand against the Nephites, with his strength and also with his great wisdom, insomuch that by sending him forth he should gain power over the Nephites—

17 Therefore he did stir them up to anger, and he did gather together his armies, and he did appoint Coriantumr to be their leader, and did cause that they should march down to the land of Zarahemla to battle against the Nephites.

18 And it came to pass that because of so much contention and so much difficulty in the government, that they had not kept sufficient guards in the land of Zarahemla; for they had supposed that the Lamanites durst not come into the heart of their lands to attack that great city Zarahemla.

19 But it came to pass that Coriantumr did march forth at the head of his numerous host, and came upon the inhabitants of the city, and their march was with such exceedingly great speed that there was no time for the Nephites to gather together their armies.

20 Therefore Coriantumr did cut down the watch by the entrance of the city, and did march forth with his whole army into the city, and they did slay every one who did oppose them, insomuch that they did take possession of the whole city.

21 And it came to pass that Pacumeni, who was the chief judge, did flee before Coriantumr, even to the walls of the city. And it came to pass that Coriantumr did smite him against the wall, insomuch that he died. And thus ended the days of Pacumeni.

The third problem of the Nephites was an old one—war. The Lamanites had learned from the Nephites and copied their armor and weapons (v. 14). They were again led by a dissenter from the Nephites (v. 15). The king of the Lamanites used the age-old tactic of Satan, stir up the people to anger (v. 17; see also 2 Nephi 28:20). The contention in the government had weakened the Nephite government, as it always has and always will (Helaman 1:18). The hawks and the doves of the Congress still defer victory and peace when the United States are involved in war.

It was a quick victory for the Lamanites (v. 20). The second chief judge was killed, one in the fortieth, and the second in the forty-first year of the judges. Each were apparently in office less than a year. The conquest of the center of the land came after the death of Pacumeni. The results of contention over government is summarized by Dr. Daniel H. Ludlow.

> "The reign of judges began in the year 92 B.C. of the Christian calendar, and from then until 52 B.C. only three chief judges had served: Alma the younger, Nephihah, and Pahoran. However, in the year 52 B.C. Pahoran died and within the next two years three additional chief judges were selected: (1) Pahoran the second was selected to succeed his father, but he was murdered by Kishkumen (Helaman 1:9): (2) Pacumeni succeeded Pahoran the second, but he was killed by Coriantumr in war (Helaman 1:21); (3) Helaman the second (the son of Helaman who was the son of Alma the younger) then became the new chief judge (Helaman 2:1–2)."[2]

Helaman 1:22–27 • The Lamanites Capture the Center of the Land

> 22 And now when Coriantumr saw that he was in possession of the city of Zarahemla, and saw that the Nephites had fled before them, and were slain, and were taken, and were cast into prison, and that he had obtained the possession of the strongest hold in all the land, his heart took courage insomuch that he was about to go forth against all the land.
>
> 23 And now he did not tarry in the land of Zarahemla, but he did march forth with a large army, even towards the city of Bountiful; for it was his determination to go forth and cut his way through with the sword, that he might obtain the north parts of the land.
>
> 24 And, supposing that their greatest strength was in the center of the land, therefore he did march forth, giving them no time to

---

[2] Dr. Daniel H. Ludlow, *A Companion to Your Study of the Book of Mormon* [1977], 239.

assemble themselves together save it were in small bodies; and in this manner they did fall upon them and cut them down to the earth.

25 But behold, this march of Coriantumr through the center of the land gave Moronihah great advantage over them, notwithstanding the greatness of the number of the Nephites who were slain.

26 For behold, Moronihah had supposed that the Lamanites durst not come into the center of the land, but that they would attack the cities round about in the borders as they had hitherto done; therefore Moronihah had caused that their strong armies should maintain those parts round about by the borders.

The success of the Lamanites turned to the advantage of the Nephites (v. 25). Was Moronihah inspired to have his armies maintain the borders of the land? Were the Lamanites led unknowingly by the Lord into the center of the land? We may learn the answers to these questions someday, but we can only speculate at the present time.

Helaman 1:28–34 • The Lamanites are Surrounded by the Nephite Armies

28 But when Moronihah had discovered this, he immediately sent forth Lehi with an army round about to head them before they should come to the land Bountiful.

29 And thus he did; and he did head them before they came to the land Bountiful, and gave unto them battle, insomuch that they began to retreat back towards the land of Zarahemla.

30 And it came to pass that Moronihah did head them in their retreat, and did give unto them battle, insomuch that it became an exceedingly bloody battle; yea, many were slain, and among the number who were slain Coriantumr was also found.

31 And now, behold, the Lamanites could not retreat either way, neither on the north, nor on the south, nor on the east, nor on the west, for they were surrounded on every hand by the Nephites.

32 And thus had Coriantumr plunged the Lamanites into the midst of the Nephites, insomuch that they were in the power of the Nephites, and he himself was slain, and the Lamanites did yield themselves into the hands of the Nephites.

33 And it came to pass that Moronihah took possession of the city of Zarahemla again, and caused that the Lamanites who had been taken prisoners should depart out of the land in peace.

34 And thus ended the forty and first year of the reign of the judges.

Although many lives were lost, the Nephites were the victors (v. 32). In spite of the contentions among the Nephites (v. 18), the Nephite leaders still respected the value of human lives and allowed the prisoners to depart in peace (v. 33).

Helaman 2:1–5 • Helaman and the Band of Kishkumen

1 And it came to pass in the forty and second year of the reign of the judges, after Moronihah had established again peace between the Nephites and the Lamanites, behold there was no one to fill the judgment-seat; therefore there began to be a contention again among the people concerning who should fill the judgment-seat.

2 And it came to pass that Helaman, who was the son of Helaman, was appointed to fill the judgment-seat, by the voice of the people.

3 But behold, Kishkumen, who had murdered Pahoran, did lay wait to destroy Helaman also; and he was upheld by his band, who had entered into a covenant that no one should know his wickedness.

4 For there was one Gadianton, who was exceedingly expert in many words, and also in his craft, to carry on the secret work of murder and of robbery; therefore he became the leader of the band of Kishkumen.

5 Therefore he did flatter them, and also Kishkumen, that if they would place him in the judgment-seat he would grant unto those who belonged to his band that they should be placed in power and authority among the people; therefore Kishkumen sought to destroy Helaman.

Although Pahoran had many sons (Helaman 1:4), none were interested or survived, or qualified to fill the judgment-seat (Helaman 2:1). As mentioned above, Helaman was probably appointed by revelation and sustained by the voice of the people (v. 2).

Kishkumen had managed to keep his previous murder of Pahoran a secret (v. 3, see Helaman 1:11–12). However, he was outsmarted by Gadianton. Again the use of flattery, another tool of the devil, was brought into play (vv. 4–5; see Jacob 7:4; Alma 30:37; 46:7,10). Gadianton used the same tactics that Amalickiah used to become the leader of the band of Kishkumen (see Alma 46:5).

Helaman 2:6–11 • The Servant of Helaman Kills Kishkumen

6 And it came to pass as he went forth towards the judgment-seat to destroy Helaman, behold one of the servants of Helaman, having been out by night, and having obtained, through disguise, a knowledge of those plans which had been laid by this band to destroy Helaman—

7 And it came to pass that he met Kishkumen, and he gave unto him a sign; therefore Kishkumen made known unto him the object of his desire, desiring that he would conduct him to the judgment-seat that he might murder Helaman.

8 And when the servant of Helaman had known all the heart of Kishkumen, and how that it was his object to murder, and also that it was the object of all those who belonged to his band to murder, and to rob, and to gain power, (and this was their secret plan, and their combination) the servant of Helaman said unto Kishkumen: Let us go forth unto the judgment-seat.

9 Now this did please Kishkumen exceedingly, for he did suppose that he should accomplish his design; but behold, the servant of Helaman, as they were going forth unto the judgment-seat, did stab Kishkumen even to the heart, that he fell dead without a groan. And he ran and told Helaman all the things which he had seen, and heard, and done.

10 And it came to pass that Helaman did send forth to take this band of robbers and secret murderers, that they might be executed according to the law.

11 But behold, when Gadianton had found that Kishkumen did not return he feared lest that he should be destroyed; therefore he caused that his band should follow him. And they took their flight

out of the land, by a secret way, into the wilderness; and thus when Helaman sent forth to take them they could nowhere be found.

As Moroni, son of Mormon, abridged the record of the Jaredites, he warned the Gentiles of the secret combinations of the latter days (Ether 8:18–26). One of the solutions he gave to the Gentiles was a commandment of the Lord to "awake to a sense of your awful situation because of this secret combination which shall be among you" (Ether 8:24). What the servant of Helaman did to Kishkumen (Helaman 2:6–9) is an example of the solution that Moroni had given. The servant learned of their plans and became awake to the awful situation of the Nephites who were under the judge-ship of Helaman. For those who react to the servant killing Kishkumen, we remind you of the Spirit telling Nephi, son of Lehi the following:

> 10 And it came to pass that I was constrained by the Spirit that I should kill Laban; but I said in my heart: Never at any time have I shed the blood of man. And I shrunk and would that I might not slay him.

> 11 And the Spirit said unto me again: Behold the Lord hath delivered him into thy hands. Yea, and I also knew that he had sought to take away mine own life; yea, and he would not hearken unto the commandments of the Lord; and he also had taken away our property.

> 12 And it came to pass that the Spirit said unto me again: Slay him, for the Lord hath delivered him into thy hands;

> 13 Behold the Lord slayeth the wicked to bring forth his righteous purposes. It is better that one man should perish than that a nation should dwindle and perish in unbelief. [1 Nephi 4:10–13]

Kishkumen had taken the life of Pahoran, he had plotted to be placed in power and authority over the people, and he sought to destroy Helaman (vv. 3–5). The law of retaliation was in effect, he had smitten the Nephites at least three times and the Lord had delivered Kishkumen into the servant's hands (see D&C 98:23–29).

Helaman's attempt to execute the band of Gadianton according to the law (v. 10) is another evidence of their wickedness. The band fleeing into the wilderness also shows their guilt (v. 11).

Helaman 2:12–14 • Mormon's Preview of Gadianton

12 And more of this Gadianton shall be spoken hereafter. And thus ended the forty and second year of the reign of the judges over the people of Nephi.

13 And behold, in the end of this book ye shall see that this Gadianton did prove the overthrow, yea, almost the entire destruction of the people of Nephi.

14 Behold I do not mean the end of the book of Helaman, but I mean the end of the book of Nephi, from which I have taken all the account which I have written.

As Mormon stated, more will be said of Gadianton later (v. 12). Mormon's declaration of Gadianton causing almost the entire destruction of the Nephites "in the end of this book," has reference to the larger plates of Nephi which he is abridging. However, it was not Gadianton himself, but the secret combination that he began. What he personally caused will be discussed in the following chapter of this work. The Gadianton band existed until the destruction of the wicked at the time of Christ (3 Nephi 8; see 3 Nephi 4:1–4; 6:27–28). "The secret oaths and combinations of Gadianton" were "again built up, and spread over all the face of the land" three hundred years after the birth of Christ (4 Nephi 1:42, 46–47). Those wicked combinations existed until the final destruction of the Nephites as a nation. The people of Nephi who were not destroyed became numbered with the Lamanites as Alma had prophesied (see Alma 45:14; Helaman 3:16; Moroni 9:24). Moroni recognized that secret combination had "caused the destruction of [the Jaredites] and also the destruction of the people of Nephi" (Ether 8:21), as he abridged the Jaredite records. We will leave further discussion of Mormon's comments for a future volume of this work.

Helaman 3:1–6 • Much Contention and Many Dissensions

1 And now it came to pass in the forty and third year of the reign of the judges, there was no contention among the people of Nephi save it were a little pride which was in the church, which did cause some little dissensions among the people, which affairs were settled in the ending of the forty and third year.

2 And there was no contention among the people in the forty and fourth year; neither was there much contention in the forty and fifth year.

3 And it came to pass in the forty and sixth, yea, there was much contention and many dissensions; in the which there were an exceedingly great many who departed out of the land of Zarahemla, and went forth unto the land northward to inherit the land.

4 And they did travel to an exceedingly great distance, insomuch that they came to large bodies of water and many rivers.

5 Yea, and even they did spread forth into all parts of the land, into whatever parts it had not been rendered desolate and without timber, because of the many inhabitants who had before inherited the land.

6 And now no part of the land was desolate, save it were for timber; but because of the greatness of the destruction of the people who had before inhabited the land it was called desolate.

The first chapter of Helaman covered two years, and the second chapter covered just one year of the reign of the judges. The third chapter covers a total of eleven years, three of which are covered very briefly (vv. 1–2). The fourth year, the forty-sixth of the reign of the judges, is described more fully than any of the eleven years in this third chapter. There is more than one full page telling of the results of the contention and dissension that arose.

The first result of their contention was a large migration to the land northward. Was the Lord involved in this movement? Nephi, son of Lehi, taught: "[the Lord] leadeth away the righteous into precious lands, and the wicked he destroyeth" (1 Nephi 17:38). Perhaps the Lord was responsible, but there is no direct evidence that he was. There is, however, indirect evidence the people of God are gathered together in any age of the world. The Prophet Joseph Smith taught us why:

> "The main object was to build unto the Lord a house whereby He could reveal unto His people the ordinances of His house and the glories of His kingdom, and teach the people the way of salvation; for there are certain ordinances and principles that, when they are taught and practiced, must be done in a place or house built for that purpose." [*TPJS*, 308]

While Mormon makes no references to a temple at this time, there was a temple in the land of Zarahemla. King Benjamin had given his speech from that temple (see Mosiah 1:18). Later, Nephi, son of Helaman, warned that unless the people of Zarahemla repented, the Lord would scatter them instead of gathering them (see Helaman 7:19). The Lord's hand was probably involved in the northern migration at this time. After all: "And in nothing doth man offend God, or against none is his wrath kindled, save those who confess not his hand in all things, and obey not his commandments" (D&C 59:21).

The people traveled an exceedingly great distance to large bodies of water (v. 4). We must be careful that contentions do not arise over where these people traveled. Some Book of Mormon students feel this is in an area in Central America. Others quote this verse as the area of the great lakes in North America. The Prophet Joseph said: "the world will prove Joseph Smith a true prophet by circumstantial evidence, in experiments" (*TPJS*, 267). In this writers opinion, all of that evidence has not yet been found, and the Lord is still expecting his people to accept the Book of Mormon on faith. When the time is right, the Lord will bring forth further evidence. The land of desolation (Helaman 3:5–6) is also a controversial geographical area. We will also wait for further verification on this point.

Helaman 3:7–12 • Expert in the Working of Cement

7 And there being but little timber upon the face of the land, nevertheless the people who went forth became exceedingly expert in the working of cement; therefore they did build houses of cement, in the which they did dwell.

8 And it came to pass that they did multiply and spread, and did go forth from the land southward to the land northward, and did spread insomuch that they began to cover the face of the whole earth, from the sea south to the sea north, from the sea west to the sea east.

9 And the people who were in the land northward did dwell in tents, and in houses of cement, and they did suffer whatsoever tree should spring up upon the face of the land that it should grow up, that in time they might have timber to build their houses, yea, their cities, and their temples, and their synagogues, and their sanctuaries, and all manner of their buildings.

10 And it came to pass as timber was exceedingly scarce in the land northward, they did send forth much by the way of shipping.

11 And thus they did enable the people in the land northward that they might build many cities, both of wood and of cement.

12 And it came to pass that there were many of the people of Ammon, who were Lamanites by birth, did also go forth into this land.

The discovery of cement has brought forth circumstantial evidence for the Book of Mormon. Dr. Hugh W. Nibley has made the following observations:

"Building Materials: The Nephites vastly preferred wood to any other building material, and only worked in cement when they were forced to by a shortage of timber. Indeed, they refused to settle otherwise good lands in the north if timber for building was lacking. (Helaman 3:5) Where they reluctantly settled in unforested areas they continued to ". . . dwell in tents, and in houses of cement," while they patiently waited for the trees to grow. (Helaman 3:9) Since cement must be made of limestone, there was no lack of stone for building in the north. Why then did they not simply build of stone and forget about the cement and wood? Because, surprising as it may seem, ancient people almost never built of stone. Even when the magnificent, ". . . King Noah built many elegant and spacious buildings," their splendor was that of carved wood and precious metal, like the palace of any great lord of Europe or Asia, with nor mention of stone. (Mos. 11:8–9.) The Book of Mormon boom cities went up rapidly (Mos. 23:5, 27:6), while the builders were living in tents. And these were not stone cities: Nephite society was even more dependent on forests that is our own.[3]

The mention of cement in the Book of Mormon (Helaman 3:7–11), has been considered as great an anachronism as that of steel. But within the last ten years or so much has been made of the surprising extent to which the ancient Americans used cement, concrete, and gypsum in their building operations. It is now suggested that the overlavish detail, the extremely high relief, and the tendency to round off all angles in the heavy and serpentine profusion of line that is so characteristic of some early American architectural adornment, are the direct heritage of a time when the builders worked in the yielding and plastic medium of cement.[4]

Since 1929 much more cement works have been discovered. While the location of cement discoveries have been mainly Central and South America, we have not been as protective of archaeological ruins in North America as they were further south. Also some may yet be discovered. Furthermore, timber was grown and shipped in to build their cities (vv. 9–11). As this happened in the north, the evidence could have been removed as new cities were built. Therefore, the jury is still out on the location of the land of desolation.

The mention of four seas: south, north, west, and east (v. 8) has led some to identify the Yucatan Peninsula as the land northward. Again, we urge caution to avoid contention. The face of the whole land may be broader than Central America. We will comment further on this subject under Helaman 6:10.

[3] Hugh W. Nibley, *An Approach to the Book of Mormon* [1957], 348.

[4] Hugh W. Nibley, *Since Cumorah* [1967], 254.

The migration of Lamanites into the north (v. 12) is also interesting in light of geography. More light may be shed on the subject as the following verses suggest.

Helaman 3:13–16 • Records Kept Chiefly by the Nephites

> 13 And now there are many records kept of the proceedings of this people, by many of this people, which are particular and very large, concerning them.
>
> 14 But behold, a hundredth part of the proceedings of this people, yea, the account of the Lamanites and of the Nephites, and their wars, and contentions, and dissensions, and their preaching, and their prophecies, and their shipping and their building of ships, and their building of temples, and of synagogues and their sanctuaries, and their righteousness, and their wickedness, and their murders, and their robbings, and their plundering, and all manner of abominations and whoredoms, cannot be contained in this work.
>
> 15 But behold, there are many books and many records of every kind, and they have been kept chiefly by the Nephites.
>
> 16 And they have been handed down from one generation to another by the Nephites, even until they have fallen into transgression and have been murdered, plundered, and hunted, and driven forth, and slain, and scattered upon the face of the earth, and mixed with the Lamanites until they are no more called the Nephites, becoming wicked, and wild, and ferocious, yea, even becoming Lamanites.

These four verses are Mormon's comments written about A.D. 385. As suggested above these particular and very large records (v. 13) should fill in many of the geographical, archaeological, and historical questions that have arisen through the years (v. 14). It will also be interesting to read the records kept by the Lamanites as implied by "kept chiefly by the Nephites" (v. 15). Were these Lamanite records also preserved? The converted Lamanites certainly kept records, and it is implied they had been placed with the Nephite records (v. 16). The records kept by unconverted Lamanites may also come forth if and when the Lord wants them restored.

Mormon's declaration that "they are no more called the Nephites" certainly identifies the time period to which he refers (v. 16), the final destruction of the Nephites occurred about A.D. 385. It also identifies "the end of the book of Nephi" referred to earlier by Mormon (see Helaman 2:14 and comments therein) as the same time period.

Helaman 3:17–22 • Helaman Fills the Judgment-seat with Justice and Equity

17 And now I return again to mine account; therefore, what I have spoken had passed after there had been great contentions, and disturbances, and wars, and dissensions, among the people of Nephi.

18 The forty and sixth year of the reign of the judges ended;

19 And it came to pass that there was still great contention in the land, yea, even in the forty and seventh year, and also in the forty and eighth year.

20 Nevertheless Helaman did fill the judgment-seat with justice and equity; yea, he did observe to keep the statutes, and the judgments, and the commandments of God; and he did do that which was right in the sight of God continually; and he did walk after the ways of his father, insomuch that he did prosper in the land.

21 And it came to pass that he had two sons. He gave unto the eldest the name of Nephi, and unto the youngest, the name of Lehi. And they began to grow up unto the Lord.

22 And it came to pass that the wars and contentions began to cease, in a small degree, among the people of the Nephites, in the latter end of the forty and eighth year of the reign of the judges over the people of Nephi.

Mormon's return to "mine account" (v. 17) refers to his abridgment work, and also shows his comments above were of his own day. He also confirms again his declaration of the end of the Nephite nation (v. 17). The forty-seventh year is given no commentary (v. 19), and the forty eighth year lightly treats the influence of Helaman during his administration as chief judge and his personal life (vv. 20–22). Justice is equated with observing the statutes, judgments, and commandments of God. Equity tells us he was no respecter of persons in his work as the chief judge. Doing right in the sight of God strongly suggests he was led by revelation, as was the case of his fathers. His prospering in the land confirms again the promise to the inhabitants of the land given to both the people of Nephi (see 2 Nephi 1:9), Jaredites, and the Gentiles of today (see Ether 2:8–12).

Helaman's two sons, Nephi and Lehi, who kept the records after their father passed on, will be prominent in the following chapters of this work. Helaman was making progress in his endeavors as the year closes (Helaman 3:22).

Helaman 3:23–26 • Continual Peace and Great Prosperity in the Church

23 And it came to pass in the forty and ninth year of the reign of the judges, there was continual peace established in the land, all save it were the secret combinations which Gadianton the robber had established in the more settled parts of the land, which at that time were not known unto those who were at the head of government; therefore they were not destroyed out of the land.

24 And it came to pass that in this same year there was exceedingly great prosperity in the church, insomuch that there were thousands who did join themselves unto the church and were baptized unto repentance.

25 And so great was the prosperity of the church, and so many the blessings which were poured out upon the people, that even the high priests and the teachers were themselves astonished beyond measure.

26 And it came to pass that the work of the Lord did prosper unto the baptizing and uniting to the church of God, many souls, yea, even tens of thousands.

The forty-ninth year of the reign of the judges saw the effects of the great leadership of Helaman. The main problem was the Gadianton band of robbers (v. 23). Being "established in the more settled parts of the land" must refer to the bigger cities. The same pattern exists in our day. The secret combinations, note they are plural, function wherever large bodies of people reside. There works of darkness and secrecy are easier to carry out among the masses. That they were "not known" by those in the government is an indication that the secret combinations of our day are farther advanced than they were in Helaman's day. Our governments know of them and their work. The government tries to control their actions and protect the people, but laws of privacy and personal rights often hampers the government in their endeavors. Certain areas of certain cities in our day seem to be controlled by the secret combinations.

The great prosperity in the church is also a parallel to our day (v. 24). Thousands and tens of thousands are today being baptized into the church (v. 26). The building of temples, the growth of business, opportunities for education, and the multi-media inventions are amazing to the older generations of the Church, and even amazing to some of the younger generations. In these prosperous times, the challenge is to remain faithful in spite of the worldly things that surround us.

Helaman 3:27–32 • Mormon's Precepts—Thus We See

27 Thus we may see that the Lord is merciful unto all who will, in the sincerity of their hearts, call upon his holy name.

28 Yea, thus we see that the gate of heaven is open unto all, even to those who will believe on the name of Jesus Christ, who is the Son of God.

29 Yea, we see that whosoever will may lay hold upon the word of God, which is quick and powerful, which shall divide asunder all the cunning and the snares and the wiles of the devil, and lead the man of Christ in a strait and narrow course across that everlasting gulf of misery which is prepared to engulf the wicked—

30 And land their souls, yea, their immortal souls, at the right hand of God in the kingdom of heaven, to sit down with Abraham, and Isaac, and with Jacob, and with all our holy fathers, to go no more out.

31 And in this year there was continual rejoicing in the land of Zarahemla, and in all the regions round about, even in all the land which was possessed by the Nephites.

32 And it came to pass that there was peace and exceedingly great joy in the remainder of the forty and ninth year; yea, and also there was continual peace and great joy in the fiftieth year of the reign of the judges.

Mormon addresses his guides to life to three different groups of people. The first group addressed are the general population or inhabitants of the land. The Lord will be merciful to every and all people if they will ask for his help (v. 27). Whether black and white, bond and free, (male and female), he remembereth the heathen, and all are alike unto God, both Jew and Gentile (see 2 Nephi 26:33). In every walk of life, and in every area of living, the Lord will answer the prayers of those who seek his blessings and want to avoid wickedness and secret abominations.

The second group addressed are those to whom the gospel is preached. Baptism, the gate to the path to eternal life (v. 28, compare 2 Nephi 31:17), is available to those who believe on the name of Jesus Christ. To believe on his name is to follow the steps given by him to obtain salvation. His is the only name whereby salvation is obtained (see Acts 4:12; 2 Nephi 31:21; Mosiah 4:8).

The third group addressed are those who have joined the church. Baptism alone will not save a person from the wickedness and secret abominations of the world. Those baptized must "lay hold upon the word of God" (Helaman 3:29). Mormon's analogy of the word of God dividing asunder (v. 29) reminds us of Nephi teaching that "the guilty taketh the truth to be hard, for it cutteth to the very center" (1 Nephi 16:2). The strait and narrow course across the gulf of misery is the path to eternal life mentioned above (see 2 Nephi 31:17–20). The gulf of misery was interpreted by Nephi, son of Lehi, as that awful hell that was prepared for the wicked, and the justice of God divided the wicked from the righteous (see 1 Nephi 15:28–30). To sit down with Abraham, Isaac, and Jacob reminds us of the parable of Lazarus and the rich man, where the rich man and Abraham are separated. "And it came to pass, that the beggar died, and was carried by the angels into Abraham's bosom: the rich man also died, and was buried; And in hell he lift up his eyes, being in torments, and seeth Abraham afar off, and Lazarus in his bosom" (Luke 16:22–23). We will not interpret the whole parable here (Luke 16:19–31). Our purpose in referring to it is to show that the separation of the wicked and the righteous in the spirit world is a biblical teaching in the Bible as well as in the Book of Mormon (see Alma 10:11–14). The word of God leads to the place where the righteous dwell, whether in the spirit world or in the kingdom of heaven (Helaman 3:30). Certainly, Mormon had a thorough knowledge of the plan of salvation and the steps to obtain it, while being in a world of temptation and contentions.

Helaman and his sons, along with other righteous men, had convinced thousands and tens of thousands to follow the plan of salvation. Peace and exceedingly great joy was experienced by this large number of people in just one year (vv. 26, 31–32). Another year is quickly covered, because they experienced the peace and joy that had been attained in the previous year (v. 32).

Helaman 3:33–36 • Pride Began to Enter into the Church

33 And in the fifty and first year of the reign of the judges there was peace also, save it were the pride which began to enter into the church—not into the church of God, but into the hearts of the people who professed to belong to the church of God—

34 And they were lifted up in pride, even to the persecution of many of their brethren. Now this was a great evil, which did cause the more humble part of the people to suffer great persecutions, and to wade through much affliction.

35 Nevertheless they did fast and pray oft, and did wax stronger and stronger in their humility, and firmer and firmer in the faith of Christ, unto the filling their souls with joy and consolation, yea, even to the purifying and the sanctification of their hearts, which sanctification cometh because of their yielding their hearts unto God.

> 36 And it came to pass that the fifty and second year ended in peace also, save it were the exceedingly great pride which had gotten into the hearts of the people; and it was because of their exceedingly great riches and their prosperity in the land; and it did grow upon them from day to day.

The fifty-first year is covered in just three verses. However, these three verses show us how persecution and affliction can have a positive effect upon faithful people. Mormon's observation that pride did not enter into the church, but into the hearts of some who professed church membership (v. 33), is astute. The church may be perfect, but the members have their agency "to chose liberty and eternal life, through the great mediator of all men, or to choose captivity and death, according to the captivity and power of the devil" (2 Nephi 2:27).

The persecution and affliction came from within the church (Helaman 3:34), but the formula to turn these negative conditions into a growth pattern is given to us by Mormon. The first step of the three step formula is to "fast and pray often" (v. 35). Note that it doesn't say how long to fast or how often to pray. Each individual must determine those times and they will vary accordingly. When the need is there, we must turn to the Lord in prayer and fasting.

The second step of the formula is to become stronger in humility (v. 35). Some may interpret humility as a weakness rather than a strength, but humility is to recognize the need for the Savior's help and turn to him for direction. As we become stronger, it is through his strength being poured out upon us. The more we rely upon him, the more power he will give us, and the stronger we become.

The third step of the formula is to become "firmer in the faith of Christ" (v. 3). To be firm in the faith of Christ is to know that you can do all things through Christ. To know you can call on his power and it will come. As Paul said "I can do all things through [the faith of] Christ which strengtheneth me" (Philippians 4:13).

Through the above formula, the people's hearts were purified and sanctified because they yielded their hearts to God (v. 35). They knew that the course they pursued was the will of God, which gave them faith unto salvation (see *Lecture of Faith* 3:7). Thus the persecutions and the afflictions, although difficult to endure, brought them to rely on the Lord, made them stronger in character, and helped them become firmer in their conviction.

Again, we see a connection between pride and prosperity (v. 36). Pride eventually destroyed the Nephites as a nation (see Moroni 8:27).

The reign of Helaman came to a close after eleven years as the chief judge. He had kept the commandment of God and brought peace and prosperity to his people. Mormon's description of his time on the judgment-seat was indeed accurate (see Helaman 3:20).

Sacred Writing

Doctrines Learned:

Helaman 3:27	The Lord is merciful to all who will call (pray) on his name.
Helaman 3:28	The gate (baptism) of heaven is open to all who will believe on the name of Jesus Christ.
Helaman 3:29–30	The word of God will lead a man through temptation of the devil to the kingdom of heaven.
Helaman 3:35	Sanctification comes by yielding one's heart to God.
Helaman 3:36	Pride comes into one's heart because of exceeding riches and prosperity.

General Authority Quotes

President Heber J. Grant • Helaman 3:5, 11

I have often said and desire to repeat here that when I was a young unmarried man, another young man who had received a doctor's degree ridiculed me for believing in the Book of Mormon. He said he could point out two lies in that book. One was that the people had built their homes out of cement and they were very skillful in the use of cement. He said there had never been found and never would be found, a house built of cement by the ancient inhabitants of this country, because the people in that early age knew nothing about cement. He said that should be enough to make one disbelieve the book. I said: "That does not affect my faith one particle. I read the Book of Mormon prayerfully and supplicated God for a testimony in my heart and soul of the divinity of it, and I have accepted it and believe it with all my heart." I also said to him, "If my children do not find cement houses, I expect that my grandchildren will." Now, since that time, houses made of cement and massive structures of the same material have been uncovered. [*Gospel Standards*, comp. G. Homer Durham [1941], 28]

Elder Milton R. Hunter • Helaman 3:5, 11

Expert in the Working of Cement: The first spot of archaeological interest which we visited in Guatemala was the ruins of Kaminaljuyu, located adjacent to the outskirts of Guatemala City. It is claimed by archaeologists that this site dates back into the early Christian period (about A.D. 320), and so its beginning was contemporaneous with the latter portion of the Book of Mormon. There are a number of mounds at that archaeological site which in ancient times were pyramids crowned with temples. Perhaps the temples were constructed of wood and have completely decomposed. Dr. Alfred V. Kidder, one of the greatest authorities on Maya archaeology, and other noteworthy scientists have done considerable work at this site and other ancient ruins in Guatemala. In some of these mounds at Kaminaljuyu they found tombs, the vaults of which were made of excellent cement. From these tombs they obtained such treasures as jade beads, jade beautifully decorated with Maya carvings, and other artifacts. These relics are housed in the National Museum in Guatemala City and photographs of some of them are shown later in the book.

As I looked at the cement vaults, I recalled the statements in the Book of Mormon wherein these ancient Nephites claimed to be experts in making cement. Certainly this cement which had remained in good condition for nearly two thousand years was good cement. [*Archaeology and The Book of Mormon*, [1956], 104–105]

Bishop Robert L. Simpson • Helaman 3:35

They did Fast and Pray, Oft, . . . to the Purifying and Sanctification of Their Hearts: In addition to the occasional fasting experience for a special purpose, each member of the Church is expected to miss two meals on the fast and testimony Sunday. To skip two consecutive meals and partake of the third normally constitutes approximately a 24-hour period. Such is the counsel.

Competent medical authorities tell us that our bodies benefit by an occasional fasting period. That is blessing number one and perhaps the least important. Second, we contribute the money saved from missing the meals as a fast offering to the bishop for the poor and the needy. And Third, we reap a particular spiritual benefit that can come to us in no other way. It is a sanctification of the soul for us today just as it was for some choice people who lived 2,000 years ago. I quote briefly from the Book of Mormon: "Nevertheless they did fast oft, and did wax stronger and stronger in their humility, and firmer and firmer in the faith of Christ, unto the filling their souls with joy and consolation, yea, even to the purifying and the sanctification of their hearts, which sanctification cometh because of their yielding their hearts unto God." (Hel. 3:35). Wouldn't you like this to happen to you? It can, you know!

Did you notice it said that those who do this have their souls filled with "joy and consolation"? You see, the world in general thinks that fasting is a time for "sackcloth and ashes," a time to carry a look of sorrow, as one to be pitied. On the contrary, the Lord admonishes: "Moreover when ye fast, be not, as the hypocrites, of a sad countenance: for they disfigure their faces, that they may appear unto men to fast. Verily I say unto you, They have their reward.

"But thou, when thou fastest, anoint thine head, and wash thy face; "That thou appear not unto men to fast, but unto thy Father which is in secret: and thy Father, which seeth in secret, shall reward thee openly." (Matthew 6:16–18). [CR, October 1967, 18]

As Challenges to Eternal Life:

1. Follow the example of Helaman in doing that which is right in the sight of God that you may prosper in the land (Helaman 3:20).

2. Determine to lay hold of the world of God that it may lead you to sit down at the right hand of God (Helaman 3:30).

3. Yield your heart to God that you may become purified and sanctified in your heart (Helaman 3:35).

4. Choose a challenge of your own from this reading and apply it to your life.

Chapter Eight

The Sole Management of Government

Helaman 4–6

H istorical Setting: The three Book of Mormon chapters included in this reading cover from the fifty-fourth year through the sixty-eighth year of the reign of the judges, a period of fifteen years. Only four of those fifteen years are described to any length, and the majority of the text speaks about one year. The geographic areas of these chapters are the lands of Zarahemla and Bountiful with their various cities. Nephi has succeeded his father Helaman as the chief judge. There is much contention and dissension as the saga continues.

Precepts of this Reading:

Now this great loss of the Nephites, and the great slaughter which was among them, would not have happened had it not been for their wickedness and their abomination which was among them; yea, and it was among those also who professed to belong to the church of God.

12 And it was because of the pride of their hearts, because of their exceeding riches, yea, it was because of their oppression to the poor, withholding their food from the hungry, withholding their clothing from the naked, and smiting their humble brethren upon the cheek, making a mock of that which was sacred, denying the spirit of prophecy and of revelation, murdering, plundering, lying, stealing,

committing adultery, rising up in great contentions, and deserting away into the land of Nephi, among the Lamanites—

13 And because of this their great wickedness, and their boastings in their own strength, they were left in their own strength; therefore they did not prosper, but were afflicted and smitten, and driven before the Lamanites, until they had lost possession of almost all their lands. [Helaman 4:11–13]

34 And thus we see that the Nephites did begin to dwindle in unbelief, and grow in wickedness and abominations, while the Lamanites began to grow exceedingly in the knowledge of their God; yea, they did begin to keep his statutes and commandments, and to walk in truth and uprightness before him.

35 And thus we see that the Spirit of the Lord began to withdraw from the Nephites, because of the wickedness and the of their hearts.

36 And thus we see that the Lord began to pour out his Spirit upon the Lamanites, because of their easiness and willingness to believe in his words. [Helaman 6:34, 36]

And thus we see that they were in an awful state, and ripening for an everlasting destruction. [Helaman 6:40]

There are many other precepts within the text of Helaman 4–6 that may be applied to our lives. An outline of these three chapters of Helaman follows as a preparation for a deeper study.

OUTLINE • HELAMAN 4–6

➤ 4:1–17　　In the fifty-fourth year there were many dissensions in the church, and a contention that caused much bloodshed.

　　　　a.　The rebellious part were slain or driven out and they went to the king of the Lamanites (vv. 2–3).

　　　　　　1.　They attempted to stir up the Lamanites to war against the Nephites.

　　　　　　2.　The Lamanites were afraid and would not hearken.

　　　　b.　In the fifty-sixth year (no mention of the fifty-fifth) other dissenters left and succeeded in stirring up the

Lamanites to anger and they prepared all that year to come to war (vv. 4–5).

   1. In the fifty-seventh year they came and commenced the work of death.

   2. In the fifty-eighth year they obtained Zarahemla and all the lands near Bountiful.

c. Moronihah's armies were driven to the land Bountiful (vv. 6–7).

   1. They fortified from the west sea to the east.

   2. It was a days journey for a Nephite on the line fortified.

d. In the fifty-eighth and fifty-ninth years, the dissenters with the army of the Lamanites had obtained all the southward lands of the Nephites (v. 8).

e. In the sixtieth year Moronihah's armies regained many cities, and in the sixty-first year they regained half of all their possessions (vv. 9–13).

   1. The great slaughter of many Nephites was because of the wickedness and abominations among those who professed to belong to the church.

   2. It was because of the pride in their hearts and because of their riches, oppression of the poor, mocking of things sacred, denying the spirit of prophecy and revelation, and their wickedness and deserting to the Lamanite Lands.

   3. They boasted in their own strength, and were left to their own strength, and thus did not prosper.

f. Moronihah, Nephi, and Lehi preached and prophesied of things to come if the Nephites did not repent (vv. 14–17).

   1. As they did repent, they began to prosper.

   2. As they repented, they regained half of their property and their land.

➤ 4:18–26   In the sixty-second year, Moronihah could regain no more lands because the Lamanites were so numerous. Therefore, they abandoned that design and employed his armies to maintain the lands they had taken.

a. The Nephites were afraid of the Lamanites overpowering them, trodding them down, and destroying them (vv. 20–22).

    1. They began to remember the prophecies of Alma, and the words of Mosiah, recognizing they had not kept the commandments of God.

    2. They had trampled and altered the laws given to Mosiah by the Lord, their laws were corrupted, and the Nephites had become wicked like the Lamanites.

b. Because of their iniquity, the Nephites began to dwindle in unbelief, disbelieving in the spirit of prophecy, and the spirit of revelation (vv. 23–24).

    1. The judgments of God did stare them in their face.

    2. The Spirit of the Lord did no more preserve them but had withdrawn because it does not dwell in unholy temples.

c. The Lord did cease to preserve the Nephites by his miraculous and matchless power (vv. 25–26).

    1. The Lamanites were more numerous than they.

    2. Except the Nephites would cleave unto the Lord they would perish.

    3. The strength of the Lamanites was as great as the Nephites strength.

    4. The Nephites transgressions had made them weak in not many years.

➤ 5:1–3 In the same year (62nd), Nephi delivered up the judgment seat to Cezoram.

a. The laws were established by the voice of the people, and those who chose evil were more numerous than those who chose good, therefore they were ripening for destruction (v. 2).

b. The Nephites were a stiffnecked people and could not be governed by law nor justice, save destruction (v. 3).

    c. Nephi became weary of the iniquity and yielded up the judgment-seat (v. 4).

➤ 5:4–13   Nephi and Lehi, his brother, chose to preach the word of God the rest of their days.

    a. Nephi and Lehi remembered the words of their father, Helaman. He taught: (vv. 5–8)

        1. Remember to keep the commandments of God and declare them to the people.

        2. I gave you the names of your first parents who came out of Jerusalem that you may remember their works, which were said and written and were good, and also that you would do good.

        3. Do not these things to boast but to lay up a treasure in heaven which is eternal, and receive that precious gift of eternal life.

    b. Remember the words of King Benjamin, there is no other way nor means for men to be saved, only through the atoning blood of Jesus Christ (v. 9).

    c. Remember the words which Amulek spoke to Zeezrom in Ammonihah that the Lord would come to redeem his people, not in their sins but from their sins (vv. 10–11).

        1. He has power given him by the Father to redeem them because of repentance.

        2. He has sent his angels to declare the conditions of repentance that bring salvation to their souls.

    d. Remember it is upon the rock of our Redeemer, who is Christ, the Son of God, that ye must build to resist the mighty storm of the devil, and it is the only sure foundation upon which to build (v. 12).

    e. Helaman taught his sons many things which are not written, and many which are (v. 13).

➤ 5:14–19   Nephi and Lehi preached the word of God beginning at Bountiful, and then on to Gid, Mulek, and among all the people of Nephi in the land southward, and then into Zarahemla among the Lamanites.

a. Nephi and Lehi preached with such power that it confounded many Nephite dissenters, and they were baptized unto repentance and returned to the Nephites to endeavor to repair the wrongs they had done (v. 17).

b. Nephi and Lehi preached to the Lamanites with great power and authority, and it was also given unto them what they should speak (vv. 18–19).

1. Eight thousand of the Lamanites were baptized unto repentance.

2. They were convinced of the wicked traditions of their fathers.

➤ 5:20–34   Nephi and Lehi went to the land of Nephi, and were taken and cast into the same prison where Ammon and his brethren were cast by Limhi's servants.

a. After many days without food, the Lamanites came to slay them (vv. 22–25).

1. Nephi and Lehi were encircled with fire and were not burned, but the Lamanites dared not lay hands on them lest they be burned.

2. They took courage when the Lamanites just stood in amazement.

b. Nephi and Lehi spoke telling them not to fear, God has shown you this marvelous thing (vv. 26–27).

1. The earth shook and the walls of the prison shook, but did not fall.

2. The Lamanites and Nephite dissenters, were in the prison.

c. The prisoners were over shadowed by a cloud of darkness and an awful solemn fear (vv. 28–34).

1. A voice spoke, as if above the darkness, saying: repent and seek no more to destroy my servants whom I have sent to declare good tidings.

2. It was not a voice of thunder, or great noise, but a still small voice of perfect mildness, as if a whisper, that did pierce even to the very soul.

3. Although the voice was mild, the earth shook and the walls trembled again, but the cloud of darkness did not disperse.

4. The voice came again; repent, the kingdom of heaven is at hand, and the earth shook again.

5. The voice came the third time, speaking marvelous words that cannot be uttered by man, and the earth shook again.

6. The Lamanites could not flee because of the cloud of darkness, but they were also immovable because of fear.

> 5:35–52 A Nephite by birth, who had dissented from the church, saw the faces of Nephi and Lehi through the darkness, shining as the faces of angels, speaking to some being whom they beheld (vv. 35–42).

a. The Nephite cried to the multitude to look, and power was given them to behold Nephi and Lehi (vv. 37–42).

1. The multitude asked, What these things mean and to whom do they converse?

2. Aminadab, the Nephite dissenter, said they conversed with the angels of God.

3. The Lamanites asked what they should do to remove the cloud of darkness.

4. Aminadab told them to repent and cry unto the voice until they had faith in Christ as taught by Alma, Amulek, and Zeezrom.

5. They cried unto the voice until the cloud was dispersed.

b. The Lamanites saw that they were encircled about by a pillar of fire, and Nephi and Lehi was in the midst of them (vv. 43–45).

1. The fire did not harm them, nor take hold of the prison walls.

2. Nephi and Lehi were filled with unspeakable joy unspeakable and full of glory.

3. The Holy Spirit of God came down and entered their hearts and filled them as if by fire, and they could speak marvelous words.

c. There came a pleasant voice unto the Lamanites, as if a whisper, saying: Peace, peace be unto you because of your faith in my Well Beloved, who was from the foundation of the world (vv. 46–49).

1. The Lamanites looked to see from whence the voice came and saw the heavens open, and angels came down and ministered to them.

2. There were about three hundred souls who saw and heard these things.

3. They were bidden to go and marvel not, nor should they doubt.

d. The three hundred souls went and ministered to the people, declaring what they had heard and seen (vv. 50–52).

1. The more part of the Lamanites were convinced because of the evidence they had received.

2. Those who were convinced laid down their weapons of war, and also their hatred and the traditions of their father.

3. Those convinced yielded the lands of their possession to the Nephites.

➤ 6:1–6 In the sixty-third year the more part of the Lamanites had become a righteous people, exceeding the Nephites because of their firmness and steadiness in the faith.

a. The Nephites had become hardened, impenitent, and grossly wicked; rejecting the word of God and all preaching and prophesying (vv. 2–3).

1. The people of the church had great joy in the conversion of the Lamanites.

       2. They fellowshipped one with another, rejoiced and experienced great joy.

  b. Many of the Lamanites came to the land of Zarahemla and declared their conversion among the Nephites, exhorting them to faith and repentance (vv. 4–6).

       1. They preached with power and authority, bringing many to be humble followers of God and the Lamb.

       2. Many of the Lamanites, and also Nephi and Lehi went to the land northward to preach.

➤ 6:7–14   In the sixty-fourth year, there was peace in the land, the Nephites going among the Lamanites, and the Lamanites going among the Nephites, to buy, sell, and get gain.

  a. Both the Lamanites and the Nephites became rich with gold, silver and precious metals in the land south and in the land north (vv. 9–11).

       1. The land south was called Lehi, and the land north was called Mulek, after the son of Zedekiah.

       2. The Lord brought Mulek into the land north, and Lehi into the land south.

       3. There was gold, silver, and ore in both lands, and also curious workmen to refine the ores.

  b. The Lamanites and Nephites did raise grain and flourish in both lands, multiplied and waxed strong, raised many flocks and herds, and the women made all manner of cloth, and linen to clothe their nakedness (vv. 12–13).

  c. The sixty-fifth year also had much joy and peace, and much preaching and prophesying (v. 14).

➤ 6:15–33   In the sixty-sixth year Cezoram was murdered upon the judgment seat by an unknown hand, and his son, who succeeded him, was also murdered.

  a. In the sixty-seventh year, the people began to grow wicked again (vv. 16).

      1.   The people began to set their hearts upon their riches, to get gain and be lifted above another.

      2.   They began to rob and plunder to get gain and commit secret murders.

  b. The Gadianton band were murderers and plunderers who were organized by Kishkumen and Gadianton (vv. 18–19).

      1.   They were more numerous among the wicked part of the Lamanites, but they were even among the Nephites.

      2.   They had murdered Cezoram and his son on the judgment-seat.

  c. The Lamanites were sorrowful to have the bands among them, and used every means to destroy them (vv. 20–24).

      1.   The hearts of the Nephites were stirred up by Satan to enter their covenants and oaths.

      2.   They would protect and preserve one another in whatever circumstances they were in, to not suffer for their crimes.

      3.   They had their secret signs and words to distinguish a brother.

      4.   They could thus do all wickedness contrary to the laws of their country and of God.

      5.   Whoso revealed unto the world their wickedness would be tried by the laws given by Gadianton and Kishkumen, not by the laws of the country.

  d. It was these secret oaths and covenants that Alma commanded his son should not go forth to the world (vv. 25–32).

      1.   They did not come to Gadianton from the records delivered to Helaman.

      2.   They were put into his heart by him who enticed our first parents to partake of the forbidden fruit.

      3.   Satan plotted with Cain to kill Abel and with Cain and his followers thereafter.

4. Satan put the building of a tower to reach heaven in the hearts of those builders.

5. The people who came to this land were led into works of darkness and abominations by him unto their destruction.

6. Satan is the author of all sin, and carries the works of darkness from generation to generation, as he can get hold of their hearts.

7. Satan got hold of the hearts of the Nephites, and they turned from righteousness.

8. All the iniquities came in not many years.

9. In the sixty-eighth year they grew in their iniquities to the sorrow and lamentation of the righteous.

➤ 6:34–40   Mormon draws his "thus we see" conclusions for the sixty-eighth year.

a. The Nephites dwindled in unbelief and wickedness, while the Lamanites grew in the knowledge of God and walked in truth and uprightness (v. 34).

b. The Lord began to withdraw his Spirit from the Nephites because of wickedness (v. 35).

c. The Lord began to pour out his Spirit upon the Lamanites because they were willing to believe in his words (vv. 36–37).

1. The Lamanites hunted out the robbers of Gadianton.

2. They preached the word of God to them, utterly destroying them among the Lamanites.

d. The Nephites supported the Gadianton band, the more wicked part, until they spread over all their land, and seduced the more part of the righteous to believe in their works and partake of their spoils (vv. 38–40).

1. They obtained the sole management of the government, and turned their backs on the poor, the meek, and the humble followers of God.

2. They were in an awful state, ripening for everlasting destruction.

NOTES AND COMMENTARY

Introduction: In modern revelation, the Lord has warned us to "beware of pride, lest ye become as the Nephites of old" (D&C 38:39). As shown in the first three chapters of the book of Helaman, pride came to the Nephites because of their riches. We will see in these next three chapters how this pride continued, and led to the sole management of the government by the Gadianton robbers. We were also warned of them in the previous chapter of this work.

Helaman 4:1–8 • The Nephites Are Driven to the Land Bountiful

1 And it came to pass in the fifty and fourth year there were many dissensions in the church, and there was also a contention among the people, insomuch that there was much bloodshed.

2 And the rebellious part were slain and driven out of the land, and they did go unto the king of the Lamanites.

3 And it came to pass that they did endeavor to stir up the Lamanites to war against the Nephites; but behold, the Lamanites were exceedingly afraid, insomuch that they would not hearken to the words of those dissenters.

4 But it came to pass in the fifty and sixth year of the reign of the judges, there were dissenters who went up from the Nephites unto the Lamanites; and they succeeded with those others in stirring them up to anger against the Nephites; and they were all that year preparing for war.

5 And in the fifty and seventh year they did come down against the Nephites to battle, and they did commence the work of death; yea, insomuch that in the fifty and eighth year of the reign of the judges they succeeded in obtaining possession of the land of Zarahemla; yea, and also all the lands, even unto the land which was near the land Bountiful.

6 And the Nephites and the armies of Moronihah were driven even into the land of Bountiful;

7 And there they did fortify against the Lamanites, from the west sea, even unto the east; it being a day's journey for a Nephite, on the line which they had fortified and stationed their armies to defend their north country.

8 And thus those dissenters of the Nephites, with the help of a numerous army of the Lamanites, had obtained all the possession of the Nephites which was in the land southward. And all this was done in the fifty and eighth and ninth years of the reign of the judges.

The above eight verses are Mormon's abridgment of six years of the record written upon the plates of Nephi by Nephi, son of Helaman. Under the new chief judge, Nephi, the dissenters were driven out of the land after much bloodshed. As servants of Satan, the Nephite dissenters attempted to stir up the Lamanites to war (vv. 1–3). We assume this contentious period lasted only the first year since Mormon makes no mention of the fifty-fifth year. The Lamanites going to war again is assumed to be caused by their previous defeats by the Nephites, and not from a fear of God. Those Lamanites who feared God were undoubtedly among the tens of thousands that had been converted to the gospel (see Helaman 3:26).

In the fifty-sixth year, other Nephite dissenters joined the pervious group and collectively they were successful in getting the Lamanites to follow Satan's plan of anger (Helaman 4:4; see 2 Nephi 28:19–20). In three years the Nephites were driven out of the entire land of Zarahemla (Helaman 4:5–6, 8). Thus one of the results of dissensions and contention is the loss of property, a primary responsibility of a government under God (see D&C 134:1–2).

Notice again that the line fortified was from the west sea to the east (v. 7) not the east sea. How much farther it was to the east sea is not given (see Alma 22:32 and commentary on that verse in volume three of this work).

Helaman 4:9–17 • Moronihah Regains Half of Their Lands

9 And it came to pass in the sixtieth year of the reign of the judges, Moronihah did succeed with his armies in obtaining many parts of the land; yea, they regained many cities which had fallen into the hands of the Lamanites.

10 And it came to pass in the sixty and first year of the reign of the judges they succeeded in regaining even the half of all their possessions.

11 Now this great loss of the Nephites, and the great slaughter which was among them, would not have happened had it not been for their wickedness and their abomination which was among them; yea, and it was among those also who professed to belong to the church of God.

12 And it was because of the pride of their hearts, because of their exceeding riches, yea, it was because of their oppression to the poor, withholding their food from the hungry, withholding their clothing from the naked, and smiting their humble brethren upon the cheek, making a mock of that which was sacred, denying the spirit of prophecy and of revelation, murdering, plundering, lying, stealing, committing adultery, rising up in great contentions, and deserting away into the land of Nephi, among the Lamanites—

13 And because of this their great wickedness, and their boastings in their own strength, they were left in their own strength; therefore they did not prosper, but were afflicted and smitten, and driven before the Lamanites, until they had lost possession of almost all their lands.

14 But behold, Moronihah did preach many things unto the people because of their iniquity, and also Nephi and Lehi, who were the sons of Helaman, did preach many things unto the people, yea, and did prophesy many things unto them concerning their iniquities, and what should come unto them if they did not repent of their sins.

15 And it came to pass that they did repent, and inasmuch as they did repent they did begin to prosper.

16 For when Moronihah saw that they did repent he did venture to lead them forth from place to place, and from city to city, even until

they had regained the one-half of their property and the one-half of all their lands.

17 And thus ended the sixty and first year of the reign of the judges.

The regaining of one-half of the Nephite lands was accomplished in two years, the sixty and sixty-first year of the judges (vv. 9–10). In Mormon's abridgments he tells why the lands had been lost (vv. 11–13) and the reasons for their lands being regained (vv. 14–15). Both observations are important, the first as a warning to us and the latter was a preventive measure for prosperity.

The wickedness and abominations that caused the loss of their lands were the effects of pride. Pride was an effect of misuse of the riches with which they had been blessed (vv. 11–12). Five years of "great slaughter" could have otherwise been avoided; three years of being driven out, and two years of regaining the losses. However, all was not regained, only one-half. The following illustrates the cause and effect of following Satan. (There is no specific correlation between the lists.)

Cause	Effect on Society
Oppression of the poor	Murder and plunder
Smiting the humble	Lying and stealing
Mocking the sacred	Dissension and contention
Denying revelation and testimony	No strength from the Lord
Boast in own strength	Afflicted and smitten

The regaining of the lands and the prosperity that the Nephites experienced were obtained because of the preaching and prophesying of Moronihah, Nephi, and Lehi (vv. 14–16). Applying their situation to our day, we have a critical choice. Do we follow the prophets, or are we willing to reap the effects of following Satan? Collectively many people in our nation are following Satan. As with the Nephites, many who prefer to belong to the Church today are also lifted up in pride (v. 11). We must use our influence to help them repent and listen to the counsel and testimony of the prophets.

Helaman 4:18–22 • The Prophecies of Alma and the Words of Mosiah

18 And it came to pass in the sixty and second year of the reign of the judges, that Moronihah could obtain no more possessions over the Lamanites.

19 Therefore they did abandon their design to obtain the remainder of their lands, for so numerous were the Lamanites that it became impossible for the Nephites to obtain more power over them; therefore Moronihah did employ all his armies in maintaining those parts which he had taken.

20 And it came to pass, because of the greatness of the number of the Lamanites the Nephites were in great fear, lest they should be overpowered, and trodden down, and slain, and destroyed.

21 Yea, they began to remember the prophecies of Alma, and also the words of Mosiah; and they saw that they had been a stiffnecked people, and that they had set at naught the commandments of God;

22 And that they had altered and trampled under their feet the laws of Mosiah, or that which the Lord commanded him to give unto the people; and they saw that their laws had become corrupted, and that they had become a wicked people, insomuch that they were wicked even like unto the Lamanites.

The remainder of the book of Helaman text covered in this chapter is about the sixty-second year of the reign of the judges. A lesson may be learned from the Nephites in their abandoning their quest for the remainder of the land (v. 19). Sometimes the making of restitution for sins committed is a long process. Had the Nephite nation been so wicked that the Lord required them not to be delivered until they had "paid the uttermost senine" for their sins? Such may have been the case. Their living in great fear (v. 20) may have also been a part of that required payment.

The fulfillment of the prophecies of Alma (v. 21) are not specified. Mormon may have been referring to what is now Alma chapter 5. Such things as pride, persecution of their brethren, and neglecting the poor are referred to in Alma's great sermon to the people of Zarahemla (see Alma 5:53–56). The laws of Mosiah (Alma 4:22) has reference to the new form of government revealed as a part of the reign of the judges (see Mosiah 29). Regardless of the generality used by Mormon in referring to both Alma and Mosiah, Alma's laws were the spiritual guidelines for the church and its members, and the laws of Mosiah were the political or governing laws revealed for a nation. The Nephites had been violating both of these kinds of laws.

Helaman 4:23–26 • The Church Had Dwindled in Unbelief

23 And because of their iniquity the church had begun to dwindle; and they began to disbelieve in the spirit of prophecy and in the spirit of revelation; and the judgments of God did stare them in the face.

24 And they saw that they had become weak, like unto their brethren, the Lamanites, and that the Spirit of the Lord did no more preserve them; yea, it had withdrawn from them because the Spirit of the Lord doth not dwell in unholy temples—

25 Therefore the Lord did cease to preserve them by his miraculous and matchless power, for they had fallen into a state of unbelief and awful wickedness; and they saw that the Lamanites were exceedingly more numerous than they, and except they should cleave unto the Lord their God they must unavoidably perish.

26 For behold, they saw that the strength of the Lamanites was as great as their strength, even man for man. And thus had they fallen into this great transgression; yea, thus had they become weak, because of their transgression, in the space of not many years.

The Nephites disbelief in the spirit of prophecy (v. 23) tells us they had been centered in Christ. The spirit of prophecy is the testimony of Jesus (see Revelation 19:10 and *TPJS*, 119). Their disbelief in the spirit of revelation (v. 23) tells us they were governing the church by the reasoning of men and not by revelation from God (see D&C 8:2–3).

King Mosiah warned his subjects that when "the voice of the people doth choose iniquity, then is the time that the judgments of God will come upon you" (Mosiah 29:27). Thus the Nephites were facing such judgment (Helaman 4:23).

Without the Spirit of the Lord (v. 24) man is left with only his natural instincts, but is also subject to the devil (see Mosiah 3:19). The body is "the temple of God" or "the temple of the Holy Ghost" (1 Corinthians 3:16; 6:19). The Spirit of the Lord withdraws when the body is involved in evil deeds. Thus the Lamanite and Nephite armies were on equal ground, but the Lamanites had the greater advantage because of their numbers (vv. 25–26).

Helaman 5:1–3 • Nephi Delivers up the Judgment-Seat

1 And it came to pass that in this same year, behold, Nephi delivered up the judgment-seat to a man whose name was Cezoram.

2 For as their laws and their governments were established by the voice of the people, and they who chose evil were more numerous than they who chose good, therefore they were ripening for destruction, for the laws had become corrupted.

3 Yea, and this was not all; they were a stiffnecked people, insomuch that they could not be governed by the law nor justice, save it were to their destruction.

Nephi had served as chief judge for nine years or more depending on the time of the fifty-third year that he was appointed (Helaman 3:37), and the time of the year that Cezoram was appointed (Helaman 5:1). These had been tumultuous years for Nephi. In spite of his "justice and equity" in the judgment-seat, and his personal righteousness in keeping "the commandments of God" (Helaman 3:37), the majority of his people were not willing to follow his example (vv. Helaman 5:2–3). Nephi was not giving up but taking another approach.

Helaman 5:4–8 • The Words of Helaman, Father of Nephi and Lehi

4 And it came to pass that Nephi had become weary because of their iniquity; and he yielded up the judgment-seat, and took it upon him to preach the word of God all the remainder of his days, and his brother Lehi also, all the remainder of his days;

5 For they remembered the words which their father Helaman spake unto them. And these are the words which he spake:

6 Behold, my sons, I desire that ye should remember to keep the commandments of God; and I would that ye should declare unto the people these words. Behold, I have given unto you the names of our first parents who came out of the land of Jerusalem; and this I have done that when you remember your names ye may remember them; and when ye remember them ye may remember their works; and when ye remember their works ye may know how that it is said, and also written, that they were good.

7 Therefore, my sons, I would that ye should do that which is good, that it may be said of you, and also written, even as it has been said and written of them.

8 And now my sons, behold I have somewhat more to desire of you, which desire is, that ye may not do these things that ye may boast, but that ye may do these things to lay up for yourselves a treasure in heaven, yea, which is eternal, and which fadeth not away; yea, that ye may have that precious gift of eternal life, which we have reason to suppose hath been given to our fathers.

In choosing "to preach the word of God" (v. 4), Nephi was following the same course as Alma, the first chief judge, although no mention is made of his doing as Alma did. Alma had resigned in the ninth year of his reign because he saw "no way that he might reclaim them save it were in bearing down in pure testimony against them" (Alma 4:20). Nephi's reason was similar but influenced by his father's admonition to both him and his brother Lehi (Helaman 5:5). Thus Nephi had help in trying to save his subjects from destruction (v. 4).

Father Helaman's desire to "declare unto the people these words" (v. 6) is not clear. He probably had reference to the words of the commandments, as indicated by the punctuation of the sentence. On the other hand, Helaman may have meant for them to declare the reason he had named them Nephi and Lehi (vv. 6–7). Regardless, the best way to teach is by personal example. As the Apostle James admonished: "be ye doers of the word, and not hearers only" (James 1:22). Furthermore, all people need to have heroes.

To lay up treasures in heaven is a principle taught in the Sermon on the Mount in the New Testament (see Matthew 6:19–21). That this principle was taught earlier in the Old Testament is evidenced by Helaman teaching the principle to his sons Nephi and Lehi (Helaman 5:8). Helaman had a copy of that part of the Old Testament inscribed on the plates of brass, and he was probably quoting from a plain and precious part of the text that is now lost from the Old Testament (see 1 Nephi 13:26–29). Helaman equates the laying up of treasures in heaven with eternal life (v. 8). In the Sermon on the Mount, Jesus is making a similar comparison, but he does not speak as directly as did Helaman. Someday we will have those plates of brass and will be able to prove that this teaching was once in the Old Testament.

Helaman 5:9–13 • Remember the Word of Past Prophets

9 O remember, remember, my sons, the words which king Benjamin spake unto his people; yea, remember that there is no other way nor means whereby man can be saved, only through the atoning blood of Jesus Christ, who shall come; yea, remember that he cometh to redeem the world.

10 And remember also the words which Amulek spake unto Zeezrom, in the city of Ammonihah; for he said unto him that the Lord surely should come to redeem his people, but that he should not come to redeem them in their sins, but to redeem them from their sins.

11 And he hath power given unto him from the Father to redeem them from their sins because of repentance; therefore he hath sent his angels to declare the tidings of the conditions of repentance, which

bringeth unto the power of the Redeemer, unto the salvation of their souls.

12 And now, my sons, remember, remember that it is upon the rock of our Redeemer, who is Christ, the Son of God, that ye must build your foundation; that when the devil shall send forth his mighty winds, yea, his shafts in the whirlwind, yea, when all his hail and his mighty storm shall beat upon you, it shall have no power over you to drag you down to the gulf of misery and endless wo, because of the rock upon which ye are built, which is a sure foundation, a foundation whereon if men build they cannot fall.

13 And it came to pass that these were the words which Helaman taught to his sons; yea, he did teach them many things which are not written, and also many things which are written.

King Benjamin's words on salvation coming only through Christ, paraphrased by Helaman, were given in his last major speech before his death "And moreover, I say unto you, that there shall be no other name given nor any other way nor means whereby salvation can come unto the children of men, only in and through the name of Christ, the Lord Omnipotent" (Mosiah 3:17; see also 4:7–8). Peter quoted the doctrine to Annas, the Jewish high priest, and his kindred in Jerusalem. "Neither is there salvation in any other: for there is none other name under heaven given among men, whereby we must be saved. (Acts 4:12). Was Peter also quoting from the Old Testament. Although this is the only reference in the Bible to the doctrine, it is quoted often in the Book of Mormon (see 2 Nephi 9:41; 25:20; 31:21).

The words of Amulek to Zeezrom regarding the impossibility of saving people "in their sins" (Helaman 5:10) are again quoted but slightly different by Helaman than by Amulek as recorded in Alma 11:34. In that incident, Zeezrom asks Amulek the question and Amulek answers in the negative, and refers to the word of God. Helaman's explanation to his sons expounds on why Amulek answered in the negative (v. 11). Zeezrom really knew better than his question implied, therefore, Amulek probably didn't need the explanation that Helaman gave his sons.

The building upon the rock of Christ admonished by Helaman (v. 12) is also a New Testament concept that is not found in our present Old Testament. The Sermon on the Mount (Matthew 5:7) concludes with a comparison of the wise man building upon the rock and the foolish man building upon a sandy foundation (see Matthew 7:24–27). The nearly identical sermon given by Jesus to the Nephites in Bountiful in A.D. 34 is prefaced with an admonition to build upon the rock of Christ so that the gates of hell will not prevail against it.

> 39 Verily, verily, I say unto you, that this is my doctrine, and whoso buildeth upon this buildeth upon my rock, and the gates of hell shall not prevail against them.
>
> 40 And whoso shall declare more or less than this, and establish it for my doctrine, the same cometh of evil, and is not built upon my rock; but he buildeth upon a sandy foundation, and the gates of hell stand open to receive such when the floods come and the winds beat upon them. [3 Nephi 11:39–40]

It seems probable that the Matthew account may have had a similar preface, which has been lost. The book of Helaman is a witness for the views that building upon the rock of Christ was once an Old Testament teaching, and also that the prevailing of the gates of hell may have been a part of the Old Testament teaching as well.

The many other things that were taught by Helaman to his sons (Helaman 5:13) may also add to our knowledge of parts lost from the Old Testament.

Helaman 5:14–19 • Nephi and Lehi Preach the Word in Many Lands

> 14 And they did remember his words; and therefore they went forth, keeping the commandments of God, to teach the word of God among all the people of Nephi, beginning at the city Bountiful;
>
> 15 And from thenceforth to the city of Gid; and from the city of Gid to the city of Mulek;

16 And even from one city to another, until they had gone forth among all the people of Nephi who were in the land southward; and from thence into the land of Zarahemla, among the Lamanites.

17 And it came to pass that they did preach with great power, insomuch that they did confound many of those dissenters who had gone over from the Nephites, insomuch that they came forth and did confess their sins and were baptized unto repentance, and immediately returned to the Nephites to endeavor to repair unto them the wrongs which they had done.

18 And it came to pass that Nephi and Lehi did preach unto the Lamanites with such great power and authority, for they had power and authority given unto them that they might speak, and they also had what they should speak given unto them—

19 Therefore they did speak unto the great astonishment of the Lamanites, to the convincing them, insomuch that there were eight thousand of the Lamanites who were in the land of Zarahemla and round about baptized unto repentance, and were convinced of the wickedness of the traditions of their fathers.

Lehi and Nephi began their teaching mission from the north to the south, to the Nephites and then to the Lamanites (vv. 15–16). The order of their preaching was determined by the geographical location of their own people. They were following the order God had prescribed as quoted by Captain Moroni to Pahoran, the chief governor at the time. "The inward vessel shall be cleansed first [the Nephites] and then shall the outer vessel be cleansed [the Lamanites] (Alma 60:23). Those who were converted and returned to preach to the Nephites, from whom they had dissented, were trying to make restitution as a part of their repentance (Helaman 5:17). In preaching to the Lamanites, Nephi and Lehi were blessed (v. 18) according to the Savior's promise in the New Testament, "it shall be given you in that same hour what ye shall speak" (Matthew 10:19 compare D&C 84:85). Was this also taught in the Old Testament? Their words must have been powerful to convince eight thousand Lamanites to enter into the waters of baptism (v. 19).

Helaman 5:20–27 • Nephi and
Lehi Are Cast into Prison

20 And it came to pass that Nephi and Lehi did proceed from thence to go to the land of Nephi.

21 And it came to pass that they were taken by an army of the Lamanites and cast into prison; yea, even in that same prison in which Ammon and his brethren were cast by the servants of Limhi.

22 And after they had been cast into prison many days without food, behold, they went forth into the prison to take them that they might slay them.

23 And it came to pass that Nephi and Lehi were encircled about as if by fire, even insomuch that they durst not lay their hands upon them for fear lest they should be burned. Nevertheless, Nephi and Lehi were not burned; and they were as standing in the midst of fire and were not burned.

24 And when they saw that they were encircled about with a pillar of fire, and that it burned them not, their hearts did take courage.

25 For they saw that the Lamanites durst not lay their hands upon them; neither durst they come near unto them, but stood as if they were struck dumb with amazement.

26 And it came to pass that Nephi and Lehi did stand forth and began to speak unto them, saying: Fear not, for behold, it is God that has shown unto you this marvelous thing, in the which is shown unto you that ye cannot lay your hands on us to slay us.

27 And behold, when they had said these words, the earth shook exceedingly, and the walls of the prison did shake as if they were about to tumble to the earth; but behold, they did not fall. And behold, they that were in the prison were Lamanites and Nephites who were dissenters.

Ammon and his brethren who were cast into prison (v. 20) were not the sons of King Mosiah who went on a mission to the Lamanites. They were Ammon and sixteen men who went to the land of Lehi-Nephi and found the people who had left Zarahemla years before. It was King Limhi, the Nephite king, who put Ammon and his brethren in prison (see Mosiah 7:1–9; Omni 1:27–30). Thus some ninety years had passed since the first imprisonment, from about 121 B.C. to about 30 B.C.

The encirclement "as if by fire" (Helaman 5:23) was undoubtedly the glory of God that may not always be discernable to the physical eye. The Prophet Joseph Smith taught: "Spirits can only be revealed in flaming fire and glory. Angels have advanced further, their light and glory being tabernacled; and hence they appear in bodily shape" (*TPJS*, 325). Apparently angels were attending to Nephi and Lehi. Nephi and Lehi recognized the presence of God in their midst (v. 26)

The shaking of the prison (v. 27) was similar to Alma and Amulek being loosed from prison in the city of Ammonihah (see Alma 14:17–29). There is also a similar incident in the Bible. Paul and Silas were loosed from prison in Philippi by an earthquake and the power of God (Acts 16:23–40).

Helaman 5:28–34 • A Voice From Above the Darkness

28 And it came to pass that they were overshadowed with a cloud of darkness, and an awful solemn fear came upon them.

29 And it came to pass that there came a voice as if it were above the cloud of darkness, saying: Repent ye, repent ye, and seek no more to destroy my servants whom I have sent unto you to declare good tidings.

30 And it came to pass when they heard this voice, and beheld that it was not a voice of thunder, neither was it a voice of a great tumultuous noise, but behold, it was a still voice of perfect mildness, as if it had been a whisper, and it did pierce even to the very soul—

31 And notwithstanding the mildness of the voice, behold the earth shook exceedingly, and the walls of the prison trembled again, as if it were about to tumble to the earth; and behold the cloud of darkness, which had overshadowed them, did not disperse—

32 And behold the voice came again, saying: Repent ye, repent ye, for the kingdom of heaven is at hand; and seek no more to destroy

my servants. And it came to pass that the earth shook again, and the walls trembled.

33 And also again the third time the voice came, and did speak unto them marvelous words which cannot be uttered by man; and the walls did tremble again, and the earth shook as if it were about to divide asunder.

34 And it came to pass that the Lamanites could not flee because of the cloud of darkness which did overshadow them; yea, and also they were immovable because of the fear which did come upon them.

The first purpose of the voice to the Lamanites was to protect the Lord's servants (v. 29). We know of no promise given to Nephi and or Lehi, but the Lord will always protect his servants until their mission is completed (see Mosiah 13:3–4; *TPJS*, 274; 328). The description of the voice (Helaman 5:30) reminds us of the "still small voice" that was heard by Elijah in Horeb, the mount of God.

11 And he said, Go forth, and stand upon the mount before the LORD. And, behold, the LORD passed by, and a great and strong wind rent the mountains, and brake in pieces the rocks before the LORD; but the LORD was not in the wind: and after the wind an earthquake; but the LORD was not in the earthquake:

12 And after the earthquake a fire; but the LORD was not in the fire: and after the fire a still small voice. [1 Kings 19:11–12]

The Prophet Joseph also referred to "the still small voice, which whispereth through and pierceth all things." [D&C 85:6]

The second time they heard the voice was an announcement of the kingdom being at hand (Helaman 5:32) The reference to the kingdom must have been to the Savior coming to the earth to establish his higher law. The voice was apparently speaking of the Lord's time since the time period was about 30 B.C. The message of the third time they heard the voice (v. 33) was not disclosed because of its sacred and divine message. Someday we may learn what was said (see 3 Nephi 26:6–12). The fear and the darkness upon the Lamanites (Helaman 5:34) made them a captive audience, which was probably the purpose desired by the hand of the Lord.

Helaman 5:35–42 • The Cloud of Darkness Is Dispersed

35 Now there was one among them who was a Nephite by birth, who had once belonged to the church of God but had dissented from them.

36 And it came to pass that he turned him about, and behold, he saw through the cloud of darkness the faces of Nephi and Lehi; and behold, they did shine exceedingly, even as the faces of angels. And he beheld that they did lift their eyes to heaven; and they were in the attitude as if talking or lifting their voices to some being whom they beheld.

37 And it came to pass that this man did cry unto the multitude, that they might turn and look. And behold, there was power given unto them that they did turn and look; and they did behold the faces of Nephi and Lehi.

38 And they said unto the man: Behold, what do all these things mean, and who is it with whom these men do converse?

39 Now the man's name was Aminadab. And Aminadab said unto them: They do converse with the angels of God.

40 And it came to pass that the Lamanites said unto him: What shall we do, that this cloud of darkness may be removed from overshadowing us?

41 And Aminadab said unto them: You must repent, and cry unto the voice, even until ye shall have faith in Christ, who was taught unto you by Alma, and Amulek, and Zeezrom; and when ye shall do this, the cloud of darkness shall be removed from overshadowing you.

42 And it came to pass that they all did begin to cry unto the voice of him who had shaken the earth; yea, they did cry even until the cloud of darkness was dispersed.

The Nephite dissenter who saw through the cloud of darkness was undoubtedly chosen by the Lord. The Lord certainly knew Aminadab would respond as he did and used him to convert the others (vv.

35–37). We do not know what caused Aminadab to dissent, but he was knowledgeable of spiritual things, as shown by the answers to the questions of the multitude of Lamanites who were captive to the cloud of darkness (vv. 38–41). Aminadab knew of the teaching of Alma, Amulek, and Zeezrom (v. 41).

Helaman 5:43–49 • The Lamanites Are Baptized with Fire

43 And it came to pass that when they cast their eyes about, and saw that the cloud of darkness was dispersed from overshadowing them, behold, they saw that they were encircled about, yea every soul, by a pillar of fire.

44 And Nephi and Lehi were in the midst of them; yea, they were encircled about; yea, they were as if in the midst of a flaming fire, yet it did harm them not, neither did it take hold upon the walls of the prison; and they were filled with that joy which is unspeakable and full of glory.

45 And behold, the Holy Spirit of God did come down from heaven, and did enter into their hearts, and they were filled as if with fire, and they could speak forth marvelous words.

46 And it came to pass that there came a voice unto them, yea, a pleasant voice, as if it were a whisper, saying:

47 Peace, peace be unto you, because of your faith in my Well Beloved, who was from the foundation of the world.

48 And now, when they heard this they cast up their eyes as if to behold from whence the voice came; and behold, they saw the heavens open; and angels came down out of heaven and ministered unto them.

49 And there were about three hundred souls who saw and heard these things; and they were bidden to go forth and marvel not, neither should they doubt.

The "pillar of fire" (v. 43) was the baptism or immersion of the Lamanites by the Holy Ghost. When Jesus spoke to the Nephites after his resurrection, he referred to the baptism and conversion of the Lamanites. "And ye shall offer for a sacrifice unto me a broken heart and a contrite spirit. And whoso cometh unto me with a broken heart and a contrite spirit, him will I baptize with fire and with the Holy Ghost, even as the Lamanites, because of their faith in me at the time of their conversion, were baptized with fire and with the Holy Ghost, and they knew it not" (3 Nephi 9:20). The Lamanites did not know it was a baptism of the Holy Ghost but they certainly knew something marvelous had happened to them.[1] The dispersion of the cloud of darkness (Helaman 5:42) was also accompanied by the cleansing or remission of the sins of the Lamanites (see Moroni 6:4; 8:25). The unspeakable joy that followed, and the Holy Spirit that entered into their hearts (Helaman 5:44–45), was what Mormon later described to his son Moroni as "the visitation of the Holy Ghost, which Comforter filleth with hope and perfect love" (Moroni 8:26). Their experience of speaking "marvelous words" (Helaman 5:45) could also be equated with King Benjamin's description of the born again person having "great views of that which is to come; and were it expedient, we could prophecy of all things" (Mosiah 5:3). The experience was great in quality and quantity. They had great faith in Christ (Helaman 5:47) and a marvelous experience individually. There were three hundred souls converted at the same time (v. 49), an amazing quantity as well.

Helaman 5:50–52 • The More Part of the Lamanites Are Converted

> 50 And it came to pass that they did go forth, and did minister unto the people, declaring throughout all the regions round about all the things which they had heard and seen, insomuch that the more part of the Lamanites were convinced of them, because of the greatness of the evidences which they had received.
>
> 51 And as many as were convinced did lay down their weapons of war, and also their hatred and the tradition of their fathers.

---

[1] For a more complete explanation of 3 Nephi 9:20 see Monte S. Nyman, *The Divine Ministry*, Granite Publishing and Distribution, LLC, Orem, UT [2003] 110, Commentary under 3 Nephi 9:20.

52 And it came to pass that they did yield up unto the Nephites the lands of their possession.

Three hundred missionaries of their own people was certainly an effective group. We don't know the total population of the Lamanites at this time, but it was certainly comparable and probably surpassed the thousands brought to the fold of God by the sons of Mosiah (see Alma 26:4), and even the tens of thousands brought into the church by Helaman and his two sons Nephi and Lehi about ten years earlier (Helaman 4:24–26). The results were three-fold; the end of war, the healing of hatred, and the return of land to the Nephites (Helaman 5:51–52).

Helaman 6:1–6 • Great Joy from the Lamanite Conversions – 62nd Year

1 And it came to pass that when the sixty and second year of the reign of the judges had ended, all these things had happened and the Lamanites had become, the more part of them, a righteous people, insomuch that their righteousness did exceed that of the Nephites, because of their firmness and their steadiness in the faith.

2 For behold, there were many of the Nephites who had become hardened and impenitent and grossly wicked, insomuch that they did reject the word of God and all the preaching and prophesying which did come among them.

3 Nevertheless, the people of the church did have great joy because of the conversion of the Lamanites, yea, because of the church of God, which had been established among them. And they did fellowship one with another, and did rejoice one with another, and did have great joy.

4 And it came to pass that many of the Lamanites did come down into the land of Zarahemla, and did declare unto the people of the Nephites the manner of their conversion, and did exhort them to faith and repentance.

5 Yea, and many did preach with exceedingly great power and authority, unto the bringing down many of them into the depths of humility, to be the humble followers of God and the Lamb.

6 And it came to pass that many of the Lamanites did go into the land northward; and also Nephi and Lehi went into the land northward, to preach unto the people. And thus ended the sixty and third year.

These six verses summarize the year (63rd) following the great conversion of the Lamanites (v. 1). The tables had turned rapidly. The Lamanites were more righteous than the Nephites (v. 1). The Nephites were now rejecting the word of God (v. 2). The Lamanites were going on missions to the Nephites and preaching with the power and authority that had been the trademark of the Nephites (v. 5). The mission of Nephi and Lehi to the land northward (v. 6) was to the Nephites who had migrated earlier (see Alma 63:4–9).

Helaman 6:7–14 • Peace in All the Land – 64th and 65th Year

7 And behold, there was peace in all the land, insomuch that the Nephites did go into whatsoever part of the land they would, whether among the Nephites or the Lamanites.

8 And it came to pass that the Lamanites did also go whithersoever they would, whether it were among the Lamanites or among the Nephites; and thus they did have free intercourse one with another, to buy and to sell, and to get gain, according to their desire.

9 And it came to pass that they became exceedingly rich, both the Lamanites and the Nephites; and they did have an exceeding plenty of gold, and of silver, and of all manner of precious metals, both in the land south and in the land north.

10 Now the land south was called Lehi and the land north was called Mulek, which was after the son of Zedekiah; for the Lord did bring Mulek into the land north, and Lehi into the land south.

11 And behold, there was all manner of gold in both these lands, and of silver, and of precious ore of every kind; and there were also curious workmen, who did work all kinds of ore and did refine it; and thus they did become rich.

12 They did raise grain in abundance, both in the north and in the south; and they did flourish exceedingly, both in the north and in the

south. And they did multiply and wax exceedingly strong in the land. And they did raise many flocks and herds, yea, many fatlings.

13 Behold their women did toil and spin, and did make all manner of cloth, of fine-twined linen and cloth of every kind, to clothe their nakedness. And thus the sixty and fourth year did pass away in peace.

14 And in the sixty and fifth year they did also have great joy and peace, yea, much preaching and many prophecies concerning that which was to come. And thus passed away the sixty and fifth year.

The prosperity of both the Nephites and the Lamanites (vv. 9–12) is evidence of the material blessing that comes from living the gospel. This is a lesson that is taught throughout the Book of Mormon (see 2 Nephi 1:20; Jarom 1:9; Mosiah 1:7; Alma 1:29–31).

The land south was called Lehi and the land north was called Mulek because of the places of their landings (Helaman 6:10). All of it was a land chosen of the Lord (see Alma 46:17). The word Mulek in Hebrew means "little king," and Mulek was the young son of Zedekiah, king of Judah at the time Babylon destroyed Jerusalem. All of his sons were killed but Mulek.[2] The exact place of either the Lehi or Mulek landing is not known and is somewhat controversial.

The brevity of the record of the sixty-fifth year is because of the peace that existed (Helaman 6:14). The Book of Mormon contains a record of a fallen people and the fullness of the gospel of Jesus Christ (D&C 20:9). When either peace of wickedness is continuous for a lengthy time, it is usually treated sparsely in the abridgment (see Helaman 6:33 for the brevity of continuous wickedness).

Helaman 6:15–19 • Two Chief Judges Killed in the Same Year—66th and 67th Year

15 And it came to pass that in the sixty and sixth year of the reign of the judges, behold, Cezoram was murdered by an unknown hand as he sat upon the judgment-seat. And it came to pass that in the same

---

[2] See Omni 1:14–16 and the commentary in volume two of this work, *These Records are True* [2004], 158–163.

year, that his son, who had been appointed by the people in his stead, was also murdered. And thus ended the sixty and sixth year.

16 And in the commencement of the sixty and seventh year the people began to grow exceedingly wicked again.

17 For behold, the Lord had blessed them so long with the riches of the world that they had not been stirred up to anger, to wars, nor to bloodshed; therefore they began to set their hearts upon their riches; yea, they began to seek to get gain that they might be lifted up one above another; therefore they began to commit secret murders, and to rob and to plunder, that they might get gain.

18 And now behold, those murderers and plunderers were a band who had been formed by Kishkumen and Gadianton. And now it had come to pass that there were many, even among the Nephites, of Gadianton's band. But behold, they were more numerous among the more wicked part of the Lamanites. And they were called Gadianton's robbers and murderers.

19 And it was they who did murder the chief judge Cezoram, and his son, while in the judgment-seat; and behold, they were not found.

The peace and prosperity was short-lived. Just as the Book of Mormon teaches continuously of prosperity when the gospel is lived, it also warns repeatedly of pride that usually comes because of those riches (see Jacob 2:13; Alma 4:6; D&C 38:39). Pride led to murders (Helaman 6:15) and the resurgence of the Gadianton robbers and murderers (vv. 17–18). These verses remind us of the death of John F. Kennedy, Robert Kennedy, and the attempt on the life of Ronald Reagan.

Helaman 6:20–24 • The Laws and Wickedness of Gadianton and Kishkumen

20 And now it came to pass that when the Lamanites found that there were robbers among them they were exceedingly sorrowful; and they did use every means in their power to destroy them off the face of the earth.

21 But behold, Satan did stir up the hearts of the more part of the Nephites, insomuch that they did unite with those bands of robbers,

and did enter into their covenants and their oaths, that they would protect and preserve one another in whatsoever difficult circumstances they should be placed, that they should not suffer for their murders, and their plunderings, and their stealings.

22 And it came to pass that they did have their signs, yea, their secret signs, and their secret words; and this that they might distinguish a brother who had entered into the covenant, that whatsoever wickedness his brother should do he should not be injured by his brother, nor by those who did belong to his band, who had taken this covenant.

23 And thus they might murder, and plunder, and steal, and commit whoredoms and all manner of wickedness, contrary to the laws of their country and also the laws of their God.

24 And whosoever of those who belonged to their band should reveal unto the world of their wickedness and their abominations, should be tried, not according to the laws of their country, but according to the laws of their wickedness, which had been given by Gadianton and Kishkumen.

It is interesting that the secret combinations were more successful among the Nephites than the Lamanites (vv. 20–21). Since the righteousness of the Lamanites did exceed that of the Nephites (see 6:1 above), the Nephites were more susceptible to Satan (v. 21). The devil takes power when commandments are broken (see *TPJS*, 181).

We notice the similarities but yet the contrast between the church and the secret combinations. The church members entered into *sacred* covenants and oaths. Secret combinations have their *secret* covenants and oaths (v. 21). Church members should be willing to lay down their lives for a brother or sister in the gospel (see 1 John 3:16). Secret combinations protect their fellow members who have murdered (Helaman 6:21). the church member recognizes fellow members as brothers and sisters in the gospel and calls them his brothers and sisters (see Matthew 12:49–50). The band of robbers had secret signs and words to recognize and protect a brother in his wickedness (Helaman 6:22–23). The church members believed "in obeying, honoring, and sustaining the law" (*Articles of Faith*, 12). The Gadianton band followed the laws of their wickedness but lived contrary to the just laws of their country and their God (Helaman 6:23–24). Thus, they followed Satan rather than Christ.

Helaman 6:25–33 • The Oaths and Covenants Come from Satan

25 Now behold, it is these secret oaths and covenants which Alma commanded his son should not go forth unto the world, lest they should be a means of bringing down the people unto destruction.

26 Now behold, those secret oaths and covenants did not come forth unto Gadianton from the records which were delivered unto Helaman; but behold, they were put into the heart of Gadianton by that same being who did entice our first parents to partake of the forbidden fruit—

27 Yea, that same being who did plot with Cain, that if he would murder his brother Abel it should not be known unto the world. And he did plot with Cain and his followers from that time forth.

28 And also it is that same being who put it into the hearts of the people to build a tower sufficiently high that they might get to heaven. And it was that same being who led on the people who came from that tower into this land; who spread the works of darkness and abominations over all the face of the land, until he dragged the people down to an entire destruction, and to an everlasting hell.

29 Yea, it is that same being who put it into the heart of Gadianton to still carry on the work of darkness, and of secret murder; and he has brought it forth from the beginning of man even down to this time.

30 And behold, it is he who is the author of all sin. And behold, he doth carry on his works of darkness and secret murder, and doth hand down their plots, and their oaths, and their covenants, and their plans of awful wickedness, from generation to generation according as he can get hold upon the hearts of the children of men.

31 And now behold, he had got great hold upon the hearts of the Nephites; yea, insomuch that they had become exceedingly wicked; yea, the more part of them had turned out of the way of righteousness, and did trample under their feet the commandments of God, and did

turn unto their own ways, and did build up unto themselves idols of their gold and their silver.

32 And it came to pass that all these iniquities did come unto them in the space of not many years, insomuch that a more part of it had come unto them in the sixty and seventh year of the reign of the judges over the people of Nephi.

33 And they did grow in their iniquities in the sixty and eighth year also, to the great sorrow and lamentation of the righteous.

Alma had commanded his son Helaman to keep the oath, covenants and agreements of the secret combinations from the people lest they fall into darkness and are destroyed (see Alma 37:27–32). These same secret oaths and covenants were prevalent among the Nephites for about fifty years (74–24 B.C.) after Alma had given that charge (Helaman 6:25). Helaman followed his father's directions (v. 26), so how were they made known? Satan can give revelation. The Prophet Joseph Smith taught that: "Some revelations are of God, some revelations are of man, and some revelations are of the devil."[3] (see also 3 Nephi 27:10–12; D&C 46:7). Gadianton had received revelation from Satan (Helaman 6:26).

In verifying Satan's part in the fall of Adam and Eve (Helaman 6:26; Genesis 3; Moses 4:1–9), Cain's murder of Abel (Helaman 6:27; Genesis 4:1–8; Moses 5:26–33), and the building of the tower of Babel (Helaman 6:28; Geneses 11:1–9), the Book of Mormon is "proving to the world that the holy scriptures are true" (D&C 20:11). This is one of the Book of Mormon's major purposes. The world rejects the above scriptural accounts and labels them as myths and legends.[4] Satan's work had continued from the time of Adam to the time of Gadianton (Helaman 6:29–30), basically the entire time of the Old Testament. His work still continues today.

---

[3] B. H. Roberts, *Comprehensive History of the Church*, 7 vols. [1925], 1:163.

[4] See Cuthbeat A. Simpson,"The Book of Genesis," in *The Interpreters Bible*, 1: 481, 561, 520.

Satan is the author or initiator of many things in the world. He is the author of sin (v. 30). He is "the father of all lies" (Moses 4:4). He is also "the father of contention" (3 Nephi 11:29). All of these are attributes or part of his works of darkness through all generations (Helaman 6:30). His work is effective and rapid in bringing wickedness among those who allow him to get hold of their hearts. The more part of the Nephites had made a near one-hundred-eighty degree turn in just two years, the sixty-sixth (v. 15), and the sixty-seventh (v. 32), and grew in inequality in the sixty-eighth (v. 33). The cycle of the Nephites from peace and prosperity to abominations and back to peace is illustrated in the table below. This cycle was a fifteen-year period. The periods of time vary.

Table 2
The Cycle of the Nephites

Year	Condition	Reference	Year Repeated	Reference
49–50	Peace & Prosperity	3:23–36	64–65	6:7–14
51–53	Pride Disbelief Dissension	3:33–36 3:33–36 4:1–4	66–67 67	6:15–17 6:18–24
57–62	Contention Abominations Preach the word Humility Conversion	4:5–16 4:14–19 4:20–26 5:20–52	67–68	6:31–33
63	Peace & Prosperity	6:1–6		

Helaman 6:34–41 • Mormon's
Summary of Year Sixty-eight

34 And thus we see that the Nephites did begin to dwindle in unbelief, and grow in wickedness and abominations, while the Lamanites began to grow exceedingly in the knowledge of their God;

yea, they did begin to keep his statutes and commandments, and to walk in truth and uprightness before him.

35 And thus we see that the Spirit of the Lord began to withdraw from the Nephites, because of the wickedness and the hardness of their hearts.

36 And thus we see that the Lord began to pour out his Spirit upon the Lamanites, because of their easiness and willingness to believe in his words.

37 And it came to pass that the Lamanites did hunt the band of robbers of Gadianton; and they did preach the word of God among the more wicked part of them, insomuch that this band of robbers was utterly destroyed from among the Lamanites.

38 And it came to pass on the other hand, that the Nephites did build them up and support them, beginning at the more wicked part of them, until they had overspread all the land of the Nephites, and had seduced the more part of the righteous until they had come down to believe in their works and partake of their spoils, and to join with them in their secret murders and combinations.

39 And thus they did obtain the sole management of the government, insomuch that they did trample under their feet and smite and rend and turn their backs upon the poor and the meek, and the humble followers of God.

40 And thus we see that they were in an awful state, and ripening for an everlasting destruction.

41 And it came to pass that thus ended the sixty and eighth year of the reign of the judges over the people of Nephi.

Mormon gave the reader four "thus we see" precepts as he recorded the events of the 68th year (vv. 33, 41). The first lesson of life is the equation of unbelief and wickedness among the Nephites. He then equates the knowledge of God with walking in truth and uprightness (v. 34). In the words of Elder Boyd K. Packer:

> "True doctrine, understood, changes attitude and behavior. The study of the doctrine of the gospel will improve behaviors quicker than a study of behavior will change behavior. Preoccupation with unworthy behavior can lead to unworthy behavior. That is why we

stress so forcefully the study of the doctrines of the gospel" [CR, Oct. 1986, 20; see also CR, Apr. 1997, 8]

The second lesson of life is the reason why the Spirit withdraws from us—wickedness (v. 35). As King Benjamin had taught to the people in Zarahemla, and Alma to the people in the land of Gideon, the Lord "dwelleth not in unholy temples" (Mosiah 2:37; Alma 7:21; see also Helaman 4:24; 1 Corinthians 3:16–17; 6:18–19). This condition is taking place again in these latter days. President Joseph Fielding Smith warned the Church in 1967 that the Spirit was withdrawing from America.

> "Now the Lord has withdrawn His Spirit from the world. Do not let this thought become confused in your minds. The Spirit He has withdrawn from the world is not the Holy Ghost (for they never had that!), but it is the light of truth, spoken of in our scriptures as the Spirit of Christ, which is given to every man that cometh into the world, as you find recorded in section 84 of the Doctrine and Covenants.
>
> "Now because of the wickedness of the world, that Spirit has been withdrawn, and when the Spirit of the Lord is not striving with men, the spirit of Satan is. Therefore, we may be sure that the time has come spoken of in section 1 of the Doctrine and Covenants, wherein the Lord says:
>
> For I am no respecter of persons, and will that all men shall know that the day speedily cometh; the hour is not yet, but is nigh at hand, when peace shall be taken from the earth, and the devil shall have power over his own dominion. [D&C 1:35]
>
> "Peace *has* been taken from the earth. The devil *has* power over *his own* dominion. The Spirit of the Lord *has* been withdrawn."[5]

America has certainly become more wicked since that warning was given, and thus that Spirit has withdrawn further.

The third lesson of life is related to the second lesson above. The Spirit began to come "upon the Lamanites because of their easiness

---

[5] Joseph Fielding Smith, "Predicted Judgments," *Speeches of the Year*, Brigham Young University Press, Provo, Utah, Mar. 21, 1967.

and willingness to believe in his words" (Helaman 6:36). The same condition is also happening again in our day. The modern-day Lamanites, those residing in Central and South America are receiving the word of God much more readily than any other place in the world. Two thirds of the converts in the years of the 1990's came from those countries.[6]

As a continuation of lesson three, Mormon observed the contrast of the Nephites and Lamanites reaction to the Gadianton robbers. Through the preaching of the word of God by the Lamanites among the more wicked part, they were eliminated (v. 37). We must assume from this statement that not all of the robbers accepted the gospel. However, many did accept the gospel which probably caused those who didn't respond to the word of God to relocate among the Nephites where the Gadianton robbers were having much success.

The spread of the secret combinations among the Nephites (v. 38), also has its parallel to our day. As the government process has incorporated more and more socialistic principles into the laws of the United States, even the more righteous are believing in the works of a welfare system because they receive financial spoils as did the Nephites (v. 38). Our leaders have consistently, warned the church against the dole system.[7]

The sole management of the government as among the Nephites (v. 39) has not happened in our day, but secret combinations have certainly been an influential element. Since the assassination of John F. Kennedy there has been much speculation and many accusations of their involvement. At the time of the Second Coming, when the sixth angel sounds his trump and reveals "the secret acts of man, and the mighty works of God" in the sixth thousand years (D&C 88:108–110), many will undoubtedly be amazed at how much influence the secret combinations have had in our own day.

[6] Daniel H. Ludlow, ed., "Much success," *Encyclopedia of Mormonism*, 5 vols. [1992], 4:1525–26.

[7] The warning of the dole system began in 1936 with the First Presidency statement on public welfare and has continued since then. See General Authority Quotes.

The fourth lesson of life is more of a warning against the awful state and ripening for destruction that came upon the Nephites (Helaman 6:40). As Nephi, son of Lehi, proclaimed, when a people are "ripe in iniquity . . . the fullness of the wrath of God [comes] upon them . . . and destroyeth the nations of the wicked" (1 Nephi 17:35–37). The Amorites in Abraham's day were not destroyed because "the iniquity of the Amorites [was] not yet full" (Genesis 15:16). The U.S. Constitution will be saved:

Elder Ezra Taft Benson:

> . . . Concerning the United States, the Lord revealed to his prophets that its greatest threat would be a vast, world-wide "secret combination" which would not only threaten the United States but also see to "over-throw the freedom of all lands, nations, and countries" (Ether 8:25).

> . . . In connection with attack on the United States, the Lord told the Prophet Joseph Smith there would be an attempt to overthrow the country by destroying the Constitution. Joseph Smith predicted that the time would come when the Constitution would hang, as it were, by a thread, and at that time, "this people will step forth and save it from the threatened destruction" (*Journal History*, Brigham Young's Speech, July 4, 1854).

> It is my conviction that the elders of Israel, widely spread over the nation, will at that crucial time successfully rally the righteous of our country and provide the necessary balance of strength to save the institutions of constitutional government (CR, Oct.1961, 70).

SACRED WRITING

Preaching Which Is Sacred:

Helaman 5:6–12   Helaman to his sons.

Revelation Which Is Great:

Helaman 5:29, 32   The Lord speaks to the Lamanites.
Helaman 5:44–48   The Lord speaks to Nephi and Lehi.

Prophesying:

Helaman 4:21–26   The fulfillment of Alma's Prophecies.

Doctrines Learned:

Helaman 4:11–13	Pride, neglect of the poor, denying revelation, and wickedness leaves a people on their own strength.
Helaman 4:24	The Spirit of the Lord did not dwell in unholy tabernacles.
Helaman 5:9	There is no other way nor means to be saved but the atoning blood of Jesus Christ.
Helaman 5:10	The Lord does not redeem his people in their sins but from their sins.
Helaman 5:12	Men must build their foundation upon the rock of Christ to prevent the devil' temptations from over-powering them (this was taught in Old Testament times).
Helaman 5:17	A part of repentance is restitution.
Helaman 5:18	The Spirit directs the Lord' servants in what they say.
Helaman 5:23	The Lord can protect his servants with a pillar of fire (Holy Ghost).
Helaman 5:29–30	The voice of the Lord is soft and mild yet pierces to the very center.
Helaman 5:41	Repentance and crying unto the Lord until ye have faith in Christ will dispel darkness.
Helaman 5:44–45	A baptism of fire and the Holy Ghost fills with joy and unspeakable glory enabling one to speak marvelous words.
Helaman 6:10	Mulek landed in the land north and Lehi in the land south.
Helaman 6:25	Secret combinations are revealed anew by Satan. Satan can give revelation.
Helaman 6:30	Satan is the author of all sin.

General Authority Quotes

President George Albert Smith • Helaman 5:6

"A number of years ago I was seriously ill, in fact, I think everyone gave me up but my wife. With my family I went to St. George, Utah, to see if it would improve my health. We went as far as we could by train, and then continued the journey in a wagon, in the bottom of which a bed had been made for me.

In St. George we arranged for a tent for my health and comfort, with a built-in floor raised about a foot above the ground, and we could roll up the south side of the tent to make the sunshine and fresh air available. I became so weak as to be scarcely able to move. It was a slow and exhausting effort for me even to turn over in bed.

One day, under these conditions, I lost consciousness of my surroundings and thought I had passed to the Other Side. I found myself standing with my back to a large and beautiful lake, facing a great forest of trees. There was no one in sight, and there was no boat upon the lake or any other visible means to indicate how I might have arrived there. I realized, or seemed to realize, that I had finished my work in mortality and had gone home. I began to look around, to see if I could find someone. There was no evidence of anyone living there, just those great, beautiful trees in front of me and the wonderful lake behind me.

I began to explore, and soon I found a trail through the woods which seemed to have been used very little, and which was almost obscured by grass. I followed this trail, and after I had walked for some time and had traveled a considerable distance through the forest, I saw a man coming towards me. I became aware that he was a very large man, and I hurried my steps to reach him, because I recognized him as my grandfather. In mortality he weighted over three hundred pounds, so you may know he was a large man. I remember how happy I was to see him coming. I had been given his name and had always been proud of it.

When grandfather came within a few feet of me, he stopped. His stopping was an invitation for me to stop. Then—and this I would like the boys and girls and young people never to forget—he looked at me very earnestly and said: "I would like to know what you have done with my name.""

Everything I had ever done passed before me as though it were a flying picture on a screen—everything I had done. Quickly this vivid retrospect came down to the very time I was standing there. My whole life passed before me. I smiled and looked at my grandfather and said: "I have never done anything with your name of which you need be ashamed."

He stepped forward and took me in his arms, and as he did so, I became conscious again of my earthly surroundings. My pillow was as wet as though water had been poured on it—wet with tears of gratitude that I could answer unashamed.

I have thought of this many times, and I want to tell you that I have been trying, more than ever since that time, to take care of that name. So I want to say to the boys and girls, to the young men and women, to the youth of the Church and all the world: Honor your fathers and mothers. Honor the names that you bear, because some day you will have the privilege and the obligation of reporting to them (and to your Father in Heaven) what you have done with their name. [*Sharing the Gospel With Others*, (1950), 110–112]

President Lorenzo Snow • Helaman 5:43–45

"I had no sooner opened my lips in an effort to pray than I heard a sound just above my head like the rushing of silken robes; and immediately the Spirit of God descended upon me, completely enveloping my whole person, filling me from the crown of my head to the soles of my feet, and oh, the joyful happiness I felt! No language can describe the almost instantaneous transition from a dense cloud of spiritual darkness into a refulgence of light and knowledge, as it was at that time imparted to my understanding. I received a perfect knowledge that God lives, that Jesus Christ is the Son of God, and of the restoration of the Holy Priesthood, and the fullness of the Gospel. It was a complete baptism—a tangible immersion in the heavenly principle or element, the Holy Ghost; and even more physical in its effects upon every part of my system than the immersion by water." [*A Comprehensive History of the Church*, 6:384]

The Prophet Joseph Smith • Helaman 6:21

"... I would further suggest the impropriety of the organization of bands or companies, by covenant or oaths, by penalties or secrecies; but let the time past of our experience and sufferings by the wickedness of Doctor Avard suffice and let our covenant be that of the Everlasting Covenant, as is contained in the Holy Writ and the things that God hath revealed unto us. Pure friendship always becomes weakened the very moment you undertake to make it stronger by penal oaths and secrecy. . . ." [*TPJS,* 146]

President John Taylor • Helaman 6:21–31

"I am sorry to see this *murderous influence* prevailing throughout the world, and perhaps this may be a fitting occasion to refer to some of these matters. The manifestation of turbulence and uneasiness which prevail among the nations of the earth are truly lamentable. . . . These feelings which tend to do away with all right, rule and government, and correct principles are not from God, or many of them are not. This feeling of *communism* and nihilism, aimed at the overthrow of rulers and men in position and authority, arises from a spirit of diabolism, which is contrary to every principle of the Gospel of the Son of God. . . ."

"These things are beginning to spread among and permeate the nations of the earth. Do we expect them? Yes. These *secret combinations* were spoken by Joseph Smith, years and years ago. I have heard him time and time again tell about them, and *he stated that when these things began to take place the liberties of this nation would begin to be bartered away.*" [President John Taylor in *Journal of Discourses,* (1831), 22:142–43]

President Joseph F. Smith • Helaman 6:21–31

". . . It is a well known truth that the counsel of the First Presidency of the Church, in all cases, has been and is against our brethren joining secret organizations for any purpose whatsoever, and that wherever any of them have already joined, they have been and are counseled to withdraw themselves from such organizations, as soon as circumstances permit and wisdom dictates. In taking this position, there has not been, neither is it intended that there shall be, any controversy with the societies, and with their aims and objects. The merits of the various orders are not considered at all; their aims may be ever so worthy and their objects ever so commendable. That matter does not enter into the discussion, so far as a member of our Church is concerned.

The gospel of Jesus Christ is true, and is a power unto salvation, temporal and spiritual. A man who complies in every respect therewith has everything that any society can offer, with countless truths and consolations added: "But seek ye first the kingdom of God, and his righteousness; and all these things shall be added unto you." The Church is divinely organized, and in that organization there is provision for the development and practice of every virtue known, every charity revealed. For this reason and for its promise of eternal life and glory, the gospel, and the Church divinely established for its promulgation, should be nearer and dearer to a follower of Christ than all other things. "No man can serve two masters; for either he will hate the one, and love the other; or else he will hold to the one and despise the other. Ye can not serve God and Mammon."

The members of our Church who have faith to heed the advice of the authorities thereof, will not ally themselves, under any pretense, with any organization not instituted by the Lord for the building up of Zion. Neither will they, for any consideration, allow themselves to imbibe the spirit of the world, or be tempted to lose their faith, which will be the result with those who divide their interests, devoting some to other organizations. This is the testimony of those who have joined and who have later withdrawn. Nothing can be permitted in the members that is calculated to bring division and weakness to the Church, yet those who have been led to join other institutions should not be dealt with harshly, but should be made to understand the position of the Church, and where it is so understood, they should shape their affairs for withdrawal, in humility and repentance, from that which threatens their standing." [*Gospel Doctrine*, (1939), 111].

The First Presidency • Helaman 6:38

"Our primary purpose was to set up, in so far as it might be possible, a system under which the curse of idleness would be done away with, the evils of a dole abolished, and independence, industry, thrift and self respect be once more established amongst our people. The aim of the Church is to help the people to help themselves. Work is to be re-enthroned as the ruling principle of the lives of our Church membership.

Our great leader, Brigham Young, under similar conditions, said:

"Set the poor to work—setting our orchards, splitting rails, digging ditches, making fences, or anything useful, and so enable them to buy meal and flour and the necessities of life."

This admonition is as timely today as when Brigham Young made it." [*Messages of the First Presidency*, Oct. 2, 1936, 6:19]

Challenges to Eternal Life:

1. Commit yourself to pay a generous fast offering that the poor may be fed, clothed and sheltered (Helaman 4:11–13).

2. Follow your ancestry to see whose name you were given and live to honor that name (Helaman 5:6).

3. Undertake a careful study of the scriptures that you may grow in knowledge and walk in truth and uprightness (Helaman 6:34).

4. Be willing to believe the words of God and his prophets that you may have the Spirit poured out upon you (Helaman 6:36).

5. Choose a challenge of your own from the reading and apply it to your life.

Chapter Nine

The Prophecy of Nephi,
The Son of Helaman

Helaman 7–10

*H*istorical Setting: The four chapters included in this reading contain three years of the record abridged by Mormon. Nephi had just returned from preaching in the land northward. He left for that mission near the end of the sixty-third year of the reign of the judges (Helaman 6:6) and returned in the sixty-ninth year. Therefore, he was gone over five years. He found the people of Zarahemla being ruled by the Gadianton robbers and living in a great state of wickedness. Nephi spends his time trying to bring the people in Zarahemla to repentance. Lehi, the brother of Nephi, went with him to preach in the land northward. Whether Lehi returned with Nephi, before or after him, is not given in the text. We do know that Lehi preached at least part of the time with Nephi in the land of Zarahemla (see Helaman 11:19, 23). The first four chapters of this reading covers a three-year time period.

Precepts of this Reading:

16 Yea, how could you have given way to the enticing of him who is seeking to hurl away your souls down to everlasting misery and endless wo?

17 O repent ye, repent ye! Why will ye die? Turn ye, turn ye unto the Lord your God. Why has he forsaken you?

18 It is because you have hardened your hearts; yea, ye will not hearken unto the voice of the good shepherd; yea, ye have provoked him to anger against you.

19 And behold, instead of gathering you, except ye will repent, behold, he shall scatter you forth that ye shall become meat for dogs and wild beasts. [Helaman 7:16–19]

4 Blessed art thou, Nephi, for those things which thou hast done; for I have beheld how thou hast with unwearyingness declared the word, which I have given unto thee, unto this people. And thou hast not feared them, and hast not sought thine own life, but hast sought my will, and to keep my commandments.

5 And now, because thou hast done this with such unwearyingness, behold, I will bless thee forever; and I will make thee mighty in word and in deed, in faith and in works; yea, even that all things shall be done unto thee according to thy word, for thou shalt not ask that which is contrary to my will. [Helaman 10:4–5]

Although neither of the above references are introduced with "thus we see" or "I will show unto you," they are guidelines to life. As Nephi said about the writings of the prophet Isaiah, "I did liken all scriptures unto us for our profit and learning" (1 Nephi 19:23), we will do with these references as our precepts. An outline of the text of Helaman 7–10 follows as a preparation for a deeper study.

OUTLINE • HELAMAN 7–10

➤ 7:1–3   In the sixty-ninth year, Nephi, son of Helaman, returned to Zarahemla from the land northward.

         a.   He had preached the word of God to them, and did prophesy many things (v. 2)

         b.   They rejected all his words and he could not stay among them (v. 3).

➤ 7:4–11   The people in Zarahemla were in awful wickedness, the Gadianton robbers filling the judgment-seat having usurped the power and authority of the land.

a. The robbers laid aside the commandments of God, not doing justice to the people (vv. 4–5).

1. They condemned the righteous because of their righteousness, and the wicked went unpunished because of their money.

2. The head of government ruled according to their wills that they might get the gain and glory of the world.

3. They easily committed adultery, stole, and killed.

b. This great iniquity had come in a few years, and Nephi exclaimed in the agony of his soul (vv. 6–9).

1. Oh that my days had been when my father Nephi first came from Jerusalem.

2. His people kept the commandments of God were quick to hearken to the word of the Lord, and were slow to do iniquity.

3. My soul would have had joy with my brethren.

4. But I am consigned to these days, and my soul is filled with sorrow because of the wickedness.

c. Nephi went to his garden, on a tower, by the highway that led to the chief market (vv. 10–11).

1. Certain men passed by and saw Nephi pouring out his soul, and they ran and told the people.

2. They gathered in multitudes to know the cause of Nephi's mourning.

➤ 7:12–29   When Nephi arose and saw the multitude; he spoke to them:

a. Why have you gathered? That I may tell you of your great iniquities? (vv. 13–17).

1. Ye marvel and should marvel because the devil has so great hold on your hearts.

2. How could you have given way to him who seeks to hurl away your sins?

3. Repent; why will ye die? Turn to the Lord your God.

    b. Why has God forsaken you? (vv. 17–23).

        1. You have hardened your hearts, and will not hearken to the voice of the good shepherd.

        2. Instead of gathering you, except you repent he will scatter you.

        3. You have forgotten God in the very day he delivered you.

        4. You have sought to get gain and to be praised of men, and have set your hearts upon riches and the vain things of the world.

        5. You murder, steal, bear false witness against your neighbor, and do all manner of iniquity.

        6. If you do not repent, this great city, and all the cities round about, shall be taken away, for the Lord will not give you strength against your enemies.

        7. Thus saith the Lord: I will not show the wicked my strength save they repent.

    c. It shall be better for the Lamanites than for you except ye repent (vv. 23–28).

        1. They are more righteous than you, for they have not sinned against great knowledge.

        2. The Lord will be merciful to them and lengthen out their days, and he will increase their seed even when you are utterly destroyed, except you repent.

        3. Wo unto you Nephites because of your uniting to that great abomination, the secret band established by Gadianton.

        4. Wo shall come because of your pride, as a result of your riches.

        5. Except ye repent, your lands will be taken from you and you will be destroyed.

    d. I do no say these things of myself, but because the Lord God has made them known unto me, and I testify that they shall be (v. 29).

➤ 8:1–9   There were men hearing Nephi speak who were judges and belonged to the secret band of Gadianton, and they were angry and cried out against him.

a.   Why do you not seize this man that he may be condemned for this crime? (vv. 1–4).

    1.   He revilest against this people and our law (Nephi had spoken many things against the corruption of the law, which cannot be written; but, nothing contrary to the commandments of God).

    2.   The judges were angry because he spoke plainly of their works of darkness, but they dared not lay their own hands on him for they feared the people.

b.   Why do you allow this man to condemn all this people, and say that our great cities will be taken from us, when this is impossible? We are powerful, our cities are great, and our enemies can have no power over us (vv. 5–6).

c.   The people were stirred up to anger against Nephi, but contentions were also raised among them (vv. 7–9).

    1.   Some said, let this man alone for he is a good man and these things will surely come.

    2.   We know he has testified right concerning our iniquities, and he knows what shall befall us.

    3.   If he were not a prophet, he could not have testified of these things.

➤ 8:10–28   The people who sought to destroy Nephi were compelled by their fear not to lay hands on him, and Nephi began to speak unto them again seeing he had gained favor of some.

a.   Nephi asked, have you not read that God gave Moses power to part the Red Sea and the Israelites, who were our fathers, passed through on dry ground, but the Egyptians were swallowed up? (vv. 11–13).

    1.   If God gave one man this power, why do you dispute and say that he has given me no power to know concerning the judgments to come except you do not repent?

2.   You do not only deny my words, but the words of our fathers, and the words of Moses concerning the Messiah.

  b. Moses bore record that the Son of God should come (vv. 14–15).

    1.   Moses lifted up a brazen serpent in the wilderness, even as the Messiah shall be lifted up.

    2.   Even as those who looked upon the serpent lived, even so shall those who look upon the Son of God with faith have eternal life.

  c. Not only Moses, but all the holy prophets from his day back to the days of Abraham, and many before Abraham, who were called by the order of God, have shown unto the people many thousands of years before Christ came, that redemption should come through him (vv. 16–20).

    1.   Abraham saw his coming and was filled with joy.

    2.   The prophet Zenos testified boldly for which he was slain.

    3.   Zenock, Ezias, Isaiah, and Jeremiah also testified.

    4.   Jeremiah also testified that Jerusalem would be destroyed, and it was according to his word.

    5.   Why would not the Son of God come according to Jeremiah's word?

  d. Will you dispute that Jerusalem was destroyed, and the sons of Zedekiah were all slain, all except Mulek? (vv. 21–23).

    1.   The seed of Zedekiah are with us and were driven out of Jerusalem.

    2.   Our father Lehi was driven out because he testified of these things.

    3.   Nephi and almost all of our fathers have testified of the coming of Christ.

    4.   Christ is our God and he did manifest himself unto them, and they were redeemed by him.

e. Ye know these things and cannot deny them except ye shall lie, and have sinned, after all these evidences both from heaven and in earth (vv. 24–26).

        1. Ye have rejected the truth and rebelled against your holy God.

        2. Ye are ripening because of your murders, fornication and wickedness, for everlasting destruction, and except ye repent it will come soon.

    f. Go into your judgment-seat and search; your judge has been murdered by his brother who seeks to sit on the judgment-seat (vv. 27–28).

        1. They both belong to your secret band.

        2. The authors of that band are Gadianton and the evil one who seeks to destroy the souls of men.

➤ 9:1–5   After Nephi had so prophesied, five men ran to the judgment-seat to see if what Nephi had said, about the chief judge being murdered, was true.

    a. The five men did not believe Nephi was a prophet, but would see if he was (v. 2).

    b. When the men came to the judgment-seat and found the chief judge lying in his blood, they believed and feared and fell to the earth in astonishment (vv. 3–5).

➤ 9:6–9   When the chief judge was murdered, his servants ran and told the people he had been murdered.

    a. The people gathered to the place of the Judgment-seat and saw the five men that had fallen to the earth (v. 7).

    b. Knowing nothing of the multitude who had gathered at the garden of Nephi, the people accused the five men of murder (vv. 8–9).

        1. They bound them and cast them into prison.

        2. A proclamation was sent abroad that the judge was slain and the murderers arrested.

➤ 9:10–18   On the morrow the people assembled to fast and mourn at the burial of the judge (vv. 10–12).

   a. The judges who had been at the garden of Nephi asked concerning the five men who were sent to the judgment-seat (v. 11).

   b. The judges were told that they knew nothing of these five, but five were arrested (v. 12).

   c. The five were brought and the judges saw that they were the five who were sent (vv. 13–15).

      1. The five testified that they saw all things as Nephi had testified, and they had fallen to the earth.

      2. They said they knew not who had murdered him, but he was dead when they arrived.

   d. The judges told the people that Nephi had agreed with some to slay the judge so he could declare it to the people and convert them to his being a prophet of God (vv. 16–18).

      1. They said they would detect him and Nephi would confess.

      2. The five were liberated and rebuked the judges one by one and confounded them.

➤ 9:19–36 Nevertheless, Nephi was bound and brought before the people and accused of the chief judge's death.

   a. Nephi was asked who his confederate was who had murdered the judge, and offered him money and freedom if he would disclose his confidante (v. 20).

   b. Nephi called them fools, and asked how long the Lord would allow them to go on in their sins (vv. 21–24).

      1. Nephi said they ought to mourn because of the destruction that awaits them, except they repent.

      2. You say I have agreed with a man to murder Seezoram, your chief judge because I showed you a sign.

   c. Nephi said he would show another sign and see if they would destroy him (vv. 25–36).

      1. Go to the house of Seantum, the brother of Seezoram, and ask him if Nephi, the pretended

prophet, has agreed with you to murder your brother?

2. He will say nay, and ask him if he has murdered his brother?

3. He will stand in fear and not know what to say.

4. He will act astonished, but declare he is innocent.

5. Examine him and you will find blood on the skirts of his cloak.

6. Ask him where it came from, and say we know this is the blood of his brother.

7. He will look pale, as if death had come upon him.

8. Tell him you know he is guilty because of his fear and paleness.

9. Greater fear will come upon him and he will confess the murder.

10. He will then say that Nephi knows nothing of the matter save it were given him by the power of God.

11. Then you will know I (Nephi) am an honest man sent from God.

➤ 9:37–43   The people went and did as Nephi said and he did confess he was the murderer.

    a. The five were set free and also Nephi (v. 38).

    b. Some of the Nephites believed on Nephi's words and others believed on the testimony of the five, for they were converted while in prison (v. 39).

    c. Some people said Nephi was a prophet (v. 40).

    d. Some said he was a god for otherwise he could not know all things (v. 41).

       1. He has told us the thoughts of our hearts.

       2. He has brought unto our knowledge the true murderer of our chief judge.

➤ 10:1–11   There arose a division among the people and they divided hither and thither leaving Nephi alone.

    a. Nephi went toward his own house pondering upon the things he had been shown (v. 2).

    b. As he was pondering, being cast down because of the wickedness of the people, a voice came to him: (vv. 3–11).

        1. Blessed art thou, Nephi, because of the things thou has done, declaring the word with unwearyingness.

        2. Thou has not feared them, nor sought thine own life, but sought my will and to keep my commandments.

        3. Thus I will bless thee forever, making thee mighty in word and deed, and faith and works.

        4. All things shall be done according to thy word, for thou shalt not ask contrary to my will.

        5. I, God, declare in the presence of mine angels that you shall have power over this people, and shall smite the earth with famine, pestilence, and destruction, according to the people's wickedness.

        6. I give you power to seal on earth and in heaven, and loose on earth and in heaven.

        7. Whatever you say to the temple, the mountain, or the people shall be done.

        8. I command you to declare unto this people that thus saith the Lord God Almighty, except ye repent ye shall be smitten to destruction.

➤ 10:12–19 Nephi did not return unto his house, but returned to the multitudes scattered upon the face of the land and declared the word unto them, to repent or be destroyed.

    a. Notwithstanding Nephi's miracle in telling them of the death of the chief judge, they hardened their hearts and did not hearken to his words (vv. 13–16).

        1. They reviled against him and sought to lay hands on him and cast him into prison.

        2. The power of God was with him; he was carried by the Spirit away from their midst.

b. Nephi went forth by the Spirit, from multitude to multitude, declaring the word of God until he had declared it or sent it among all people (vv. 17–18).

       1. They would not hearkened to his words.

       2. They were divided against themselves and began to slay one another.

    c. The seventy-first year ended (v. 19).

NOTES AND COMMENTARY

Introduction: What comes to mind when a person is referred to as a prophet? Many people will see in their mind a man that is old, with a long, white beard who foretells the future. Such a concept is possibly drawn from a scripture in the Old Testament.

> "And if thou say in thine heart, How shall we know the word which the LORD hath not spoken? When a prophet speaketh in the name of the LORD, if the thing follow not, nor come to pass, that is the thing which the LORD hath not spoken, but the prophet hath spoken it presumptuously: thou shalt not be afraid of him." [Deuteronomy 18:21–22]

While a prophet may and often does foretell the future, he has many other characteristics. The chapters in Helaman we are discussing now give us many others characteristics. We will notice them those as we proceed, and summarize them at the conclusion.

Helaman 7:1–3 • Nephi in the Land Northward

> 1 Behold, now it came to pass in the sixty and ninth year of the reign of the judges over the people of the Nephites, that Nephi, the son of Helaman, returned to the land of Zarahemla from the land northward.

> 2 For he had been forth among the people who were in the land northward and did preach the word of God unto them, and did prophesy many things unto them;

3 And they did reject all his words, insomuch that he could not stay among them, but returned again unto the land of his nativity.

As mentioned previously, Nephi went preaching in the land northward for over five years, we have no record of his work in those years, but we will look forward to learning of the things he prophesied (v. 2) when the unabridged records come forth (see 3 Nephi 26:6–12). The text seems to suggest that he could not stay (Helaman 7:3) because it was unsafe after he was rejected. However, his return might also have been directed by revelation, and he would not go against the Lord's will. Mormon was not impressed to speak further on the matter.

Helaman 7:4–11 • The Gadianton Robbers Fill the Judgment-seats

4 And seeing the people in a state of such awful wickedness, and those Gadianton robbers filling the judgment-seats—having usurped the power and authority of the land; laying aside the commandments of God, and not in the least aright before him; doing no justice unto the children of men;

5 Condemning the righteous because of their righteousness; letting the guilty and the wicked go unpunished because of their money; and moreover to be held in office at the head of government, to rule and do according to their wills, that they might get gain and glory of the world, and, moreover, that they might the more easily commit adultery, and steal, and kill, and do according to their own wills—

6 Now this great iniquity had come upon the Nephites, in the space of not many years; and when Nephi saw it, his heart was swollen with sorrow within his breast; and he did exclaim in the agony of his soul:

7 Oh, that I could have had my days in the days when my father Nephi first came out of the land of Jerusalem, that I could have joyed with him in the promised land; then were his people easy to be entreated, firm to keep the commandments of God, and slow to be led to do iniquity; and they were quick to hearken unto the words of the Lord—

8 Yea, if my days could have been in those days, then would my soul have had joy in the righteousness of my brethren.

9 But behold, I am consigned that these are my days, and that my soul shall be filled with sorrow because of this the wickedness of my brethren.

10 And behold, now it came to pass that it was upon a tower, which was in the garden of Nephi, which was by the highway which led to the chief market, which was in the city of Zarahemla; therefore, Nephi had bowed himself upon the tower which was in his garden, which tower was also near unto the garden gate by which led the highway.

11 And it came to pass that there were certain men passing by and saw Nephi as he was pouring out his soul unto God upon the tower; and they ran and told the people what they had seen, and the people came together in multitudes that they might know the cause of so great mourning for the wickedness of the people.

Any resemblance of these verses to modern-day politicians is probably not coincidental. Mormon wrote "the things which have been commanded me" (see 3 Nephi 26:12), as a witness and a warning to this generation (see Mormon 3:16–22). Commandments of God (Helaman 7:4) are being laid aside today when laws are interpreted to make a display of the ten commandments illegal. The guilty and the wicked are set free through the work of high-priced lawyers (v. 5). Immorality (v. 5) has been made common by men in the highest offices of government. We do need the message of the book of Helaman in our day.

Nephi's wish for having lived in another day shows his human element, a common wish among many. However, he also teaches us the first characteristic of a prophet. Each prophet has a foreordained calling. Jeremiah was told by the Lord: "Before I formed thee in the belly I knew thee; and before thou camest forth out of the womb I sanctified thee, and I ordained thee a prophet unto the nations" (Jeremiah 1:5.) Jeremiah is undoubtedly typical of all Old Testament Prophets. Peter's name was changed to Cephas by Jesus the first time they met. "Cephas, which is, by interpretation, a seer, or a stone" (JST, John 1:42). Peter went on to become the prophet, seer, and revelator of the Church in the Meridian of Time.

12 And also with Peter, and James, and John, whom I have sent unto you, by whom I have ordained you and confirmed you to be apostles, and especial witnesses of my name, and bear the keys of your ministry and of the same things which I revealed unto them;

13 Unto whom I have committed the keys of my kingdom, and a dispensation of the gospel for the last times; and for the fulness of times, in the which I will gather together in one all things, both which are in heaven, and which are on earth;" [D&C 27:12–13; see also D&C 7:7]

Joseph Smith was told by the angel Moroni:

He called me by name, and said unto me that he was a messenger sent from the presence of God to me, and that his name was Moroni; that God had a work for me to do; and that my name should be had for good and evil among all nations, kindreds, and tongues, or that it should be both good and evil spoken of among all people. [Joseph Smith–History 1:33]

It is obvious that each of the Prophet Joseph Smith's successors were likewise foreordained.

Nephi's praying upon a tower in his garden was probably not by chance. Had the Lord led him there in order to have him warn the people of Zarahemla? While that is only the likely possibility, it did attract a multitude, and he was able to testify and prophesy to many people (Helaman 7:10–11).

Helaman 7:12–23 • Nephi Calls the Multitude to Repentance

12 And now, when Nephi arose he beheld the multitudes of people who had gathered together.

13 And it came to pass that he opened his mouth and said unto them: Behold, why have ye gathered yourselves together? That I may tell you of your iniquities?

14 Yea, because I have got upon my tower that I might pour out my soul unto my God, because of the exceeding sorrow of my heart, which is because of your iniquities!

15 And because of my mourning and lamentation ye have gathered yourselves together, and do marvel; yea, and ye have great need to marvel; yea, ye ought to marvel because ye are given away that the devil has got so great hold upon your hearts.

16 Yea, how could you have given way to the enticing of him who is seeking to hurl away your souls down to everlasting misery and endless wo?

17 O repent ye, repent ye! Why will ye die? Turn ye, turn ye unto the Lord your God. Why has he forsaken you?

18 It is because you have hardened your hearts; yea, ye will not hearken unto the voice of the good shepherd; yea, ye have provoked him to anger against you.

19 And behold, instead of gathering you, except ye will repent, behold, he shall scatter you forth that ye shall become meat for dogs and wild beasts.

20 O, how could you have forgotten your God in the very day that he has delivered you?

21 But behold, it is to get gain, to be praised of men, yea, and that ye might get gold and silver. And ye have set your hearts upon the riches and the vain things of this world, for the which ye do murder, and plunder, and steal, and bear false witness against your neighbor, and do all manner of iniquity.

22 And for this cause wo shall come unto you except ye shall repent. For if ye will not repent, behold, this great city, and also all those great cities which are round about, which are in the land of our possession, shall be taken away that ye shall have no place in them; for behold, the Lord will not grant unto you strength, as he has hitherto done, to withstand against your enemies.

23 For behold, thus saith the Lord: I will not show unto the wicked of my strength, to one more than the other, save it be unto those who repent of their sins, and hearken unto my words. Now therefore, I would that ye should behold, my brethren, that it shall be better for the Lamanites than for you except ye shall repent.

These verses illustrate a second characteristic of a prophet. Each prophet calls the people to repentance. The sin for which they must repent will vary, but there is a call to repentance whether spoken of directly or indirectly. In Nephi's call he was very direct. He spoke of their yielding to the devil (vv. 15–16). He declared of the Lord's displeasure over their actions (vv. 17–18). He further warned them of what the Lord would do if they did not repent (v. 19). A very important doctrinal point is pronounced here by Nephi. The Prophet Joseph Smith taught that "One of the most important points in the faith of the Church of the Latter-day Saints through the fullness of the everlasting gospel, is the gathering of Israel" (*TPJS*, 92). The Lord told the people of Judah (as well as the Nephites): "How often would I have gathered thy children together" (Matthew 23:37; see 3 Nephi 10:4–7). If they were to be gathered often, they must have been intermittently scattered. Nephi here gives the reason why Israel was scattered, they did not repent (Helaman 7:19). He warned again of their destruction and being taken away (scattered) if they do not repent (v. 23). In Nephi's day one of the sins was priestcraft. They sought the gain and praise of men (v. 21). Nephi, son of Lehi, had earlier defined priestcraft in those terms (see 2 Nephi 26:29).

John the Baptist is known for his call to repentance as he prepared the way for the kingdom and the Messiah (see Matthew 3:1–3; Mark 1:2–4; Luke 3:2–6). Again, the Old Testament gives the same message by the prophets (see Amos 9:8–9; Jonah 1:1–2). The Prophet Joseph Smith warned: "Hear it, all ye ends of the earth—all ye priests, all ye sinners, and all men. Repent! repent! Obey the Gospel. Turn to God; for your religion won't save you, and you will be damned." (*TPJS*, 361).

Nephi, son of Helaman, taught the Nephites that God was no respecter of persons. He then warned them that it would be better for the Lamanites than for them except they repent (Helaman 7:23). He then expounded upon that warning.

Helaman 7:24–29 • Why it Was More Tolerable for the Lamanites

24 For behold, they are more righteous than you, for they have not sinned against that great knowledge which ye have received; therefore the Lord will be merciful unto them; yea, he will lengthen out their days and increase their seed, even when thou shalt be utterly destroyed except thou shalt repent.

25 Yea, wo be unto you because of that great abomination which has come among you; and ye have united yourselves unto it, yea, to that secret band which was established by Gadianton!

26 Yea, wo shall come unto you because of that pride which ye have suffered to enter your hearts, which has lifted you up beyond that which is good because of your exceedingly great riches!

27 Yea, wo be unto you because of your wickedness and abominations!

28 And except ye repent ye shall perish; yea, even your lands shall be taken from you, and ye shall be destroyed from off the face of the earth.

29 Behold now, I do not say that these things shall be, of myself, because it is not of myself that I know these things; but behold, I know that these things are true because the Lord God has made them known unto me, therefore I testify that they shall be.

The scattering of the Nephites would be determined by whether or not they repented of several things. First, it was more serious for the Nephites because they had been given more knowledge (v. 24; see also Alma 9:15–16). "Unto whom much is given much is required" (D&C 82:3; Luke 12:48). Secondly, the Nephites had united with the Gadianton band (Helaman 7:25). Thirdly, they were guilty of pride because of their great riches (v. 26), a recurring problem in the Book of Mormon. What they had worked so hard to regain a few years before was threatened to be lost again, their lands (v. 28).

Nephi now gives us a third characteristic of a prophet, his message is not his own, but comes from the Lord (v. 29). Again, it is the same for Old and New Testament prophets. Amos was sent to northern Israel to call them to repentance. Amaziah, the priest of Bethel sent Amos away but Amos responded.

> 7 Thus he shewed me: and, behold, the Lord stood upon a wall made by a plumbline, with a plumbline in his hand.

> 8 And the LORD said unto me, Amos, what seest thou? And I said, A plumbline. Then said the Lord, Behold, I will set a plumbline in the midst of my people Israel: I will not again pass by them any more:

> 9 And the high places of Isaac shall be desolate, and the sanctuaries of Israel shall be laid waste; and I will rise against the house of Jeroboam with the sword.

> 10 Then Amaziah the priest of Beth-el sent to Jeroboam king of Israel, saying, Amos hath conspired against thee in the midst of the house of Israel: the land is not able to bear all his words.

> 11 For thus Amos saith, Jeroboam shall die by the sword, and Israel shall surely be led away captive out of their own land.

> 12 Also Amaziah said unto Amos, O thou seer, go, flee thee away into the land of Judah, and there eat bread, and prophesy there:

> 13 But prophesy not again any more at Beth-el: for it is the king's chapel, and it is the king's court.

> 14 Then answered Amos, and said to Amaziah, I was no prophet, neither was I a prophet's son; but I was an herdman, and a gatherer of sycomore fruit:

> 15 And the LORD took me as I followed the flock, and the LORD said unto me, Go, prophesy unto my people Israel. [Amos 7:4–15]

The high priest in Jerusalem commanded Peter and the apostles not to teach in the name of Christ. They answered: "We ought to obey God rather than man," and continued their message, which had been commissioned to them by Jesus (Acts 4:27–32).

The Prophet Joseph Smith declared: "I am a rough stone. The sound of the hammer and chisel was never heard on me until the Lord took me in hand" (*TPJS*, 307). The Prophet had previously compared himself to "a smooth and polished shaft [of the arrow] in the quiver of the Almighty," a symbol used by Isaiah, as a servant of the Lord in the latter days (Isaiah 49:2; 1 Nephi 21:2; *TPJS*, 304). The Prophet's message was certainly from the Lord, as was Nephi's, the son of Helaman.

Helaman 8:1–9 • The Gadianton Judges Cry Against Nephi

1 And now it came to pass that when Nephi had said these words, behold, there were men who were judges, who also belonged to the secret band of Gadianton, and they were angry, and they cried out against him, saying unto the people: Why do ye not seize upon this man and bring him forth, that he may be condemned according to the crime which he has done?

2 Why seest thou this man, and hearest him revile against this people and against our law?

3 For behold, Nephi had spoken unto them concerning the corruptness of their law; yea, many things did Nephi speak which cannot be written; and nothing did he speak which was contrary to the commandments of God.

4 And those judges were angry with him because he spake plainly unto them concerning their secret works of darkness; nevertheless, they durst not lay their own hands upon him, for they feared the people lest they should cry out against them.

5 Therefore they did cry unto the people, saying: Why do you suffer this man to revile against us? For behold he doth condemn all this people, even unto destruction; yea, and also that these our great cities shall be taken from us, that we shall have no place in them.

6 And now we know that this is impossible, for behold, we are powerful, and our cities great, therefore our enemies can have no power over us.

7 And it came to pass that thus they did stir up the people to anger against Nephi, and raised contentions among them; for there were some who did cry out: Let this man alone, for he is a good man, and those things which he saith will surely come to pass except we repent;

8 Yea, behold, all the judgments will come upon us which he has testified unto us; for we know that he has testified aright unto us

concerning our iniquities. And behold they are many, and he knoweth as well all things which shall befall us as he knoweth of our iniquities;

9 Yea, and behold, if he had not been a prophet he could not have testified concerning those things.

The majority of the people had chosen a contrary course, as King Mosiah had warned (see Mosiah 29:27), thus the few who recognized the truth (Helaman 8:7) feared that judgments would follow (v. 8). Those few took the position that Nephi would not be able to know what he knew if he was not a prophet (v. 9).

The anger of the secret band of Gadianton was typical of a fourth characteristic of a prophet; he is always unpopular with the wicked, while the righteous defend him. Jeremiah was the epitome of the Old Testament prophets unpopularity. He was placed in stocks at the gate by the temple where all could see him (see Jeremiah 20:1–2). He also suffered other persecutions (see Jeremiah 12). In the New Testament, Stephen was stoned to death because he testified to the wicked San-hedrin (see Acts 7:51–60). Joseph Smith was treated with great contempt by the very minister who had inspired him to go into the grove and pray, leading to his first vision (see Joseph Smith–History 1:21–23). Also, the angel Moroni told Joseph that his "name should be had for good and evil among all nations, kindreds, and tongues, or that it should be both good and evil spoken of among all people" (Joseph Smith–History 1:33).

Helaman 8:10–20 • The People Are Afraid to Lay Hands on Nephi

10 And it came to pass that those people who sought to destroy Nephi were compelled because of their fear, that they did not lay their hands on him; therefore he began again to speak unto them, seeing that he had gained favor in the eyes of some, insomuch that the remainder of them did fear.

11 Therefore he was constrained to speak more unto them saying: Behold, my brethren, have ye not read that God gave power unto one man, even Moses, to smite upon the waters of the Red Sea, and they

parted hither and thither, insomuch that the Israelites, who were our fathers, came through upon dry ground, and the waters closed upon the armies of the Egyptians and swallowed them up?

12 And now behold, if God gave unto this man such power, then why should ye dispute among yourselves, and say that he hath given unto me no power whereby I may know concerning the judgments that shall come upon you except ye repent?

13 But, behold, ye not only deny my words, but ye also deny all the words which have been spoken by our fathers, and also the words which were spoken by this man, Moses, who had such great power given unto him, yea, the words which he hath spoken concerning the coming of the Messiah.

14 Yea, did he not bear record that the Son of God should come? And as he lifted up the brazen serpent in the wilderness, even so shall he be lifted up who should come.

15 And as many as should look upon that serpent should live, even so as many as should look upon the Son of God with faith, having a contrite spirit, might live, even unto that life which is eternal.

16 And now behold, Moses did not only testify of these things, but also all the holy prophets, from his days even to the days of Abraham.

17 Yea, and behold, Abraham saw of his coming, and was filled with gladness and did rejoice.

18 Yea, and behold I say unto you, that Abraham not only knew of these things, but there were many before the days of Abraham who were called by the order of God; yea, even after the order of his Son; and this that it should be shown unto the people, a great many thousand years before his coming, that even redemption should come unto them.

19 And now I would that ye should know, that even since the days of Abraham there have been many prophets that have testified these things; yea, behold, the prophet Zenos did testify boldly; for the which he was slain.

20 And behold, also Zenock, and also Ezias, and also Isaiah, and Jeremiah, (Jeremiah being that same prophet who testified of the destruction of Jerusalem) and now we know that Jerusalem was

destroyed according to the words of Jeremiah. O then why not the Son of God come, according to his prophecy?

Continuing to speak because the multitude was paralyzed with fear and because he gained the favor of some who listened, Nephi turned to the scriptures. He cited Moses' parting of the Red Sea, an apparent favorite with the Nephites (see 1 Nephi 4:2; 1 Nephi 17:26–27; Mosiah 7:19; Alma 36:28), as evidence that the power God had been given to one man before and therefore could be given to Nephi (Helaman 8:12–13).

The account of the serpent made of brass that Moses lifted up in the wilderness (v. 14) is found in the Old Testament:

> 6 And the LORD sent fiery serpents among the people, and they bit the people; and much people of Israel died.
>
> 7 Therefore the people came to Moses, and said, We have sinned, for we have spoken against the LORD, and against thee; pray unto the LORD, that he take away the serpents from us. And Moses prayed for the people.
>
> 8 And the LORD said unto Moses, Make thee a fiery serpent, and set it upon a pole: and it shall come to pass, that every one that is bitten, when he looketh upon it, shall live.
>
> 9 And Moses made a serpent of brass, and put it upon a pole, and it came to pass, that if a serpent had bitten any man, when he beheld the serpent of brass, he lived. [Numbers 21:6–9]

The Gospel of John refers to the incident and gives us the symbolism of Christ being lifted up. "And as Moses lifted up the serpent in the wilderness, even so must the Son of man be lifted up. That whosoever believeth in him should not perish, but have eternal life." (John 3:14–15)

Nephi, son of Lehi, tells us why the people were not benefited or healed by Jehovah at that time.

> 41 And he did straiten them in the wilderness with his rod; for they hardened their hearts, even as ye have; and the Lord straitened them because of their iniquity. He sent fiery flying serpents among them;

and after they were bitten he prepared a way that they might be healed; and the labor which they had to perform was to look; and because of the simpleness of the way, or the easiness of it, there were many who perished. [1 Nephi 17:41]

Alma expanded upon the lesson given by Nephi.

19 Behold, he was spoken of by Moses; yea, and behold a type was raised up in the wilderness, that whosoever would look upon it might live. And many did look and live.

20 But few understood the meaning of those things, and this because of the hardness of their hearts. But there were many who were so hardened that they would not look, therefore they perished. Now the reason they would not look is because they did not believe that it would heal them.

21 O my brethren, if ye could be healed by merely casting about your eyes that ye might be healed, would ye not behold quickly, or would ye rather harden your hearts in unbelief, and be slothful, that ye would not cast about your eyes, that ye might perish? [Alma 33:19–21]

Therefore, that this great type of Christ was taught by Nephi, son of Helaman (Helaman 8:15) serves as a another witness of the biblical account. It was also taught in the apocrypha:

For when the horrible fierceness of beasts came upon these, and they perished with the stings of crooked serpents, thy wrath endured not forever: But they were troubled for a small season, that they might be admonished, having a sign of salvation, to put them in remembrance of the commandment of thy law. For he that turned himself toward it was not saved by the thing that he saw, but by thee, that art the Saviour of all. And in this thou madest thine enemies confess, that it is thou who deliverest from all evil. ["The Wisdom of Solomon," *The Missing Books of the Bible*, 16:226).

Nephi, son of Helaman, bore testimony that all the prophets back to Abraham, and before Abraham knew of Christ (Helaman 8:16–18). This testimony adds some additional insights concerning what plain and precious parts have been lost from the Bible. The Gospel of John confirms that Abraham saw the coming of Christ as Nephi testified

(v. 17). Jesus testified to the Jews that "your father Abraham rejoiced to see my day: and he saw it, and was glad" (John 8:56). Furthermore, the Prophet Joseph Smith restored the account of Abraham's vision of the Savior to the Genesis record:

> 9 And Abram said, Lord God, how wilt thou give me this land for an everlasting inheritance?
>
> 10 And the Lord said, Though thou wast dead, yet am I not able to give it thee?
>
> 11 And if thou shalt die, yet thou shalt possess it, for the day cometh, that the Son of man shall live; but how can he live if he be not dead? he must first be quickened.
>
> 12 And it came to pass, that Abram looked forth and saw the days of the Son of man, and was glad, and his soul found rest, and he believed in the Lord; and the Lord counted it unto him for righteousness. [JST, Genesis 15:9–12]

Nephi's list of prophets who had testified of the coming of the Son of God names three prophets whose accounts are no longer in the Bible: Zenos, Zenock and Ezias (Helaman 8:19–20). Other parts of the Book of Mormon quote from Zenos and Zenock (see 1 Nephi 19:10–17; Jacob 5:1; Alma 33:3–17; 3 Nephi 10:16). Helaman 8:20 is the only mention of the prophet Ezias. If all of these prophets were listed in chronological order, which is implied by Abraham, Isaiah, and Jeremiah being in chronological order, we may have some insight into the time period when Zenos, Zenoch, and Ezias lived on earth. The plates of brass will certainly verify their time periods.

The fifth characteristic of a prophet is drawn from Nephi's testimony of the prophets who had testified (Helaman 8:11–20). A prophet's testimony will be consistent with other testimonies of Christ and with other scriptures. Isaiah invites his people to turn "To the law [of Moses] and to the testimony [of the prophets]; and if they speak not according to this word, it is because there is no light in them" (Isaiah 8:20; 2 Nephi 18:20). Jesus opened up the scriptures to the two men on the road to Emmaus to testify of himself, and also later to the apostles.

27 And beginning at Moses and all the prophets, he expounded unto them in all the scriptures the things concerning himself.

44 And he said unto them, These are the words which I spake unto you, while I was yet with you, that all things must be fulfilled, which were written in the law of Moses, and in the prophets, and in the psalms, concerning me.

45 Then opened he their understanding, that they might understand the scriptures. [Luke 24:27, 44–45]

There is consistency in the scriptures and in the prophets. Joseph Smith also testified that "Christ was the Great High Priest" (*TPJS*, 158) and that "none ever were perfect but Jesus; and why was he perfect? Because he was the Son of God, and had the fullness of the Spirit, and greater power than any man" (*TPJS*, 187–88).

Helaman 8:21–23 • Evidence of the Destruction of Jerusalem

21 And now will you dispute that Jerusalem was destroyed? Will ye say that the sons of Zedekiah were not slain, all except it were Mulek? Yea, and do ye not behold that the seed of Zedekiah are with us, and they were driven out of the land of Jerusalem? But behold, this is not all—

22 Our father Lehi was driven out of Jerusalem because he testified of these things. Nephi also testified of these things, and also almost all of our fathers, even down to this time; yea, they have testified of the coming of Christ, and have looked forward, and have rejoiced in his day which is to come.

23 And behold, he is God, and he is with them, and he did manifest himself unto them, that they were redeemed by him; and they gave unto him glory, because of that which is to come.

Nephi declared that "Jeremiah . . . testified of the destruction of Jerusalem" (v. 20 above). Jeremiah prophesied just prior to Lehi's party leaving Jerusalem, about 600 B.C. Therefore, they would have known of Jeremiah's prophecies. The book of Jeremiah records many of his prophecies concerning the destruction of Jerusalem (see

Jeremiah 1:13–16; 4:27–29; 5:14–20; 7:32–34; 8:1–22). The significance of Jeremiah's prophecies being known and spoken of among the Nephites about six hundred years after they were given is twofold: first, that the Nephites came to their promised land just prior to the fulfillment of Jeremiah's prophecies; and second, how they knew that Jeremiah's prophecies had been fulfilled. The second point needs further analysis.

The first way that the Nephites knew that Jeremiah's prophecies had been fulfilled was through a vision given to father Lehi showing that Jerusalem had been destroyed (2 Nephi 1:4). Later, the righteous Nephites, in journeying north, discovered the people of Zarahemla (Omni 1:12–14). These people had left "Jerusalem at the time that Zedekiah, king of Judah, was carried away captive into Babylon" just prior to the destruction of Jerusalem (Omni 1:15). Among these people was one of Zedekiah's sons named Mulek (Helaman 8:21). Thus, the Nephites had a spiritual witness (vision) and a physical one that Jerusalem had been destroyed, as prophesied by Jeremiah.

The contribution of the above passage in Helaman verifies and clarifies a number of Bible prophecies concerning the Mulekites, a Book of Mormon people who lived in America after the time of Jerusalem's destruction about 589 B.C. (Book of Mormon dating). The first reference to Mulek is made in Mosiah 25:2 regarding the people of Zarahemla "who was a descendant of Mulek, and those who came with him into the wilderness." The next reference to Mulek is a comment by Mormon, identifying the land north being "called Mulek, which was after the son of Zedekiah" (Helaman 6:10). Nephi's comment, cited previously, that all of Zedekiah's sons were slain except Mulek (8:21), seems to contradict the Bible since both Jeremiah and the author of Kings states that all of Zedekiah's sons were killed (Jeremiah 39:6; 2 Kings 25:6–7). However, there are two Bible prophecies that would sustain the idea that some of Zedekiah's seed did escape the conquest of Babylon in 589 B.C. (Book of Mormon dating).

The Lord gave Ezekiel a parable concerning the king of Judah and his seed being taken into Babylon (Ezekiel 17:1–21). As an apparent addendum to this prophecy, the Lord said:

> Thus saith the Lord God; I will also take of the highest branch of the high cedar, and will set it; I will crop off from the top of his young twigs a tender one, and will plant it upon an high mountain and eminent:
>
> In the mountain of the height of Israel will I plant it: and it shall bring forth boughs, and bear fruit, and be a goodly cedar: and under it shall dwell all fowl of every wing; in the shadow of the branches thereof shall they dwell (Ezekiel 17:22–23).

Elder Orson Pratt, who himself had a special gift of prophecy (see D&C 34:10), interpreted these verses as a prophecy concerning the Mulekites:

> When Zedekiah, king of Judah, was carried away captive into Babylon, the Lord took one of his sons, whose name was Mulok [sic.], with a company of those who would hearken unto His words, and brought them over the ocean, and planted them in America. This was done in fulfillment of the 22nd and 23rd verses of the seventeenth chapter of Ezekiel . . .By reading this chapter, it will be seen that the Jews were the "high cedar," that Zedekiah the king was the "highest branch," that the "tender one" cropped off from the top of his young twigs, was one of his sons, whom the Lord brought out and planted him and his company upon the choice land of America, which He had given unto a remnant of the tribe of Joseph for an inheritance, in fulfillment of the blessing of Jacob and Moses upon the head of that tribe.[1]

The last phrase of the Ezekiel prophecy, "in the shadow of the branches thereof shall they dwell," (17:23) may be an allusion to their dwelling with the Nephites and Lamanites. The Nephites were branches of Joseph who were to "run over the wall . . .unto the utmost bound of the everlasting hills [America]" (see Genesis 49:22–26).

---

[1] Orson Pratt, *Orson Pratt's Works,* comp. Packer Pratt Robinson, Deseret News Press, Salt Lake City, Utah, [1945] 280–281.

Further evidence that the young son Mulek escaped from Jerusalem is found in the writings of the Jewish historian Josephus:

> . . . when Zedekiah was sensible of it, he took his wives and his children and his captains and friends, and with them fled out of the city, through the fortified ditch, and through the desert; and when certain of the deserters had informed the Babylonians of this, at break of day, they made haste to pursue after Zedekiah, and overtook him not far from Jericho, and encompassed him about. But for those friends and captains of Zedekiah who had fled out of the city with him, when they saw their enemies near them, they left him and dispersed themselves, some one way and some another, and every one resolved to save himself; so the enemy took Zedekiah alive, when he was deserted by all but a few, with his children and his wives, and brought him to the king.[2]

This account by Josephus can be read as indicating that one of Zedekiah's young sons could have escaped to America. Another evidence that Mulek was a son of Zedekiah is the name Mulek. The Hebrew letters, written without vowels (or points-as called in the Hebrew), "mem," "lamet," "koph," whose equivalent in English is mlk, means king. The English equivalent that includes vowels is thus "mulek."

There is another prophecy of the Mulekites in Isaiah, although it does not specifically say the remnant who escaped had the son of Zedekiah among them. In answer to King Hezekiah's prayer, the Lord sent Isaiah to him to calm his concern about the threats of Assyria. In addition, an angel made a prediction concerning the Mulekites:

> And the remnant that is escaped of the house of Judah shall again take root downward, and bear fruit upward;
>
> For out of Jerusalem shall go forth a remnant; and they that escape out of Jerusalem shall come up upon mount Zion; the zeal of the Lord of hosts shall do this. [JST, Isaiah 37:31–32; emphasis added]

---

[2] *Josephus. Complete Works*, trans. William Whiston. Grand Rapids, MI: Kregel, [1960], 220.

Since this prophecy is about a remnant of the house of Judah that escapes, it seems to be a prophecy of the Mulekites rather than one about the Nephites who were of Joseph. The prophecy states that they would come to Mount Zion, which was identified by the Prophet Joseph as "the whole of America is Zion itself from north to south, and is described by the Prophets" (*TPJS*, 362). Thus, through the book of Helaman we can verify Bible prophecies of the Mulekites, and clarify other biblical passages regarding the Mulekites.[3]

A sixth characteristic of a prophet is shown in these verses from Helaman and the comments above. External evidences will sustain the prophet's words. This evidence may not come for years afterwards, but it will come. Artifacts, archaeology, and historical records verify what prophets have said in both the Old and the New Testament. The Prophet Joseph Smith proclaimed: "The world will prove Joseph Smith a true prophet by circumstantial evidence" (*TPJS*, 267). That evidence comes as the Lord sees it is timely and necessary.

Father Lehi and his son Nephi testified of Christ. They knew that Christ was the Old Testament God, and gloried in his coming (Helaman 8:22–23).

Helaman 8:24–28 • The Judge Murdered by His Brother

> 24 And now, seeing ye know these things and cannot deny them except ye shall lie, therefore in this ye have sinned, for ye have rejected all these things, notwithstanding so many evidences which ye have received; yea, even ye have received all things, both things in heaven, and all things which are in the earth, as a witness that they are true.

---

[3] The information under Helaman 8:21–23 above was originally published in the *Book of Mormon: Helaman through 3 Nephi 8, According to the Word* "the Restoration of Plain and Precious Parts: The Book of Helaman," Monte S. Nyman, ed. Monte S. Nyman and Charles D. Tata Jr. Religious Study Center, Brigham Young University, distributed by Deseret Book Company, Salt Lake City, Utah [1992].

25 But behold, ye have rejected the truth, and rebelled against your holy God; and even at this time, instead of laying up for yourselves treasures in heaven, where nothing doth corrupt, and where nothing can come which is unclean, ye are heaping up for yourselves wrath against the day of judgment.

26 Yea, even at this time ye are ripening, because of your murders and your fornication and wickedness, for everlasting destruction; yea, and except ye repent it will come unto you soon.

27 Yea, behold it is now even at your doors; yea, go ye in unto the judgment-seat, and search; and behold, your judge is murdered, and he lieth in his blood; and he hath been murdered by his brother, who seeketh to sit in the judgment-seat.

28 And behold, they both belong to your secret band, whose author is Gadianton and the evil one who seeketh to destroy the souls of men.

The rejection of the truth instead of laying up treasure in heaven was a New Testament concept also taught in the Old Testament (v. 25, see also Helaman 5:8 and comments there).

When the circumstances are right, a prophet will utter current prophecies. Giving current prophecies is a seventh characteristic of a prophet. Nephi told of the judge being murdered (Helaman 8:27–28), probably to leave his listeners without excuse. With such evidence how could they doubt? Nevertheless, they did try other explanations to refute his being a prophet, as will be shown in Helaman chapter 9.

The Old Testament gives examples of prophets giving current prophecies. The Lord revealed to Samuel who should be the leader of Israel, and the circumstances of where he would find him.

15 Now the LORD had told Samuel in his ear a day before Saul came, saying,

16 To morrow about this time I will send thee a man out of the land of Benjamin, and thou shalt anoint him to be captain over my people Israel, that he may save my people out of the hand of the Philistines: for I have looked upon my people, because their cry is come unto me.

17 And when Samuel saw Saul, the LORD said unto him, Behold the man whom I spake to thee of! this same shall reign over my people.

18 Then Saul drew near to Samuel in the gate, and said, Tell me, I pray thee, where the seer's house is.

19 And Samuel answered Saul, and said, I am the seer: go up before me unto the high place; for ye shall eat with me to day, and to morrow I will let thee go, and will tell thee all that is in thine heart.

20 And as for thine asses that were lost three days ago, set not thy mind on them; for they are found. And on whom is all the desire of Israel? Is it not on thee, and on all thy father's house? [1 Samuel 9: 15:20]

In the New Testament, a Prophet named Agabus, of whom we know little, foretold what would happen to Paul.

10 And as we tarried there many days, there came down from Judaea a certain prophet, named Agabus.

11 And when he was come unto us, he took Paul's girdle, and bound his own hands and feet, and said, Thus saith the Holy Ghost, So shall the Jews at Jerusalem bind the man that owneth this girdle, and shall deliver him into the hands of the Gentiles.

12 And when we heard these things, both we, and they of that place, besought him not to go up to Jerusalem. [Acts 21:10–12]

The Prophet Joseph Smith told Judge Stephen A. Douglas:

"Judge, you will aspire to the presidency of the United States; and if ever you turn your hand against me or the Latter-day Saints, you will feel the weight of the hand of the Almighty upon you; and you will live to see and know that I have testified the truth to you; for the conversation of this day will stick to you through life." [_TPJS_, 303]

The Prophet Joseph also "prophesied, in the name of the Lord Jesus Christ, that Orrin Porter Rockwell would get away honorably from the Missourians" (_TPJS_, 285). His prophecy was fulfilled shortly.

While the foretelling of the future is often equated with being a prophet, it is only one of many characteristics that identify him. The list will continue.

Helaman 9:1–9 • The Murder of the Chief Judge Is Verified

1 Behold, now it came to pass that when Nephi had spoken these words, certain men who were among them ran to the judgment-seat; yea, even there were five who went, and they said among themselves, as they went:

2 Behold, now we will know of a surety whether this man be a prophet and God hath commanded him to prophesy such marvelous things unto us. Behold, we do not believe that he hath; yea, we do not believe that he is a prophet; nevertheless, if this thing which he has said concerning the chief judge be true, that he be dead, then will we believe that the other words which he has spoken are true.

3 And it came to pass that they ran in their might, and came in unto the judgment-seat; and behold, the chief judge had fallen to the earth, and did lie in his blood.

4 And now behold, when they saw this they were astonished exceedingly, insomuch that they fell to the earth; for they had not believed the words which Nephi had spoken concerning the chief judge.

5 But now, when they saw they believed, and fear came upon them lest all the judgments which Nephi had spoken should come upon the people; therefore they did quake, and had fallen to the earth.

6 Now, immediately when the judge had been murdered—he being stabbed by his brother by a garb of secrecy, and he fled, and the servants ran and told the people, raising the cry of murder among them;

7 And behold the people did gather themselves together unto the place of the judgment-seat—and behold, to their astonishment they saw those five men who had fallen to the earth.

8 And now behold, the people knew nothing concerning the multitude who had gathered together at the garden of Nephi; therefore

they said among themselves: These men are they who have murdered the judge, and God has smitten them that they could not flee from us.

9 And it came to pass that they laid hold on them, and bound them and cast them into prison. And there was a proclamation sent abroad that the judge was slain, and that the murderers had been taken and were cast into prison.

Although these five men did not believe (v. 2), they were still willing to find out for themselves. Too many people will take the word of others without personally testing them. As the Apostle John taught, "Try the Spirits whether they are of God" (1 John 4:1). When knowledge of the truth came to the five men, they fell to the earth in astonishment and fear (Helaman 9:4–5). Had they been in touch with the Spirit, they would have believed Nephi's words. When truth comes by the Spirit, it testifies or brings light and a good feeling (see D&C 50:17–20). The Lord "will cause that your bosom shall burn within you; therefore; you shall feel that it is right" (D&C 9:8). The story line in these chapters is self-explanatory, but the characteristics of a prophet are given so that we may decide for ourselves who qualifies as a prophet of the Lord.

Helaman 9:10–15 • The Five Men Verify Nephi's Words

10 And it came to pass that on the morrow the people did assemble themselves together to mourn and to fast, at the burial of the great chief judge who had been slain.

11 And thus also those judges who were at the garden of Nephi, and heard his words, were also gathered together at the burial.

12 And it came to pass that they inquired among the people, saying: Where are the five who were sent to inquire concerning the chief judge whether he was dead? And they answered and said: Concerning this five whom ye say ye have sent, we know not; but there are five who are the murderers, whom we have cast into prison.

13 And it came to pass that the judges desired that they should be brought; and they were brought, and behold they were the five who

were sent; and behold the judges inquired of them to know concerning the matter, and they told them all that they had done, saying:

14 We ran and came to the place of the judgment-seat, and when we saw all things even as Nephi had testified, we were astonished insomuch that we fell to the earth; and when we were recovered from our astonishment, behold they cast us into prison.

15 Now, as for the murder of this man, we know not who has done it; and only this much we know, we ran and came according as ye desired, and behold he was dead, according to the words of Nephi.

There are always those who are quick to seek alternate explanations of incidents rather than accept the evident truth. It is ironic in this situation that the people made God responsible in their justification of what had happened (v. 8). In spite of the five men being innocently cast into prison, it did give them and opportunity to tell the truth to the multitude. God's hand was certainly involved, but not in the way the people thought.

Helaman 9:16–20 • Nephi Is Accused of the Murder

16 And now it came to pass that the judges did expound the matter unto the people, and did cry out against Nephi, saying: Behold, we know that this Nephi must have agreed with some one to slay the judge, and then he might declare it unto us, that he might convert us unto his faith, that he might raise himself to be a great man, chosen of God, and a prophet.

17 And now behold, we will detect this man, and he shall confess his fault and make known unto us the true murderer of this judge.

18 And it came to pass that the five were liberated on the day of the burial. Nevertheless, they did rebuke the judges in the words which they had spoken against Nephi, and did contend with them one by one, insomuch that they did confound them.

19 Nevertheless, they caused that Nephi should be taken and bound and brought before the multitude, and they began to question him in divers ways that they might cross him, that they might accuse him to death—

20 Saying unto him: Thou art confederate; who is this man that hath done this murder? Now tell us, and acknowledge thy fault; saying, Behold here is money; and also we will grant unto thee thy life if thou wilt tell us, and acknowledge the agreement which thou hast made with him.

The modern-day spin tactics of turning upon the accuser (Nephi), and making him the accused, is a tool of Satan and has always been used by his followers (vv. 16–17). As with the five who investigated the chief judge being murdered, Nephi is given an opportunity to testify again (v. 20). We should also note how the five became Nephi's advocates (v. 18). What the Lord told Joseph Smith applies here: "All these things shall give thee experience, and shall be for thy good" (D&C 122:7).

Helaman 9:21–24 • Nephi Testifies Again

21 But Nephi said unto them: O ye fools, ye uncircumcised of heart, ye blind, and ye stiffnecked people, do ye know how long the Lord your God will suffer you that ye shall go on in this your way of sin?

22 O ye ought to begin to howl and mourn, because of the great destruction which at this time doth await you, except ye shall repent.

23 Behold ye say that I have agreed with a man that he should murder Seezoram, our chief judge. But behold, I say unto you, that this is because I have testified unto you that ye might know concerning this thing; yea, even for a witness unto you, that I did know of the wickedness and abominations which are among you.

24 And because I have done this, ye say that I have agreed with a man that he should do this thing; yea, because I showed unto you this sign ye are angry with me, and seek to destroy my life.

Nephi does not pull any punches. The names he calls them (v. 21) are certainly fitting of their present character, but it is not a way to win friends. Perhaps he was angry because of their thinking they could buy him off (v. 20 above). His next purpose, however, was to show them he knew of their wickedness. Since he had been absent while preaching in the north, they may have thought he hadn't been back long enough to find out the extent of their wickedness and abominations (v. 23).

Helaman 9:25–36 • Nephi
Gives the Nephites a Sign

25 And now behold, I will show unto you another sign, and see if ye will in this thing seek to destroy me.

26 Behold I say unto you: Go to the house of Seantum, who is the brother of Seezoram, and say unto him—

27 Has Nephi, the pretended prophet, who doth prophesy so much evil concerning this people, agreed with thee, in the which ye have murdered Seezoram, who is your brother?

28 And behold, he shall say unto you, Nay.

29 And ye shall say unto him: Have ye murdered your brother?

30 And he shall stand with fear, and wist not what to say. And behold, he shall deny unto you; and he shall make as if he were astonished; nevertheless, he shall declare unto you that he is innocent.

31 But behold, ye shall examine him, and ye shall find blood upon the skirts of his cloak.

32 And when ye have seen this, ye shall say: From whence cometh this blood? Do we not know that it is the blood of your brother?

33 And then shall he tremble, and shall look pale, even as if death had come upon him.

34 And then shall ye say: Because of this fear and this paleness which has come upon your face, behold, we know that thou art guilty.

35 And then shall greater fear come upon him; and then shall he confess unto you, and deny no more that he has done this murder.

36 And then shall he say unto you, that I, Nephi, know nothing concerning the matter save it were given unto me by the power of God. And then shall ye know that I am an honest man, and that I am sent unto you from God.

The Savior said: "An evil and adulterous generation seeketh after a sign" (Matthew 12:39; 16:4). But one who seeks for a sign is different than one whom the Lord chooses to give signs. The eighth characteristic of a prophet, given in these chapters, is that God gives signs when they are necessary. Nephi called his first disclosure of the high priest's assassination a sign (Helaman 9:24 above). The Savior called the Prophet Jonas a sign of "the Son of man [being] three days and three nights in the heart of the earth" (Matthew 12:40). This was stated at the time of his chastising the scribes and Pharisees for seeking a sign. Elijah gave a sign to the prophets of Baal in mount Carmel (see 1 Kings 18:17–40). The viper that fastened itself to Paul, and he was not affected by it, was a sign given to the people on the island of Melita (see Acts 28:1–6). The Prophet Joseph Smith confirmed the Savior's teaching of a sign seeker.

> "When I was preaching in Philadelphia, a Quaker called out for a sign. I told him to be still. After the sermon, he again asked for a sign. I told the congregation the man was an adulterer; that a wicked and adulterous generation seeketh after a sign; and that the Lord had said to me in a revelation, that any man who wanted a sign was an adulterous person. "It is true," cried one, "for I caught him in the very act," which the man afterwards confessed when he was baptized" (Feb. 9, 1843). [*TPJS*, 278]

However, the healing of the sick is a sign of the person's sins being forgiven.

> 14 Is any sick among you? let him call for the elders of the church; and let them pray over him, anointing him with oil in the name of the Lord:
>
> 15 And the prayer of faith shall save the sick, and the Lord shall raise him up; and if he have committed sins, they shall be forgiven him. (James 5:14–15)

The Lord chooses when and to whom his servants give signs.

Helaman 9:37:41 • Nephi Is Recognized by Some as a Prophet

37 And it came to pass that they went and did, even according as Nephi had said unto them. And behold, the words which he had said were true; for according to the words he did deny; and also according to the words he did confess.

38 And he was brought to prove that he himself was the very murderer, insomuch that the five were set at liberty, and also was Nephi.

39 And there were some of the Nephites who believed on the words of Nephi; and there were some also, who believed because of the testimony of the five, for they had been converted while they were in prison.

40 And now there were some among the people, who said that Nephi was a prophet.

41 And there were others who said: Behold, he is a god, for except he was a god he could not know of all things. For behold, he has told us the thoughts of our hearts, and also has told us things; and even he has brought unto our knowledge the true murderer of our chief judge.

After Nephi's sign was proven true (v. 27) some, but not the majority, were converted. Others were converted though the testimony of the first five investigators (v. 39). Some others were over-converted in believing Nephi was a God (v. 41). However, a prophet may know the thoughts of the heart. Ammon perceived the thought of the Lamanite king (Alma 18:16). Ammon was also told things about his brothers being imprisoned in the land of Middoni (Alma 20:3–5). A prophet is not a God, but he can tell you things that only God could know. We honor a prophet but we worship God.

Helaman 10:1–11 • The Lord Blesses Nephi Forever

1 And it came to pass that there arose a division among the people, insomuch that they divided hither and thither and went their ways, leaving Nephi alone, as he was standing in the midst of them.

2 And it came to pass that Nephi went his way towards his own house, pondering upon the things which the Lord had shown unto him.

3 And it came to pass as he was thus pondering—being much cast down because of the wickedness of the people of the Nephites, their secret works of darkness, and their murderings, and their plunderings, and all manner of iniquities—and it came to pass as he was thus pondering in his heart, behold, a voice came unto him saying:

4 Blessed art thou, Nephi, for those things which thou hast done; for I have beheld how thou hast with unwearyingness declared the word, which I have given unto thee, unto this people. And thou hast not feared them, and hast not sought thine own life, but hast sought my will, and to keep my commandments.

5 And now, because thou hast done this with such unwearyingness, behold, I will bless thee forever; and I will make thee mighty in word and in deed, in faith and in works; yea, even that all things shall be done unto thee according to thy word, for thou shalt not ask that which is contrary to my will.

6 Behold, thou art Nephi, and I am God. Behold, I declare it unto thee in the presence of mine angels, that ye shall have power over this people, and shall smite the earth with famine, and with pestilence, and destruction, according to the wickedness of this people.

7 Behold, I give unto you power, that whatsoever ye shall seal on earth shall be sealed in heaven; and whatsoever ye shall loose on earth shall be loosed in heaven; and thus shall ye have power among this people.

8 And thus, if ye shall say unto this temple it shall be rent in twain, it shall be done.

9 And if ye shall say unto this mountain, Be thou cast down and become smooth, it shall be done.

10 And behold, if ye shall say that God shall smite this people, it shall come to pass.

11 And now behold, I command you, that ye shall go and declare unto this people, that thus saith the Lord God, who is the Almighty: Except ye repent ye shall be smitten, even unto destruction.

Undoubtedly discouraged because he had not been more successful, Nephi was given a blessing few people are given. Was his calling and election made sure? Peter admonished the saints "Wherefore the rather, brethren, give diligence to make your calling and election sure: for if ye do these things, ye shall never fall:" (2 Peter 1:10).

Nephi had seemingly been thoroughly proven of the Lord who found "that the man [was] determined to serve Him at all hazards, then the man [had found] his calling and his election made sure" (*TPJS*, 150). He had been blessed forever. The Lord knew that he would not ask for anything contrary to his will (Helaman 10:5). While it may be argued that his calling and election was not made sure, it really doesn't matter. That assurance was between Nephi and the Lord. We do recognize though, the ninth characteristic of a prophet.

Nephi was granted power. Prophets are granted power. Joshua was promised that "the Lord thy God is with thee whithersoever thou goest" (Joshua 1:9). Elijah was given power to bring famine by causing the rains to cease (see 1 Kings 17:1–7). Jesus promised the twelve apostles he ordained "that whatsoever ye shall ask of the Father in my name, he may give it you" (John 15:16). The Lord knew these men would not ask anything contrary to his will, just as he knew Nephi wouldn't. The Nephite Twelve were given the same blessing (see 3 Nephi 27:28). Peter James and John were given the same power as Nephi (Helaman 10:7): "whatsoever thou shalt bind on earth shall be bound in heaven; and whatsoever thou shalt loose on earth shall be loosed in heaven" (Matthew 16:19). The Prophet Joseph was indeed a prophet and was granted these same powers. He testified:

"The Lord once told me that what I asked for I should have. I have been afraid to ask God to kill my enemies, lest some of them should, peradventure, repent.

I asked a short time since for the Lord to deliver me out of the hands of the Governor of Missouri, and if it needs must be to accomplish it, to take him away; and the next news that came pouring down from there was, that *Governor Reynolds had shot himself.* And I would not say, Beware, O earth how you fight against the Saints of God and shed innocent blood; for in the days of Elijah, his enemies came upon him, and fire was called down from heaven and destroyed them." [*TPJS*, 340]

Nephi was indeed a prophet and so was Joseph Smith.

Jacob, brother of Nephi had power over the elements (Jacob 4:6) just as Nephi, son of Helaman was given in these verses (Helaman 10:8–9). The Nephites and the Jaredites were smitten unto destruction. The prophets warned them just as the Lord told Nephi to warn the Nephite people (vv. 10–11; see also Mormon 8:6–8; Ether 15:19). Prophets are granted power.

Helaman 10:12–19 • The Power of God Is with Nephi

12 And behold, now it came to pass that when the Lord had spoken these words unto Nephi, he did stop and did not go unto his own house, but did return unto the multitudes who were scattered about upon the face of the land, and began to declare unto them the word of the Lord which had been spoken unto him, concerning their destruction if they did not repent.

13 Now behold, notwithstanding that great miracle which Nephi had done in telling them concerning the death of the chief judge, they did harden their hearts and did not hearken unto the words of the Lord.

14 Therefore Nephi did declare unto them the word of the Lord, saying: Except ye repent, thus saith the Lord, ye shall be smitten even unto destruction.

15 And it came to pass that when Nephi had declared unto them the word, behold, they did still harden their hearts and would not hearken unto his words; therefore they did revile against him, and did seek to lay their hands upon him that they might cast him into prison.

16 But behold, the power of God was with him, and they could not take him to cast him into prison, for he was taken by the Spirit and conveyed away out of the midst of them.

17 And it came to pass that thus he did go forth in the Spirit, from multitude to multitude, declaring the word of God, even until he had declared it unto them all, or sent it forth among all the people.

18 And it came to pass that they would not hearken unto his words; and there began to be contentions, insomuch that they were divided against themselves and began to slay one another with the sword.

19 And thus ended the seventy and first year of the reign of the judges over the people of Nephi.

The blessing given to Nephi by the Lord was beginning to be fulfilled immediately. He also immediately did what the Lord requested. He did not go to his house but to warn the people of the impending destruction (vv. 12–14). This reminds us of President Spencer W. Kimball's motto, "do it now." The blessing of power over the people was demonstrated when they were not able to take him and cast him into prison. Being conveyed out of their midst by the Spirit (v. 17) was a blessing given to Elijah (see 1 Kings 18:8–15). It was also experienced by Phillip in the New Testament times (see Acts 8:36–40).

We learn another characteristic of a prophet, the tenth one in this reading. Miracles will attend and protection will be with a prophet (Helaman 10:16–17). Elisha, Elijah's successor in the Old Testament, had many miracles associated with his life (see 2 Kings 3–7). Peter, the prophet of the New Testament church, as he passed through all quarters of the church, healed and even raised a woman from the dead (see Acts 9:32–41). Joseph Smith cast the devil out of Newell Knight (*HC*, 1:82–83), and healed the sick in Montrose, Iowa.[4] Miracles are not published, but many miracles have been performed throughout the history of the church.

---

[4] There are two more characteristics of a prophet in Helaman chapter eleven. These two characteristics are discussed in the following chapter and a chart illustrates all twelve of the characteristics see Table 3 on pages 375 and 376.

The events summarized in verses 17 through 19 are probably a general treatise of the seventieth and seventy-first year of the judges, since all of the events in Helaman 7:1–10:16 were apparently a record of the sixty-ninth year. Nephi had returned in the sixty-ninth year (see Helaman 7:1), and all the following events happened as he saw the conditions of the people in Zarahemla and went to his garden to pray (see Helaman 7:4–10). Although the seventieth year is not mentioned, it seems to be covered with the seventy-first year (Helaman 10:19).

SACRED WRITING

Preaching Which Is Sacred:

Helaman 7:13–29	Nephi to the multitude in Zarahemla.
Helaman 8:11–26	Nephi again to the multitude in Zarahemla.

Revelation Which Is Great:

Helaman 10:4–11	The Lord blesses Nephi and gives him power.

Prophesying:

Helaman 8:27–28	Nephi prophecies of the chief judge's murder.
Helaman 9:21–36	Nephi prophecies about the chief judge's brother.

Doctrines Learned:

Helaman 7:9	A prophet is foreordained to come in a certain day.
Helaman 7:19	The Lord scatters people instead of gathering them when they get wicked.
Helaman 7:29	The Lord God makes his will known to his prophets.
Helaman 8:11	Moses parted the waters of the Red Sea.
Helaman 8:13–15	Those who look upon the Son of God with faith, having a contrite spirit, will have eternal life. Moses symbolized this with a brazen serpent.
Helaman 8:16–20	All the prophets from before Abraham to Jeremiah testified of Christ.
Helaman 8:19–20	The writings of many prophets have been lost.

Helaman 8:21	Mulek, son of Zedekiah, escaped out of Jerusalem 589 B.C.
Helaman 8:27–28	A prophet can know of current events by revelation.
Helaman 9:25-ff	A prophet will give a sign when necessary.
Helaman 9:41	A prophet can know the thoughts of a person's heart.
Helaman 10:4–5	A prophet will not ask contrary to the will of God.
Helaman 10:6–11	A prophet is granted power to seal and loose in earth and in heaven.
Helaman 10:17	A prophet can be conveyed from place to place by the Spirit.

General Authority Quotes:

Elder Marion G. Romney • Helaman 10:5

"The time will come when we shall know the will of God before we ask. Then everything for which we pray will be "expedient." Everything for which we ask will be "right." That will be when as a result of righteous living we shall so enjoy the companionship of the Spirit that He will dictate what we ask. On this point the Lord has said, "He that asketh in the Spirit asketh according to the will of God; wherefore it is done even as he asketh" (D&C 46:30), and again, "And if ye are purified and cleansed from all sin, ye shall ask whatsoever you will in the name of Jesus and it shall be done. But know this, it shall be given you what you shall ask." (D&C 50:29, 30.) Nephi, the son of Helaman, so lived. He with unwearyingness declared the word of God. He sought not his own life but the will of God, and to keep his commandments continually, and to him the Lord said, ". . . all things shall be done unto thee according to thy word, for thou shalt not ask that which is contrary to my will." [CR, Oct.1944, 55–56]

Challenges to Eternal Life:

1. Realize that you were assigned to come in these days and were foreordained to do certain things. Read your patriarchal blessing and follow its guidelines (Helaman 7:9).
2. Be determined to be a part of the gathering of Israel wherever you reside and follow your leaders instructions.

3. Make a commitment to be like Nephi and seek the Lord's will and keep his commandments that you may be blessed forever (Helaman 10:5).

4. Choose a challenge of your own from this reading and apply it to your life.

Chapter Ten

True Points of Doctrine

Helaman 11–12

Historical Setting: Helaman chapter eleven is a very brief synopsis of fourteen years of the record abridged by Mormon, the seventy-second through the eighty-fifth year of the reign of the judges. Helaman chapter twelve is Mormon's comments about the last seventeen years, as abridged in Helaman 7–11. Only three of those years are labeled as peaceful and prosperous. The record centers around the land of Zarahemla, the seat of government. Eleven of the fourteen years in chapter eleven are covered in one or two verses each or less.

Precepts of this Reading:

The entire twelfth chapter of Helaman are precepts inserted by Mormon. However, we will cite the three main precepts as introduced by the now notorious "thus we see."

> And thus we can behold how false, and also the unsteadiness of the hearts of the children of men; yea, we can see that the Lord in his great infinite goodness doth bless and prosper those who put their trust in him. Helaman 12:1
>
> Yea, and we may see at the very time when he doth prosper his people, yea, in the increase of their fields, their flocks and their herds, and in gold, and in silver, and in all manner of precious things of every kind and art; sparing their lives, and delivering them out of the hands of their enemies; softening the hearts of their enemies that they should

not declare wars against them; yea, and in fine, doing all things for the welfare and happiness of his people; yea, then is the time that they do harden their hearts, and do forget the Lord their God, and do trample under their feet the Holy One—yea, and this because of their ease, and their exceedingly great prosperity. [Helaman 12:2]

And thus we see that except the Lord doth chasten his people with many afflictions, yea, except he doth visit them with death and with terror, and with famine and with all manner of pestilence, they will not remember him. [Helaman 12:3]

Mormon wrote "the things which have been commanded me of the Lord" (3 Nephi 26:12). Therefore, the above three precepts and the entire twelfth chapter were written for the readers of the Book of Mormon in these latter days. An outline of the text of Helaman 11:12 follows as a preparation for a deeper study.

OUTLINE • HELAMAN 11–12

➤ 11:1–6   Contentions increased in the seventy-second year, and there were wars through out the year and the seventy-third also.

    a. The secret band of robbers carried out the work of destruction and wickedness (v. 2).

    b. Nephi cried to the Lord to not let the people be destroyed by the sword, but let there be a famine to stir them to repentance (vv. 3–4).

    c. There was a great famine in the land, among all the people of Nephi, in the seventy-third, fourth, and fifth year (vv. 5–6).

        1. The work of destruction ceased by the sword but became sore by famine.

        2. The earth was dry and did not yield grain, even among the Lamanites, and thousands perished in the more wicked parts of the land.

➤ 11:7–16   As the people perished by famine they began to remember the Lord, and the words of Nephi.

a.   The people began to plead with their chief judges and leaders that they would acknowledge Nephi as a man of God and ask him to cry unto God that he take away the famine (v. 8).

    b.   The judges did cry unto Nephi, and Nephi saw that the people had repented (v. 9).

    c.   Nephi cried unto the Lord these words (vv. 9–16).

        1.   This people have repented and have swept away the band of Gadianton.

        2.   Because of their humility let thine anger be appeased in the destruction of these wicked men.

        3.   Cause that the famine cease in the land.

        4.   According to my words send forth rain on the earth, to bring forth fruit and grain.

        5.   The people have repented because of famine and pestilence, turn away thing anger so they can try again to serve you and thou canst bless them.

➤ 11:17–21   In the seventy-sixth year, the Lord caused rain to come on the earth.

    a.   The rain brought forth fruit and grain in the season (vv. 17–20).

        1.   The people did rejoice and glorify God.

        2.   They no more sought to destroy Nephi, but esteemed him a great prophet and man of God, having power and authority given him of God.

        3.   Lehi, his brother, was not a whit behind him in righteousness.

        4.   The people began to prosper in the land and build up the waste places, and to multiply and spread until they covered the whole land northward and southward, from the sea west to the sea east.

    b.   The seventy-sixth year ended in peace, and the seventy-seventh year began in peace and so ended (v. 21).

        1.   The church spread throughout the land.

2. The more part of the Nephites and the Lamanites did belong to the church.

➤ 11:22–38 There was peace in the seventy-eight year, but for a few contentions over the doctrine laid down by the prophets.

a. In the seventy-ninth year, there was much strife, but Nephi, Lehi, and many of their brethren who knew the true points of doctrine, having daily revelations, preached to the people and put down the strife (v. 23).

b. In the eightieth year, some Nephite dissenters, who had taken the name of Lamanites earlier, stirred up some of the Lamanites to come to war against the Nephites (vv. 24–27).

    1. They murdered and plundered and then retreated to their secret places in the wilderness and many dissenters were added to them daily.

    2. In a few years they became a great band of robbers.

    3. They searched out the secret plan of Gadianton and became Gadianton robbers.

    4. They made great havoc among both the Nephites and the Lamanites.

c. An army was sent into the wilderness to destroy this band of robbers but they were driven back into their own lands (vv. 28–35).

    1. In the eighty-first year the army went again against the robbers and did destroy many, but they also suffered much destruction.

    2. They were forced to return out of the wilderness and the mountain to their own lands because of the number of the robbers.

    3. The robbers still increased and defied the armies of the Nephites and the Lamanites and caused great fear.

    4. They visited many parts of the land and did great destruction, killing many, and carrying many captive, especially women and children.

5. This great evil stirred them up again to remember the Lord their God.

d. The eighty-second through the eighty-fifth year saw them growing stronger in pride and wickedness, and ripening for destruction (vv. 36–38).

12:1–26   Mormon draws his "thus we see" conclusion.

a. The hearts of men are false and unsteady (v. 1).

b. The Lord in his great infinite goodness blesses and prospers those who put their trust in him (v. 1).

c. At the very time when he prospers his people in their fields, animals, and precious things of every kind, and delivers them from their enemies and wars, and does all things for their welfare and happiness, they harden their hearts, forget the Lord, and trample him under their feet (v. 2).

d. Except the Lord chastens his people with many afflictions, i.e. death, terror, famine, and pestilence, they will not remember him (v. 3).

e. How foolish, vain, evil, devilish, and quick to do iniquity, but slow to do good are the children of men (v. 4).

f. How quick are they to be lifted up in pride and to boast, and slow to remember God and his counsels, and to walk in wisdom's paths (v. 5).

g. They do not desire the God who created them should rule over them in spite of his great goodness and mercy, but set at naught his counsels and guidance (v. 6).

h. The children of men are as nothing and even less than the dust of the earth (vv. 7–19).

1. The dust moves hither and thither at his command.

2. The mountains, valleys, and the whole earth obeys his voice, and the foundations rock.

3. The earth goes back and lengthens its day and it appears that the sun stands still, which it does, for the earth moves and not the sun.

> 4. The waters of the great deep dry up, or the moun-
>   tains fall upon a city at his command.
>
> 5. If man hides up treasures and the Lord curses it
>   because of man's iniquity, and says it shall not be
>   found, it shall not.

i. If the Lord curses a man, or cuts him off from his
   presence, it shall be so (vv. 20–22).

> 1. Wo to his of whom this is said because it is for his
>   iniquity.
>
> 2. He cannot be saved and for this cause of the Lord
>   hath declared repentance.

j. Blessed are they who repent and hearken to the voice
   of God for they are saved (vv. 23–26).

> 1. May God grant men repentance unto good works
>   that they may be restored grace for grace.
>
> 2. May all men repent, but we read that in the great
>   and last day some will be cast off.
>
> 3. They will be consigned to endless misery, fulfilling
>   the words which say: they that have done good shall
>   have everlasting life, and they who have done evil
>   shall have everlasting damnation.

NOTES AND COMMENTARY

Helaman 11:1–6 • A Summary of the Next Four Years—72nd–75th

1 And now it came to pass in the seventy and second year of the reign of the judges that the contentions did increase, insomuch that there were wars throughout all the land among all the people of Nephi.

2 And it was this secret band of robbers who did carry on this work of destruction and wickedness. And this war did last all that year; and in the seventy and third year it did also last.

3 And it came to pass that in this year Nephi did cry unto the Lord, saying:

4 O Lord, do not suffer that this people shall be destroyed by the sword; but O Lord, rather let there be a famine in the land, to stir them up in remembrance of the Lord their God, and perhaps they will repent and turn unto thee.

5 And so it was done, according to the words of Nephi. And there was a great famine upon the land, among all the people of Nephi. And thus in the seventy and fourth year the famine did continue, and the work of destruction did cease by the sword but became sore by famine.

6 And this work of destruction did also continue in the seventy and fifth year. For the earth was smitten that it was dry, and did not yield forth grain in the season of grain; and the whole earth was smitten, even among the Lamanites as well as among the Nephites, so that they were smitten that they did perish by thousands in the more wicked parts of the land.

The power granted to Nephi to smite the earth was now exercised. The famine was into the third year (73rd–75th), causing thousands to perish (vv. 2–6). The above six verses are certainly a brief account of an almost four-year period (72nd–75th). A little more is said about the fourth year as the record continues.

Helaman 11:7–16 • Nephi Asks the Lord for Rain

7 And it came to pass that the people saw that they were about to perish by famine, and they began to remember the Lord their God; and they began to remember the words of Nephi.

8 And the people began to plead with their chief judges and their leaders, that they would say unto Nephi: Behold, we know that thou art a man of God, and therefore cry unto the Lord our God that he turn away from us this famine, lest all the words which thou hast spoken concerning our destruction be fulfilled.

9 And it came to pass that the judges did say unto Nephi, according to the words which had been desired. And it came to pass that when Nephi saw that the people had repented and did humble themselves in sackcloth, he cried again unto the Lord, saying:

10 O Lord, behold this people repenteth; and they have swept away the band of Gadianton from amongst them insomuch that they have become extinct, and they have concealed their secret plans in the earth.

11 Now, O Lord, because of this their humility wilt thou turn away thine anger, and let thine anger be appeased in the destruction of those wicked men whom thou hast already destroyed.

12 O Lord, wilt thou turn away thine anger, yea, thy fierce anger, and cause that this famine may cease in this land.

13 O Lord, wilt thou hearken unto me, and cause that it may be done according to my words, and send forth rain upon the face of the earth, that she may bring forth her fruit, and her grain in the season of grain.

14 O Lord, thou didst hearken unto my words when I said, Let there be a famine, that the pestilence of the sword might cease; and I know that thou wilt, even at this time, hearken unto my words, for thou saidst that: If this people repent I will spare them.

15 Yea, O Lord, and thou seest that they have repented, because of the famine and the pestilence and destruction which has come unto them.

16 And now, O Lord, wilt thou turn away thine anger, and try again if they will serve thee? And if so, O Lord, thou canst bless them according to thy words which thou hast said.

The people were compelled by the famine to be humble (vv. 7–8). We have no record of how and when the band of Gadianton was swept away (v. 10). Alma is convinced enough of their repentance to ask God to cause rain on the land and end the famine (vv. 11–13). Notice Nephi's request for the Lord to give them another chance (v. 16). This seems to be a request for the people to "try again," not the Lord. Nephi places a condition of the people serving God. Regardless, the Lord responds to Nephi's request as the record continues.

Helaman 11:17–21 • The Lord Turns Away His Anger 76th–77th Year

17 And it came to pass that in the seventy and sixth year the Lord did turn away his anger from the people, and caused that rain should

fall upon the earth, insomuch that it did bring forth her fruit in the season of her fruit. And it came to pass that it did bring forth her grain in the season of her grain.

18 And behold, the people did rejoice and glorify God, and the whole face of the land was filled with rejoicing; and they did no more seek to destroy Nephi, but they did esteem him as a great prophet, and a man of God, having great power and authority given unto him from God.

19 And behold, Lehi, his brother, was not a whit behind him as to things pertaining to righteousness.

20 And thus it did come to pass that the people of Nephi began to prosper again in the land, and began to build up their waste places, and began to multiply and spread, even until they did cover the whole face of the land, both on the northward and on the southward, from the sea west to the sea east.

21 And it came to pass that the seventy and sixth year did end in peace. And the seventy and seventh year began in peace; and the church did spread throughout the face of all the land; and the more part of the people, both the Nephites and the Lamanites, did belong to the church; and they did have exceedingly great peace in the land; and thus ended the seventy and seventh year.

The Lord blessing the land with rain (v. 17) reminds us of Alma's admonition to the Zoramites.

13 And now, because ye are compelled to be humble blessed are ye; for a man sometimes, if he is compelled to be humble, seeketh repentance; and now surely, whosoever repenteth shall find mercy; and he that findeth mercy and endureth to the end the same shall be saved.

14 And now, as I said unto you, that because ye were compelled to be humble ye were blessed, do ye not suppose that they are more blessed who truly humble themselves because of the word?

15 Yea, he that truly humbleth himself, and repenteth of his sins, and endureth to the end, the same shall be blessed—yea, much more blessed than they who are compelled to be humble because of their exceeding poverty. [Alma 32:13–15]

The joy of the gospel (v. 18) can only be understood by experiences. Nephi and Ammon experienced similar joy (see Alma 26). The total reversal of the people's attitude toward Nephi (v. 18) must have also made him rejoice. We probably don't express enough appreciation to our leaders for their dedication to God and the Church.

The eleventh characteristic of a prophet is also shown at this time with Nephi. The people did esteem Nephi as a prophet (v. 18). The Lord always establishes his prophets in the eyes of the people. Elisha parted the Jordan River. He cured the water at Jericho (2 Kings 2:12–15). The house of Israel knew he had replaced Elijah. The young prophet Samuel is another good example.

> 19 And Samuel grew, and the LORD was with him, and did let none of his words fall to the ground.
>
> 20 And all Israel from Dan even to Beer-sheba knew that Samuel was established to be a prophet of the LORD. [1 Samuel 3:19–20]

When Peter raised the woman named Dorcas from death "it was known throughout all Joppa; and many believed in the Lord" (Acts 9:42).

Joseph Smith was established in the eyes of many as he began the restoration of the gospel in these latter days. John Taylor is a good example since he met the Prophet when he was being criticized similar to Nephi, son of Helaman.

> "In March 1837, John Taylor went to Kirtland, Ohio, and had the opportunity to meet the Prophet Joseph Smith for the first time and learn more about the principles of the newly restored gospel. At the time of John Taylor's visit to Kirtland, many Church members had become critical of the Prophet Joseph. Even some members of the Quorum of the Twelve were caught up in this dissenting spirit, including Parley P. Pratt, who had approached him and shared some of his doubts about the Prophet, Brother Taylor replied:
>
> 'I am surprised to hear you speak so, Brother Parley. Before you left Canada you bore a strong testimony to Joseph Smith being a Prophet of God, and to the truth of the work he has inaugurated; and

you said you knew these things by revelation, and the gift of the Holy Ghost. You gave to me strict charge to the effect that though you or an angel from heaven was to declare anything else I was not to believe it. Now Brother Parley, it is not man that I am following, but the Lord. The principles you taught me led me to Him, and I now have the same testimony that you then rejoiced in. If the work was true six months ago, it is true today; if Joseph Smith was then a prophet, he is now a prophet.' To Elder Pratt's credit, he soon repented of his feelings and continued to be a valiant servant of the Lord." [*Teachings of Presidents of the Church;* John Taylor, 77]

Little has been said about Lehi, but the tribute paid to him by Mormon (v. 19) should whet our appetites to learn more of him when the opportunity comes. The Lord usually provides a close friend to bolster his prophet when persecution and trials are prevalent. Sam was always in support of Nephi, son of Lehi (see 2 Nephi 4:11). Jonathan was a comfort to King David (see 1 Samuel 23:16–18). Hyrum Smith was a true friend to his brother Joseph (see D&C 135:6–7). The list could go on.

Once more Mormon bears witness of the prosperity of the church members, and the church itself, when the gospel is lived, and its peaceful effect is upon the entire land (Helaman 11:20–21). What an effect we could have on the world today if we all lived as we should.

Helaman 11:22–23 • Contention over Points of Doctrine 78th–79th Year

22 And also they had peace in the seventy and eighth year, save it were a few contentions concerning the points of doctrine which had been laid down by the prophets.

23 And in the seventy and ninth year there began to be much strife. But it came to pass that Nephi and Lehi, and many of their brethren who knew concerning the true points of doctrine, having many revelations daily, therefore they did preach unto the people, insomuch that they did put an end to their strife in that same year.

Peace did not last long. Just two years after the famine was over, contention began over doctrine. Doctrine was established by the prophets (v. 22). As stated above, Satan is "the father of contention" (see 3 Nephi 11:29). The president of the Church is responsible for correct doctrine (see D&C 28:2, 43:2–3). Therefore, Nephi with the help of Lehi was fulfilling that role when they put an end to strife over true doctrine in the second year (Helaman 11:23). This gives us the twelfth characteristic of a prophet, the establishment of true doctrine.

Through Abraham, Jehovah established his covenant with Abraham's seed (see Genesis 12:1–3; Abraham 2:8–11). The Lord spoke face to face with Moses to give the new but lower law to the children of Israel (see Deuteronomy 5). Peter taught the New Testament saints:

> 20 Knowing this first, that no prophecy of the scriptures is given of any private will of man.
>
> 21 For the prophecy came not in old time by the will of man; but holy men of God spake as they were moved by the Holy Ghost. [JST, 2 Peter 1:20]

The Lord instructed modern-day saints to preach only the words of the apostles and prophets.

> 9 And let them journey from thence preaching the word by the way, saying none other things than that which the prophets and apostles have written, and that which is taught them by the Comforter through the prayer of faith. (D&C 52:9)

He gave the same instructions regarding the teaching of families (52:36). The Prophet Joseph Smith very tactfully corrected Elder Orson Hyde on some points of doctrine (see D&C 130 section heading, which cites HC, 5:323–35).

Thus, Helaman 5–11 gives us twelve characteristics of a prophet that will enable the people to know he is a prophet. The writer has taken this criteria and tested it with many of the fifteen prophets who succeeded the Prophet Joseph Smith and found striking evidence for sustaining each one of these great men. Space does not lend itself to including that evidence here, but the accompanying chart shows the comparison of Nephi with the prophets of the Old Testament, the New Testament, and with the Prophet Joseph Smith. The chart does not include all the references used in the commentary above.

Table 3
Helaman 7–11

Recognition of a prophet	Book of Mormon Hel. 7–11	Old Test.	New Test.	Joseph Smith
1. Each prophet has a foreordained mission. Obtains his errand.	Hel. 7:8–9 Jacob 1:17	Jer. 1:5	Acts 9:5–6	JS–History 1:33
2. Each prophet declares repentance	Hel. 7:17	Jonah 1:1–2	Mark 1:4	"I love you all; but I hate some of your deeds." *TPJS*, 361
3. A prophet's message is not his own.	Hel. 7:29 Alma 5:45–46	Amos 7:14–16	Acts 4:18–20 & 5:29–32	"I am a rough stone. The sound of the hammer and chisel was never heard on me until the Lord took me in hand." *TPJS*, 304–307
4. A prophet is unpopular to the wicked. Righteous defend. Protected until finished.	Hel. 8:7–8 Mosiah 13:3–9	Jer. 20:1–2	Acts 7:51–60 Matt. 21:23–27	JS–Hist. 1:21
5. His message will be consistent with the scriptures, testifying of Jesus Christ.	Hel. 8:16–19 Jacob 7:11	Isaiah 9:6 Luke 24:27	1 Cor. 2:12	"Christ is the Great High Priest." *TPJS*, 158

Recognition of a prophet	Book of Mormon Hel. 7–11	Old Test.	New Test.	Joseph Smith
6. External evidences will support the prophet.	Hel. 8:21	Artifacts & Discoveries	Acts 7:51–60	"The world will prove Joseph Smith a true prophet by circumstantial evidence." *TPJS*, 267
7. Prophets will utter current prophecies which will be fulfilled.	Hel. 8:27	1 Sam. 9:15–20	Acts 21:10–12	(Judge Stephen A. Douglas) 'You will aspire to the presidency of the U.S.; ... turn your hand against me or the Latter-day Saints, you will feel the weight of the Almighty.' *TPJS*, 302
8. Signs are given if and when needed.	Hel. 9:23–41	1 Kings 18:17–40	Acts 28:1–6	Any man who wanted a sign was an adulterous person. *TPJS*, 278
9. Prophets are granted power	Hel. 10:5	Josh. 1:9	John 15:16	Lord gave this power to Joseph Smith. *TPJS*, 340
10. Miracles will attend. Protected.	Hel. 10:16–17	2 Kings 3–7	Acts 9:32–41; 8:39	Newell Knight HC 1:82–83
11. Prophets will be established in the eyes of the people.	Hel. 11:18	2 Kings 2:12–15 1 Sam. 3:19–20	Acts 9:42	John Taylor Parley P. Pratt *HC*, 2:488–89 (Note)
12. True doctrine is established	Hel. 11:22–23	Deut. ch. 5 Gen. 12:1–3 Abr. 2:8–11	2 Peter 1:20	Corrections to Orson Hyde *HC*, 5:323–34

Helaman 11:24–27 • The Revival of the Gadianton Robbers—80ᵗʰ Year

24 And it came to pass that in the eighteenth year of the reign of the judges over the people of Nephi, there were a certain number of the dissenters from the people of Nephi, who had some years before gone over unto the Lamanites, and taken upon themselves the name of Lamanites, and also a certain number who were real descendants of the Lamanites, being stirred up to anger by them, or by those dissenters, therefore they commenced a war with their brethren.

25 And they did commit murder and plunder; and then they would retreat back into the mountains, and into the wilderness and secret places, hiding themselves that they could not be discovered, receiving daily an addition to their numbers, inasmuch as there were dissenters that went forth unto them.

26 And thus in time, yea, even in the space of not many years, they became an exceedingly great band of robbers; and they did search out all the secret plans of Gadianton; and thus they became robbers of Gadianton.

27 Now behold, these robbers did make great havoc, yea, even great destruction among the people of Nephi, and also among the people of the Lamanites.

Satan does not sit idly by as the kingdom is being built. When "we revolt at anything which comes from God, the devil takes power" (*TPJS*, 181). The Nephite dissenters stirred up the Lamanites again, and it was undoubtedly begun by their revolting against the things of God (vv. 24–25). Their growth seems to cover more than just the eightieth year. As Mormon is abridging; he is speaking of not many years, but probably more than one (vv. 26–27).

Helaman 11:28–35 • An Army Searches out the Robbers 80ᵗʰ–81ˢᵗ Year

28 And it came to pass that it was expedient that there should be a stop put to this work of destruction; therefore they sent an army of strong men into the wilderness and upon the mountains to search out this band of robbers, and to destroy them.

29 But behold, it came to pass that in that same year they were driven back even into their own lands. And thus ended the eightieth year of the reign of the judges over the people of Nephi.

30 And it came to pass in the commencement of the eighty and first year they did go forth again against this band of robbers, and did destroy many; and they were also visited with much destruction.

31 And they were again obliged to return out of the wilderness and out of the mountains unto their own lands, because of the exceeding greatness of the numbers of those robbers who infested the mountains and the wilderness.

32 And it came to pass that thus ended this year. And the robbers did still increase and wax strong, insomuch that they did defy the whole armies of the Nephites, and also of the Lamanites; and they did cause great fear to come unto the people upon all the face of the land.

33 Yea, for they did visit many parts of the land, and did do great destruction unto them; yea, did kill many, and did carry away others captive into the wilderness, yea, and more especially their women and their children.

34 Now this great evil, which came unto the people because of their iniquity, did stir them up again in remembrance of the Lord their God.

35 And thus ended the eighty and first year of the reign of the judges.

Since the robbers were among the Lamanites, it must have been impossible to preach the word of God unto them as they had done before (see Helaman 6:37). Therefore, the Nephites resorted to another principle taught earlier, "whatsoever evil we cannot resist with our words, yea, such as rebellions and dissensions, let us resist them with our swords, that we may retain our freedom" (Alma 61:14; see also 31:5). The Nephites' own iniquity was a reason for the sword not being as effective as it might have been (Helaman 11:34).

Helaman 11:36–38 • Ripening for Destruction 82nd – 85th Year

> 36 And in the eighty and second year they began again to forget the Lord their God. And in the eighty and third year they began to wax strong in iniquity. And in the eighty and fourth year they did not mend their ways.
>
> 37 And it came to pass in the eighty and fifth year they did wax stronger and stronger in their pride, and in their wickedness; and thus they were ripening again for destruction.
>
> 38 And thus ended the eighty and fifth year.

Four years are summarized in just two verse (36–37). A fitting conclusion is drawn by Mormon, "ripening again for destruction." The same ingredients as always, pride and wickedness (v. 37).

Helaman 12:1–2 • Mormon's Conclusions for the Seventeen Years 69–85

> 1 And thus we can behold how false, and also the unsteadiness of the hearts of the children of men; yea, we can see that the Lord in his great infinite goodness doth bless and prosper those who put their trust in him.
>
> 2 Yea, and we may see at the very time when he doth prosper his people, yea, in the increase of their fields, their flocks and their herds, and in gold, and in silver, and in all manner of precious things of every kind and art; sparing their lives, and delivering them out of the hands of their enemies; softening the hearts of their enemies that they should not declare wars against them; yea, and in fine, doing all things for the welfare and happiness of his people; yea, then is the time that they do harden their hearts, and do forget the Lord their God, and do trample under their feet the Holy One—yea, and this because of their ease, and their exceedingly great prosperity.

The first conclusion is a contrast between false and unsteady hearts and those who put their trust in the Lord (v. 1). The list of things that God had done for the Nephites (v. 2) is a recognition of the Lord's "hand in all things" (D&C 59:21). The Nephites forgetting the Lord their God in their great prosperity (v. 2) was certainly caused by pride, even though Mormon does not mention it (see Jacob 2:13; Alma 4:6–8).

Helaman 12:3–6 • Why the Lord Chastens His People?

> 3 And thus we see that except the Lord doth chasten his people with many afflictions, yea, except he doth visit them with death and with terror, and with famine and with all manner of pestilence, they will not remember him.
>
> 4 O how foolish, and how vain, and how evil, and devilish, and how quick to do iniquity, and how slow to do good, are the children of men; yea, how quick to hearken unto the words of the evil one, and to set their hearts upon the vain things of the world!
>
> 5 Yea, how quick to be lifted up in pride; yea, how quick to boast, and do all manner of that which is iniquity; and how slow are they to remember the Lord their God, and to give ear unto his counsels, yea, how slow to walk in wisdom's paths!
>
> 6 Behold, they do not desire that the Lord their God, who hath created them, should rule and reign over them; notwithstanding his great goodness and his mercy towards them, they do set at naught his counsels, and they will not that he should be their guide.

The Apostle Paul wrote to the Hebrews explaining why the Lord chastens those whom he loves (Hebrews 12:5–11). Mormon is giving similar counsel to the Book of Mormon reader (Helaman 12:3–6). The Lord revealed the same concept to Joseph Smith in the latter days:

> 1 Verily, thus saith the Lord unto you whom I love, and whom I love I also chasten that their sins may be forgiven, for with the chastisement I prepare a way for their deliverance in all things out of temptation, and I have loved you—
>
> 2 Wherefore, ye must needs be chastened and stand rebuked before my face; [D&C 95:1–2]

Another reason for chastisement is given by Mormon, "to remember the Lord" (vv. 3, 5). The Lord wants his people to remember him so he can bless them.

> 20 There is a law, irrevocably decreed in heaven before the foundations of this world, upon which all blessings are predicated—
>
> 21 And when we obtain any blessing from God, it is by obedience to that law upon which it is predicated. [D&C 130:20–21]

However, as Mormon points out, it is not the natural manner of man to follow the Lord but to hearken to the evil one (vv. 4–6).

Helaman 12:7–20 • Man Is Less Than the Dust of the Earth

> 7 O how great is the nothingness of the children of men; yea, even they are less than the dust of the earth.
>
> 8 For behold, the dust of the earth moveth hither and thither, to the dividing asunder, at the command of our great and everlasting God.
>
> 9 Yea, behold at his voice do the hills and the mountains tremble and quake.
>
> 10 And by the power of his voice they are broken up, and become smooth, yea, even like unto a valley.
>
> 11 Yea, by the power of his voice doth the whole earth shake;
>
> 12 Yea, by the power of his voice, do the foundations rock, even to the very center.
>
> 13 Yea, and if he say unto the earth—Move—it is moved.
>
> 14 Yea, if he say unto the earth—Thou shalt go back, that it lengthen out the day for many hours—it is done;
>
> 15 And thus, according to his word the earth goeth back, and it appeareth unto man that the sun standeth still; yea, and behold, this is so; for surely it is the earth that moveth and not the sun.
>
> 16 And behold, also, if he say unto the waters of the great deep—Be thou dried up—it is done.

17 Behold, if he say unto this mountain—Be thou raised up, and come over and fall upon that city, that it be buried up—behold it is done.

18 And behold, if a man hide up a treasure in the earth, and the Lord shall say—Let it be accursed, because of the iniquity of him who hath hid it up—behold, it shall be accursed.

19 And if the Lord shall say—Be thou accursed, that no man shall find thee from this time henceforth and forever—behold, no man getteth it henceforth and forever.

20 And behold, if the Lord shall say unto a man—Because of thine iniquities, thou shalt be accursed forever—it shall be done.

The doctrine of the depravity of man, which Mormon might be accused of teaching (v. 7) is false. There is no better explanation of why man is less than the dust of the earth, as some people imply,[1] than Mormon's treatise of it here. When God speaks to the earth it obeys (vv. 8–14). The earth was created by God speaking to the elements of the earth and they obeyed.[2]

In support of Mormon's words, Jacob, brother of Nephi, bears witness of the righteous Nephites commanding the parts of the earth.

6 Wherefore, we search the prophets, and we have many revelations and the spirit of prophecy; and having all these witnesses we obtain a hope, and our faith becometh unshaken, insomuch that we truly can command in the name of Jesus and the very trees obey us, or the mountains, or the waves of the sea. [Jacob 4:6]

The Jaredites had the same power according to Moroni.

---

[1] See Isaiah 40:17, Daniel 4:35 As pointed out in Moses 1:8–11, the nothingness of individual man is in comparison to the worlds and their inhabitants which God has created. It should be remembered in light of what Moses learned, man became immortal and eternal (Moses 1:39).

[2] The Genesis account reads "And God said" (Genesis 1:3, 6, 9, 14 etc). The Book of Moses reads "And I, God, said (Moses 2:3, 6, 9, 14 etc). The Abraham account says the Gods organized and formed the heavens (Abraham 1:1, 3, 6, 9, 14 etc). The word Barou in Hebrew means to organize (see *TPJS*, 348–350).

> 30 For the brother of Jared said unto the mountain Zerin,
> Remove—and it was removed. And if he had not had faith it would
> not have moved; wherefore thou workest after men have faith. [Ether
> 12:30; see also Helaman 10:9]

Jesus promised his disciples the power to move mountains (see Matthew 17:20).

Mormon also had a knowledge of astronomy, he knew that the earth moved and not the sun (Helaman 12:15). As Abraham learned the sun is one of the fixed plants (see Abraham facsimile No.2, figure 5). The Lord revealed a knowledge of the planets to Abraham (Abraham 3) and apparently it was handed down to the Nephites, or they learned it anew.

There is still evidence of a knowledge of astronomy among the ancient Americans.

> They were so capable at natural astrology, the said "Toltecs," that
> they were the first that had counted and calculated the days of the year
> and the night and its hours and the difference of time. They knew very
> well those (days) that were helpful and those that were harmful, which
> they left identified by 20 figures or characters. They also invented
> the art of interpreting dreams and they were so able and wise that they
> knew the movements of the heavens . . .[3]

The next chapter of this work will comment on the treasures of earth being moved (see Helaman 3:17 and commentary). Man is certainly less than the dust of the earth in obedience to the Lord.

Helaman 12:20–26 • Repentance May Bring the Salvation of Men

> 20 And behold, if the Lord shall say unto a man—Because of thine
> iniquities, thou shalt be accursed forever—it shall be done.

---

[3] Milton R. Hunter and Thomas Stuart Ferguson, *Ancient America and the Book of Mormon*, Oakland: Kolob Book Company, [1950], 291.

21 And if the Lord shall say—Because of thine iniquities thou shalt be cut off from my presence—he will cause that it shall be so.

22 And wo unto him to whom he shall say this, for it shall be unto him that will do iniquity, and he cannot be saved; therefore, for this cause, that men might be saved, hath repentance been declared.

23 Therefore, blessed are they who will repent and hearken unto the voice of the Lord their God; for these are they that shall be saved.

24 And may God grant, in his great fulness, that men might be brought unto repentance and good works, that they might be restored unto grace for grace, according to their works.

25 And I would that all men might be saved. But we read that in the great and last day there are some who shall be cast out, yea, who shall be cast off from the presence of the Lord;

26 Yea, who shall be consigned to a state of endless misery, fulfilling the words which say: They that have done good shall have everlasting life; and they that have done evil shall have everlasting damnation. And thus it is. Amen.

Those men who will hearken unto the voice of the Lord their God can be saved through repentance (vv. 22–23). "Restored unto grace for grace, according to their works" (v. 24) shows what man must do as often as he has repented. Alma "labored without ceasing, that I might bring souls to repentance" (Alma 36:24). Jesus did not receive a fullness of glory "at the first, but received grace for grace" (D&C 93:12). As one works to help others he retains a forgiveness of sins (Jesus excepted). As King Benjamin taught, if we live as we should we will "be filled with the love of God, and always retain a remission of [our] sins" (Mosiah 4:12).

Mormon's closing wish was that all might be saved, but he knew some would not (Helaman 12:25). His last sentence (v. 26) is almost identical to John 5:29, which are Jesus' words to the Jews who sought to kill him. Was Mormon quoting from the plates of brass, another Old Testament teaching lost from the Bible (1 Nephi 13:26–29), or is it one of the "hundredth part of the things which Jesus did truly teach unto the people" (3 Nephi 26:6)? Mormon could have known of it but it was not included in his abridgment of Jesus teachings. Someday that question will be answered.

The time of the birth of Jesus is drawing nigh. What will the next few years bring among the Nephites?

SACRED WRITING

Preaching Which Is Sacred:

Helaman 11:10–16	Nephi prays to have the heavens open again.

Doctrines Learned:

Helaman 11:23	Through revelation prophets know true points of doctrine.
Helaman 12:7–8ff	Man is less than the dust of the earth because the earth obeys God and man does not always do so.
Helaman 12:22–23	Men may be saved from iniquity if they repent and hearken to the voice of the Lord their God.
Helaman 12:24	Men may be restored from grace to grace according to their works.
Helaman 12:25–26	Some men will not be saved, but cast out and consigned to endless misery.

General Authority Quotes:

President Ezra Taft Benson • Helaman 7–11

In 1980 Pres. Benson gave a devotional talk at BYU titled "Fourteen Fundamentals in Following the Prophet." It is published in parts in *The Teachings of Ezra Taft Benson*, pp. 131–143 along with other quotes about the Prophet—President of the Church. It is too lengthy for inclusion here, but a summary of the fourteen fundamentals is included here.

1. The prophet is the only man who speaks for the Lord in everything.

2. The living prophet is more vital to us than the standard works.

3. The living prophet is more important to us than a dead prophet.

4. The prophet will never lead the Church astray.

5. The prophet is not required to have any particular earthly training or credentials to speak on any subject or act on any matter at any time.

6. The prophet does not have to say "Thus saith the Lord" to give us scripture.

7. The prophet tells us what we need to know, not always what we want to know.

8. The prophet is not limited by men's reasoning.

9. The prophet can receive revelation on any matter, temporal or spiritual.

10. The prophet may be involved in civic matters.

11. The two groups who have the greatest difficulty in following the prophet are the proud who are learned and the proud who are rich.

12. The prophet will not necessarily be popular with the world or the worldly.

13. The prophet and his counselors make up the First Presidency—the highest quorum in the Church.

14. The prophet and the presidency—the living prophet and the First Presidency—follow them and be blessed; reject them and suffer.

President Harold B. Lee • Helaman 12:2–3

"Isn't that a terrible indictment, and yet that is happening before us today. We are seeing that affluence. Never was there such prosperity in this country. We have been forgetting God, and we have turned aside from His teachings, and we are paying a terrible price. It is the test that, if we survive, will perhaps take some of the punishments that this prophet said would be necessary to bring us back to our knees and seek for the Lord to guide and direct us." [*The Teachings of Harold B. Lee,* 329]

Elder Neal A. Maxwell • Helaman 12:3

"Only greater consecration will cure ambivalence and casualness in any of us! As already noted, the tutoring challenges arising from increased consecration may be severe but may reflect the divine mercy necessary to induce further consecration (see Helaman 12:3). If we have grown soft, hard times may be necessary. Deprivation may prepare us for further consecration, though we shudder at the thought. If we are too easily contented, God may administer a dose of divine discontent. His long-suffering thus becomes very necessary to maximize our agency and development. But He is not an indulgent Father." ["Consecration," CR Oct. 1992, 90–91]

Elder Henry B. Eyring • Helaman 12:4–6

"From those three short verses of scripture, we see three causes for the sad drift away from humble prayer. First, while God implores us to pray, the enemy of our souls belittles and then derides it. The warning from 2 Nephi is true:

'And now, my beloved brethren, I perceive that ye ponder still in your hearts; and it grieveth me that I must speak concerning this thing. For if ye would hearken unto the Spirit which teacheth a man to pray ye would know that ye must pray; for the evil spirit teacheth not a man to pray but teacheth him that he must not pray.'

Second, God is forgotten out of vanity. A little prosperity and peace, or even a turn slightly for the better, can bring us feelings of self-sufficiency. We can feel quickly that we are in control of our lives, that the change for the better is our own doing, not that of a God who communicates to us through the still, small voice of the Spirit. Pride creates a noise within us, which makes the quiet voice of the Spirit hard to hear. And soon, in our vanity, we no longer even listen for it. We can come quickly to think we don't need it.

The third cause is rooted deeply within us. We are spirit children of a loving Heavenly Father, who placed us in mortality to see if we would choose—freely choose—to keep His commandments and come unto His Beloved Son. They do not compel us. They cannot, for that would interfere with the plan of happiness. And so there is in us a God-given desire to be responsible for our own choices." [CR Oct. 2001, 16]

President Harold B. Lee • Helaman 12:3–6

"*Sometimes we need chastening.* It's an interesting thing that sometimes it takes calamity to drive us together. It's a terrifying thing to think that that's necessary, but the Lord said through one of His prophets that sometimes we have to have the chastening hand of the Almighty before we will wake up and humble ourselves to do the thing that He has asked us to do (see Helaman 12:3–6). In talking about the conditions that would come, He warned the people that death and destruction and all sorts of difficulties would have to come before people would listen, before they would obey, and He removes His hand and lets these things occur, or our people would not repent and come unto the Lord." [*The Teachings of Harold B. Lee*, 191]

President Ezra Taft Benson • Helaman 12:6, 17

"The proud cannot accept the authority of God giving direction to their lives (see Helaman 12:6). They pit their perceptions of truth against God's great knowledge, their abilities versus God's priesthood power, their accomplishments against His mighty works.

Our enmity toward God takes on many labels, such as rebellion, hard-heartedness, stiff-neckedness, unrepentant, puffed up, easily offended, and sign seekers. The proud wish God would agree with them. They aren't interested in changing their opinions to agree with God's." [CR, Apr. 1989, 4]

President Ezra Taft Benson • Helaman 15:3

"God will have a humble people. Either we can choose to be humble or we can be compelled to be humble. Alma said, "Blessed are they who humble themselves without being compelled to be humble" (Alma 32:16).

Let us choose to be humble

We can choose to be humble ourselves by conquering enmity toward our brothers and sisters, esteeming them as ourselves, and lifting them as high or higher than we are (see D&C 38:24; 81:5; 84:106).

We can choose to humble ourselves by receiving counsel and chastisement "(see Jacob 4:10; Helaman 15:3; D&C 63:55; 101:4–5; 108:1; 124:61, 84; 136:31; Proverbs 9:8). ("Compelled to be Humble," CR Apr. 1989, 6]

Elder Russell M. Nelson • Helaman 16:22

"To understand why the Lord has commanded us not to "contend one with another," we must know the true source of contention. A Book of Mormon prophet revealed this important knowledge even before the birth of Christ:

'Satan did stir them up to do iniquity continually; yea, he did go about spreading rumors and contentions upon all the face of the land, that he might harden the hearts of the people against that which was good and against that which should come.'" ["Contention," CR, Apr. 1989, 85]

Challenges to Eternal Life:

1. Resolve to listen to the prophets and know concerning the true points of doctrine that you not have strife and contention in your life (Helaman 11:12–13).
2. Try not to be one whit behind Nephi and Lehi pertaining to righteousness (Helaman 11:19).
3. When you are chastened, search your life to see why you need to repent (Helaman 12:3).
4. Choose a challenge of your own form this reading and apply it to your life.

Chapter Eleven

The Prophecies of Samuel the Lamanite

Helaman 13–16

H *istorical Setting:* Helaman 13–16 covers five years of the record of the Nephites, the eighty-sixth through the ninetieth. However, only one year of those five years has much recorded about it, the eighty-sixth year. There is only one event covered in that one year, the prophecies of Samuel the Lamanite that he made from the wall of the city of Zarahemla. Three of the other years (87–89) have only one verse each about them. The fifth year (90) has a little more said about it, and this is mainly a reaction of the people to the prophecies of Samuel.

Precepts of this Reading:

11 And ye shall hear my words, for, for this intent have I come up upon the walls of this city, that ye might hear and know of the judgments of God which do await you because of your iniquities, and also that ye might know the conditions of repentance;

12 And also that ye might know of the coming of Jesus Christ, the Son of God, the Father of heaven and of earth, the Creator of all things from the beginning; and that ye might know of the signs of his coming, to the intent that ye might believe on his name.

13 And if ye believe on his name ye will repent of all your sins, that thereby ye may have a remission of them through his merits. [Helaman 14:11–13]

There are no precepts in these chapters of Helaman as identified by "thus we see," or "I will show unto you." However, the purpose and message of Samuel the Lamanites coming to Zarahemla are also applicable to us as the day of the Second Coming draws near.

An outline of the four chapters of Helaman follows as a preparation for a deeper study.

OUTLINE • HELAMAN 13–16

➤ Superscription: The prophecy of Samuel, the Lamanite, to the Nephites.

➤ 13:1–4   In the eighty-sixth year, the Nephites remained in great wickedness, while the Lamanites observed the commandments of God according to the law of Moses.

     a.   Samuel, a Lamanite, came into Zarahemla and did preach to the people (v. 2).

     b.   He preached repentance many days and they cast him out (v. 2).

     c.   The voice of the Lord told him to return and prophesy the things that came into his heart (v. 3).

     d.   They would not let him into the city, so he climbed upon the wall and prophesied the things that came into his heart (v. 4).

➤ 13:5–39   The words of Samuel, the Lamanite, that the Lord put into his heart.

     a.   The sword of justice hangs over this people, and four hundred years pass not away save the sword shall fall (vv. 5–10).

        1.   Heavy destruction awaits this people and nothing can save them but repentance and faith on the Lord.

2. An angel of the Lord brought glad tidings to me, and sent me to declare it to you, but you would not receive me.

3. The Lord said because of the hardness of the Nephites' hearts, I will take away my word, and withdrew my Spirit from them unless they repent.

4. Those of the fourth generation who shall live, of your enemies, shall behold your destruction.

b. If you repent and return unto the Lord you will be blessed, but wo if you do not (vv. 11–14).

   1. Wo unto the great city of Zarahemla for it is only saved by those who are righteous.

   2. If it were not for the righteous, I would cause fire to come down and destroy it.

   3. When you cast out the righteous, ye shall be ripe for destruction.

c. Wo unto the city of Gideon, and all the Nephite cities, because of the wickedness and abominations a curse shall come upon the land (vv. 15–17).

d. Thus saith our great and true God, those who hide up treasures in the earth shall find them no more because of the curse of the land, save it be a righteous man who hides it up unto the Lord (vv. 18–23).

   1. None hideth up treasures unto me save the righteous.

   2. The day comes when those who set their hearts on riches will hide them up and both they and their treasures shall be cursed.

   3. The hearts of the people of this city are not drawn out to the Lord, but swell with pride unto boasting, and a curse is upon the land.

e. Wo unto this people because ye cast out the prophets, mock them, stone them, and slay them (vv. 24–29).

   1. You say if you had been in the days of our fathers we would not have slain the prophets.

2. You are worse than they, for when a prophet comes you cast him out and say he is a false prophet.

3. If a man comes and says to walk after your own heart and follow your own desires, you receive him and say he is a prophet.

4. You give him your substance, gold, silver, and costly apparel, because he flatters you and says all is well.

5. How long will you follow blind guides and choose destruction rather than light?

f. The anger of the Lord is kindled against you, and he hath cursed the land because of your iniquity (vv. 30–37).

1. The time comes when he curses your riches, and they become slippery and you cannot hold them.

2. In the days of your poverty, you cry unto the Lord in vain.

3. You will say, O had I repented and not killed the prophets.

4. Had we remembered the Lord, our riches would not have become slippery.

5. We lay a tool here, and tomorrow it's gone, our swords are taken from us in the day of battle.

6. We are surrounded by demons, angels of the devil, canst thou not turn away thine anger.

g. Your days of probation are past, you have procrastinated the day of your salvation until it is everlastingly too late, for your destruction is made sure (v. 38).

1. Ye have sought all the days of your life what you could not obtain.

2. You have sought for happiness in doing iniquity, which is contrary to the nature of the righteousness which is in our great and Eternal head.

h. I pray you would repent and the anger of the Lord be turned away, and you be saved (v. 39).

➤ 14:1   Samuel the Lamanite prophesied a great many more things that cannot be written.

➤ 14:2–9   Prophecies of Samuel that were written:

a. A sign; five more years and the Son of God will come to redeem all those who shall believe on his name (v. 2).

b. Signs at the time of his coming, great lights in heaven the night before, and no darkness insomuch it shall appear as if it was day (vv. 3–6).

1. There shall be one day, a night, and a day, as if it were one day.

2. You will know of the rising of the sun and it setting and know of a surety that it is two days and a night before he is born.

3. A new star shall arise.

4. Many signs and wonders shall be in the heavens.

c. You shall all be amazed and wonder, and shall fall to the earth (v. 7).

d. Whosoever shall believe on the Son of God, shall have everlasting life (v. 8).

e. An angel came from the Lord to tell me to prophesy those things, and for you to repent and prepare the way of the Lord (v. 9).

➤ 14:10–31   Because I am a Lamanite and have spoken what the Lord commanded me, you are angry, seek to destroy me, and have cast me out from among you.

a. You shall hear my words, for this intent I have come on the walls of this city:

1. To hear and know of the judgments of God that await you because of your iniquities.

2. To know the conditions of repentance.

3. To know of the coming of Jesus Christ.

4. To know of the signs of his coming.

b. If you believe on his name, you will repent of your sins, and have them remitted.

c. It is expedient that Christ die, to bring the resurrection of the dead, and bring you into the presence of the Lord (vv. 15–19).

1. His death bringeth the resurrection and redemption of all mankind from spiritual death.

2. All mankind, by the fall of Adam, are cut off from the presence of the Lord and are considered as dead to temporal and spiritual things.

3. Those who repent are not hewn down and cast into the fire.

4. Those who do not repent are hewn down and there cometh again a spiritual death.

5. Therefore repent and do not bring yourself under condemnation, or a second death.

d. The angel gave Samuel a sign of his death, there shall be thunderings and lightnings for three hours, and darkness for three days (vv. 14, 20–27).

1. The sun shall be darkened, the moon, and the stars, and there shall be no light for the space of three days, until he shall rise from the dead.

2. When Christ yields up the ghost, there shall be thunderings and lightnings for many hours, and the earth tremble and shake.

3. The rocks above and beneath the earth, or the more part of it that are now solid, shall be broken up.

4. They shall ever after be found in seams and cracks and broken fragments.

5. There shall be great tempests, many mountains laid low, and valleys become mountains.

6. Highways shall be broken up, and cities become desolate.

7. Graves shall be opened, yield up their dead, and many saints appear unto many.

e. The angel said that many shall see greater things than these that they might believe these signs, and there be no cause for unbelief (vv. 28–30).

1. Whosoever will believe will be saved and a righteous judgment will come on those who do not believe.

2. Those condemned will bring upon themselves their own condemnation.

f. You are free and permitted to act for yourself; God has given you knowledge and has made you free (vv. 30–31).

1. You may know good from evil and you may choose life or death.

2. You can do good and be restored to good, or be evil and have evil restored to you.

➤ 15:1–30   Samuel continues his prophecies concerning those who do not repent.

a. Your houses shall be left desolate (v. 1).

b. Your woman shall have cause to mourn in the day they shall give suck (v. 3).

1. They shall attempt to flee and there will be no place of refuge.

2. Those with child, shall be heavy, be trodden down and left to perish.

c. Wo shall come to the Nephites, for they have been a chosen people, loved and chastened by the Lord because he loveth them (v. 3).

➤ 15:4   The Lamanites have been hated by the Lord because of the traditions of their fathers.

a. Salvation had come to them through the preaching of the Nephites (vv. 4–9).

1. For this intent the Lord hath prolonged their days.

2. The more part of them walk before God and observe his commandments.

        3. They strive to bring their brethren to the knowledge of the truth, and many are added to their numbers daily.

        4. They are led to believe the scriptures, the written prophecies of the holy prophets, which leads to faith unto repentance and a change of heart.

        5. They are firm and steadfast in the faith, and have been made free.

        6. They have buried their weapons of war, and will allow themselves to be trodden down because of their faith in Christ.

    b. Because of the Lamanites' firmness when they are once enlightened, the Lord will bless them and prolong their days in spite of their iniquity (vv. 10–13).

        1. If they should dwindle in unbelief the Lord will prolong their days until the time spoken of by our fathers, the prophet Zenos, and many other prophets concerning the restoration of the Lamanites again to the knowledge of the truth.

        2. The promises of the Lord have been extended to the Lamanites, and the Lord will be merciful to them after their afflictions and persecutions.

        3. This is according to the prophecy of their being brought to the true knowledge of their Redeemer, the true shepherd, and be numbered among his sheep.

    c. It shall be better for the Lamanites than for the Nephites except you repent (vv. 14–17).

        1. If the mighty works had been shown to them that have been shown to you, they never would again have dwindled in unbelief.

        2. The Lord says he will not utterly destroy them, but in the day of his wisdom, they shall return to him.

        3. If the Nephites do not repent, the Lord will utterly destroy them.

➤ 16:1–12   Many believed the words of Samuel, the Lamanite, and sought out Nephi, and were baptized after confessing their sins.

    a. Many who did not believe were angry with him, and cast stones and shot arrows at him as he stood on the wall (vv. 2–5).

        1. The Spirit of the Lord was with him insomuch that the arrows and the stones could not hit him.

        2. When they saw they could not hit him, many more believed and went to Nephi to be baptized.

        3. Nephi was baptizing, prophesying, preaching repentance, and working miracles among the people that they might know that Christ would shortly come.

    b. The more part of the Nephites did not believe in the words of Samuel, asking their captains to bind him for the power of the devil was preventing their stones and arrows from hitting him (vv. 6–9).

        1. As they went to bind him, he cast himself down from the wall, fled to his own country, and began to preach and prophesy there.

        2. He was never heard from among the Nephites again.

        3. Thus ended the eighty-sixth year of the judges.

    c. In the eighty-seventh year, the more part of the people remained in pride and wickedness, the lesser part following after God (vv. 10–12).

        1. The same conditions existed in the eighty-eighth year.

        2. The people began to be more hardened in iniquity and do more contrary to the commandments of God in the eighty-ninth year.

➤ 16:13–25   In the ninetieth year, there were great signs and wonders, the words of the prophets began to be fulfilled, and angels appeared declaring glad tidings of great joy.

a. The more part of the people hardened their hearts, and began to depend upon their own strength and wisdom, both among the Nephites and the Lamanites (vv. 15–21).

    1. They said some of the fulfilling of the prophets were correct guesses, but all those marvelous works cannot come to pass.

    2. It was not reasonable for such a being as Christ to come.

    3. If he is the Son of God, why will he not appear to us as well as in Jerusalem.

    4. This is a wicked tradition of our fathers, to cause us to believe in something in a far distant land, to keep us in ignorance, for we cannot witness these things with our own eyes.

    5. They will work some great mystery by the cunning of the evil one to keep us servants to their word and to them.

b. Many more foolish and vain things did the people imagine in their hearts (vv. 22–25).

    1. They were much disturbed by Satan who was stirring them up to do iniquity continually.

    2. He spread rumors and contentions throughout the land against that which was good and that which was to come.

    3. In spite of signs and miracles wrought among the people of the Lord, Satan got great hold upon the hearts of the people.

    4. Thus ended the record of Helaman and his sons.

NOTES AND COMMENTARY

Introduction: In the October General Conference of the Church in 1987, Elder Dean L. Larsen said: "I am much more concerned about understanding the admonitions of Samuel the Lamanite as he stood on the walls of the city of Zarahemla and called the rebellious Nephites to repentance than I am about identifying the location of that city in today's geography" (*Ensign*, Oct. 1987, 11).

These chapters contain what was said by Samuel the Lamanite from the walls of Zarahemla. Let us endeavor to understand as much of what he said as is possible.

> *Superscription:* The prophecy of Samuel, the Lamanite, to the Nephites. Comprising chapters 13 to 15 inclusive.

Helaman 13:1–4 • Samuel on the Wall of Zarahemla – 86ᵗʰ Year

> 1 And now it came to pass in the eighty and sixth year, the Nephites did still remain in wickedness, yea, in great wickedness, while the Lamanites did observe strictly to keep the commandments of God, according to the law of Moses.
>
> 2 And it came to pass that in this year there was one Samuel, a Lamanite, came into the land of Zarahemla, and began to preach unto the people. And it came to pass that he did preach, many days, repentance unto the people, and they did cast him out, and he was about to return to his own land.
>
> 3 But behold, the voice of the Lord came unto him, that he should return again, and prophesy unto the people whatsoever things should come into his heart.
>
> 4 And it came to pass that they would not suffer that he should enter into the city; therefore he went and got upon the wall thereof, and stretched forth his hand and cried with a loud voice, and prophesied unto the people whatsoever things the Lord put into his heart.

The preaching of Samuel the Lamanite for many days, and then being cast out, is almost a duplicate experience of Alma going to the city of Ammonihah (see Alma 8:13). However, this time it is a Lamanite instead of a Nephite (Helaman 13:2). An angel appeared to Alma (Alma 8:14), but the voice of the Lord came to Samuel. Alma entered the city of Ammonihah by another way (Alma 8:18), and Samuel climbed on the wall to preach (Helaman 13:4). Being on the wall was probably to attract attention to him. While Samuel prophesied whatsoever things the Lord put into his heart (v. 4), he later gave four reasons why he came upon the wall: (1) that they might know the judgments of God that awaited them because of their iniquities; (2) that they might know the conditions of repentance; (3) that they might know of the coming of Jesus Christ, the Son of God, the Father of heaven and earth, the Creator of all things from the beginning; and (4) that they might know of the signs of his coming, to the intent they might believe on his name (Helaman 14:11–12). These four reasons for his coming upon the wall will be treated in the order that he speaks about them, which is in a slightly different order than he listed them.

Helaman 13:5–11 • The Judgments of God That Await the Nephites

5 And he said unto them: Behold, I, Samuel, a Lamanite, do speak the words of the Lord which he doth put into my heart; and behold he hath put it into my heart to say unto this people that the sword of justice hangeth over this people; and four hundred years pass not away save the sword of justice falleth upon this people.

6 Yea, heavy destruction awaiteth this people, and it surely cometh unto this people, and nothing can save this people save it be repentance and faith on the Lord Jesus Christ, who surely shall come into the world, and shall suffer many things and shall be slain for his people.

7 And behold, an angel of the Lord hath declared it unto me, and he did bring glad tidings to my soul. And behold, I was sent unto you to declare it unto you also, that ye might have glad tidings; but behold ye would not receive me.

8 Therefore, thus saith the Lord: Because of the hardness of the hearts of the people of the Nephites, except they repent I will take away my word from them, and I will withdraw my Spirit from them, and I will suffer them no longer, and I will turn the hearts of their brethren against them.

9 And four hundred years shall not pass away before I will cause that they shall be smitten; yea, I will visit them with the sword and with famine and with pestilence.

10 Yea, I will visit them in my fierce anger, and there shall be those of the fourth generation who shall live, of your enemies, to behold your utter destruction; and this shall surely come except ye repent, saith the Lord; and those of the fourth generation shall visit your destruction.

11 But if ye will repent and return unto the Lord your God I will turn away mine anger, saith the Lord; yea, thus saith the Lord, blessed are they who will repent and turn unto me, but wo unto him that repenteth not.

Samuel begins speaking by testifying that he is speaking by the revelation (v. 5). The first judgment of God that he mentions is "the sword of justice" that hangs over the Nephites. As an attribute of God, justice is what the people deserve. It is based upon the keeping of the law or the breaking of the law. In this case it was the law of Moses (v. 1 above). The sword depicts war or destruction, thus the Nephites were facing destruction. However, this destruction was not to come for four hundred years (v. 5). Would this cause much anxiety today if a prophet told you that your city and its inhabitants would be destroyed in four hundred years? Probably not. Alma had given Helaman, his son, the same prophecy nearly seventy years before (Alma 45:12–13) and it hadn't had too much effect since that time.

Perhaps the four-hundred-year prophecy was just a reminder or an attention getter. It may have been an appeal to their pride as a people as well. Whatever the reason, the Lord did inspire Samuel to say it. He only warns the present inhabitants of their imminent danger after he warns them of the future destruction more thoroughly (Helaman 13:12–39).

Repentance as the condition for not being destroyed was based on the assured coming of Christ (v. 6). Since the time of his coming had been foretold for nearly six hundred years (1 Nephi 10:4; 19:8; 2 Nephi 25:19), and the time was almost there (about 6 B.C.), it was appropriate for the occasion.

The angel who declared it to Samuel (Helaman 13:7) may have been an earlier appearance than the voice of the Lord that had sent him again to the city. The angel's appearance being earlier is implied by Samuel's reference to his earlier rejection (v. 7). The continued warning also implies that the very generation to which Samuel is speaking will have the word of God and the Lord's Spirit taken away if they do not repent (v. 8). Also, the four hundred year, fourth generation destruction will still take place (v. 9–10). The condition of repentance is held out to both generations, then and four hundred years later (v. 11).

Helaman 13:12–16 • Wo Unto the City of Zarahemla

12 Yea, wo unto this great city of Zarahemla; for behold, it is because of those who are righteous that it is saved; yea, wo unto this great city, for I perceive, saith the Lord, that there are many, yea, even the more part of this great city, that will harden their hearts against me, saith the Lord.

13 But blessed are they who will repent, for them will I spare. But behold, if it were not for the righteous who are in this great city, behold, I would cause that fire should come down out of heaven and destroy it.

14 But behold, it is for the righteous' sake that it is spared. But behold, the time cometh, saith the Lord, that when ye shall cast out the righteous from among you, then shall ye be ripe for destruction; yea, wo be unto this great city, because of the wickedness and abominations which are in her.

15 Yea, and wo be unto the city of Gideon, for the wickedness and abominations which are in her.

16 Yea, and wo be unto all the cities which are in the land round about, which are possessed by the Nephites, because of the wickedness and abominations which are in them.

Having reminded the inhabitants of Zarahemla of the four-hundred-year prophecy, Samuel turns to focus on those of their specific city. If it weren't for the fewer numbers but more righteous citizens of the city, it would be destroyed right then (vv. 12–13). As a further warning, when the righteous are cast out they will be destroyed (v. 14).

The city of Zarahemla was destroyed at the time of the crucifixion of Christ, and it was destroyed by fire as the Lord threatened at this time (see 3 Nephi 8:8). The same principle that applies to the nations apparently applies to the cities: "He leadeth away the righteous into precious lands, and the wicked he destroyeth, and curseth the land unto them for their sakes" (1 Nephi 17:38). This cursing Samuel also foretold (see below).

The city of Gideon, which Samuel also warned along with other cities (Helaman 13:15–16), may have repented. When the Savior spoke to the Nephites after he was crucified, he mentioned many cities that were destroyed (3 Nephi 9:2–10), Mormon mentioned three of those in this abridgment (3 Nephi 8:8–10), but Gideon was not mentioned.

Helaman 13:17–23 • A Curse to Come upon the Land

17 And behold, a curse shall come upon the land, saith the Lord of Hosts, because of the peoples' sake who are upon the land, yea, because of their wickedness and their abominations.

18 And it shall come to pass, saith the Lord of Hosts, yea, our great and true God, that whoso shall hide up treasures in the earth shall find them again no more, because of the great curse of the land, save he be a righteous man and shall hide it up unto the Lord.

19 For I will, saith the Lord, that they shall hide up their treasures unto me; and cursed be they who hide not up their treasures unto me; for none hideth up their treasures unto me save it be the righteous; and he that hideth not up his treasures unto me, cursed is he, and also the treasure, and none shall redeem it because of the curse of the land.

20 And the day shall come that they shall hide up their treasures, because they have set their hearts upon riches; and because they have set their hearts upon their riches, and will hide up their treasures when they shall flee before their enemies; because they will not hide them up unto me, cursed be they and also their treasures; and in that day shall they be smitten, saith the Lord.

21 Behold ye, the people of this great city, and hearken unto my words; yea, hearken unto the words which the Lord saith; for behold,

he saith that ye are cursed because of your riches, and also are your riches cursed because ye have set your hearts upon them, and have not hearkened unto the words of him who gave them unto you.

22 Ye do not remember the Lord your God in the things with which he hath blessed you, but ye do always remember your riches, not to thank the Lord your God for them; yea, your hearts are not drawn out unto the Lord, but they do swell with great pride, unto boasting, and unto great swelling, envyings, strifes, malice, persecutions, and murders, and all manner of iniquities.

23 For this cause hath the Lord God caused that a curse should come upon the land, and also upon your riches, and this because of your iniquities.

The curse upon the land that those who hide up treasures in the earth shall find them no more (v. 18) may seem very unusual. However, the cause of the curse was their having set their hearts upon their riches, and they weren't able to take the riches with them (v. 20). This curse was fulfilled prior to the time of the destruction of the Nephites as a nation (Mormon 1:18). The curse was conditional, the righteous who hid their treasures up to the Lord would be able to get them again (Helaman 13:19). Those who had riches were to thank the Lord their God for them (v. 22). More will be said of this curse later.

When the heart is not turned to God, Samuel lists several effects of having riches (v. 22). Are these progressive or sequential effects? The list begins with pride and ends with murder and iniquities. Pride comes when because of prosperity we think we are better than others (Jacob 2:13). Thus, we begin to boast about ourselves. Boasting makes us conceited or self-centered (swelling). The next step is envy of those who really do have more character than we do. Envy causes strife or conflict. When we experience strife, we feel malice towards others. Malice brings us to persecuting others and ends up with murders and other iniquities, which brings spiritual death.[4] There seems to be a

---

[4] My good friend and colleague, Dennis Largey, suggested the progressive nature of this verse.

progressive pattern in these effects, which may explain why the Lord warns us against setting our hearts on riches.

Helaman 13:24–29 • You Cast out the Prophets and Mock Them

24 Yea, wo unto this people, because of this time which has arrived, that ye do cast out the prophets, and do mock them, and cast stones at them, and do slay them, and do all manner of iniquity unto them, even as they did of old time.

25 And now when ye talk, ye say: If our days had been in the days of our fathers of old, we would not have slain the prophets; we would not have stoned them, and cast them out.

26 Behold ye are worse than they; for as the Lord liveth, if a prophet come among you and declareth unto you the word of the Lord, which testifieth of your sins and iniquities, ye are angry with him, and cast him out and seek all manner of ways to destroy him; yea, you will say that he is a false prophet, and that he is a sinner, and of the devil, because he testifieth that your deeds are evil.

27 But behold, if a man shall come among you and shall say: Do this, and there is no iniquity; do that and ye shall not suffer; yea, he will say: Walk after the pride of your own hearts; yea, walk after the pride of your eyes, and do whatsoever your heart desireth—and if a man shall come among you and say this, ye will receive him, and say that he is a prophet.

28 Yea, ye will lift him up, and ye will give unto him of your substance; ye will give unto him of your gold, and of your silver, and ye will clothe him with costly apparel; and because he speaketh flattering words unto you, and he saith that all is well, then ye will not find fault with him.

29 O ye wicked and ye perverse generation; ye hardened and ye stiffnecked people, how long will ye suppose that the Lord will suffer you? Yea, how long will ye suffer yourselves to be led by foolish and blind guides? Yea, how long will ye choose darkness rather than light?

Many prophets have been killed after their missions were completed (see Matthew 23:37). The Lord will protect them until that mission is finished (see Mosiah 13:3; *TPJS*, 274, 328). He allows the prophet to be killed to "seal his testimony with his blood, that he might be honored and the wicked might be condemned" (D&C 136:39). We have no record of Nephite prophets being slain at this time, but apparently they were (Helaman 13:24).

During his earthly ministry, the Savior gave a chastisement to the scribes and Pharisees for slaying the prophets similar to the one Samuel gave to the Nephites (v. 25, see Matthew 23:30–31). Samuel said the Nephites were worse than the generation who killed the prophets because they labeled the true prophets as false prophets, and accepted the false prophets as true prophets (Helaman 13:26–28). Isaiah described a similar problem among the Israelites of his day: "That this is a rebellious people, lying children, children that will not hear the law of the LORD: Which say to the seers, See not; and to the prophets, Prophesy not unto us right things, speak unto us smooth things, prophesy deceits: Get you out of the way, turn aside out of the path, cause the Holy One of Israel to cease from before us" (Isaiah 30:9–11). Nephi gave a figuration description of "the very God of Israel do men trample under their feet, but I would speak in other words—they set him at naught, and hearken not to the voice of his counsels" (1 Nephi 19:7).

In desperation Samuel asks the Nephites how long they will be led by foolish and blind guides (instead of the prophets), and choose darkness rather than light (Helaman 13:29). The blood of the saints, and prophets are also saints (see Revelation 18:24), shall cry from the ground for vengeance, whether it be physical blood or spiritual rejection and trampling to death (see 2 Nephi 28:10; D&C 7:7).

Helaman 13:30–37 • O That We Had Not Killed the Prophets

30 Yea, behold, the anger of the Lord is already kindled against you; behold, he hath cursed the land because of your iniquity.

31 And behold, the time cometh that he curseth your riches, that they become slippery, that ye cannot hold them; and in the days of your poverty ye cannot retain them.

32 And in the days of your poverty ye shall cry unto the Lord; and in vain shall ye cry, for your desolation is already come upon you, and your destruction is made sure; and then shall ye weep and howl in that day, saith the Lord of Hosts. And then shall ye lament, and say:

33 O that I had repented, and had not killed the prophets, and stoned them, and cast them out. Yea, in that day ye shall say: O that we had remembered the Lord our God in the day that he gave us our riches, and then they would not have become slippery that we should lose them; for behold, our riches are gone from us.

34 Behold, we lay a tool here and on the morrow it is gone; and behold, our swords are taken from us in the day we have sought them for battle.

35 Yea, we have hid up our treasures and they have slipped away from us, because of the curse of the land.

36 O that we had repented in the day that the word of the Lord came unto us; for behold the land is cursed, and all things are become slippery, and we cannot hold them.

37 Behold, we are surrounded by demons, yea, we are encircled about by the angels of him who hath sought to destroy our souls. Behold, our iniquities are great. O Lord, canst thou not turn away thine anger from us? And this shall be your language in those days.

The topic turns again to the land being cursed (v. 30). The curse is two-fold concerning riches: first, they will become slippery that you cannot hold them; and secondly, in the days of poverty you cannot retain them (v. 31. Samuel speaks of the second one first, the days of poverty (v. 32–33). Hindsight is always better than foresight. Their riches may have been lost because of poor management, inflation, or other reasons, but the main reason is that they had not remembered the Lord and had killed the prophets (v. 33). Their tools and swords also became "slippery" (vv. 31, 34) and are added to their riches. The tools and swords may have been stolen or lost, not remembering where they were left, but the treasures that were hid up would slip away (vv. 34–35). The Lord was involved here. As spoken of by Mormon in chapter 12, the Lord apparently spoke and the treasure was moved, or the earth relocated it at the Lord's command (see Helaman

12:18–19). President Brigham Young relates an interesting experience that certainly has a connection to the land of the Nephites being cursed.

I presume there are some present who have heard me narrate a circumstance with regard to the discovery of a gold mine in Little Cottonwood Canyon, and I will here say that the specimens taken from it, which I have in my possession today, are as fine specimens of gold as ever were found on this continent. A man whom some of you will well know, brought to me a most beautiful nugget. I told him to let the mine alone.

When General Conner came here, he did considerable prospecting; and in hunting through the Cottonwoods, he had an inkling that there was gold there. Porter, as we generally call him, came to me one day, saying, "They have struck within four inches of my lode, what shall I do?" He was carried away with the idea that he must do something. I therefore told him to go with the other brethren interested, and make his claim. When he got through talking I said to him, "Porter, you ought to know better; you have seen and heard things which I have not, and are a man of long experience in this Church. I want to tell you one thing; they may strike within four inches of that lode as many times as they have a mind to, and they will not find it." They hunted and hunted, hundreds of them did; and I had the pleasure of laughing at him a little, for when he went there again, he could not find it himself." (Laughter.)

Sometimes I take the liberty of talking a little further with regard to such things. Orin P. Rockwell is an eyewitness to some powers of removing the treasure of the earth. He was with certain parties that lived near by where the plates were found that contain the records of the Book of Mormon. There were a great many treasures hid up by the Nephites. Porter was with them one night where there were treasures, and they would find them easy enough, but they could not obtain them.

I will tell you a story which will be marvelous to most of you. It was told me by Porter, whom I would believe just as quickly as any man that lives. When he tells a thing he understands, he will tell it just as he knows it; he is a man that does not lie. He said that on this night, when they were engaged hunting for this old treasure, they dug around the end of a chest for some twenty inches. The chest was about three feet square. One man who was determined to have the contents of that chest, took his pick and struck into the lid of it, and split through the chest. The blow took off a piece of the lid, which a certain lady kept in her possession until she died. That chest of money went into the bank. Porter describes it so (making a rumbling sound); he says this is just as true as the heavens are. I have heard others tell the same story. I relate this because it is marvelous to you. But to those who understand these things, it is not marvelous. [*Journal of Discourses*, 19:37–38]

All things had become slippery (v. 36). It apparently pertained to more than tools, swords, and treasures.

The Nephites beings surrounded by the devil's angels (v. 37) may be describing the time of the Nephite destruction in the fourth generation, or the destruction at the time of Christ's crucifixion, or both. The veil of light would obviously be taken away, and that would leave them subject to the darkness of Satan's world. The Lord even foretells their language.

Helaman 13:38–39 • Your Destruction Is Made Sure

38 But behold, your days of probation are past; ye have procrastinated the day of your salvation until it is everlastingly too late, and your destruction is made sure; yea, for ye have sought all the days of your lives for that which ye could not obtain; and ye have sought for happiness in doing iniquity, which thing is contrary to the nature of that righteousness which is in our great and Eternal Head.

39 O ye people of the land, that ye would hear my words! And I pray that the anger of the Lord be turned away from you, and that ye would repent and be saved.

Just as a person may have his calling and election made sure (see 2 Peter 1:1–11), a person may make his everlasting destruction sure (Helaman 13:38, see also v.32). To make one's calling and election sure, "the Lord has thoroughly proved him, and finds that the man is determined to serve Him at all hazards" (*TPJS*, 150). A person who has sought all the days of his or her life for things that could not be obtained, and sought for happiness in doing iniquity, will have his or her eternal destruction made sure (v. 38). Things they could not obtain (v. 38) must refer to power and glory which comes only through the priesthood. Before quoting verse 38, President Spencer W. Kimball wrote: "As we have seen, one can wait too long to repent. Many of the Nephites did."[5]

Samuel prayed for the Nephites to avoid destruction (v. 39). Many did but many didn't (see 3 Nephi 8). At the time near the final destruction of the Nephites, Mormon described his people as having their destruction made sure. He recognized that "the day of grace was passed with them, both temporally and spiritually, for I saw thousands of them hewn down in open rebellion against their God" (Mormon 2:15). As the Second Coming approaches, more and more people will make their destruction sure because we know the wicked will be destroyed (see D&C 76:98–112).

The nature of our great and Eternal Head (God) is one of total righteousness. This righteousness God obtained by living eternal laws. He will not and cannot change because he is an eternal being. We can become like him (see 1 John 1:2–3; Moroni 7:48). Peter urges us to become "partakers of the divine nature" (2 Peter 1:4), and "be ye holy for I am holy" (1 Peter 1:13–16). The followers of the devil become carnal, sensual, and devilish in their nature. Abinadi warns:

> But remember that he that persists in his own carnal nature, and goes on in the ways of sin and rebellion against God, remaineth in his fallen state and the devil hath all power over him. Therefore, he is as though there was no redemption made, being an enemy to God; and also is the devil an enemy to God. [Mosiah 16:5]

Such a state of nature brings everlasting destruction of the body and soul.

---

[5] Spencer W. Kimball, *The Miracle of Forgiveness,* [1969], 15.

Helaman 14:1–9 • The Signs of the Birth of the Son of God

1 And now it came to pass that Samuel, the Lamanite, did prophesy a great many more things which cannot be written.

2 And behold, he said unto them: Behold, I give unto you a sign; for five years more cometh, and behold, then cometh the Son of God to redeem all those who shall believe on his name.

3 And behold, this will I give unto you for a sign at the time of his coming; for behold, there shall be great lights in heaven, insomuch that in the night before he cometh there shall be no darkness, insomuch that it shall appear unto man as if it was day.

4 Therefore, there shall be one day and a night and a day, as if it were one day and there were no night; and this shall be unto you for a sign; for ye shall know of the rising of the sun and also of its setting; therefore they shall know of a surety that there shall be two days and a night; nevertheless the night shall not be darkened; and it shall be the night before he is born.

5 And behold, there shall a new star arise, such an one as ye never have beheld; and this also shall be a sign unto you.

6 And behold this is not all, there shall be many signs and wonders in heaven.

7 And it shall come to pass that ye shall all be amazed, and wonder, insomuch that ye shall fall to the earth.

8 And it shall come to pass that whosoever shall believe on the Son of God, the same shall have everlasting life.

9 And behold, thus hath the Lord commanded me, by his angel, that I should come and tell this thing unto you; yea, he hath commanded that I should prophesy these things unto you; yea, he hath said unto me: Cry unto this people, repent and prepare the way of the Lord.

Rather than enlarge on Samuel the Lamanite's other prophecies (v. 1), Mormon gives us the essential prophecies of the third reason Samuel came upon the wall—the coming of the Son of God. We assume the prophecies that were not written pertained to the destruction of the Nephites. The reason why they "cannot be written" was probably because of their grossness. Mormon's second epistle to his son Moroni (Moroni 9) is extremely gross, but Samuel's prophesies must have been even worse than Mormon described. Another reason it couldn't be written may have been tied to the abomination of the secret combinations. Previously Alma had commanded that they not be written (see Alma 37:27–32).

There were essentially four signs of the Saviors birth given by Samuel. While they are quite obvious from the text, we will summarize them here:

First, five years until Christ would be born (Helaman 14:2). Was this prophecy given on the exact calendar day five years before, or the general time? Based upon the day it was fulfilled it seems to have been considered the exact day for his future birth. At least the unbelievers set a day to put all the believers to death if the sign was not given (see 3 Nephi 1:9).

Secondly, there were to be great lights in the heavens, and there would be a day and a night with no darkness, or a total of two days and a night with the people knowing of the sun rising and setting (Helaman 14:3–4). How this happened could again have been by the power of God speaking to the earth and the earth obeying. Certainly, he who created an earth could control the light as well. There is no record of this sign being given in Jerusalem but perhaps it wasn't desired there because of the natural birth through which he entered the world. Regardless, the sign was very appropriate because Christ was the light and life of the world. (see 3 Nephi 9:18; John 1:4–5). There will be a similar sign given at his Second Coming. "And it shall come to pass in that day, that the light shall not be clear, nor dark: But it shall be one day which shall be known to the LORD, not day, nor night: but it shall come to pass, that at evening time it shall be light" (Zechariah 14:6–7).

The third sign was a new star appearing in the heavens (Helaman 14:5). This sign was apparently given in the East, at least in some places. "There came wise men from the east to Jerusalem, Saying, Where is he that is born King of the Jews? for we have seen his star in the east, and are come to worship him" (Matthew 2:1–2). These magi may have been descendants of Judah who had not returned from Babylon in 538 B.C.

The fourth sign was not specific. There would be many signs and wonders in the heavens; but so amazing would this be that many would fall to the earth. This sign again was literally fulfilled (see 3 Nephi 1:16–17).

Those who believed on the Son of God would receive eternal life (v. 8) seems to refer to all four signs not just the fourth one. Of course it would be almost impossible to believe in one sign and not the others.

Samuel again refers to an angel instructing him to come and tell these things (v. 9). As mentioned above, this may have been prior to his first visit to them when he was cast out (13:2).

Helaman 14:10–13 • You Are Angry Because I Am a Lamanite

10 And now, because I am a Lamanite, and have spoken unto you the words which the Lord hath commanded me, and because it was hard against you, ye are angry with me and do seek to destroy me, and have cast me out from among you.

11 And ye shall hear my words, for, for this intent have I come up upon the walls of this city, that ye might hear and know of the judgments of God which do await you because of your iniquities, and also that ye might know the conditions of repentance;

12 And also that ye might know of the coming of Jesus Christ, the Son of God, the Father of heaven and of earth, the Creator of all things from the beginning; and that ye might know of the signs of his coming, to the intent that ye might believe on his name.

13 And if ye believe on his name ye will repent of all your sins, that thereby ye may have a remission of them through his merits.

Samuel being rejected because he was a Lamanite is another evidence of the Nephite's pride. The Nephites at this time supposed they were better than the Lamanites (see Jacob 2:10; Alma 5:54). Why Samuel inserted his lineage and his purpose in coming on the wall at this time in his prophecy is not known. Perhaps some were ridiculing or questioning his authority or right to speak. In our day, many General Authorities are called from other nations. From the words of Samuel, may we take caution against assuming they are not as qualified or prepared as any others who may be called.

The four reasons for his coming on the wall (Helaman 14:11–12) were described under Helaman 13:1–4. We will now discuss the second reason for his coming on the wall. Of course all four reasons were given as a basis for the Nephites to repent (v. 13).

Helaman 14:14–19 • Known of the Death of Christ

14 And behold, again, another sign I give unto you, yea, a sign of his death.

15 For behold, he surely must die that salvation may come; yea, it behooveth him and becometh expedient that he dieth, to bring to pass the resurrection of the dead, that thereby men may be brought into the presence of the Lord.

16 Yea, behold, this death bringeth to pass the resurrection, and redeemeth all mankind from the first death—that spiritual death; for all mankind, by the fall of Adam being cut off from the presence of the Lord, are considered as dead, both as to things temporal and to things spiritual.

17 But behold, the resurrection of Christ redeemeth mankind, yea, even all mankind, and bringeth them back into the presence of the Lord.

18 Yea, and it bringeth to pass the condition of repentance, that whosoever repenteth the same is not hewn down and cast into the fire; but whosoever repenteth not is hewn down and cast into the fire; and there cometh upon them again a spiritual death, yea, a second death, for they are cut off again as to things pertaining to righteousness.

19 Therefore repent ye, repent ye, lest by knowing these things and not doing them ye shall suffer yourselves to come under condemnation, and ye are brought down unto this second death.

In addition to knowing of the birth of Christ, Samuel was to tell the Nephites of Christ's death. He began by saying he would give a sign of his death, but this sign is not given until verse 20 and will be discussed in the next section of Helaman 14.

Samuel gave two reasons for Christ to die. Christ was to bring salvation, or immortality, by dying and bringing to pass the resurrection of the dead. His death also redeemed all mankind and brought them back into the presence of the Lord (v. 15). This part of his Redemption is often misunderstood. It is often taught that the resurrection is universal but the atonement is conditional, referring to the Atonement which brings us eternal life. As Samuel explains, the resurrection and the redemption of all mankind are unconditional (v. 17). All are brought back into God's presence. The conditional part is whether we are prepared to remain there, or will be cast out and suffer a second spiritual death (v. 18). Those who are not prepared will be cast out. This casting out may be to a terrestrial degree of habitation, a telestial degree, or a complete second death being cast into outer darkness. The Atonement is infinite and eternal (see Alma 34:10). The doctrine of the Atonement bringing all mankind into God's presence is taught throughout the Book of Mormon. Father Lehi taught the doctrine to his son Jacob.

> And because of the intercession for all, all men come unto God; wherefore, they stand in the presence of him, to be judged of him according to the truth and holiness which is in him. Wherefore, the ends of the law which the Holy One hath given, unto the inflicting of the punishment which is affixed, which punishment that is affixed is in opposition to that of the happiness which is affixed, to answer the ends of the atonement— [2 Nephi 2:10]

Alma taught the doctrine to Zeezrom.

12 And Amulek hath spoken plainly concerning death, and being raised from this mortality to a state of immortality, and being brought before the bar of God, to be judged according to our works.

13 Then if our hearts have been hardened, yea, if we have hardened our hearts against the word, insomuch that it has not been found in us, then will our state be awful, for then we shall be condemned. [Alma 12:12–13]

Moroni taught the doctrine during his final days of recording on the plates.

13 And because of the redemption of man, which came by Jesus Christ, they are brought back into the presence of the Lord; yea, this is wherein all men are redeemed, because the death of Christ bringeth to pass the resurrection, which bringeth to pass a redemption from an endless sleep, from which sleep all men shall be awakened by the power of God when the trump shall sound; and they shall come forth, both small and great, and all shall stand before his bar, being redeemed and loosed from this eternal band of death, which death is a temporal death.

14 And then cometh the judgment of the Holy One upon them; and then cometh the time that he that is filthy shall be filthy still; and he that is righteous shall be righteous still; he that is happy shall be happy still; and he that is unhappy shall be unhappy still. [Mormon 9:13–14]

Thus Samuel invited the Nephites to repent (v. 19) after clearly teaching them the doctrine of the infinite (all inclusive) and unconditional (eternal) Atonement.

Helaman 14:20–28 • The Signs of Christ's Death

20 But behold, as I said unto you concerning another sign, a sign of his death, behold, in that day that he shall suffer death the sun shall be darkened and refuse to give his light unto you; and also the moon and the stars; and there shall be no light upon the face of this land, even from the time that he shall suffer death, for the space of three days, to the time that he shall rise again from the dead.

21 Yea, at the time that he shall yield up the ghost there shall be thunderings and lightnings for the space of many hours, and the earth shall shake and tremble; and the rocks which are upon the face of this earth, which are both above the earth and beneath, which ye know at this time are solid, or the more part of it is one solid mass, shall be broken up;

22 Yea, they shall be rent in twain, and shall ever after be found in seams and in cracks, and in broken fragments upon the face of the whole earth, yea, both above the earth and beneath.

23 And behold, there shall be great tempests, and there shall be many mountains laid low, like unto a valley, and there shall be many places which are now called valleys which shall become mountains, whose height is great.

24 And many highways shall be broken up, and many cities shall become desolate.

25 And many graves shall be opened, and shall yield up many of their dead; and many saints shall appear unto many.

26 And behold, thus hath the angel spoken unto me; for he said unto me that there should be thunderings and lightnings for the space of many hours.

27 And he said unto me that while the thunder and the lightning lasted, and the tempest, that these things should be, and that darkness should cover the face of the whole earth for the space of three days.

28 And the angel said unto me that many shall see greater things than these, to the intent that they might believe that these signs and these wonders should come to pass upon all the face of this land, to the intent that there should be no cause for unbelief among the children of men—

There are also four signs of Christ's death predicted by Samuel. The first sign was darkness for three days. The sun, moon, and stars would refuse to give their light. This was fulfilled (see 3 Nephi 8:19–23). What is meant by the sun, moon, and stars refusing to give their light is not known. The fulfillment of the sign was described as a vapor of darkness. Perhaps those heavenly bodies can show their light or withheld it similar to a resurrected being containing his glory or appearing in it. (see *TPJS*, 325).

The second sign was the terrible storm that would break up the rocks, mountains, valleys, highways, and cities (vv. 21–24). The storm lasted for about three hours at the time it was fulfilled (see 3 Nephi 8:19). Cities were destroyed and the whole face of the land was changed (see 3 Nephi 8:5–18). Evidence of the rocks being broken up could be tested today by the sedimentation process of dating now used by scientists. Based upon the rate of materials seeping or falling into a crevice of the earth, it is determined how long the crevice has been there. That should be a challenge for a young LDS scientist to test. Evidence of highways having been broken up and cities having been destroyed has been discovered.[6]

The third sign was the graves being opened and resurrected beings going forth (v. 25). This was also fulfilled, but Nephi had forgotten to record it. Jesus later commanded that it be recorded (see 3 Nephi 23:10–13). There was also a resurrection in Jerusalem.

> 50 Jesus, when he had cried again with a loud voice, yielded up the ghost.
>
> 51 And, behold, the veil of the temple was rent in twain from the top to the bottom; and the earth did quake, and the rocks rent;
>
> 52 And the graves were opened; and many bodies of the saints which slept arose. [Matthew 27:50–52]

The fourth sign was not specified except that there would be greater signs than the ones listed, which would leave no reason for unbelief (Helaman 14:28). These greater things were not identified in the fulfillment of these signs either, unless it was the voice of Jesus Christ and the message he gave to those who survived the terrible tempest (3 Nephi 9). "All the people of the land did hear these sayings" (3 Nephi 10:1), which was certainly a greater miracle. There was no cause for unbelief.

---

[6] The author will not enter into archeological discoveries in this work. For those interested see Paul R. Cheesman, *The World of the Book of Mormon*.

Helaman 14:29–31 • The Conditions of Repentance

29 And this to the intent that whosoever will believe might be saved, and that whosoever will not believe, a righteous judgment might come upon them; and also if they are condemned they bring upon themselves their own condemnation.

30 And now remember, remember, my brethren, that whosoever perisheth, perisheth unto himself; and whosoever doeth iniquity, doeth it unto himself; for behold, ye are free; ye are permitted to act for yourselves; for behold, God hath given unto you a knowledge and he hath made you free.

31 He hath given unto you that ye might know good from evil, and he hath given unto you that ye might choose life or death; and ye can do good and be restored unto that which is good, or have that which is good restored unto you; or ye can do evil, and have that which is evil restored unto you.

The condition of repentance was listed second of the four reasons Samuel gave for coming upon the wall, but was given last in his prophesy. The first condition is that those who believe (and repent) might be saved. Their were two classes of people who survived the destruction after his death: those who received the prophets (celestial type beings), and those who did not shed the blood of the saints (terrestrial type beings). Many telestial type beings were killed, drowned, burned, or buried (3 Nephi 10:12; 8:10–15).

The second condition was a righteous judgment would come. Therefore, those who were condemned were responsible for their own actions. The people were free to choose; they had their agency. They had been taught to know good from evil, and they chose life or death. They could choose to repent and not be destroyed, or to do evil and have evil restored to them (Helaman 14:30–31). Alma taught the same doctrine to his son Corianton. The justice of God requires a judgment and a restoration to good through repentance or a restoration unto evil (see Alma 41:2–4). Other conditions follow.

Helaman 15:1–3 Except You Repent
Your Houses Will Be Left Desolate

1 And now, my beloved brethren, behold, I declare unto you that except ye shall repent your houses shall be left unto you desolate.

2 Yea, except ye repent, your women shall have great cause to mourn in the day that they shall give suck; for ye shall attempt to flee and there shall be no place for refuge; yea, and wo unto them which are with child, for they shall be heavy and cannot flee; therefore, they shall be trodden down and shall be left to perish.

3 Yea, wo unto this people who are called the people of Nephi except they shall repent, when they shall see all these signs and wonders which shall be showed unto them; for behold, they have been a chosen people of the Lord; yea, the people of Nephi hath he loved, and also hath he chastened them; yea, in the days of their iniquities hath he chastened them because he loveth them.

The third condition of repentance was to repent and be prepared when catastrophe comes. The Lord always warns his people in advance. If they are prepared, those who are pregnant or have small children will be able to gather elsewhere early (v. 2). The Savior gave a similar warning to Judea regarding the Romans destruction of the temple in 70 A.D. "And wo unto them that are with child, and unto them that give suck in those days; Therefore, pray ye the Lord that your flight be not in the winter, neither on the Sabbath day;" (JS–Matthew 1:16–17, see also Matthew 24:19–20).

The fourth condition of repentance was to listen to the Lord's chastening and keep his commandments. Those chastened were a chosen and covenant people and the Lord loved them, but they had to repent when he chastened them (Helaman 15:3). "Unto whom much is given much is required" (D&C 82:3, see also Luke 12:48).

Helaman 15:4–13 • The Lamanites
Followed Their Fathers Traditions

4 But behold my brethren, the Lamanites hath he hated because their deeds have been evil continually, and this because of the iniquity of the tradition of their fathers. But behold, salvation hath come unto them through the preaching of the Nephites; and for this intent hath the Lord prolonged their days.

5 And I would that ye should behold that the more part of them are in the path of their duty, and they do walk circumspectly before God, and they do observe to keep his commandments and his statutes and his judgments according to the law of Moses.

6 Yea, I say unto you, that the more part of them are doing this, and they are striving with unwearied diligence that they may bring the remainder of their brethren to the knowledge of the truth; therefore there are many who do add to their numbers daily.

7 And behold, ye do know of yourselves, for ye have witnessed it, that as many of them as are brought to the knowledge of the truth, and to know of the wicked and abominable traditions of their fathers, and are led to believe the holy scriptures, yea, the prophecies of the holy prophets, which are written, which leadeth them to faith on the Lord, and unto repentance, which faith and repentance bringeth a change of heart unto them—

8 Therefore, as many as have come to this, ye know of yourselves are firm and steadfast in the faith, and in the thing wherewith they have been made free.

9 And ye know also that they have buried their weapons of war, and they fear to take them up lest by any means they should sin; yea, ye can see that they fear to sin—for behold they will suffer themselves that they be trodden down and slain by their enemies, and will not lift their swords against them, and this because of their faith in Christ.

10 And now, because of their steadfastness when they do believe in that thing which they do believe, for because of their firmness when they are once enlightened, behold, the Lord shall bless them and prolong their days, notwithstanding their iniquity—

11 Yea, even if they should dwindle in unbelief the Lord shall prolong their days, until the time shall come which hath been spoken

of by our fathers, and also by the prophet Zenos, and many other prophets, concerning the restoration of our brethren, the Lamanites, again to the knowledge of the truth—

12 Yea, I say unto you, that in the latter times the promises of the Lord have been extended to our brethren, the Lamanites; and notwithstanding the many afflictions which they shall have, and notwithstanding they shall be driven to and fro upon the face of the earth, and be hunted, and shall be smitten and scattered abroad, having no place for refuge, the Lord shall be merciful unto them.

13 And this is according to the prophecy, that they shall again be brought to the true knowledge, which is the knowledge of their Redeemer, and their great and true shepherd, and be numbered among his sheep.

The Lord was more patient with the Lamanites because they were not given as many opportunities as the Nephites. Therefore, the Lord would not destroy them, but would leave them upon the land (v. 4). The more part of the Lamanites at this time were observing the law of Moses (v. 5). Missionary work was thriving among them (v. 6). They believed the holy scriptures and were firm and steadfast in the faith (vv. 7–8). They had also buried their weapons of war and feared to sin (v. 9). Those are the reasons the Lord will prolong their days upon the land (v. 10).

Zenos and many other prophets had spoken of the restoration of the Lamanites in the latter days even though they would be scattered and smitten (vv. 11–12; see also Alma 9:16). The Lamanites shall come to a true knowledge of their Redeemer, their great and true shepherd (v. 13). The Redeemer and true shepherd is not the Christian concept of God today, but the knowledge of Jesus Christ, the creator, and administrator of the world. He is "the author and the finisher of their faith" (Moroni 6:4; Hebrews 12:2).

Helaman 15:14–17 • Better for the Lamanites than the Nephites Unless They Repent

14 Therefore I say unto you, it shall be better for them than for you except ye repent.

15 For behold, had the mighty works been shown unto them which have been shown unto you, yea, unto them who have dwindled in unbelief because of the traditions of their fathers, ye can see of yourselves that they never would again have dwindled in unbelief.

16 Therefore, saith the Lord: I will not utterly destroy them, but I will cause that in the day of my wisdom they shall return again unto me, saith the Lord.

17 And now behold, saith the Lord, concerning the people of the Nephites: If they will not repent, and observe to do my will, I will utterly destroy them, saith the Lord, because of their unbelief notwithstanding the many mighty works which I have done among them; and as surely as the Lord liveth shall these things be, saith the Lord.

The Nephites had been shown mighty works, and the Lamanites were the victims of the traditions of their wicked fathers. Thus the Lord would be more merciful to the Lamanites. Justice does not always come in this life. The time that people are sent to the earth is determined "on account of their exceeding faith and good works; in the first (pre-mortal) place" (Alma 13:3). Justice is a deciding factor. As the balance between justice and mercy changes in this life, it may again be adjusted in the spirit world. However, there will be a perfect balance at the end of all three experiences. Truth will prevail "and truth is a knowledge of things as they are [on earth], and as they were [in the pre-mortal], and as they are to come [post mortal]" (D&C 93:24).

Helaman 16:1–12 • Many Believe but Do Not Believe—86th – 89th Year

1 And now, it came to pass that there were many who heard the words of Samuel, the Lamanite, which he spake upon the walls of the city. And as many as believed on his word went forth and sought for Nephi; and when they had come forth and found him they confessed unto him their sins and denied not, desiring that they might be baptized unto the Lord.

2 But as many as there were who did not believe in the words of Samuel were angry with him; and they cast stones at him upon the wall, and also many shot arrows at him as he stood upon the wall; but

the Spirit of the Lord was with him, insomuch that they could not hit him with their stones neither with their arrows.

3 Now when they saw that they could not hit him, there were many more who did believe on his words, insomuch that they went away unto Nephi to be baptized.

4 For behold, Nephi was baptizing, and prophesying, and preaching, crying repentance unto the people, showing signs and wonders, working miracles among the people, that they might know that the Christ must shortly come—

5 Telling them of things which must shortly come, that they might know and remember at the time of their coming that they had been made known unto them beforehand, to the intent that they might believe; therefore as many as believed on the words of Samuel went forth unto him to be baptized, for they came repenting and confessing their sins.

6 But the more part of them did not believe in the words of Samuel; therefore when they saw that they could not hit him with their stones and their arrows, they cried unto their captains, saying: Take this fellow and bind him, for behold he hath a devil; and because of the power of the devil which is in him we cannot hit him with our stones and our arrows; therefore take him and bind him, and away with him.

7 And as they went forth to lay their hands on him, behold, he did cast himself down from the wall, and did flee out of their lands, yea, even unto his own country, and began to preach and to prophesy among his own people.

8 And behold, he was never heard of more among the Nephites; and thus were the affairs of the people.

9 And thus ended the eighty and sixth year of the reign of the judges over the people of Nephi.

10 And thus ended also the eighty and seventh year of the reign of the judges, the more part of the people remaining in their pride and wickedness, and the lesser part walking more circumspectly before God.

11 And these were the conditions also, in the eighty and eighth year of the reign of the judges.

> 12 And there was but little alteration in the affairs of the people, save it were the people began to be more hardened in iniquity, and do more and more of that which was contrary to the commandments of God, in the eighty and ninth year of the reign of the judges.

As usual there were two extreme reactions to Samuel's words. Those who believed Samuel went to Nephi. They apparently knew from Samuel's words that Nephi, who was preaching and prophesying at the same time, had the authority to baptize (vv. 1, 4). Those who did not believe tried to shoot the messenger. They tried to vent the anger which had been stirred up by Satan and Samuel was their target. The Spirit of the Lord obviously shielded him, as implied in the text (v. 2). With another witness, more repented and sought out Nephi (v. 3). The majority were still unbelievers, and turned to their spin tactics and attributed his protection to Satan (v. 6). At least they recognized that he had been protected, another witness to the believers that the Spirit of the Lord had been his shield. Samuel served his mission, and was thereafter transferred to another field of labor, his own people (v. 8). A lengthy coverage was given of one year (86), but it was still just one event and its aftermath that were covered. The unabridged plates should tell us much more.

There was little change in the next two years (vv. 10–11), and a slight worsening of conditions in the third year (v. 12). The birth of Christ was just two years away.

Helaman 16:3–25 • Great Signs, Wonders, Prophets, Angels – 90th Year

> 3 Now when they saw that they could not hit him, there were many more who did believe on his words, insomuch that they went away unto Nephi to be baptized.
>
> 4 For behold, Nephi was baptizing, and prophesying, and preaching, crying repentance unto the people, showing signs and wonders, working miracles among the people, that they might know that the Christ must shortly come—

5 Telling them of things which must shortly come, that they might know and remember at the time of their coming that they had been made known unto them beforehand, to the intent that they might believe; therefore as many as believed on the words of Samuel went forth unto him to be baptized, for they came repenting and confessing their sins.

6 But the more part of them did not believe in the words of Samuel; therefore when they saw that they could not hit him with their stones and their arrows, they cried unto their captains, saying: Take this fellow and bind him, for behold he hath a devil; and because of the power of the devil which is in him we cannot hit him with our stones and our arrows; therefore take him and bind him, and away with him.

7 And as they went forth to lay their hands on him, behold, he did cast himself down from the wall, and did flee out of their lands, yea, even unto his own country, and began to preach and to prophesy among his own people.

8 And behold, he was never heard of more among the Nephites; and thus were the affairs of the people.

9 And thus ended the eighty and sixth year of the reign of the judges over the people of Nephi.

10 And thus ended also the eighty and seventh year of the reign of the judges, the more part of the people remaining in their pride and wickedness, and the lesser part walking more circumspectly before God.

11 And these were the conditions also, in the eighty and eighth year of the reign of the judges.

12 And there was but little alteration in the affairs of the people, save it were the people began to be more hardened in iniquity, and do more and more of that which was contrary to the commandments of God, in the eighty and ninth year of the reign of the judges.

13 But it came to pass in the ninetieth year of the reign of the judges, there were great signs given unto the people, and wonders; and the words of the prophets began to be fulfilled.

14 And angels did appear unto men, wise men, and did declare unto them glad tidings of great joy; thus in this year the scriptures began to be fulfilled.

15 Nevertheless, the people began to harden their hearts, all save it were the most believing part of them, both of the Nephites and also of the Lamanites, and began to depend upon their own strength and upon their own wisdom, saying:

16 Some things they may have guessed right, among so many; but behold, we know that all these great and marvelous works cannot come to pass, of which has been spoken.

17 And they began to reason and to contend among themselves, saying:

18 That it is not reasonable that such a being as a Christ shall come; if so, and he be the Son of God, the Father of heaven and of earth, as it has been spoken, why will he not show himself unto us as well as unto them who shall be at Jerusalem?

19 Yea, why will he not show himself in this land as well as in the land of Jerusalem?

20 But behold, we know that this is a wicked tradition, which has been handed down unto us by our fathers, to cause us that we should believe in some great and marvelous thing which should come to pass, but not among us, but in a land which is far distant, a land which we know not; therefore they can keep us in ignorance, for we cannot witness with our own eyes that they are true.

21 And they will, by the cunning and the mysterious arts of the evil one, work some great mystery which we cannot understand, which will keep us down to be servants to their words, and also servants unto them, for we depend upon them to teach us the word; and thus will they keep us in ignorance if we will yield ourselves unto them, all the days of our lives.

22 And many more things did the people imagine up in their hearts, which were foolish and vain; and they were much disturbed, for Satan did stir them up to do iniquity continually; yea, he did go about spreading rumors and contentions upon all the face of the land, that he might harden the hearts of the people against that which was good and against that which should come.

23 And notwithstanding the signs and the wonders which were wrought among the people of the Lord, and the many miracles which they did, Satan did get great hold upon the hearts of the people upon all the face of the land.

24 And thus ended the ninetieth year of the reign of the judges over the people of Nephi.

25 And thus ended the book of Helaman, according to the record of Helaman and his sons.

In preparation for the birth of Christ, the wise were more blessed, but the people in general responded to Satan's effort to discredit the work of the prophets and the Spirit, and to trust in the power of man (vv. 14–15). How many people today follow similar rationalizations as those advocated by the unbelievers here? Do we look to our own strength rather than to the power of God? Do we trust in our wisdom rather than in the revelations of God? Do we attribute the miracles of today to be of the evil one (vv. 16–22)? As the Second Coming draws nearer, we can expect more and more of these explanations to be used against us and the church. Satan is real and he is working overtime against the good (v. 22). Satan has great hold upon many hearts today, but there are miracles happening among the people of God (v. 23). May we learn to look to God, trust in his revelations, and recognize the miracles of God as we study the Record of Helaman, son of Alma and also the record of Helaman and his sons, Nephi and Lehi.

SACRED WRITING

Prophesying:

Helaman 13:5–39	Samuel prophesies of the Nephite destruction.
Helaman 14:2–15:17	Samuel prophecies of the birth, death and resurrection of Christ.

Doctrines Learned:

Helaman 13:12–14	A few righteous can save a city, but when they are cast out the city is ripe for destruction.
Helaman 13:38	A person's destruction can be made sure (just as their calling and election can be made sure).
Helaman 13:38	Our great and Eternal Head has a nature of righteousness.

Helaman 14:2–6, 20–25	The Lord gives signs to those righteous people who look for them.
Helaman 14:15	It was expedient that Christ die to bring about the resurrection of the dead, and to bring them back into his presence.
Helaman 14:16	Christ redeemed all mankind from the first death, by the fall of Adam all mankind were cut off from the presence of the Lord being considered dead spiritually and temporally.
Helaman 14:17–18	The resurrection brings man back into the presence of God and if they are not repentant they suffer a second death, cut off from things pertaining to righteousness.
Helaman 14:25	Many were resurrected at the time of Christ's resurrection.
Helaman 14:29	Signs are given for those who believe to be saved, and for those who do not believe they may have a righteous judgment – to their own condemnation.
Helaman 14:30–31	Men are free to act for themselves based on the knowledge God has given them to know good from evil. Men shall be rested good for good or evil for evil.
Helaman 15:2–3	The Lord warns before the destruction comes upon the unrepentant.
Helaman 15:3	The Lord chastens those whom he loves.
Helaman 15:4–10	The Lord prolonged the days of the Lamanites because of their father's iniquity.
Helaman 15:11–16	Zenos and other prophets foretold the restoration of truth to the Lamanites.

General Authority Quotes:

President Joseph Fielding Smith • Helaman 13:37–38

In relation to the Nephites spoken of by Jacob, Alma, Samuel, and others, we should remember that these were once members of the Church who had turned away and denied the truth and fought to destroy it. They were not like the people in the gentile nations who never received the truth. These Nephites had received the light, rebelled, and then attempted to destroy it. After the visitation of our Lord, both Nephites and Lamanites lived in unity in the light of the gospel for nearly two hundred years. The Lord established his Church in all its fullness among them, and when they began to rebel they did it knowingly. This is clearly indicated in the words of Mormon. They had the guidance of the Nephite twelve, and three of them remained until in the extreme wickedness of the people the Lord would not permit them to remain. Samuel's castigation of these Nephites was fully justified in his accusation and prophecy of their punishment.

"Behold, we are surrounded by demons, yea, we are encircled about by the angels of him who hath sought to destroy our souls. Behold, our iniquities are great. O Lord, canst thou not turn away thing anger from us? And this shall be your language in those days.

"But behold, your days of probation are past; ye have procrastinated the day of your salvation until it is everlastingly too late, and your destruction is made sure; yea, for ye have sought all the days of your lives for that which ye could not obtain; and ye have sought for happiness in doing iniquity, which thing is contrary to the nature of that righteousness which is in our great and Eternal Head." [Helaman 13:37–38]

And again the words of Mormon:

"And it came to pass that when I, Mormon, saw their lamentation and their mourning and their sorrow before the Lord, my heart did begin to rejoice within me, knowing the mercies and the long-suffering of the Lord, therefore supposing that he would be merciful unto them that they would again become a righteous people.

"But behold this my joy was vain, for their sorrowing wad not unto repentance, because of the goodness of God; but it was rather the sorrowing of the damned, because the Lord would not always suffer them to take happiness in sin" (Mormon 2:12–13). [*Answers to Gospel Questions* 1:79]

The Prophet Joseph Smith • Helaman 14:12

"The coming of the Son of Man never will be—never can be till the judgments spoken of for this hour are poured out: which judgments are commenced. Paul says, "Ye are the children of the light, and not of the darkness, that that day should overtake you as a thief in the night," It is not the design of the Almighty to come upon the earth and crush it and grind it to powder, but he will reveal it to His servants the prophets.

Judah must return, Jerusalem must be rebuilt, and the temple, and water come out from under the temple, and the waters of the Dead Sea be healed. It will take some time to rebuild the walls of the city and the temple, &c.; and all this must be done before the Son of Man will make His appearance. There will be wars and rumors of wars, signs in the heavens above and on the earth beneath, the sun turned into darkness and the moon to blood, earthquakes in divers places, the seas heaving beyond their bounds; then will appear one grand sign of the Son of Man in heaven. But what will the world do? They will say it is a planet, a comet, etc. But the Son of man will come as the sign of the coming of the Son of Man, which will be as the light of the morning cometh out of the east." [*TPJS*, 286–7]

President Ezra Taft Benson • Helaman 15:3

"God will have a humble people. Either we can choose to be humble or we can be compelled to be humble. Alma said, "Blessed are they who humble themselves without being compelled to be humble" (Alma 32:16).

Let us choose to be humble.

We can choose to be humble ourselves by conquering enmity toward our brothers and sisters, esteeming them as ourselves, and lifting them as high or higher than we are (see D&C 38:24; 81:5; 84:106).

We can choose to humble ourselves by receiving counsel and chastisement (see Jacob 4:10; Helaman 15:3; D&C 63:55; 101:4–5; 108:1; 124:61; 84; 136:31; Proverbs 9:8). [CR, April 1989, 6]

President Harold B. Lee • Helaman 16:18–20

"Our best hope of maintaining doctrinal purity rests with a membership that knows and understands doctrinal implications because they have "witnessed for themselves." Without that conviction, our members—under the pressures of a changing society, which less and less shares with us the basic teachings of Christ—may become like the members and nonmembers on this continent prior to the Savior's birth: they rationalized the pronouncements and predictions of the prophets by saying, "It is not reasonable that such a being as a Christ shall come"; they complained about His birthplace because it was to occur "in a land which is far distant, a land which we know not," and, therefore, they could not "witness with [their] own eyes" (Helaman 16:18–20). This kind of agnosticism infected some in the Church then and could in our time if our members rationalize, question, and lack a personal conviction. We can, if we will, combine our efforts to do a better job of showing the power and majesty of the doctrines of the Church and their implications and applications in the lives of individual members." *[The Teachings of Harold B. Lee*, 439]

Elder Russell M. Nelson • Helaman 16:22

President Ezra Taft Benson in his keynote address yesterday described contention as "another face of pride."

My concern is that contention is becoming accepted as a way of life. From what we see and hear in the media, the classroom, and the workplace, all are now infected to some degree with contention. How easy it is, yet how wrong it is, to allow habits of contention to pervade matters of spiritual significance, because contention is forbidden by divine decree:

"The Lord God hath commanded that men should not murder; that they should not lie; that they should not steal; that they should not take the name of the Lord their God in vain; that they should not envy; that they should not have malice; that they should not contend one with another" (2 Nephi 26:32).

To understand why the Lord has commanded us not to "contend one with another," we must know the true source of contention. A Book of Mormon prophet revealed this important knowledge even before the birth of Christ:

"Satan did stir them up to do iniquity continually; yea, he did go about spreading rumors and contentions upon all the face of the land, that he might harden the hearts of the people against that which was good and against that which should come" (Helaman 16:22). [CR, April 1989, 85]

Challenges to Eternal Life:

1. Make a commitment to listen to and study the General Conference talks that you may follow the advice of the Prophets (Helaman 13:26).

2. Thank the Lord for your treasures and lay them up to him as appropriate (Helaman 13:22).

3. Learn the signs of the Second Coming and watch for their fulfillment that you may believe and not be deceived (Helaman 14:12).

4. Choose a challenge of your own from this reading and apply it to your life.

Scripture Index

OLD TESTAMENT

NEW TESTAMENT

BOOK OF MORMON

DOCTRINE AND COVENANTS

PEARL OF GREAT PRICE

Topical Index

wicked traditions of their fathers,
280, 431

Truth

and righteousness, 181, 211

and soberness, 129, 133, 147, 148

Tubaloth

son of Ammoron, 242, 252

Twelve Apostles, 68, 362

—V—

Voice of God , 374, 390, 391

hearken to, 374

Voice of Jesus Christ, 426

Voice of the good shepherd, 324, 326, 337

Voice of the Lord, 316, 398, 407, 409

Voice of the people, 69, 98, 99, 112-114,
211, 241, 243, 249-251, 255, 278,
292

Voice of the Spirit, 393

Voice of thunder, 281, 299

—W—

War years, vii, 1

Wars and contentions, 12, 81, 115, 222,
225, 246, 248, 264

Wax exceedingly strong, 226, 306

meaning of, 226

Wickedness, 108, 110, 276, 277, 312

Wickedness and abominations, 241, 248,
267, 275-277, 288, 289, 308, 311,
339, 357, 358, 399, 410, 411

Widtsoe, John A., 47, 48

Discourses of Brigham Young (book),
89

Wisdom of Solomon, 345

The Missing Books of the Bible
(book), 345

—Y—

Young, Brigham, 63, 89, 169, 321, 416

Journal History (book), 315

—Z—

Zarahemla, 14, 95, 98, 131, 138, 140-142,
144, 177, 179, 190, 192, 193,
222, 223, 242-244, 252, 277, 280,
298, 324, 365, 398, 407

city of, 159, 198, 207, 209, 224, 252,
253, 255, 335, 397, 399, 406,
410, 411

inhabitants of, 95, 410

land of, 5, 36, 47, 51, 54, 55, 66, 69,
75, 78, 82, 93, 95, 105, 106, 113,
118, 129, 145, 146, 159, 164-167,
170-172, 175, 185, 196, 205, 207,
211, 212, 221, 227, 239, 252-254,
259, 260, 267, 275, 283, 286,
287, 297, 304, 323, 333, 369, 407

people of, 260, 291, 313, 323, 324,
336, 348, 365

Zenock, 328, 343, 346

Zenos, 328, 343, 346, 404, 430, 437

Zion

definition of, 64